NEW!

2nd edition

Denise & Alan Fields
Authors of the Best-seller, Bridal Bargains

BABY BARGAINS

S E C R E T S

to saving 20% to 50% on

baby furniture, equipment,

clothes, toys, maternity wear

and much, much more!

Copyright Page, Credits and Zesty Lo-Cal Recipes

Saxophone, lead guitar and breast-feeding by Denise Fields
Drums, rhythm guitar and father stuff by Alan Fields
Congas on "Grandparents" by
Max & Helen Coopwood, Howard & Patti Fields
Cover design and keyboard solo by Epic Design
Baby-sitting and harmony vocals by Margot Voorhies
Pre-natal care by Dr. Marlene Kaniuk
Screaming guitar solos on "(Let's Go) Perego" by
Charles & Arthur Troy
Additional guitar work on "Diaper Changing Blues"
by Ed Robertson and Steven Paige
Backing vocals on "(She's Got A) Five-Point Car Seat" by Ric Ocasek
Band photography by Deb Kogan

This book was written to the music of Barenaked Ladies,
which probably explains a lot.

Special Thanks to our experts panel of
juvenile products retailers—your insights were invaluable.

Distribution to the book trade by Publisher's Group West, 4065 Hollis St., Emeryville, CA 94608. 1-800-788-3123. Thanks to the entire staff of PGW for their support.

All rights reserved. Copyright © 1997 by Denise & Alan Fields. Published Windsor Peak Press, Boulder, CO. This book may not be reproduced in whole or in part by any means without the expressed written permission of the authors.

To order this book, call 1-800-888-0385. Or send $13.95 plus $3 shipping (or, in Canada, $19.75 plus $4 shipping) to Windsor Peak Press, 436 Pine Street, Boulder, CO 80302. Questions or comments? Please call the authors at (303) 442-8792. Or fax them a note at (303) 442-3744. Or write to them at the above address in Boulder, CO.

E-mail the authors at adfields@aol.com. Updates to this book are posted on the web at www.windsorpeak.com

Library Cataloging in Publication Data

Fields, Denise
Fields, Alan
Baby Bargains: Secrets to saving 20% to 50% on baby furniture, equipment, clothes, toys maternity wear and much, much more/ Denise & Alan Fields
352 pages.
Includes index.
ISBN 1-889392-00-6
1. Child Care—Handbooks, manuals, etc. 2. Infants' supplies—Purchasing—United States, Canada, Directories. 3. Children's paraphernalia—Purchasing—Handbooks, manuals. 4. Product Safety—Handbooks, manuals. 5. Consumer education.
649'.122'0296—dc20.   1997.

We miss you Dee Dee.

Contents

Chapter 3

Baby Bedding

Chapter 4

The Reality Layette: Little Clothes for Little Prices

Chapter 5

Maternity/Nursing Clothes & Feeding Baby

Chapter 6

Around the House: Baby Monitors, Toys, Bath, Foods, High Chairs, and Swings

Chapter 7

Places to Go! Car Seats, Strollers, Carriers & More

Chapter 8

Affordable Baby Proofing

Chapter 9

The Best Gifts for Baby

Chapter 10

Etcetera: Books, Web Sites, Child Care & More

Chapter 11

Do it By Mail: The Best Mail-order Catalogs for Clothes, Baby Products, and More

Chapter 12

Conclusion: What Does It All Mean?

Appendix

Canada: Car Seat Info, Cribs and More

The Icons

 Sources

 The Name Game

 When Do You Need This Stuff

 Do it by Mail

 What Are You Buying?

 Safe and Sound

 Wastes of Money

 Smart Shopper Tips

 Money Saving Tips

 Spotlight on Best Buys

 E-Mail From the Real World

 Bottom Line

Chapter 1

"It's Going to Change Your Life"

That had to be the silliest comment we heard while we were pregnant with our first baby. Believe it or not, we even heard this refrain more often than "Do you want a boy or a girl?" and "I'm sorry. Your insurance doesn't cover that." For the friends and relatives of first-time parents out there, we'd like to point out that this a pretty stupid thing to say. Of course, we knew that a baby was going to change our lives. What we didn't realize was how much a baby was going to change our *pocketbook*.

Oh sure, we knew that we'd have to buy triple our weight in diapers and be subjected to dangerously high levels of Barney. What we didn't expect was the endless pitches for cribs, bedding, toys, clothing, and other items parents are required to purchase by FEDERAL BABY LAW.

We quickly learned that having a baby is like popping on the Juvenile Amusement Park Ride from Consumer Hell. Once that egg is fertilized, you're whisked off to the Pirates of the Crib ride. Then it's off to marvel at the little elves in StrollerLand, imploring you to buy brands with names you can't pronounce. Finally, you take a trip to Magic Car Seat Mountain, where the salespeople are so real, it's scary.

Consider us your tour guides—the Yogi Bear to your Boo Boo Bear, the Fred to your Ethyl, the . . . well, you get the idea. Before we enter BabyLand, let's take a look at the Four Truths That No One Tells You About Buying Stuff For Baby.

The Four Truths That No One Tells You About Buying Stuff for Baby

1 BABIES DON'T CARE IF THEY'RE WEARING DESIGNER CLOTHES OR SLEEPING ON DESIGNER SHEETS. Let's be realistic. Babies just want to be comfortable. They can't even distinguish between the liberals and conservatives on CNN's "Crossfire," so how would they ever be able to tell the difference between Laura Ashley crib bedding and another less famous brand that's just as comfortable, but 50% less expensive? Our focus is on making your baby happy—at a price that won't break the bank.

2   YOUR BABY'S SAFETY IS MORE IMPORTANT THAN YOUR
    CONVENIENCE. Here are the scary facts: 70,000 babies
per year are injured by juvenile products, according to government estimates. Each chapter of this book has a section
called "Safe & Sound," which arms you with in-depth advice
on keeping your baby out of trouble. We'll tell you which
products we think are dangerous and how to safely use other
potentially hazardous products.

3   MURPHY'S LAW OF BABY TOYS SAYS YOUR BABY'S HAPPI-
    NESS WITH A TOY IS INVERSELY RELATED TO THE TOY'S
PRICE. Buy a $200 shiny new wagon with anti-lock brakes,
and odds are baby just wants to play with your keys. In
recognition of this reality, we've included "wastes of money"
in each chapter that will steer you away from frivolous items.

4   IT'S GOING TO COST MORE THAN YOU THINK. Whatever
    amount of money you budget for your baby, get ready
to spend more. Here's a breakdown of the average costs of
bringing a baby into the world today:

The Average Cost of Having a Baby

*(based on industry estimates for
a child from birth to age one)*

Crib, mattress, dresser, rocker	$1500
Bedding / Decor	$ 300
Baby Clothes	$ 500
Disposable Diapers	$ 600
Maternity/Nursing Clothes	$1200
Nursery items, high chair, toys	$ 400
Baby Food / Formula	$ 600
Stroller, Car Seat, Carrier	$ 300
Miscellaneous	$ 500
TOTAL	**$5900**

*The above figures are based on buying name brand
products at regular retail prices. We surveyed over 1000
parents to arrive at these estimates*

*Bedding/Decor includes not only bedding items but
also any decor (lamp, wall paper, etc.) for your baby's
nursery. Baby Food/Formula assumes you'd breastfeed
for the first six months and then feed baby jarred baby
food ($100) and formula ($500) until age one. If you
plan to bottlefeed instead of breastfeed, add another
$500 on to that figure.*

You probably noticed the numbers on the previous page didn't include prenatal care, the medical bills from the actual delivery, or day-care expenses—sorry, that's all extra. How much should you budget for day care and medical expenses? That depends on several factors. Later in this book, we'll discuss the different day care options and their approximate costs. Suffice to say, full-time day care isn't cheap—you can spend from anywhere from $3000 to $30,000 per year. Medical bills for first year routine check-ups and immunizations can cost $700 or more. (Of course, your health insurance may pay for all or part of this figure).

Add in those extras (day care, medical bills, etc.) and you'll end up spending a total of $9000 to $14,000 to raise an "average" baby for the first year, according to U.S. government statistics. (The lower figure is for middle-income parents; upper-income parents end up spending closer to the larger number). Sure, you do get an automatic tax write-off for that bundle of joy, but that only amounts to $2650 for 1997. As you can see, the expenses will far out-strip that deduction.

Of course, when it comes to calculating the financial impact of a child, there's more than just increased expenses. Another "indirect" cost you may want to consider is the loss of income if one spouse cuts back on work to care for the baby. If you don't already, now is a great time to start tracking your finances (affordable software programs like Quicken help organize your income and expenditures).

Reality Check: Does it Really Cost that Much to Have a Baby?

 No, you can spend less. And that's what this book is all about: how to save money and still buy the best for your baby. Follow all the tips in this book, and we estimate the above items will cost you $3740. Yes, that's a savings of over $2000!

Now, at this point, you might be saying "No way! I suppose you'll recommend buying all the cheap stuff, from polyester clothes to no-name cribs." On the contrary, we'll show you how to get *quality* name brands at discount prices. For example, we've got outlets and catalogs that sell all-cotton clothing at 20% to 40% off retail. You'll also learn how to get a name-brand car seat for free. And much more. Yes, we've got the maximum number of bargains allowed by federal law.

A word on bargain shopping: when interviewing hundreds of parents for this book, we realized bargain seekers fall into two frugal camps. There's the "do-it-yourself" crowd and the "quality at a discount" group. As the name implies, "do-it-yourselfers" are resourceful folks who like to take second-hand products and refurbish them. Others use creative tricks to make home-made versions of baby care items like baby wipes and diaper rash creme.

While that's all well and good, we fall more into the second camp of bargain hunters. We love discovering a hidden factory outlet that sells goods at 50% off. Or finding a great mail-order source that discounts name-brand strollers at rock-bottom prices. We also realize savvy parents save money by not *wasting* it on inferior goods or useless items.

While we hope that *Baby Bargains* pleases both groups of bargain hunters, the main focus of this book is not on do-it-yourself projects. Books like the *Tightwad Gazette* (check your local library for a copy) do a much better job on this subject. Our main emphasis will be on discount catalogs, outlet stores, brand reviews and identifying best buys for the dollar.

What? There's no advertising in this book?

Yes, it's true. This book contains zero percent advertising. We have never taken any money to recommend a product or company and never will. We make our sole living off the sales of this and other books. (So, when your friend asks to borrow this copy, have them buy their own book!) Our publisher, Windsor Peak Press, also derives its sole income from the sale of this book and our other publications. No company recommended in this book paid any consideration or was charged any fee to be mentioned in it. As consumer advocates, we believe this ensures our objectivity. The opinions in the book are just that—ours and those of the parents we interviewed.

Please note that the prices quoted in this book were accurate as of the date of publication. While the publisher makes every effort to ensure their accuracy, errors and omissions may exist. That's why we've established a web site where you can get the latest updates on this book for free (www.windsorpeak.com). You can talk directly to us: call (303) 442-8792 or e-mail to adfields@aol.com to ask a question, report a mistake, or just give us your thoughts. You can also write to us at "Baby Bargains," 436 Pine Street, Suite 700, Boulder, CO 80302.

Of course, the prices quoted in this book may change at any time. Inflation and other factors may affect the actual prices you discover in shopping for your baby.

What about the phone numbers listed in this book? We list contact numbers for manufacturers so you can find a local dealer near you that carries the product (or request a catalog, if available). Unless otherwise noted, these manufacturers do NOT sell directly to the public.

So, Who Are You Guys Anyway?

Why do a book on saving money on baby products? Don't new parents throw caution to wind when buying for their baby, spending whatever it takes to insure their baby's safety and comfort?

Ha! When our first son was born in 1993, we quickly realized how darn expensive this guy was. Sure, as a new parent, you know you've got to buy diapers, clothes and toys . . . but who would have guessed you have to navigate a maze of juvenile gizmos and gadgets, all claiming to be the best thing for parents since sliced bread.

Of course, as people who make their living writing about consumer topics, you'd think we'd know better. Sure, we researched all matters of scams and rip-offs in the wedding business for our first book, *Bridal Bargains*. Yet, we found the baby business to be perilous in other ways—instead of outright fraud or scam artists, we instead discovered a bewildering array of baby products, some with dubious value and others that there outright dangerous. We were surprised to learn how most juvenile items faced little (or no) government scrutiny, leaving parents to sort out conflicting safety claims.

So, we went on a quest to find the best baby products, at prices that won't send you to the poor house. Sure, we sampled many of these items first hand. But this book is much more than our experiences—we interviewed over 1000 new parents to learn their experiences with products. We also attend juvenile product trade shows to interview manufacturers and retailers on what's hot and what's not. The insights from retailers are especially helpful, since these folks are on the front lines and often see which items are returned by unhappy parents.

Our focus was on safety and durability: which items stood up to real world conditions and which didn't. Interestingly, we found many products for baby are sold strictly on price . . . and sometimes a great "bargain" broke, fell apart or shrunk after a few uses. Hence, you'll note some of our top recommendations for items that are slightly more expensive than the competition. To be sensitive to those on really tight budgets, we try to identify "good, better and best" bets in different price ranges.

Let's go shopping!

Now that all the formal introductions are done, let's move on to the good stuff. As your tour guides to BabyLand, we'd like to remind you of a few park rules before you go:

1 NO FEEDING THE SALESPEOPLE. Remember, the juvenile products industry is a $3.7 BILLION DOLLAR business. While all those baby stores may want to help you, they are first and foremost in business to make a profit. As a consumer, you should arm yourself with the knowledge necessary to make smart decisions. If you do, you won't be taken for a ride.

2 KEEP YOUR PERSPECTIVE INSIDE THE VEHICLE AT ALL TIMES. With all the hormones coursing through the veins of the average pregnant woman, now is not the time to lose it. As you visit baby stores, don't get caught in the hype of the latest doo-dad that converts a car seat to a toaster.

3 HAVE A GOOD TIME. Oh sure, sifting through all those catalogs of crib bedding and convertible strollers will frazzle your mind. Just remember the goal is to have a healthy baby—so, take care of yourself first and foremost.

What's New in This Edition?

We're proud to announce several additions and improvements in the second edition of *Baby Bargains*. You asked for us more brand name reviews and we listened—check out the greatly expanded reviews of cribs, bedding, strollers, car seats and more. Sprinkled throughout most chapters, you'll also notice "E-Mail from the Real World," handy suggestions sent in by readers. This edition also includes new outlets and catalogs, plus web site addresses for many sources. We've added new sections on playpens, baby bottles, formula, plus money-saving advice on day care and the latest news on car seat safety. Of course, we've updated prices and info on everything from nursery furniture to high chairs. Finally, check out the tear-out sheet in the back of the book—you'll find quick tips and advice to take along with you while shopping.

Questions or comments? Did you discover a bargain you'd like to share? Call the authors at (303) 442-8792 or e-mail adfields@aol.com! Updates to this book are posted at *www.windsorpeak.com*

Chapter 2

Nursery Necessities:
Cribs, Dressers and More

How can you save 20% to 50% off cribs, dressers, and other furniture for your baby's room? In this chapter, you'll learn these secrets, plus discover the six smart shopper tips to getting the most for your money. Then, you'll learn which juvenile furniture has safety problems and a toll-free number you can call to get the latest recall info. Next, we'll rate and review the 22 top brands for cribs and spotlight several baby store chains that offer unbelievably low prices. Finally, you'll learn which crib mattress is best, how to get a deal on a dresser, and four more items you'll want for your baby's room.

Getting Started: When Do You Need This Stuff?

So, you want to buy a crib for Junior? And, what the heck, why not some other furniture, like a dresser to store all those baby gifts and a changing table for, well, you know. Just pop down to the store, pick out the colors, and set a delivery date, right?

Not so fast, o' new parental one. Once you get to that baby store, you'll discover that most don't have all those nice cribs and furniture in stock. No, that would be too easy, wouldn't it? You will quickly learn that you have to *special order* all that booty. (Baby trivia note: What's the difference between an order and a *special* order? A special order takes twice as long and costs three times more than a regular order. Just kidding.)

Most baby specialty stores told us it takes four to six weeks to order many furniture brands. And here's the shocker: some imported cribs can take 12 to 16 weeks. It's hard to believe that it takes this long for companies to ship a simple crib or dresser—we're not talking space shuttle parts here. The way it's going, you'll soon have to order the crib *before* you conceive.

Obviously, this policy is more for the benefit of the retailer than the consumer. Most baby stores are small operations and they tell us that stocking up on cribs, dressers, and the like means an expensive investment in inventory and storage space. Frankly, we could care less. Why you can't get a crib in a week or less is one of the mysteries of modern retailing that will have to be left to future generations to solve. What if you don't have that much time? There are a couple of solutions: some stores sell floor models and others actually keep a limited number of styles in stock. Discounters (Target, Toys R Us, and others) stock cribs—the only downside is that while the price is low, often so is the quality.

Here's an idea given to us by one new mother: don't buy the crib until *after* the baby is born. The infant can sleep in a bassinet or cradle for the first few weeks or even months, and you can get the furniture later. (This may also be an option for the superstitious who don't want to buy all this stuff until the baby is actually born.) The downside to waiting? The last thing you'll want to do with your newborn infant is go furniture shopping. There will be many other activities (such as sleep deprivation experiments) to occupy your time.

So, when should you make a decision on the crib and other furniture for the baby's room? We recommend you place your order in the sixth or seventh month of your pregnancy. By that time, you're pretty darned sure you're having a baby, and the order will arrive several weeks before the birth. (The exception: if your heart is set on an imported crib, you may have to order in your fourth or fifth month to ensure arrival before Junior is born).

Cribs

Sources: Where to Shop

There are four basic sources for finding a crib, each with its own advantages and drawbacks:

1 BABY SPECIALITY STORES. Baby specialty stores are pretty self-explanatory—shops that specialize in the retailing of baby furniture, strollers, and accessories. Some also sell clothing, car seats, swings, and so on. While there are a few large chains, most are small mom-and-pop operations. On the plus side, specialty stores have a good selection of the best name brands. Generally, you get good service—most stores have knowledgeable staffers (usually the owner or manager) who can answer questions. We also like the extra services, like set-up and delivery. The downside: you're gonna pay for that service with high prices—sky high in some cases. Later, we'll give

you some money-saving tips if you want to go this route.

2 DISCOUNTERS/DEPARTMENT STORES. Big stores like Target, Montgomery Ward and Toys R Us carry cribs, albeit with a very small selection. You'll see lower-end brands (like Cosco's metal cribs) and no-name imports. Prices are low, but so is the quality. Delivery and set-up? Forget it; you're often on your own. Another negative: the salespeople (if you can find any) often seem to have the IQ of a rutabaga.

3 MAIL-ORDER CATALOGS. Yes, you can order a crib from mail-order catalogs. JCPenney (800-222-6161) has two catalogs with baby furniture, accessories, maternity wear, and more (check out the review of Penney's catalogs in Chapter 11 for more information). The prices aren't that bad—we noticed a white Child Craft hard wood crib with a single drop side for $179. Other brand names available include Cosco, Stork Craft, Bassett, Okla Homer Smith and Penney's own in-house brands "Bright Future" and "Forever Mine." Of course, if you go mail order, you have to set up the crib yourself. Most mail-order prices are about the same as regular retail, making this more of an option for those who live in remote areas or in a town where the local baby stores are charging sky-high prices for name brands.

4 BABY MEGA-STORES. In the past few years, a new breed of baby store has emerged as a very attractive alternative to specialty stores: the mega-store. With huge stores that top 30,000 square feet, mega-stores combine the best of both worlds: a good selection of the best brand names AND discount prices. And those prices are hard to beat—sometimes 20% to 40% below retail. We review two of the best mega-stores, LiL' Things and Babies R Us/Baby Superstore, later in this section under "Best Buys." Service at the baby mega-stores is variable—some have knowledgeable staffers who can answer questions and others at least tag their cribs and furniture with information on features, accessories, and color options.

5 REGULAR FURNITURE STORES. You don't have to go to a "baby store" to buy juvenile furniture. Many regular furniture stores sell name-brand cribs, dressers and other nursery items. Since these stores have frequent sales, you may be able to get a better price than at a juvenile specialty store. On the other hand, the salespeople many not be as knowledgeable about brand and safety issues.

What Are You Buying?

 While you'll see all kinds of fancy juvenile furniture at baby stores, focus on the items that you really need. First and foremost is a crib, of course. Mattresses are sold separately, as you might expect, so you'll need one of those. Another nice item is a dresser or chest to hold clothes, bibs, wash cloths, etc. A changing table is an optional accessory; some parents just use the crib for this (although that can get messy) or buy a combination dresser and changing table. Some dressers have a removable changing table on top, while others have a "flip top": a hinged shelf that folds up when not in use.

So, how much is this going to cost you? Crib prices start at $80 to $100 for an inexpensive metal crib. A hard wood crib by such popular manufacturers as Simmons or Child Craft (see reviews later in this chapter) start at about $180 and go up to $400. Super-expensive import brands can range from $300 to $700—Bellini (the chain of exclusive baby stores that sells its own cribs—see review later) has cribs that top out at close to $800!

Fortunately, mattresses for cribs aren't that expensive. Basic mattresses start at about $40 and go up to $150 for fancy varieties. Later in this chapter, we'll have a special section on mattresses that includes tips on what to buy and how to save money.

Dressers and changing tables (known in the baby business as case pieces) have prices that are all over the board. A basic four-drawer dresser (made from white laminate) sells for $100 to $200, while name brand, all wood styles would be $300 to $400. We've seen five-drawer dressers by the Canadian manufacturer Ragazzi top out at $750! If you want to go all out, Ragazzi even has an armoire for baby at a whopping $1000.

If you want a "flip-top" dresser/changing table combination, expect to spend another $50 to $100 over the price of a regular dresser. A better solution may be the new "hi-low" combo dressers/changers pioneered by Rumble Tuff (see review later this chapter). Such styles run $350 to $500. If you want a separate changing table, expect to spend $70 to $180 for basic styles, and up to $300 for fancy brands.

So, you can see that your quest for a crib, mattress, dresser, and changing table could cost you as little as $300 or more than $1000.

Smart Shopper Tips

Smart Shopper Tip #1

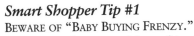

BEWARE OF "BABY BUYING FRENZY."

"I went shopping with my friend at a baby store last week, and she just about lost it. She started buying all kinds of fancy accessories and items that didn't seem that necessary. First there was a $50 womb sound generator and finally the $200 Star Trek Diaper Changing Docking Station. There was no stopping her. The salespeople were egging her on—it was quite a sight. Should we have just taken her out back and hosed her down?"

Yes, you probably should have. Your friend has come down with a severe case of what we call Baby Buying Frenzy—that overwhelming emotional tug to buy all kinds of stuff for Junior. And baby stores know all about this disease and do their darnedest to capitalize on it. Check out this quote from *Juvenile Merchandising* (October 1993) advising salespeople on how to sell to expectant parents: "It's surprising how someone who is making a purchase (for baby) sometimes can be led into a buying frenzy." No kidding. Some stores encourage their staff by giving them bonuses for every additional item sold to a customer. Be wary of stores that try to do this, referred to in the trade as "building the ticket." Remember what you came to buy and don't get caught up in the hype.

Smart Shopper Tip #2

GET IT DELIVERED AND SET-UP.

"My wife and I thought we'd save some money buying an unassembled crib and putting it together ourselves. Big mistake. Five hours later, the crib wasn't set up, and we were missing a part that had to be special ordered from Tanzania. What could we have done differently?"

Yes, it costs extra to have a crib delivered and set up (about $25 to $50 in most cities). But the cost may be worth it. We've spoken to folks who actually deliver and set up cribs for a living, and they tell us stories of cribs that are often missing crucial parts. Even for name brands, you may discover a missing screw here or a defective part there. We'd prefer to let someone else deal with this hassle.

On the other hand, putting a crib together isn't exactly rocket science. Most can be assembled in a short time with basic household tools. And cribs from mail-order catalogs always come unassembled. If you don't live near a baby store or department store that delivers, mail-order may be the only option, and you'll have no choice but to set up the crib yourself.

Another side issue: sales taxes. If you live outside a city, the savings in sales tax may pay for the delivery and set-up. Why? When you purchase an item for delivery, you're only charged the sales tax rate where you live, not where the store is. For example, the nearest city to us has a 7.25% sales tax. Yet we live just outside the city in a county that has a 4.05% sales tax rate. On a $350 crib and a $300 dresser, you'd save about $20. That nearly covers the delivery and set-up fee at many baby stores. Mail-order purchases are even a better deal—in most states, purchase an item from a mail-order catalog and you don't have to pay any sales tax.

Smart Shopper Tip #3
The Art and Science of Selecting the Right Crib.

"How do you evaluate a crib? They all look the same to me. What really makes one different from another?"

Selecting a good crib is more than just picking out the style and finish. You should look under the hood, so to speak. Here are our eight key points to look for when shopping for a crib:

♣ *Mattress support.* Look underneath that mattress and see what is holding it up. You might be surprised. Some lower-end cribs use cheap vinyl straps. Others use metal bars. One crib we saw actually had a cardboard deck holding up the mattress—boy, that looked real comfortable for baby. The best option: a set of springs that provides both mattress support and a springy surface to stand on when Junior gets older. Remember, your infant won't just lay there for long. Soon, Junior will be standing up in the crib, jumping up and down, and causing general mayhem.

♣ *Ease of release.* At least one side of the crib has a railing that lowers down so you can pick up your baby. The railing's ease of release varies widely from crib to crib. Some just have a hand release, but most require you to lift up the side while depressing a foot bar. We suggest trying it out several times. Do you need more than one hand? Is the foot mechanism easy to use? One mother complained to us about how loud many crib locking mechanisms are. If you're putting a sleeping baby to bed, the last thing you need is a crib side that locks into place with a loud CLANK! Unfortunately, most crib makers have yet to figure out how to make silent release mechanism for the side rail. (The exception may be Canadian crib maker Ragazzi, which makes one of the quietest releases on the market. We review Ragazzi later in this chapter).

♣ *Mattress height adjustment.* Most cribs have several height levels for the mattress—you use the highest setting when the baby is a newborn. Once she starts pulling up, you adjust the mattress to the lowest level so she won't be able to punt herself over the railing. Cheaper cribs use a screw system—you adjust the mattress by loosening a screw on each of the four posts. The problem: the holes can become stripped, weakening the support system.

A better system is a series of hooked brackets—the mattress lays on top of springs, anchored to the crib frame by hooked brackets. Child Craft and others uses this system, and we believe it provides superior mattress support and safety— there's even a little catch to prevent a sibling from getting under the crib and pushing the mattress upward. While Simmons has a similar system, it's missing that little catch. As a result, you can accidentally dislodge the mattress by pushing up from the bottom—a potential death trap if Junior has adventurous siblings or pets.

♣ *How stable is the crib?* Go ahead and abuse that crib set up in the baby store. Push it and see if it wobbles. Wobbling is not good. Most cribs we recommend are quite stable. The cribs with a drawer under the mattress are the most stable. Unfortunately, all this extra stability comes at a price—models with this feature start at $300 and can go up to $500 or $600. Keep in mind that some cribs may be wobbly because the store set them up incorrectly. Check out the same model at a couple of different stores if you have stability concerns.

♣ *Check those casters.* Metal are much better than plastic. We also prefer wide casters to those thin, disk-shaped wheels. You'll be wheeling this crib around more than you think—to change the sheets, to move away from a drafty part of the room, etc. One solution: if you find a good buy on a crib that has cheap casters, you can easily replace them. Hardware stores sell the good, thick, metal casters for $10 to $20—or less.

♣ *How easy is it to assemble?* Ask to see those instructions— most stores should have a copy lying around. Make sure they are not in Greek.

♣ *Compare the overall safety features of the crib.* In a section later in this book, we discuss crib safety in more detail.

♣ *Consider other special needs.* As we noted above, noisy crib railing release mechanisms can be a hassle—and this seems especially so for short people (or, in politically correct terms, the vertically-challenged). Why? Taller folks (above 5' 8") may be able to place the baby into a crib *without* lowering the side rail (when the mattress is in the highest position). Shorter parents can't reach over the side rail as easily, forcing them to use the release mechanism more often than not. Hence, a quieter release on a more expensive brand might be worth the extra investment.

Disabled parents also may find the foot bar difficult or impossible to operate. In that case, we recommend a crib that has a two-handed release (Simmons, reviewed below, makes such a model).

The Name Game: Reviews of Selected Manufacturers

 Here is a look at some of the best known brand names for cribs. There are over 100 companies in the U.S. that manufacture and/or import cribs, but, because of space limitations, we can't review each one. We decided to concentrate on the best and most common brand names. If you've discovered a brand that we didn't review, feel free to share your discovery by calling us at (303) 442-8792.

How did we evaluate the brands? First, we looked at samples of cribs at retail stores. With the help of veteran juvenile furniture retailers, we checked construction, release mechanisms, mattress support, and overall fit and finish.

Then we stood back and asked the question, "Would we put our baby in this crib?" We checked safety features and inquired about delivery schedules. Of course, we also evaluated the prices and how they compared to the competition. To supplement our own field research, we also interviewed dozens of new parents about their cribs. What did they like? Which cribs held up to real world abuse? Our highest ratings went to cribs that combined good quality with affordable prices.

We should note that the following ratings apply *only* to cribs. You'll see these same name brands on a myriad of other products, including "case goods" (dressers, changing tables, etc.), crib mattresses, high chairs, rockers, and much more. Of course, just because a company makes a great crib at an affordable price doesn't necessarily mean that their dressers or rockers are good deals. Later in this chapter, we'll take a look at crib mattresses and the "name game" for case goods.

The Ratings

★★★★ EXCELLENT—*our top pick!*

★★★ GOOD—*above average quality, prices, and creativity.*

★★ FAIR—*could stand some improvement.*

★ POOR—*yuck! could stand some major improvement.*

Angel Line ....★★
17 Peak Place, Sewell, NJ 08080, Call (800) 889-8158 or (609) 227-5505 for a dealer near you. Internet: www.voicenet.com/~aline This low priced line has good quality even though the styling is rather boring. Their entry-level Jenny Lind-style crib sells for $100 to $150, but other more contemporary styles are in the $150 to $250 range. Typical of the plain vanilla styling is the Angel II crib with curved headboard and single dropside. The available finishes are rather limited too—choose from natural, white, maple, white wash, oak and cherry. As for the quality, we liked the hardware, overall construction and large casters. On the downside, the mattress support attaches to the crib frame with a screw, which is not our preferred method. Angel Line (whose parent is Longwood Forest Products) also makes canopy cribs, changing tables, cradles, rockers and high chairs.

Baby's Dream ....★★ ¹/₂
PO Box 579, Buena Vista, GA 31803, Call (912) 649-4404 for a dealer near you. Baby's Dream's claim to fame is their "Crib 4 Life," a product which converts from a crib to a youth bed to a twin bed to an adult bed to, finally, a thermonuclear weapon. Just kidding on that last one. But seriously . . . with all these uses, you'd think Baby's Dream would be a good value. Well, yes and no. The cribs are good quality, made of solid wood (pine, sycamore, oak and beech are the options) and available in a variety of finishes. Yet the prices start at around $300 for pine (which we wouldn't recommend since this soft wood nicks and scratches) and soar to $600 to $700 for more expensive woods and styles. Not bad for all those uses, you think? Hold it—in order to morph the crib into a twin or adult bed, you have buy a separate "conversion kit." This could set you back another $30 to $200, depending on the model. In the end, you've probably spent just as much as, or more than, the cost to buy a simple crib and twin bed.

As for safety, Baby's Dream cribs are JPMA safety-certified, which is nice, but we don't like the railing release on the Crib 4 Life (as well as on the similar "Crib 2 College" and "Generation" crib models). Instead of using a rail release that drops down (as most cribs have), Baby's Dream uses a folding design, where the rail folds down to give you access to the baby. As we'll note later about a similar model made by Child Craft (the Crib N Bed), we find this dangerous. Why? As your baby starts standing up, she can use this extra ledge to get a foothold to climb out of the crib. The fact that the JPMA certifies such a crib as "safe" creates doubt in our mind into how useful this safety certification is.

Fortunately, Baby's Dream does make other models that

use a conventional drop-side (the Madonna, made from beech, is one example). So, we have to give Baby's Dream a mixed review. With the exception of the folding side rail on certain models, the cribs are well-made and styled. And while we applaud their efforts to make a crib that a child can use through college, the hefty initial investment and later "conversion" kit expenses makes this crib no bargain.

Bassett ....★★
Main Street, Bassett, VA 24055. Call (540) 629-6000 for a dealer near you. Internet: www.bassettfurniture.com Bassett cribs are sold to stores in large truckloads; hence, you're more likely to see them at chain stores like Sears and JCPenney. In fact, Penney's catalog features several Bassett models, including an oak contemporary design with curved headboard for $200. And that's Bassett's key advantage—a pretty good crib at an affordable price. Some Bassett cribs can be had for as little as $150. *Consumer Reports* ranked Bassett third overall (based on convenience and durability factors) in a recent report. The two top-ranked crib makers (Child Craft and Simmons) are generally higher in price. As for style, Bassett is conservative and somewhat behind when it comes to trends; the company just added a two-tone color line (combining natural wood with a color accent), several years after such color combinations became popular in the market. As for safety, we thought the Bassett cribs we saw were passable, but the mattress support bracket could use some beefing up. Another negative: it's also difficult to get replacement parts from the company.

Bonavita ....★★
121 Ethel Rd. West, Unit 4, Piscataway, NJ 08854. Call (800) 560-5624 or (908) 572-9733 for a dealer near you. Formerly know as Bambolina, this company has been importing Italian-made cribs into the U.S. since 1993. As with other Italian brands like Pali (reviewed later), Bonavita cribs have hidden hardware, an under-crib storage drawer, and sturdy construction. The Italians seem to take pride in making a crib with super thick headboards and Bonavita is no exception—some of these styles are built like tanks. Of course, all this heavy-duty construction ain't cheap. Bonavita's cribs retail for $300 to $700. While the styling isn't as fashionable as the Canadian brands Morigeau and Ragazzi, Bonavita does have a new "antique white" finish which was interesting.

Bellini ....★★¹/₂
2216 Agate Ct., Unit A, Simi Valley, CA 93065. Call (805) 520-0974 for a store location near you. Bellini's cribs are sold exclusively in Bellini stores (50+ locations, mostly on the East

and West coasts). And that's a good thing, because when you consider the prices they're charging, it's doubtful they'd sell anywhere else. And just how expensive are these cribs? Well, prices *start* at $400 and range up to an astronomical $750. At that price, we expect the cribs to be works of art with side rails that are gilded in platinum or some other exotic metal. Sadly, they're just made out of wood. And the styling, surprisingly, is rather conservative—contemporary but hardly exciting. For example, the "Katie" is a simple design with a low headboard. That's it. Price: $500! At least for that price you do get a under-the-crib drawer (useful for storing silver spoons, we suppose). The drawer helps stabilize the crib, which is a nice safety feature. Also, most Bellini cribs convert into youth beds, which the company claims can be used up to four or five years of age.

Despite the high prices, fans of Bellini cite the stores' superior service as a good selling point. And, we discovered that the prices on other items in the Bellini store (strollers, for example) can be very competitively priced—depending on the market.

C&T International ....★★
170 Roosevelt Place, Palisades Park, NJ 07650. Call (201) 461-9444 for a dealer near you. This importer sells Italian-made cribs and other juvenile items under their name and "Brevi." All the cribs are made from Italian beech hardwood and feature one-handed drop side systems and storage drawers. Like other Italian brands, C&T's cribs feature hidden hardware—unlike Simmons and Child Craft, you don't see any metal bars or kick plates on the release mechanisms. The prices are rather high ($300 to $500), considering the styling is more plain vanilla than other Italian cribs. Typical of the styling is the Alexandra, which has a subtlety curved head and footboard. In the "natural" finish, the beech wood looks similar to maple. There are no over the top designs like Pali nor any wide variety of finishes (just white, natural, whitewash and cognac, although not all styles are available in all finishes). All in all, these are sturdy, if not somewhat boring cribs. C&T/Brevi's distribution is limited to a small number of cities on the East and West coasts (plus Chicago).

Child Craft ....★★★★
PO Box 444, Salem, IN 47167. Call (812) 883-3111 for a dealer near you. Internet: www.childcraftind.com. This is one of our favorite brands for cribs—and after you shop the competition, we think you'll agree. We like Child Craft for three reasons: styling, safety, and price. The designs (all in wood) run the gamut from contemporary to traditional. For example, we liked the "Sculptures" line with a curved headboard ($229).

The safety features are top notch—the mattress height adjustment/locking system is the best on the market. The simple release mechanism (with a foot bar) is easy to use. Best of all, you get a stylish and safe crib at a very reasonable price. Retail prices range from about $200 to $400—but we've seen a single-drop side Child Craft for as low as $179 at LiL' Things (see review later in this chapter). Delivery takes 12 to 16 weeks on most orders. New this year at Child Craft is a "watered silk" finish (sort of a southwestern white-washed look). Also new is a style with an under-crib drawer (for $299).

If we had one complaint about Child Craft, it would have to be that the company still markets Crib N Beds ($400 to $550), combination crib/youth beds with attached dressers. In our opinion, all these products should be withdrawn from the market for safety reasons (see the Safe & Sound section later in this chapter for more details). The quality of the Crib N Bed is also a concern: the product has sharp corners on the changing table and sharp edges on the bottom of the attached drawers. That's unacceptable at this price level.

Speaking of quality concerns, we also have found the quality of the low-end (the "Child Line" and other cribs under $200) Child Craft cribs to be a problem. Compared to similarly-priced cribs from Simmons, we found the entry-level Child Craft cribs to be lacking in construction and finish quality. Fortunately, these problems didn't exist on cribs that were over $200 (the vast majority of the Child Craft line). Despite these complaints, we still like Child Craft and pick them as one of the best crib makers in the country.

The rain in Spain . . .

In "My Fair Lady," Professor Higgins could tell a person exactly where they lived in England by listening to a few words of their accent. Oddly enough, cribs in the U.S. follow a similar pattern. Tell us your crib color and we can tell you where you live, down to the zip code. Well, it's not that precise, but there seems to be a strong regional flavor to crib colors and finishes. Some of this is related to interior fashion—how a home is decorated often influences nursery furnishings. As a result, it's not to surprising that you'd see white-wash cribs in the Desert Southwest. In the traditional Midwest, you'll find traditional oak cribs sell best. Yet other areas have less obvious crib fashion trends. In Southern states like Texas and Georgia, white cribs outsell all other colors by a mile. White is also popular on the West Coast, while maple is the preferred crib finish in Colorado. And what about cherry? These cribs sell best in New England and, to a lesser extent, other parts of the East Coast.

Cosco ....★★
2525 State St., Columbus, IN 47201. Call (812) 372-0141 for
a dealer near you. Internet: www.coscoinc.com Cosco's claim
to fame is their very inexpensive metal cribs (one in four cribs
sold in the U.S. is a metal crib). In fact, we saw these cribs for
as low as $78 at discount stores (retail prices are $90 to $180).
But what do you get for that money? Not much, as it turns
out. Like most metal cribs, the mattress doesn't rest on a set of
springs but instead sits on a series of straps or metal bars,
which is inadequate in our opinion. The welding of the joints
looks sloppy, and the mattress height adjustment mechanism
consists of a metal bar that screws into the side post. The
problem? Those screws can strip and the mattress could con-
ceivably disconnect from the frame. Our advice: spend some
extra money to get a basic wood crib with a spring mattress
support and better safety features. New this year at Cosco is a
crib that combines a metal frame with wood slats—a funky
look for $179. Thanks to their low prices, Cosco's metal cribs
are best-sellers. The company claims to be the largest crib
maker in North America, shipping 250,000 cribs each year.
Cosco does have an outlet store (with savings of up to 50%)
that sells cribs as well as many of the other products they manufacture (see the section "Outlets" later in this chapter).

Delta ....★★
175 Liberty Ave., Brooklyn, NY 11212. Call (718) 385-1000
for a dealer near you. Imported from Indonesia, Delta makes a
crib that looks like a knock-off of a Bellini style with an oval-
shaped headboard. This double-drop side crib is made of
"Ramin wood with a white finish" (Ramin is a hard wood
from Southeast Asia) and has a hand-release side mechanism.
Cost: $269. (Most Delta cribs sell for $150 to $300). Our
biggest complaint with Delta—the crib's mattress rests on a
wood platform, instead of bed springs. Delta claims its wood
platform is better for baby's back, but we remain unconvinced.
We also wouldn't recommend Delta for folks who live in dry
climates. Why? Plastic rail release triggers and tracks have broken when the crib's wood frame shrinks (caused by low humidity). We spoke with one baby store in Denver who reported
return problems with Delta cribs for exactly those reasons.

On the upside, all the cribs are JPMA safety-certified and
feature double drop-sides and heavy-duty furniture-style casters. We also like the easy of assembly with Delta cribs—they
ship pre-assembled and require no tools. The styling is also
more contemporary than other lower-priced cribs.

Generation 2 Worldwide ....★★$^1/_2$
113 Anderson Court, PO Box 2208, Dothan, AL 36302. For a dealer near you, call (800) 736-1140 or (334) 792-1144. This company used to be known as Nelson, a low-end crib maker that was always an also-ran in the crib market. The name change in 1996 was more than just a cosmetic makeover, though. The company has new designs and features that are impressive. Generation 2's cribs now feature the "Guardian Lock" railing releases—this "dual action" drop side can only be activated by an adult with an arm span of 53". The company claims this guards against younger children accidentally releasing the drop side of the crib. For parents who don't like the kick-plate releases common on other American-made cribs, this might be an option to consider.

Generation 2 divides its cribs into two groups: Child Design and Next Generation. Child Design cribs are lower-priced models sold in mass-market, discount stores for $89 to $149. Next Generation designs are slightly more expensive ($119 to $199) and feature more fancy styling. While all cribs feature the Guardian Lock drop-sides, dual-wheeled casters and metal spring mattress supports, the more expensive models have a few more doo-dads (teething rail guards on both sides, a three versus two position mattress height adjustment, etc.).

The hardware on the crib is made from Dupont Zytel, which is a combination of nylon and plastic. The company calls this system "Quiet-Glide" and claims the crib rail can be raised or lowered without any squeaks or clanks. As we noted above in a review of a similar crib rail release by Delta, however, we're concerned about cracking problems with such hardware caused by wood shrinkage in dry climates. While we have yet to hear of any reports of trouble with Generation 2 cribs, we urge parents in such climates to consult with a local store about this issue before buying. Despite these concerns, we liked Generation 2's cribs—all the models are JPMA safety certified and the cribs come pre-assembled (the company claims the cribs can be assembled in 15 minutes or less). While it remains to be seen if Generation 2 can breathe new life into a moribund brand, the signs are encouraging.

Kindercraft ....★$^1/_2$
For contact information, see Babies R Us/Baby Superstore's review later in this chapter. Kindercraft is Baby Superstore's in-house crib brand. While we like the Baby Superstore for many things, the styling, construction and finish of these cribs isn't one of the them. In short, they're just average. And the future status of this brand is very much up in the air. With Toys R Us acquisition of Baby Superstore in 1996, there's a question as to whether the combined Babies

Certifications—Do they really matter?

As you shop for cribs and other products for your baby, you'll no doubt run into "JPMA-Certified" products sporting a special seal. But who is the JPMA and what does their certification mean?

The Juvenile Products Manufacturers Association (JPMA) is a group of over 225 companies that make juvenile products, both in the United States and Canada. Twenty years ago, in a stroke of marketing genius, the group started a testing program to help weed out unsafe products. Instead of turning this into a propaganda effort, they actually enlisted the support of the Consumer Products Safety Commission and the American Society of Testing and Materials to develop standards for products in several categories: carriages/strollers, cribs, play yards, high chairs, safety gates, portable hook-on chairs, and walkers (which we think are dangerous, but more on this later).

Manufacturers must have their product tested in an independent testing lab and, if it passes, they can use the JPMA seal. To the group's credit, the program has been so successful that the JPMA seal carries a good deal of credibility with many parents we interviewed. But does it really mean a product is safe? Well, yes and no. First, with any product, you must follow instructions for assembly and use very carefully. Second, the testing program (and standards) are voluntary and manufacturers aren't required to certify all the products in a line of merchandise. Hence, if a manufacturer wants to make a cheap version of a popular product that wouldn't meet the guidelines, they just don't have it certified. The result: confusion at the store level, where some products carry the JPMA seal and others don't, even though they're made by the same manufacturer.

To be fair, we should note that just because you don't see the JPMA seal on a product does not mean that it failed to meet the safety standards—the Consumer Products Safety Commission sets minimum requirements that *all* manufacturers have to meet. (When it comes to cribs, the JPMA's voluntary standards are stricter versions of the CPSC rules. As for other products, the association merely requires additional warning labels and other educational info for parents). Nevertheless, to clear up this confusion and give the program some teeth, we'd like to see safety testing be a mandatory requirement for all JPMA members. As with all industries that pledge to police themselves, the JPMA certification does have its weaknesses—the fact that they can certify walkers as "safe" is a glaring example. Yet, despite the fact that the cynical side of us wonders whether the fox can ever watch the hen house, we have to give a hand to the JPMA for creating a successful certification program. With some fine-tuning, it might be a model for other juvenile-related industries as well. To contact the JPMA for a list of certified products, you can call (609) 231-8500, write to JPMA, 236 Route 38 West, Suite 100, Moorestown, NJ 08057 or check out their web site at *www.jpma.org*. A safety brochure (in both English and Spanish) is available—send a self-addressed stamped business size envelope to the above address.

R Us/Baby Superstore outlets will sell their own in-house brand of cribs or rely more on outside sources. As a result, parents who buy a Kindercraft crib may be out of luck when it comes to finding replacement parts or service for a broken railing if the brand is discontinued. We suggest waiting to see how this shakes out in the coming months before investing in a Kindercraft crib. Watch our web page at www.windsorpeak.com for updates on this situation.

Lexington ....★★$^1/_2$
Call (800) 539-4636 or (910) 249-5300 for a brochure or a dealer near you. Juvenile furniture companies aren't the only ones who make cribs. "Adult" furniture makers have tip-toed into the market too. Furniture-giant Lexington is a good example—this well-known brand makes a line of cribs that have caught the eye of many parents-to-be. Why? Lexington's cribs have what is often lacking in the market today: style. Several of their cribs look like antique reproductions, with unique color finishes and other features. While the metal hardware is similar to Child Craft or Simmons, the styling is definitely head and shoulders above other cribs on the market today. Unfortunately, the pricing is also head and shoulders above the competition—a Lexington crib can set you back $700 to $800! Yet, a sharp reader of our previous edition noticed you can order Lexington furniture from North Carolina discounters at substantially lower prices. An example: a crib from Lexington's "Imaginations" collection retailed for $741, with a matching dresser for $572. Yet a quick call to discounter Loftin-Black Furniture (800) 334-7398 reveals their price is just $380 for the crib and $300 for the dresser. Even when you tack on delivery and set-up charges, the savings is dramatic (and remember you also don't pay any sales tax in most states on mail-order purchases). Check out the classified ads in such magazines as "Southern Living" for other furniture discounters.

Little Miss Liberty..★★$^1/_2$
3040 N. Avon St., Burbank, CA 91504. Call (800) RND-CRIB or (818) 556-3505 for a dealer near you. Internet: www.crib.com. Little Miss Liberty has two claims to fame. First, they are one of the very few companies that makes round cribs. Second, they are the only crib maker owned by the wife of the cartoon voice of Shaggy (of Scooby Doo fame). Yes, actress Jean Kasem (who played Loretta Tortelli on "Cheers" and is the wife of Casey "America's Top 40" Kasem) is the driving force behind this company, which took over the country's largest round crib maker a few years ago. The company plays up it's Hollywood connec-

tion to the hilt, with Jean dropping celebrity client names (Melanie Griffith, Roseanne) on her many talk show appearances to plug the cribs.

So, what's so special about a round crib, except for its price tag? The company points out that the first cribs commissioned for European royalty were round or oval. In press materials, Jean says "those who want the best cribs favor the rounded shape because they don't restrict the child's view. They can focus on the whole world and they are the center of it." Uh huh.

Well, we can say one thing about Little Miss Liberty—that unrestricted world view isn't cheap. A basic model starts at $500 and many fancy styles with canopies run $600 to $700. While those prices include a foam mattress, the special bedding needed for a round crib is extra. Since few traditional bedding companies make round crib bedding, Little Miss Liberty offers their own bedding, which will set you back another $200 to $700.

It's apparent the company realized those prices were a wee bit high for those of us non-Hollywood types and has since introduced a low-price crib model (and bedding). Their new "Dura Crib" is made from molded "poly-plastic" components (the regular round cribs are made of wood) and features a canopy. The price: about $225, which is definitely more realistic. The new bedding ("Bedding in a Bag") sells for about $250.

So, is it worth it? Well, we don't buy Little Miss Liberty's argument that round cribs are safer than rectangular ones. We monitor the federal government's reports on injuries caused by juvenile products and see no evidence that rectangular cribs are a problem. So, if you're going to go for a round crib, do it because you like the crib's aesthetics. And save up those pennies—when you add in the bedding, this investment can soar above $1000 quickly.

Million Dollar Baby ....★
855 Washington Blvd., Montebello, CA. Call (800) 282-3886 or (213) 722-2288 for a dealer near you. Internet: www.milliondollarybaby.com We just didn't like these cheap imported cribs, which are made in Taiwan. One Jenny Lind-style crib at a discount store was about $140. In our opinion, construction was just barely passable—we noted that the crib didn't seem very stable when we shook it and that the finish was poor. One baby store manager we spoke to claimed they've received returns on low-end Million Dollar Baby cribs who's spindles have broken. On the plus side, the company uses the same hardware (release mechanisms, etc.) as Child Craft and Simmons. Million Dollar Baby's budget line of cribs starts at

around $100 and goes up to $200. At press time, we heard from a reader who saw a new Million Dollar Baby crib that's imported from Italy. She was impressed with the quality (hidden hardware, sturdy under-crib drawer) for the price, which was $290. Since we haven't seen this model yet, we're reserving judgment, but it's an encouraging sign.

Morigeau/Lepine ....★★★
2625 Rossmoor Dr., Pittsburgh, PA 15241. Call (800) 326-2121 or (412) 942-3583 for a dealer near you. Based in Quebec, Canada, this family-run juvenile furniture company has been in business for over 50 years. Their pricey cribs are quite stylish, with a Shaker sensibility. Morigeau cribs run $475 to $750, while a five-drawer dresser topped $579. The cribs (which have just two mattress levels) have a weird locking mechanism that we found awkward. On the upside, Morigeau sells a wide assortment of accessories, including coordinating desks, armoires, and even baby entertainment centers. As for the finishes, we thought the white looked the best, although Morigeau boasts a wide variety of finishes for each crib style (including such interesting options as cinnamon and cognac). One style that caught our eye was a "moon" crib, featuring a crescent shaped moon headboard (style 795) available in a variety of painted finishes for $575. Other innovative headboard styles featured carousel and swan designs. Morigeau's sister line is "Lepine," a smaller collection of cribs at slightly lower prices. Lepine cribs feature similarly whimsical designs in a smaller number of finishes (white, natural, cherry) for $450 to $660. Morigeau/Lepine is mainly available through baby specialty stores.

Double Duty: A Crib for Twins

And you thought buying for *one* baby was expensive. Parents of twins face an unpleasant economic reality—they often need two of everything, including two cribs, two mattresses, etc. Well, to the rescue comes California-based NeNe Quality Baby Products (213-890-4449, internet: www.nene.com), which has introduced "Double Delight," the first crib for twins. The L-shaped crib, which is designed to fit into a corner and lets two infants sleep in the same crib, isn't cheap at $800. But that price does include a mattress and custom-made bedding, available in three styles. When you compare that to a regular crib (which can cost $200 to $400 for just the wood crib alone), the Double Delight may not be that expensive after all.

Okla Homer Smith ....★ ¹/₂
*416 S. 5th St., PO Box 1148, Ft. Smith, AR 72902. Call
(501) 783-6191 for a dealer near you.* Owned by baby
products giant Century, this mass market brand is available
in many stores and through the JCPenney catalog. We saw
a shaker-style single-drop side crib that sells for $199 in the
Penney's catalog. Frankly, we weren't very impressed by
this crib—it was made of pine, a soft wood that tends to
scratch and nick easily (we prefer hard woods like maple
and oak for cribs). On the upside, many Okla Homer Smith
cribs come with optional under-mattress drawers (an extra
$80 or so), which make the cribs more stable. As far as ease
of use goes, Okla Homer Smith gets a mixed review. Their
"Nod-A-Way" style crib scored dead last in *Consumer
Reports* recent crib survey, which cited "difficult to release
drop-sides." We should note that in the same survey, an
Okla Homer Smith crib made for Sears was rated much
higher. The bottom line: you can find a higher-quality single-drop side crib made by Child Craft or Simmons for the
same price at most discount stores.

Pali ....★★★
*Imported by R. Levine Distributor, 125 W. Front St., Suite
154, Wheaton, IL 60187. Call (630) 690-6143 for a dealer
near you.* In business since 1920, Italian-made Pali cribs
enjoy a good reputation for two reasons: quality and delivery. The contemporary-styled cribs feature better than
average construction and safety features. Pali, which is the
largest crib maker in Europe, churns out cribs with con-
cealed hardware (no metal bars or rods are visible on the
railing), which some parents like for their more stream-
lined look. All Pali cribs have under-crib storage drawers
(a nice feature) and a one-handed drop side mechanism.
While there are few available finishes (white, natural,
bleach and honey ash are among the choices), there are
quite a few cribs which are definitely not "run-of-the-
mill." We liked the "Venus" crib, which featured a molded
sea shell headboard accented by "golden plating." Or how
about the "Marline" crib, whose molded headboard is
highlighted by spring flowers with pastel accents? New
this year at Pali is a rocker crib, a new combination crib
and day bed and a new line of dressers made in Montreal,
Canada. So how much does all this creativity cost?
Surprisingly, not as much as you might think. We saw a
Pali crib that was on sale for $249 in San Diego, although
most retail in the $300 to $500 range. Shipping from their
Illinois-based distributor takes only six weeks or so—not
bad for a foreign-made crib.

Ragazzi .... ★ $^{1}/_{2}$
*8965 Pascal Gagnon, St. Leonard, Quebec H1P 1Z4. Call
(514) 324-7886 for a dealer near you.* This Canadian import
features very adult-looking furniture at very-adult prices. Cribs
run a whopping $469 to $510, while a five-drawer dresser will
set you back an amazing $749. Ragazzi's claim to fame is their
two-tone wood finishes in contemporary colors (forest green,
deep burgundy, etc.). For example, the base of the dresser is a
natural finish wood, with the knobs and top finished in color.
This two-color look has become so popular that almost every
other crib manufacturer has knocked it off today. As a result,
you can get a Ragazzi look at a much lower price.

As for the cribs themselves, parents we've interviewed say
they love Ragazzi's crib rail release—it's one of the quietest in
the market. We didn't like the mattress height adjustment system, however, which had metal straps that screwed to the side
post (unusual for this price level). The quality of Ragazzi's
cribs disappointed us; for the money, you can find a much better crib than this. Even if you can find a Ragazzi crib on sale
for $300 or so (as some of our readers have reported), they
still seem overpriced.

While we liked the *style* of Ragazzi's furniture, we're less
thrilled with Ragazzi's customer service. In a word, it stinks.
One baby store owner we interviewed said he dropped Ragazzi
after the company shipped the wrong color cribs and was very
slow to fix defective products. Also, we encountered Ragazzi's
president Jerry Schwartz at a trade show recently and found his
arrogant and obnoxious behavior reflected poorly on his company. All in all, if you want a stylish Canadian crib, we suggest
buying from Morigeau (reviewed earlier).

Simmons ....★★★ $^{1}/_{2}$
*613 E. Beacon Ave., New London, WI 54961. Call (414) 982-
2140 for a dealer near you.* Another high-quality maker of cribs,
Wisconsin-based Simmons makes an incredibly wide variety of
styles and designs. In fact, we counted nearly 30 coordinating sets
of cribs, dressers, and other furniture! One design that caught our
eye was the Camden, a sleigh-style crib with Queen Anne, turned
spindles. Like many Simmons cribs, this is available in vintage
cherry, snow white, and aspen white finishes. The price: $389 at
a discount store (Baby Superstore). If that's too much, simpler
designs start at $180 and run to $300. The Matino, for example,
features a "contemporary maple design with arced top and
tapered spindles." A single-drop side version of this crib was just
$179 at a discount store. LiL' Things carries a Simmons sleigh-
style also for $179. Better yet, we were impressed with the quality
of these cribs. Despite the low prices, the $179 Simmons cribs
were made much better than similar low-end cribs by other

brands. The safety features of the cribs are good, but we wish the mattress locked into place when the height is adjusted. On the upside, Simmons cribs are widely available, at both pricey specialty shops and discount stores. Simmons' customer service is also excellent. Delivery takes 12 to 16 weeks. One interesting trivia note: one of the original owners of the company was Thomas Alva Edison, of light bulb fame.

Stork Craft ....★★ *¹/₂*
11511 No. 5 Road, Richmond, British Columbia, Canada, V7A4E8. For a dealer near you, call (604) 274-5121. Internet: www.storkcraft.com/storkcraft Unlike other Canadian crib makers that concentrate on the upper-end markets, Stork Craft's cribs are priced for the rest of us. Most are in the $150 to $250 range (although a few reach $400) and are sold in such places as Baby Superstore and other chain stores. Manufactured in Mississauga, Ontario (just outside Toronto), Stork Craft's cribs feature two different releases. Some models use the standard metal hardware/foot-bar release, similar to Child Craft and Simmons. Others use a two-handed plastic trigger drop-side. As mentioned earlier in this section, we're concerned such plastic hardware might crack, especially in dry climates where low humidity leads to wood shrinkage. Nonetheless, the styling of Stork Craft cribs is pleasing. Most are plain vanilla, although a few echo Italian cribs with curvy headboards, heavy white wood finishes, etc. A few styles even have under-crib drawers.

Tracers ....★★ *¹/₂*
30 Warren Place, Mt. Vernon, NY 10550. Call (914) 668-9372 for a dealer near you. This crib brand was highly rated by *Consumer Reports*, but we think they're slightly wrong on this one. One style of Tracers cribs is made from plastic and molded wood, giving it a contemporary feel. Although the hardware is good, we've heard reports from retailers that the cribs' finish cracks and chips. We also didn't like the metal straps that hold up the mattress and the side rails with no teething guards. Tracer's single-drop side crib is rather pricey, retailing for $350 to $375 (though we saw it on sale for as little as $200 in one store). On the upside, Tracers wood cribs are much better quality—similar to Bellini, but more affordable. All of Tracer's cribs convert into day beds and the upper-end models have under-crib drawers. New this year at Tracers is an expanded case good (dresser) line with eight different collections. You can choose from five finishes in a variety of color combinations.

Welsh .... ★★
1535 S. 8th St., St. Louis, MO 63104. Call (314) 231-8822 for a dealer near you. If you like traditional styling, you'll like

Welsh. This St. Louis-based company churns out cribs with turned spindles and basic finishes like cherry and oak. A single-drop side crib runs $239—about middle of the road as far as pricing goes. Other models go for as little $100. We saw this brand more at department stores than at specialty shops. While we thought the cribs were OK, we did receive a complaint about a Welsh dresser. A reader of a previous edition of this book was disappointed in the quality of a Welsh dresser she purchased through JCPenney's catalog.

Other obscure crib brands. Besides the major crib makers mentioned above, there are a small number of other juvenile products companies that make cribs. For example, *Gerry* makes a handful of cribs that are sold through Sears, among other stores. We also saw a crib or two from *Evenflo*, who are better known for their car seats than nursery furniture. To be honest, we wouldn't buy any crib with an obscure brand name. Why? We'd rather buy a crib from a company that makes just cribs (or whose major business is cribs). Such companies have better designs, stock replacement parts and generally are on the forefront of safety research. Companies who make the obscure brands, however, are usually just marketing a "me-too" crib that's sold strictly on price.

E-MAIL FROM THE REAL WORLD
IKEA fans love ready-to-assemble furniture

 Bargain shoppers on both the East and West coasts are probably very familiar with IKEA, the European furniture superstore with stylish furniture at down-to-earth prices. What you might not realize is IKEA also offers nursery furniture at great prices. Here's an e-mail we received from one IKEA fan:

"We outfitted our entire nursery for just $300 at IKEA. The crib was $79, a basic dresser was $110, while the changing table top was $50. The beauty of Ikea is that many of the furnishings come flat-packed, ready to take home and assemble yourself—don't fret, though, each pieces comes with easy-to-follow, logical instructions. Only drawback: IKEA furniture isn't for traditionalists. Most items are made of beech, wood veneer or laminate and particle board. Despite this, they are very durable and of high quality." ✍

Note: There are only a dozen or so IKEA's in the U.S, most of which are on the East and West coasts (there is also one in Houston, TX). To find a store near you, call 610-834-0180.

Who Is Jenny Lind?

You can't shop for cribs and not hear the name "Jenny Lind." Here's an important point to remember: Jenny Lind isn't a *brand* name; it refers to a particular *style* of crib. But how did it get this name? Jenny Lind was a popular Swedish soprano during the 19th century. During her triumphal U.S. tour, it was said that Lind slept in a "spool bed." Hence, cribs that feature turned spindles (which look like stacked spools of thread) became known as Jenny Lind cribs. All this begs the question—what if today we still named juvenile furniture after famous singers? Could we have Whitney Houston cribs and Melissa Ethridge dressers? Nah.

Safe & Sound: Safety Tips and Advice

 Here's a little fact to keep you up at night: cribs are associated with more children's deaths than any other juvenile product. That's right, number one. In the latest year for which statistics are available, over 13,000 injuries and 50 deaths were blamed on cribs alone. Altogether, nursery equipment and furniture account for over 92,000 injuries serious enough to require emergency room treatment each year.

Now, before you get all excited, let's point out that the vast majority of injuries related to cribs were caused by *old* cribs. Surprisingly, these old cribs may not be as old as you think— some models from the 1970s and early 1980s have caused many injuries and deaths. Nearly all *new* cribs sold in the United States meet the current safety standards designed to prevent injuries. These facts brings us to our biggest safety tip on cribs:

♣ *Don't buy a used or old crib.* Let's put that into bold caps: **DON'T BUY A USED OR OLD CRIB.** And don't take a hand-me-down from a well-meaning friend or relative. Why? Because old cribs can be death traps—spindles that are too far apart, cut-outs in the headboard, and other hazards that could entrap your baby's head. Decorative trim (like turned posts) that looks great on adult beds are a major no-no for cribs—they present a strangulation hazard. Other cribs have lead paint, a dangerous peril for a teething baby.

It may seem somewhat ironic that a book on baby bargains would advise you to go out and spend your hard-earned money on a new crib. True, we find great bargains at consignment and second-hand stores. However, you have to draw the line at your baby's safety. Certain items are great deals at these stores—toys and clothes come to mind. However, cribs (and, as you'll read later, car seats) are no-no's, no matter how tempting the bargains.

Readers of the first edition of this book wondered why we didn't put in tips for evaluating old or hand-me-down cribs. The reason is simple: it's hard to tell whether an old crib is dangerous just by looking at it. Cribs don't have "freshness dates"—most manufacturers don't stamp the date of manufacture on their cribs. Was the crib made before or after the current safety standards went into effect in the 1980's? Who knows?

Today's safety regulations are so specific (like the allowable width for spindles) that you just can't judge a crib's safety with a cursory examination. Cribs made before the 1970's might contain lead paint, which is difficult to detect unless you get it tested. Another problem: if the brand name is rubbed off, it will be hard to tell if the crib has been involved in a recall. Obtaining replacement parts is also difficult for a no-name crib.

What if a relative insists you should use the "family heirloom" crib? We've spoken to dozens of parents who felt pressured into using an old crib by a well-meaning relative. There's a simple answer: don't use it. As a parent, you sometimes have to make unpopular decisions that are best for your child's safety. This is just the beginning.

♣ *Cribs with fold-down railings or attached dressers are a major safety hazard.* Most cribs have a side rail that drops to give you access to an infant. However, a few models have fold-down railings—to gain access to the crib, the upper one-third of the railing is hinged and folds down.

What's the problem? Well, toddlers can get a foothold on the hinged rail to climb out of the crib, injuring themselves as they fall to the floor. Attached dressers (like on the Child Craft Crib N Bed model) pose a similar problem. Children can climb onto the dresser and then out of the crib. One mother we interviewed was horrified to find her 10-month-old infant sitting on top of a four-foot-high dresser one night.

So what's the appeal of these cribs? Well, manufacturers like Child Craft and Baby's Dream (whose Crib 4 Life has a fold-down rail) say the design lets you easily convert the crib into a youth bed (a small size bed that uses the crib mattress). We say big deal—most children can go directly from a crib to a twin bed, making the "youth" bed an unnecessary item. Another point to remember: if you plan to have subsequent children, you can't use the crib again (because the older child is using it's frame for his bed).

And the prices of these items are amazing—Child Craft's Crib N Bed is nearly $500 and many Baby's Dream models sell for similar prices. For that kind of money, you can buy a decent (and safe) crib with a normal drop-side release *and* a twin bed. Yet our biggest beef with these products comes down to safety. We urge the Consumer Products Safety Commission to initiate an investigation as to whether cribs with fold-down side rails should be banned.

♣ *Metal beds.* Metal cribs are cheap (under $100 retail), but they have safety problems. First, sloppy welding between parts of the crib can leave sharp edges. Clothing can snag and fingers can get cut. Remember that when your baby starts to stand, she will be all over the crib—chewing on the railing, handling the spindles, and more. We've also noticed that inexpensive metal cribs tend to have inadequate mattress support. In many models, the mattress is held up with cheap vinyl straps. Despite these problems, a new metal crib is still a better buy from a safety point of view than an old crib or a crib with a fold-down railing.

♣ *Forget about no-name cribs.* Many less-than-reputable baby stores import cheap cribs from some third world country whose standards for baby safety are light years behind the U.S. Why would stores do this? Bigger profits—cheap imports can be marked up big-time and still be sold to unsuspecting parents at prices below name-brand cribs.

Take the Baby Furniture Outlet of Marathon, Florida. These scam artists imported cribs and playpens that grossly failed to meet federal safety standards. From the construction to the hardware, the cribs were a disaster waiting to happen. As a result, 19 babies were injured, and the Consumer Products Safety Commission permanently banned the items in 1987. Sold under the "Small Wonders" brand name at the Baby Furniture Outlet (and other outlets nationwide), parents were undoubtedly suckered in by the "outlet" savings of these cheap cribs. Instead of recalling the cribs, the company declared bankruptcy and claimed it couldn't pay to fix the problem.

♣ *Watch out for sharp edges.* It amazes us that any company today would market a baby furniture item with sharp edges. Yet, there are still some on the market. We've seen changing tables with sharp edges and dressers with dangerous corners. A word to the wise: be sure to check out any nursery item carefully before buying.

What's the lesson? Stick to brand names, like the ones we review earlier in this chapter. Also check to see if the crib has the Juvenile Products Manufacturers Association (JPMA) seal. In a box earlier in this chapter, we explained how they certify cribs by major brands.

Recalls: Where to Find Information

The U.S. Consumer Product Safety Commission has a toll-free hotline at (800) 638-2772 for the latest recall information on cribs and other juvenile furniture. It's easy to use—the hotline is a series of recorded voice mail messages that you access by following the prompts. You can also report any potential hazard you've discovered or an injury to your child caused by a product. Write to the U.S. Consumer Products Safety Commission, Washington, D.C. 20207.

Another good source: Toys R Us posts product recall information at the front of their stores. Although they don't sell much in the way of furniture, you will find recall information on a myriad of other products like high chairs, bath seats, and toys.

Money Saving Secrets

1 GO FOR A SINGLE INSTEAD OF DOUBLE. Cribs that have a single-drop side are usually less expensive ($50 to $100 cheaper) than those with double-drop sides. Sure, double-drop side cribs are theoretically more versatile (you can take the baby out from either side), but ask yourself if your baby's room is big enough to take advantage of this feature. Most small rooms necessitate that the crib be placed against a wall—a double-drop side crib would then be a tad useless, wouldn't it?

2 FORGET THE DESIGNER BRANDS. What do you get for $500 when you buy a crib with such fancy names as Bellini or Ragazzi? Safety features that rival the M-1 tank? Exotic wood from Bora Bora? Would it surprise you to learn that these cribs are no different than those that cost $180 to $300? Oh sure, "Italian-designed" Bellini throws in an under-crib drawer for storage and Canadian-import Ragazzi has designer colors like "persimmon." But take a good look at these cribs—we found them to be surprisingly deficient in some ways. See our reviews earlier in this chapter for more details.

3 CONSIDER MAIL-ORDER. Say you live in a town that has one baby shop. One baby shop that has sky-high prices. What's the antidote? Consider mail-order. JCPenney and Sears sell such famous (and quality) name brands as Child Craft and Bassett. Granted, they don't sell them at deep discount prices (you'll find them at regular retail). But this may be more preferable than the price-gouging local store that thinks it has a license from God to overcharge everyone on cribs and juvenile furniture. Another good source: North Carolina furniture discounters. As mentioned earlier in the review of Lexington, Loftin-Black Furniture (800) 334-7398

offers great discounts on a couple brands of cribs and juvenile furniture (including Bassett) and ships the items direct to your home. One note of caution: be sure to compare delivery costs and policies. See the box E-Mail from the Real World about a story on this subject later in this chapter.

4 Shop around. We found the same crib priced $100 less at one store than at a competitor down the street. Use the manufacturers' phone numbers (printed earlier in this chapter) to find other dealers in your area for price comparisons. Take the time to visit the competition, and you might be pleasantly surprised to find that the effort will be rewarded.

5 Go naked. Naked furniture, that is. We see an increasing number of stores that sell unfinished (or naked) furniture at great prices. Such places even sell the finishing supplies and give you directions (make sure to use a non-toxic finish). The prices are hard to beat. At a local unfinished furniture store, we found a three-drawer pine dresser (23" wide) for $90, while a four drawer dresser (38" wide) was $160. Compare that to baby store prices, which can top $300 to $600 for a similar size dresser. A reader in California e-mailed us with a great bargain find in the Bay Area: "Bus Van" has two locations in San Francisco (900 Battery, 415-981-1405 and 244 Clement 415-752-5353) that sell unfinished furniture. She found a five-drawer dresser in pine for just $109 there and other good deals on glider-rockers. While we haven't seen an unfinished crib at these places (yet), naked furniture stores at least offer affordable alternatives for dressers, bookcases, and more.

6 Shop at regular furniture stores for rockers, dressers, etc. Think about it—most juvenile furniture looks very similar to regular adult furniture. Rockers, dressers, and bookcases are, well, just rockers, dressers, and bookcases. And don't you wonder if companies slap the word "baby" on an item just to raise the price 20%? To test this theory, we visited a local discount furniture store. The prices were incredibly low. A basic three-drawer dresser was $56. Even pine or oak three-drawer dressers were just $129 to $189. The same dresser at a baby store by a "juvenile" manufacturers would set you back at least $300, if not twice that. We even saw cribs by such mainstream names as Bassett at decent prices in regular furniture stores. What's the disadvantage to shopping there? Well, if you have to buy the crib and dresser at different places, the colors might not match exactly. But, considering the savings, it might be worth it. The baby can't tell.

Best Buys: Baby Mega-Stores

BEST BUY There was a time not too long ago when going shopping for baby meant hitting a dozen or so stores. You might have viewed cribs at a specialty store, then driven to a department store to check out bedding and clothes. Safety items? It was on to a third store, perhaps a discount chain that had great prices but very little selection. By the time you shopped for a car seat, high chair or stroller, you would have logged a good number of miles on the odometer.

Well, all that's changed. In the early 1990's, a new breed of baby retail was born: the mega-store. With 30,000 or more square feet, these stores stocked everything a parent needed, from necessities like diapers to luxuries like the latest strollers from Europe.

There are three companies competing in this segment: Baby Superstore (which was bought in 1996 by Toys R Us), LiL' Things, and Baby Depot/Totally for Kids, which is part of the Burlington Coat Factory chain. In this section, we'll look at the strengths and weaknesses of each store.

Baby Superstore (call 864-968-9292 for a store near you; internet: *www.bsst.com*) was the first company to launch this concept nationwide. Jack Tate, who started the company with a series of small baby shops in South Carolina, quickly realized the future of the business in 1991 when he opened his first "large" Baby Superstore. Their motto was "prices were born here and raised elsewhere."

Baby Superstore was at the right place at the right time. When the company went pubic a few years later, investors snapped up their stock with the zeal usually reserved for high-tech wunderkinds. Baby Superstore used this windfall to launch an aggressive expansion and by 1996, they had 70 stores nationwide. From their base in the Southeast, they expanded as far west as Arizona and as far north as Chicago. At the same time, the Baby Superstore concept was refined— gone was the early "warehouse look" and in came a slicker store layout with bright signage and better displays.

Yet, like all high flyers on Wall Street, Baby Superstore soon learned it couldn't defy gravity for long. The company quickly became a victim of its own success—sales at existing stores slumped as management was distracted with the task of putting up the latest new store. Consumers complained to us about inconsistent service: some stores had helpful staff, while others didn't seem to care. The company also shot itself in the foot with a series of missteps—an accounting scandal gave Baby Superstore a black eye and the company never reached its own rosy projections in terms of sales and profits. As a result, Wall Street pounced, sending the stock diving 75% in value in a few short weeks.

At the same time all this was happening with Baby Superstore, alarm bells were going off at House of Geoffrey—Toys R Us, the industry behemoth, was getting nervous. As Baby Superstore and others were expanding across the country, the company noticed a disturbing trend. Instead of stealing customers from fancy specialty stores, Baby Superstore was poaching more parents-to-be from discounters like Toys R Us.

In a belated reaction to the competition, Toys R Us launched their own baby mega-store concept in 1996, dubbed (as you might guess) *Babies R Us*. Instead of cheap, low-brow brands carried in their main stores, Babies R Us focused on higher-quality merchandise. The company quickly opened a half dozen Babies R Us in locations like Long Island, New York and Atlanta, with more to come in Southern California.

Yet, when Baby Superstore stumbled, Toys R Us saw an opportunity. It would take years to build their own baby mega-store chain. Hey! Why not buy an existing company and leap frog over the competition? Hence, the deal was sealed in October 1996—Toys R Us swallowed Baby Superstore whole.

At the time of this writing, it's unclear what exact plans Toys R Us has in mind for Baby Superstore. It's a safe bet the company will merge its operations with that of Babies R Us, probably moving Baby Superstore's headquarters to New Jersey in the process. Hence, it may be a good bet to keep the Babies R Us phone number (201) 599-7840 handy when looking for these stores. We hear that new stores will be called "Babies R Us: Your Baby Superstore."

Whether the merchandise in Baby Superstore will change is also up in the air. If Babies R Us dumps quality brand names like Peg Perego strollers and Simmons cribs, that would be a shame. The latest Baby Superstores feature an impressive array of brands in all price points—sure, you can buy a basic stroller for $30, but they also have European and Japanese options that top $300. Another plus: we love Baby Superstore's wide assortment of items like baby monitors, diapers and feeding supplies.

If Babies R Us could improve anything with Baby Superstore, it would have to be their displays. We've never liked the way Baby Superstore merchandised items like cribs and bedding. Instead of having one area with furniture, the cribs are scattered across several aisles, divided by color/finish (white, oak, maple, cherry, etc.). Baby Superstore's selection of clothes, toys and videos could also be improved.

By contrast, our favorite entry in this category *LiL' Things* (for a store near you, call 817-649-6100) has a much more logical layout. This Texas-based chain has 20+ stores in places like Dallas/Ft. Worth, Houston, Austin, Tulsa, Oklahoma City, Denver, Phoenix and San Jose. LiL' Things has taken the baby mega-store concept to another level—sure, you'll find strollers, cribs and car seats to your heart's content, but the stores also have services like a hair salon (LiL' Cuts) and photo studio.

LiL' Things is better-designed than other similar stores, with bright signage that points to areas like safety items, shoes, clothes and more. The store is also more hands-on—their toy area features displays where your child can play with an item before you buy. The "LiL' Land" of slides, trucks and cars is always buzzing with activity.

If we had to criticize LiL Things on any point, it would have to be brand selection in certain categories. Areas like baby monitors and crib bedding lack the better quality brand names we'd like to see. (To be fair, Baby Superstore also falls short in the bedding category as well—both of the chains seem to have more success with the "mass market" bedding brands like Pooh than upper-end bedding with 200 thread counts). On the upside, you can find Child Craft cribs at LiL Things, as well as strollers from Peg Perego, Aprica and Combi. Another plus is the service—we found the employees here much more knowledgeable about products and brands than other baby stores.

Clothing seems to be evolving into a critical piece of both LiL' Things and Baby Superstore's merchandising mix. Both chains now put these high-margin items on display in the middle of the store for maximum visibility. Once again, we have to give the edge to LiL' Things in this category—they carry better brands and have many more options with items like shoes than the Baby Superstore.

What about *Baby Depot*? The third entry in the baby mega-store sweepstakes is a chain owned by Burlington Coat Factory (call 800-444-COAT or 609-386-3314 for a store near you). To be honest, we don't know what to make of Baby Depot—we visited three different Depots and came away with vastly different impressions. In Dallas, we visited a Baby Depot that was tucked in an ancient Burlington Coat Factory that felt more like a warehouse than a factory. Yet, even crammed in a small portion of the store, the Depot had its plusses—cribs from Child Craft, Evenflo car seats and strollers from Peg Perego. Best of all were the prices; they were darn low. And we soon noticed the Baby Depot has frequent sales, where they slice those price tags even more.

Our visit to a Baby Depot in Denver was a completely different experience. This Depot was a department in a brand-new Burlington Coat Factory that looked more like a nice department store. The selection and prices were much the same, although the displays and stock quantities were much better than Dallas.

Finally, we visited the Baby Depot in Milpitas, California (outside of San Jose). Except this wasn't called Baby Depot—nope, this was a "Totally for Kids." It turns out that Burlington has a handful of these stores on both the East and West Coast (why they went with the other name is baffling). Totally For Kids is a huge store that looks more like Baby Superstore or LiL' Things, with much more selection and options. Despite this, we were not as impressed—the whole store seemed chaotic, employees were non-existent and the displays were all jumbled together. Yet, the prices were, once again, fantastic. If you know exactly what you want and have one of these stores nearby, it's definitely worth the visit.

So, which baby mega-store should you shop at? Heck, we'd hit them all. For those lucky enough to have both (or all three) stores in one town, we'd compare prices and selection. You'll find one has that new high chair you want, while another may run a special close-out on a stroller that's a steal.

E-MAIL FROM THE REAL WORLD
Bargains for parents in the Northeast

 While there is a Babies R Us on Long Island (NY), there aren't too many other superstore options for those folks who live in the Northeast. For some reason, Baby Superstore and LiL' Things have concentrated their expansion in other parts of the country. But don't fret—that doesn't mean you can't find great deals in that part of the U.S. Here's an e-mail from a mother-to-be who found a great crib deal in New Jersey:

"There aren't too many bargain baby places near where we live in New York City, but we did found a few crib stores in New Jersey that are pretty competitive, price-wise—though I must say, my husband went through sticker-shock at first! We shopped *Crib Outlet*, 1603A Route 22W, Union, New Jersey (908) 686-6733 and *Crib City*, #130 on Route 22, Springfield, New Jersey (201) 379-2229. We stumbled onto a GREAT deal at Crib City: A Child Craft crib in white with turned spindles all the way around, a three drawer dresser/flip top changing table and four-drawer dresser, plus mattress and changing pad—all for $950!! It was a floor model on sale . . . but the big bonus was they had an extra boxed set, so we got it brand new!"

Outlets

Very few manufacturers of cribs and juvenile furniture have outlets. In fact, we only found one. If you discover an outlet that you'd like to share with our readers, call us at (303) 442-8792.

Cosco

2525 State St., Columbus, IN 47201. (812) 372-0141.

Located inside their factory in Columbus, Indiana, Cosco's outlet store sells cribs, high chairs, play pens, and more. In fact, the store sells nearly every product that bears the Cosco name. Prices are up to 50% off retail, and both new and slightly damaged merchandise is on display. As we mentioned in the Name Game, we're not wild about Cosco's metal cribs, but their other products (most notably baby monitors, high chairs, and other accessories) are good buys. The store is only open weekdays, 10-6.

Special thanks to the *Joy of Outlet Shopping* magazine for helping us track down the Cosco outlet. To order a copy of the magazine, call 1-800-344-6397.

Wastes of Money

1 "CONVERTIBLE" CRIBS. Convertible to what, you might ask? Manufacturers pitch these more expensive cribs as a money-saver since they are convertible to "youth beds," which are smaller and narrower than a twin bed. But, guess what? Most kids can go straight from a crib to a regular twin bed with no problem whatsoever. So, the youth bed business is really a joke. Another rip-off: some manufacturers sell cribs that convert to adult-size beds. The catch? You have to pay for a "conversion kit," which will set you back another $30 to $200. And that's on top of the hefty prices ($400 to $600) that many of these models cost initially. Also, if you have more than one child, you'll have to buy another crib (because the older child is using the "convertible" crib frame for their bed).

2 BASSINET. Do you really need one? A newborn infant can sleep in a regular crib just as easily as a cradle. And you'll save a bundle on that bundle of joy—cradles run $100 to $400. Of course, the advantage of having the baby in a cradle is you can keep it in your room for the baby's first few weeks, making midnight (and 2 am and 4 am) feedings more convenient. If you want to go this way, consider a bassinet instead of a cradle (bassinets are baskets set on top of a stand, while cradles are wooden miniature versions of cribs that rock). We priced bassinets at only $40 to $180, much less than cradles. Is it worth the extra money? It's up to you, but our baby slept in his crib from day one, and it worked out just fine. If the distance between your room and the baby's is too far and you'd like to give a bassinet a try, see if you can find one at a consignment or second-hand store. (A good brand of affordable bassinets is Badger Basket; call 847-381-6200 for a dealer near you).

E-MAIL FROM THE REAL WORLD
Get all the details on delivery before you mail-order furniture

 A mom-to-be in Chicago discovered Sears was a much better deal than JCPenney for her nursery furniture. Here's her story:

"While I was searching for major baby furniture, I thought JCPenney's would be a good choice. The catalog gave me a large selection to choose from and it would be less time consuming than hitting all the little shops. So, I put in an order for a crib and mattress and a four-drawer dresser. The prices on the furniture were pretty good (about $150 less than in other stores). However, the furniture has to be shipped directly from the warehouse to your home. Shipping and handling would have been $110 and the shipping company would only drop off the material at the front door—not into the home (or, in our case, a second floor apartment!) I could hardly believe it! If I had to spend over a hundred dollars extra on shipping, I would rather spend it on a higher quality crib and dresser than on shipping and handling. Hence, the search continued.

"So, next I went to Sears where they had the 'Sculptured' series Child Craft crib and the matching flip-top dresser. The prices were reasonable, you could pick the delivery day (including Saturdays) and they would deliver and set up for just $25! They had these items in stock, so we got it in two days. Even if it did have to be shipped from the main warehouse, however, we would still only be charged the $25 fee and would have to wait at most four weeks. Needless to say, we bought the crib and dresser at Sears!"

3 CRIBS WITH "SPECIAL FEATURES." It may be tempting to buy a special crib (like the round cribs from Little Miss Liberty, reviewed earlier in this chapter), but watch out. A special crib may require special additional expenses, such as custom-designed mattresses or bedding. While Little Miss Liberty includes a round foam mattress with every crib it sells, the special bedding it sells is extra . . . prepare to spend another $200 to $800. And since few companies make bedding for round cribs, your choices are limited. The best advice: make sure you price out the total investment (crib, mattress, bedding) before falling in love with an unusual brand.

4 CHANGING TABLES. Separate changing tables are a big waste of money. Don't spend $70 to $200 on a piece of furniture you won't use again after your baby gives up diapers. A better bet: buy a dresser that can do double duty as a changing table. A good example are the hi-low dressers (pioneered by Rumple Tuff, reviewed later in this chapter) which start at $350 (not much more than a regular dresser). Best of all, a hi-low dresser doesn't look like a changing table and can be used as a real piece of furniture as your child grows older. Another solution: buy a dresser with a flip-top changing table. Child Craft makes one for about $430. Other parents we interviewed did away with the changing area altogether—they used a crib, couch or floor to do diaper changes.

Do it by Mail: The Best Mail-Order Sources for Cribs and Baby Furniture

JCPenney.

To Order Call: (800) 222-6161. Ask for the following catalogs: "For Baby" and "Maternity Collection"
Shopping Hours: 24 hours a day, seven days a week.
Credit Cards Accepted: MC, VISA, JCPenney, AMEX, Discover.

 JCPenney has been selling baby clothes, furniture, and more for over 90 years. Their popular mail-order catalog has two free "mini-catalogs" that should be of particular interest to parents-to-be.

"For Baby" is Penney's main furniture catalog, with over 50 pages of cribs, bedding, mattresses, safety items, car seats, strollers, swings, and even a few pages of baby clothes. The crib section features such famous brand names as Child Craft, Okla Homer Smith, Stork Craft and Bassett. An example of Penney's prices: a Child Craft "Child Line" hardwood crib with a single-drop side is $180. If you buy both the crib and mattress, Penney's offers discounts of $15 to $50 off the crib—a pretty good deal. Other crib offerings range from a Cosco metal crib for $130 to a Bassett hand-painted crib for $299.

Looking for a bassinet? Penney's sells a basic model with hood for $40, plus a wide variety of accessories like liners, skirts, and hood covers. Crib mattresses run from $35 for a foam mattress to $100 for a Sealy Baby Posturpedic.

New this year in the catalog are Dutailier glider rockers in three styles with six fabric choices ($200 to $270). The ottomans are $110 each. You can also find high chairs like the Evenflo Phases (reviewed later in this book), strollers by Century, Gerry and Kolcraft and car seats by Evenflo, Century and Cosco.

The catalogs could be organized better—the furniture catalog mixes prices for cribs, linens, and other accessories on the same page, making price comparisons somewhat difficult. Nevertheless, if you live in a remote area or in a town with sky-high prices, the Penney's catalog offers a good deal—name brands at decent prices.

Mattresses

Now that you've just spent several hundred dollars on a crib, you're done, right? Wrong. Despite price tags that can soar over $500, most cribs don't come with mattresses. So, here's our guide to buying the best quality mattress for the lowest price.

Smart Shopper Tips

Smart Shopper Tip #1
FOAM OR COIL?

"It seems the choice for a crib mattress comes down to foam or coil? Which is better? Does it matter?"

Yes, it does matter. After researching this issue, we've come down on the foam side of the debate. Why? Foam mattresses are lighter than those with coils, making it easier to change the sheets in the middle of the night when Junior reenacts the Great Flood in his crib. Foam mattresses typically weigh less than five pounds, while coil mattresses can top 20 pounds! Another plus: foam mattresses are less expensive, running $35 to $90. Coil mattresses cost $50 to $150.

We get quite a few calls from readers on this issue. Many baby stores only sell coil mattresses, claiming that coil is superior to foam. One salesperson even told a parent that foam mattresses aren't safe for babies older than six months. Please. We've consulted with pediatricians and industry experts on this issue and have come to the conclusion that the best course is to choose a *firm* mattress for baby—it doesn't matter whether it's a firm coil mattress or a firm foam one. We suspect some stores only sell coil because they can get fatter profit margins from such items.

Smart Shopper Tip #2
COIL OVERKILL AND CHEAP FOAM MATTRESSES

"How do you tell a cheap quality coil mattress from a better one? How about foam mattresses—what makes one better than the next?"

Evaluating different crib mattresses isn't easy. Even the cheap ones claim they are "firm" and comparing apples to apples is difficult. When it comes to coil mattresses, the number of coils seems like a good way to compare mattresses, but even that can be deceiving. For example, is a 150 coil mattress better than an 80 coil mattress?

Well, yes and no. While an 80 coil mattress probably won't be as firm as one with 150 coils, it's important to remember that a large number of coils does not necessarily mean the mattress is superior. Factors such as the wire gauge, number of turns per coil and the temper of the wire contribute to the firmness, durability and strength of the mattress. Unfortunately, most mattresses only note the coil count (and no other details). Hence, the best bet would be to buy a good brand that has a solid quality reputation (we'll recommend specific choices after this section).

What about foam mattresses? The cheapest foam mattresses are made of low-density foam (about .9 pounds per cubic foot). The better foam mattresses are high-density with 1.5 pounds per cubic foot. Easy for us to say, right? Once again, foam mattresses don't list density on their packing, leaving consumers to wonder whether they're getting high or low density. As with coil mattresses, you have to rely on a reputable brand name to get a good foam mattress (see the next section for more details).

Smart Shopper Tip #3
DO FOAM MATTRESSES HAVE A GAS PROBLEM?

"I read on the Internet that some foam mattresses have an out-gassing problem. Is this true?"

We've noticed that several eco-catalogs have raised concerns that standard crib mattresses are a possible health hazard. One even went on to say that such mattresses are "unhealthy combinations of artificial foams, fluorocarbons, synthetic fibers and formaldehyde, all materials that give off toxic fumes." The solution? Buy *their* organic cotton crib mattress for a whopping $650 and your baby won't have to breathe that nasty stuff.

Hold it. We checked with pediatricians and industry experts and found no evidence that such a problem exists. While it is possible that a foam or coil mattress might give off a few vapors when you first take it out of the packaging, there's no ongoing fume problem in our opinion. There are also no medical studies linking, say, lower SAT scores to kids who slept on foam mattresses as babies. While it is possible that a few children who have extreme chemical sensitivities might do better on "organic" mattresses, it's doubtful such products will make any difference to the vast majority of infants.

We think it's irresponsible of such eco-crusaders to raise bogus issues intended to scare parents without providing corresponding proof of their claims.

Top Picks: Brand Recommendations

When it comes to mattresses, it's best not to scrimp. Go for the best mattress you can afford. Besides, the price differences between the cheap products and the better quality ones is often small, about $50 or so.

♣ *Foam Mattresses.* Our top brand recommendation is *Colgate* (call 404-681-2121 for a dealer near you). This Georgia-based company makes a full line of foam mattresses which range from $42 to $100. Among the best of Colgate's offerings is the "Classica," a group of five-inch foam mattresses with varying firmnesses. The Classica II was top-rated by *Consumer Reports* and is available in stores like LiL' Things and mail-order catalogs like Baby Catalog of America (1-800-PLAYPEN) for about $80 to $90. Colgate's Grand Premier is their top-of-the line five-inch "super firm" mattress.

♣ *Coil Mattresses. Simmons* (see the review of Simmons cribs earlier in this chapter for contact info) makes a good line of coil mattresses, including the "Super Maxipedic" 9200 mattress with 160 coils constructed of heavy-gauge tempered steel. It sells for $100 to $125. Once again, we also like the *Colgate* line, which offers 16 options. The Colgate "Cradletyme Deluxe Ultra II 150 coil" is a typical offering at about $100. We recommend a coil mattress with 150 coils in general (keeping in mind the previous discussion about wire gauge, etc.). Fewer coils makes the mattress too soft; more coils (say 250 or 280) is overkill.

Still can't decide between foam or coil? Well, Colgate has a solution—a "2 in 1" mattress that is half foam and half coil. The company suggests the extra-firm foam side for infants. When your baby reaches toddlerhood, you flip the mattress over to the coil side. While this sounds nice, we were put off by the product's hefty price tag ($160 in some stores). As a result, we still think a good foam mattress is still your best bet.

Safe & Sound

 Babies don't have the muscle strength to lift their heads up when put face-down into soft or fluffy bedding—some have suffocated as a result. The best defense: buy a firm mattress (foam or coil) and don't place your baby face down in soft, thick quilts, wool blankets, pillows, or toys. (Futon mattresses are also a no-no). Never put the baby down on a vinyl mattress without a cover or sheet since vinyl can also contribute to suffocation. In addition, you should know that several studies into the causes of Sudden Infant Death Syndrome (SIDS) have found that a too-soft sleep surface (such as the items listed above) and environmental factors (a too-hot room, cigarette smoke) are related to crib death, though exactly how has yet to be determined. Experts therefore advise against letting infants sleep on a too-soft surface. Another important tip: make sure you put your baby to sleep on her side or back. Studies suggest that babies who are put to sleep on their stomachs have an increased risk of SIDS.

Dressers & Changing Tables

The trade refers to dressers, changing tables, and the like as "case pieces" since they are essentially furniture made out of a large case (pretty inventive, huh?). Now that you've got a place for the baby sleep (and a mattress for the baby to sleep on), where are you going to put all those cute outfits that you'll get as gifts? And let's not forget that all too important activity that will occupy so many of your hours after the baby is born: changing diapers.

The other day we calculated that by our baby's first birthday, we had changed over 2400 diapers! Wow! To first-time parents, that may seem like an unreal number, but babies actually do go through 70 to 100 diapers a week for the first six months or so. That translates into 10 to 15 changes a day. Hence, you'll need some place to change those diapers.

What are You Buying

 1 DRESSERS. As you shop for baby furniture, you'll note a wide variety of dressers—three drawer, four drawer, armoires, combination

dresser/changing tables, and more. No matter which type you choose, we do have two general tips for getting the most for your money. First, choose a dresser whose drawers roll out on roller bearings. Cheap dressers have drawers that simply sit on a track. As a result, they don't roll out as smoothly and are prone to come off the track. Our second piece of advice: make sure the dresser top is laminated. If you're in a rush and put something wet on top, you want to make sure you don't damage the finish. Also, unlaminated tops are more prone to scratches and dings.

2 CHANGING AREA. Basically, you have two options here. You can buy a separate changing table or a combination dresser/changing table. As mentioned earlier, we think a separate changing table is a waste of money (as well as a waste of space).

A better option is the combo package, a dresser and changing table all rolled into one. These come in two varieties: the flip-top and the hi-low. Flip-top dressers have a top unit that flips forward to provide a space to change the baby. Some of these models convert to regular dressers (the changing table top detaches and can be removed). A good example is Child Craft's flip-top dresser (about $400). The large changing surface of this changing table would be great for parents of twins. The only downside? It's kind of a pain to flip the changing area over each time you want to use it. Also, there's a limited area for changing supplies in the small space under the flip-top.

Hi-low dressers are another option. These dressers (pioneered by Rumble Tuff, reviewed later in this section) are popular for a good reason—their two-tier design provides a convenient space to change diapers while not looking like a diaper changing table. Most parents keep diaper changing supplies in the upper drawer, while the lower dresser functions as clothing storage, etc. Hi-low dressers start at $350 and range up to $500.

Let's say you're on a really tight budget. What should you do? Forget the diaper changing station altogether! Some mothers we interviewed just change their baby in the crib.

Of course, there are a couple of disadvantages. First, there's not a convenient place for diapers and supplies. This could be solved by a rolling nursery cart (cost: about $25 in many catalogs). Another disadvantage: if you have a boy, he could spray the crib sheets, bumper pads, and just about anything else in the crib with his little "water pistol." Hence, you might find yourself doing more laundry.

One mom sent us an e-mail with a solution to the

changing table dilemma—she bought a "Rail Rider," changing table that fits across a crib and can be removed when the baby is sleeping. For $28, it did the trick. Made by Burlington Basket Company (for a dealer near you, call 800-553-2300 or 319-754-6508), the Rail Rider does have a few drawbacks: it doesn't fit all cribs and shorter folks find it more difficult to use.

Nursery in a closet
New York City parents make do with less

It always amazes us about how some folks in New York City can squeeze their life into a tiny studio apartment. And where do you put the nursery when the kitchen is crammed into a hallway?

For some parents, a closet is the only place they have left for Junior's room. (Of course, make sure the closet is baby-proofed and a fan is installed for adequate ventilation). In such cases, space saving juvenile furniture and equipment isn't a luxury for New Yorkers, it's a requirement.

We found two items that should be of interest to those who have to make do with less—a combo dresser/changing table/bathtub as well as a folding high chair, both made by Peg Perego, the Italian manufacturer of baby products.

The PrimeBolle "bathinette" is one of the most inventive products we've seen in years. What the heck is a bathinette? Popular in Europe for it's space saving design, the bathinette combines a dresser, changing table and baby bath all in one piece of furniture.

The PrimeBolle is made of lightweight injection-molded plastic and sits on casters, so it can be easily wheeled about. There's even a built-in towel rack and shelf that hide away when not in use. It ain't cheap (about $400 retail), but it might do the trick for those who with a nursery in the closet.

We'll also review another space-saver from Peg Perego later in this book—the Prima Poppa high chair, the only full-feature high chair that actually folds up to store out of the way. Call (219) 482-8191 to find a Peg Perego dealer near you.

The Name Game: Reviews of Selected Manufacturers

The Ratings

★★★★ EXCELLENT—*our top pick!*
  ★★★ GOOD—*above average quality, prices, and creativity.*
    ★★ FAIR—*could stand some improvement.*
     ★ POOR—*yuck! could stand some major improvement.*

Simmons .... ★★ ¹/₂

613 E. Beacon Ave., New London, WI 54961. For a dealer near you, call (414) 982-2140. While we liked Simmons cribs, we weren't as wild about their case pieces. Why? The prices are just too high. For example, a basic four-drawer dresser weighs in at a pricey $400. And that price is from one of the baby mega-store discounters. For your money, you at least get drawers with solid wood sides (cheaper dressers have pressed-board drawer sides). But this feature is really overkill when it comes to juvenile furniture. Another negative: the dressers we saw did not have laminated tops.

Child Craft ....★★★
PO Box 444, Salem, IN 47167. For a dealer near you, call (812) 883-3111. Child Craft is a better buy when it comes to dressers and other case pieces. A four-drawer dresser starts at $300, while flip-top dressers/changing tables are in the $400 range. Child Craft uses roller bearings for their drawers, giving them a smooth pull. The only negative: the drawer sides are not solid wood. On the upside, however, the tops of the pieces are laminated. New for 1997 is a line of four-drawer dressers in the "Heirloom" style group which feature side drawer glides (for a smoother glide). These dressers are taller and wider than Child Craft's other dressers and retail for about $400 to $450.

Rumble Tuff ....★★★★
1186 North Industrial Park Dr., Orem, UT 84057. (800) 524-9607. (801) 226-2648. Rumble Tuff is our pick as the best buy in juvenile furniture. A small manufacturer based in Utah, Rumble Tuff has won fans nationwide with their affordable and stylish dressers. Their strategy is to knock-off the big guys, making similar furniture styles in the exact same finishes as Child Craft and Simmons. And the prices are fantastic—we noticed that Rumble Tuff is often 10% to 25% less than the competition.

Rumble Tuff's claim to fame is their popular "hi-low" combo dresser. This unit combines both a three-drawer dresser/changing table and a taller base cabinet and drawer. Price: $400 to $500, depending on the finish. These hi-low units have proven so popular that they've been knocked off by other furniture makers (including Osage which sells a similar unit for $350 at discount stores like LiL' Things, reviewed earlier in this chapter).

All in all, Rumble Tuff makes 30 different pieces, in both contemporary and traditional finishes. The quality is excellent: all of Rumble Tuff's drawers feature roller bearings. While the drawer sides are not solid wood, we found the overall construction to be good. We bought a Rumble Tuff dresser and bookshelf unit and have been very happy—it matches our Child Craft crib exactly and we saved about $80. Rumble Tuff is available in stores nationwide (especially on the East and West Coasts), but they're somewhat hard to find in certain metro areas (most notably in the Southeast). As a side note, Rumble Tuff also makes pads for changing tables which are excellent.

Safe & Sound

Just like the crib, you must also think about the safety aspects of the other pieces of furniture in your baby's room. Here are our tips:

♣ *Anchor those shelves.* A nice bookcase (whether on the floor or on top of the dresser) can become a tip-over hazard as the baby begins pulling up on objects. The best advice is to attach any shelves to a wall to provide stability.

♣ *Baby proof the diaper station.* If your diaper changing area has open shelves, you may have to baby proof the bottom shelves. As the baby begins to climb, you must remove any dangerous medicines or supplies from easily accessible shelves.

♣ *Choose a dresser that doesn't have drawer pulls.* Those little knobs can make it easy for baby to open the drawers—and it's those open drawers that can be used as a step stool to scale the dresser. A good tip is to buy a dresser without drawer pulls; quite a few styles have drawers with grooves that let you open the drawer from below. While this isn't totally baby proof, it reduces the attraction for baby. Another good tip: anchor the dresser to the wall. In case baby does find a way to climb it, at least the unit won't tip over.

Even More Stuff To Spend Money On

Just because to this point you have spent an amount equivalent to the gross national product of Peru on baby furniture doesn't mean you're done, of course. Nope, we've got four more items to consider for your baby's room:

1 ROCKER-GLIDER. We're not talking about the rocking chair you've seen at grandma's house. No, we're referring to the high-tech modern-day rockers that are so fancy they aren't mere rockers—they're "glider-rockers." What's the difference? Market-leader *Dutailier* (298 Chaput, St-Pie, Quebec, Canada J0H 1W0; call 800-363-9817 or 514-772-2403 for a dealer near you) says their glider-rockers have a "unique bearing system (tested to six million cycles) that ensures the best rocking sensation money can buy!" Wow! Sounds like the same system used on the Stealth bomber.

Basically, what all this hoo-hah means is gliders rock more easily than plain rocking chairs. We were somewhat skeptical about this before we bought our glider, but after doing a test drive we're convinced they're worth the extra money.

And how much money are we talking about here? A basic Dutailier (pronounced due-TAL-yea) glider starts at $210 (without cushions, or $250 with basic cushions), with some leather versions topping out at $600 or more. An optional accessory is the ottoman that glides too. This starts at $99 without a cushion, but most cost $125 to $150 with cushions.

We suggest forgetting the ottoman and ordering an inexpensive "nursing" footstool (about $30 to $40 in catalogs like Motherwear 800-950-2500). Why? Some moms claim the ottoman's height puts additional strain on their backs while breastfeeding. While the nursing footstool doesn't rock, it's lower height puts less strain on your back.

Is a glider-rocker a waste of money? Some parents have written to us with that question, assuming you'd just use the item for the baby's first couple of years. Actually, a glider-rocker can have a much longer life. You can swap the cushions after a couple of years (most companies let you order these items separately) and move the glider-rocker to a family room.

So, how can you get a deal on a Dutailier? Well, the brand is so popular that you can find them in discount baby stores like Baby Superstore and LiL' Things (see reviews earlier in this chapter). Even the JCPenney catalog (800) 222-6161 sells a few basic styles of Dutailier gliders for $270. We also discovered the Baby Catalog of America (800-PLAYPEN) sells Dutailier at a discount.

Of course, there are several other companies that make

glider-rockers for nurseries. While we think these brands are good alternatives, Dutailier is still our pick. Why? Consider the styling—while other glider-rockers make a basic number of styles, Dutailier is the fashion leader. For example, they're the only company with a "sleigh back" glider-rocker that matches similar style cribs. Dutailier also has a much wider choice of fabrics than other brands—just this year, they've released 17 new styles (including a teddy bear tapestry).

Finally, Dutailier does a better job at shipping and customer service than its rivals. In 1996, the company introduced its "Express" line—a selection of 17 chair styles in two or three different fabric choices that are in stock for shipment in two weeks. (Glider-rockers from other makers and Dutailier's regular line must be special ordered and that can take six to eight weeks). As for quality, we've never received a complaint about Dutailier glider-rockers.

Nonetheless, here are few other brands of glider-rockers to consider:

♣ *Brooks* (Call 800-427-6657 or 423-626-1111 for a dealer near you). Tennessee-based Brooks has been around for 40 years, but only entered the glider-rocker business in 1988. Their glider-rockers retail for $169 to $399, while the ottomans are $100-$200. Unlike Dutailier, all their fabrics are available on any style chair. Brooks chairs feature solid base panels (Dutailier has an open base), which the company touts as more safe. While we liked Brooks' styles and fabrics, one baby store owner told us he found the company very disorganized with poor customer service.

♣ *Conant Ball* (In the U.S., call 800-363-2635 for dealer near you or 800-556-1515 or 819-566-1515 for a dealer in Canada). We saw this brand at LiL' Things and other chain stores. The gliders retail for $170-$190 (without cushions), while ottomans start at $80. The quality is better than average and Conant Ball offers a good selection of cushions. Conant Ball is manufactured in Sherbrooke, Quebec (Canada).

♣ *Towne Square* (Call 800-356-1663 for a dealer near you). Hillsboro, Texas-based Towne Square has a lifetime warranty for all its glider-rockers. Their glider-rockers feature solid base panels for safety and a "long-glide" rocking system that has no ball bearings that can wear out. Towne Square's gliders sell for $300 to $500. Their "exclusive glider nursing ottoman" is quite unusual looking—low to the ground at a height that the manufacturer claims is "ideal for nursing."

Who is Dutailier?

Dutailier, Inc., is to glider-rockers what Microsoft is to software. But how did this company from Quebec come to dominate the glider-rocker market here in the United States?

First, consider the glider-rocker itself. It's really cool. Dutailier (call 800-363-9817 or 514-772-2403 to find a dealer near you) has an incredible selection of 45 models, 12 finishes, and 70 different fabrics. The result: over 37,000 possible combinations. All wood is solid maple or oak and features non-toxic finishes. You have to try real hard to avoid seeing a Dutailier—the company has an amazing 3500 retail dealers, from small specialty stores to major retail chains.

Dutailier offers three basic lines: The "Express" line of quick-ship styles (explained earlier in this chapter), the "Eagle" line (small chairs with basic cushions that retail for $199 to $249) and the regular "Dutailier" line (larger chairs with swivel bases, plush cushions and arm pads that retail for $259 to $999).

If we had to criticize Dutailier on something, it would have to be their cushions. Most are not machine washable (the covers can't be zipped off and put into the washing machine). As a result, you'll have to take them to a dry cleaner and pay big bucks to get them looking like new. A few of our readers have solved this problem by sewing slip covers for their glider-rockers (most fabric stores carry books with patterns for glider-rockers). Of course, if the cushions are shot, you can always order different ones when you move the glider-rocker into a family room.

2 CLOSET ORGANIZERS. Most closets are a terrible waste of space. While a simple rod and shelf might be fine for adults, the basic closet doesn't work for babies. Wouldn't it be better to have small shelves to store accessories, equipment and shoes? Or wire baskets for blankets and t-shirts? What about two or three more additional rods at varying heights to allow for more storage? The solution is closet organizers and you can go one of two routes. For the do-it-yourself crowd, consider a storage kit from such brands as Closet Maid (call 800-874-0008 for a store near you), Storage Pride (800) 441-0337 or Lee Rowan (800) 325-6150. Three catalogs that sell

storage items include Hold Everything (800) 421-2264, LL Bean (800) 341-4341 and the Container Store (800) 733-3532. A basic storage kit made of laminated particle board ranges from $50 to $120 (that will do an average size closet). Kits made of coated wire run $30 to $60.

What if you'd rather leave it to the professionals? For those parents who don't have the time or inclination to install a closet organizer themselves, consider calling Closet Factory (call 800-692-5673 for a dealer near you) or California Closets (call 800-274-6754 for a dealer near you). You can also check your local phone book under "Closets" for local companies that install closet organizers. Professionals charge about $400 to $500 for a typical closet.

While a closet organizer works well for most folks, it may be especially helpful in cases where baby's room is small. Instead of buying a separate dresser or bookshelves, you can build-in drawer stacks and shelves in a closet to squeeze out every possible inch of storage. We did this for our second child's room and were more than pleased with the results.

3 A STEREO. During those sleep deprivation experiments, it's sure nice to have some soothing music to make those hours just whiz by. Sure, you could put a cheap clock radio in the baby's room, but that assumes you have decent radio stations. And even the best radio station will be somewhat tiring to listen to for the many nights ahead. Our advice: buy (or get someone to get you as a gift) one of those CD/cassette boom box radios that run $100 to $300 in most electronics stores. Another hint: get one with digital tuning, where you can hit preset buttons to find stations. We made the mistake of buying one with analog tuning—just try to tune in that fuzzy talk-radio station at 2 am with one hand in the dark, and you'll know why digital is the way to go.

4 DIAPER PAIL. Well, those diapers have to go somewhere. Sure you could buy a basic diaper pail, but we like the Diaper Genie, that wonderful invention by a parent who apparently smelled one too many diaper pails. In Chapter 4, we'll explore the Eighth Wonder of the World: The Diaper Genie. A safety note on this subject: many basic diaper pails come with "deodorizers," little cakes that are supposed to take the stink out of stinky diapers. The only problem: many of these deodorizers contain toxic chemicals that can be poisonous if toddlers get their hands on them. A new solution to this problem comes from Sassy (call 616-243-0767 for a dealer near you).This Michigan-based company has introduced *Dream Scents*, a new line of nursery air fresheners and deodorant cakes for diaper pails that are completely non-toxic.

THE BOTTOM LINE:
A Wrap-Up of Our Best Buy Picks

 For cribs, it's hard to beat the single-drop side crib by Simmons for just $179 at LiL' Things. We also liked Child Craft cribs (except for the lowest-priced models under $200). Of all the brands, Child Craft combines the best safety features and styling at the most reasonable of prices. A double-drop side crib will set you back more ($200 to $350), but it's a nice feature if you have the room to take advantage of it.

For mattresses, we like the Colgate Classica foam mattress at $80 to $90 retail. For coil, the Simmons "Super Maxipedic" 9200 mattress with 160 coils is reasonable at $100 to $125. Colgate "Cradletyme Deluxe Ultra II 150 coil" is another good buy at about $100.

As far as stores go, we thought the baby mega-stores LiL' Things, Baby Depot, and Baby Superstore had incredible prices, although we liked LiL' Things furniture selection best. For the best selection of cribs via mail order, it's hard to beat the brand names available from JCPenney and Sears.

Dressers and other case pieces by Rumble Tuff were great deals—they exactly match the finishes of Child Craft and Simmons, but at prices 10% to 25% less than the competition. We liked their three-drawer combo unit that combines a changing table and a dresser for $415.

Finally, we recommend the Dutailier line of glider-rockers. At $330 (retail), the basic model isn't cheap but is better made than the competition. A matching ottoman runs $150 to $180. Once again, the baby mega-stores had the best prices when we checked, about 10% to 30% less than retail. For example, LiL' Things sells a basic Dutailier glider for $250 (or with matching ottoman for about $350). So, here's the total damage so far:

Simmons single drop-side crib	$179
Colgate foam mattress	$80
Rumble Tuff Hi-Lo dresser	$415
Dutailier glider-rocker	$250
Miscellaneous	$200
TOTAL	$1124

By contrast, if you bought a Bellini crib ($500), a 200-coil mattress ($160), a designer-brand dresser ($750), a fancy glider-rocker ($500), separate changing table ($200) and miscellaneous items ($200) at full retail, you'd be out $2310 by this point.

Of course, you don't have any sheets for your baby's crib yet. Nor any clothes for Junior to wear. So, next we'll explore those topics and save more of your money.

Chapter 3

Baby Bedding

How can you find brand new, designer-label bedding for 25% off the retail price? We've got the answer in this chapter, plus you'll find nine smart shopper tips to getting the most for your money. Then, we'll share six important tips that will keep your baby safe and sound. Finally, we've got reviews of the best bedding designers and an interesting list of seven top money-wasters.

Getting Started: When Do You Need This Stuff?

Begin shopping for your baby's linen pattern in the sixth month of your pregnancy, if not earlier. Why? If you're purchasing these items from a baby specialty store, they usually must be special-ordered—allow at least four to eight weeks for delivery. If you leave a few weeks for shopping, you can order the bedding in your seventh month and be assured it arrives before the baby does.

If you're buying bedding from a store or catalog that has your pattern in stock, you can wait until your eighth month. It still takes time to comparison shop, and some stores may only have certain pieces you need in stock, while other accessories (like wall hangings, etc.) may need to be ordered.

Sources:

There are four basic sources for baby bedding:

1 BABY SPECIALTY STORES. These stores tend to have a limited selection of bedding in stock. Typically, you're expected to choose the bedding by seeing what you like on sample cribs or by looking through manufacturers' catalogs. Since the stores don't stock the bedding, you have to special-order your choices and wait four to eight weeks for arrival. And that's the main disadvantage to buying linens at a specialty store: you can't always touch the merchandise. Plus, it's no fun having to wait so long. On the upside, most specialty stores do carry high-quality brand names. On the downside, you'll pay through the nose for them.

2 DISCOUNTERS/DEPARTMENT STORES. Who are the discounters? Well, they include a range of chain stores, from K-Mart and Target to Marshalls and TJ Maxx. Even Toys R Us sells baby bedding, clothes, and diapers.

Compared to specialty stores, discount stores like Toys R Us certainly carry more bedding items in stock, but the brand names are of lower quality. Prices are very affordable, but don't expect the items to last long—synthetic fabrics and cheaper construction may not withstand repeated washings.

Meanwhile, the selection of baby bedding at department stores is all over the board. Some chains have great baby departments and others need help. For example, JCPenney carries linen sets by such companies as NoJo and Cotton Tale (see the reviews of these brands later in this chapter), while Foley's (part of the May Department Store chain) seems to only have a few blankets and sheets. Prices at department stores vary as widely as selection; however, you can be guaranteed that they will hold occasional sales, making them a better deal.

3 BABY MEGA-STORES. As we mentioned in the last chapter, the major baby mega-stores LiL' Things, Babies R Us/Baby Superstore and others are an incredible resource for name brands at low prices—especially for bedding. These stores stock a good selection of bedding sets by well-known brand names at up to 50% savings off retail. We even found such premium labels as Glenna Jean at Babies R Us/Baby Superstore. The baby mega-stores also offer a special-order service similar to specialty stores. These chains tend to stock designs that have broad appeal, so if you're looking for the unusual, you may need to special-order.

4 MAIL-ORDER. Some of the big catalogs like JCPenney carry a limited selection of linens, and they tend to be lower-end options. Other catalogs like Garnet Hill offer high-quality bedding, but expect to pay for the privilege. Later in this chapter, we spotlight one mail-order company that offers the best of both worlds: famous brand names at discounted prices.

What Are You Buying?

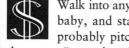 Walk into any baby store, announce you're having a baby, and stand back: the eager salespeople will probably pitch you on all types of bedding items that you "must buy." We call this the "Diaper Stacker Syndrome," named in honor of that useless (but expensive) linen item that allegedly provides a convenient place to store diapers. Most parents aren't about to spend the equivalent of

the Federal Deficit on diaper stackers. So, here's our list of the absolute necessities for your baby's linen layette:

♣ *Fitted sheets—at least three to four.* We like cotton flannel sheets because we live in a cold climate, and flannel is less of a cold shock to our baby when we lay him down. In warmer climates, regular woven cotton sheets (or knit cotton sheets) would be a good choice. If you plan to use a bassinet/cradle, you'll need a few of these special-size sheets as well. One mom called us with a great money-saving tip on this subject: just use pillow cases as bassinet/cradle sheets! King-size pillow cases should fit fine.

♣ *Mattress cover/protector.* While most baby mattresses have water-proof vinyl covers, many parents use a sheet protector to keep from having to re-make the entire bed when the baby leaks or spits-up. A sheet protector is a non-fitted sheet with a rubber backing to protect against leaking. If the baby's diaper leaks, it's easy to simply remove the sheet protector and throw it in the wash (instead of the fitted crib sheets).You can buy sheet protectors in most baby stores or catalogs, or simply use an extra receiving blanket in your baby's crib or bassinet/cradle.

♣ *A good blanket.* Baby stores love to pitch expensive quilts to parents and many bedding sets include them as part of the package. Yet, all most babies need is a simple cotton blanket. Not only are thick quilts overkill for most climates, they can also be dangerous. The latest report from the Consumer Product Safety Commission on Sudden Infant Death Syndrome (SIDS) concluded putting babies face down on such soft bedding may contribute to as many as 30% of SIDS deaths (that's 1800 babies) each year in the U.S. (As a side note, there is no explanation for the other 70% of SIDS cases, although environmental factors like smoking near the baby and a too-hot room are suspected). Some baby bedding companies have responded to these concerns by rolling out decorative flannel-backed blankets (instead of quilts) in their collections.

But what if you live in a cold climate and think a cotton blanket won't cut it? Consider crib blankets made from Polartec (a lightweight 100% polyester fabric brushed to a soft fleece finish) available from Land's End "Coming Home" catalog (800) 345-3696 for about $25. Or how about a "coverlet," which is lighter than a quilt but more substantial than a blanket. A cotton flannel crib coverlet from Land's End is about $25 too. Of course, Polartec blankets are also available from mainstream bedding companies like California Kids (see review later in this chapter).

E-Mail from The Real World
Sheet savers make for easy changes

 Baby bedding sure looks cute, but the real work is changing all those sheets. Karen Naide found a product that makes changes easier:

"One of our best buys was 'The Ultimate Crib Sheet.' I bought one regular crib sheet which matched the bedding set, and two Ultimate Crib Sheets. This product is waterproof (vinyl on the bottom, and soft white cotton on the top) and lies on top of your regular crib sheet. It has six elastic straps which snap around the bars of your crib. When it gets dirty or the baby soils it, all you have to do is unsnap the straps, lift it off, put a clean one on, and that's it! No taking the entire crib sheet off (which usually entails wrestling with the mattress and bumper pads)... it's really quick and easy! While the white sheet may not exactly match your pattern, it can only be seen from inside the crib, and as you have so often stated, it's not like the baby cares about what it looks like. From the outside of the crib, you can still see the crib sheet which matches your bedding. Anyway, I think it's a wonderful product, and really a must. It costs about $15.95 and Baby Superstore/Babies 'R Us carries it."

♣ *Bumper pads.* In the last edition of this book, we called bumper pads "an important safety item." We've since changed our mind and now consider them to be an optional accessory. Why the change of heart? All the warnings about SIDS and soft bedding (see the previous page) make us wonder whether any fluffy, soft bedding should be in a crib, even if bumpers are designed as a "safety item." After having two babies of our own, we also question their usefulness, since you're suppose to remove them after baby begins pulling himself up (so he doesn't use them as a stepstool to get out of the crib). Besides, most parents today use foam blocks or rolled up towels to keep babies sleeping on their backs or sides and these devices also keep baby from rolling into the side of a crib.

If you choose to purchase bumpers, don't buy the ultra-thick kind. Check to see if you can machine-wash them—thinner bumpers can be popped into a washing machine, while ultra-thick bumpers may have to be dry-cleaned. Some parents are concerned that the chemical residue from dry-cleaning might be harmful to their baby.

Another interesting option is the Bumpa Bed, available by mail from Baby Jogger (800) 241-1848, internet: *www. babyjogger.com* This sculpted foam mattress features "built-in" bumper pads which provide protection from crib rails without the risk of entanglement, entrapment or threat of suffocation. The cost: $219 (plus $15 shipping), which includes two sheets, which Velcro to the mattress for easy removal. All in all, the Bumpa Bed isn't inexpensive (and additional sheets are $35 for a pair), but it can be used later out of the crib (to keep a toddler from rolling off her bed) and then with a foam insert (included) to become a toddler mattress. The product does come with a money-back guarantee.

Smart Shopper Tips
PILLOW TALK: LOOKING FOR MR. GOOD BEDDING
"Pooh and more Pooh—that seemed to be the basic choice in baby bedding at our local juvenile store. Since it all looks alike, is the pattern the only difference?"

There's more to it than that. And buying baby bedding isn't the same as purchasing linens for your own bed—you'll be washing these pieces much more frequently, so they must be made to hold up to extra abuse. Since baby bedding is more than just another set of sheets, here are nine points to keep in mind:

1 RUFFLES SHOULD BE FOLDED OVER FOR DOUBLE THICK-NESS—instead of a single thickness ruffle with hemmed edge. Double ruffles hold up better in the wash.

2 COLORED DESIGNS ON THE BEDDING SHOULD BE PRINTED ONTO THE FABRIC like you'd see with any calico print fabric), not stamped (like you'd see on a screen-printed t-shirt). Stamped designs on sheets will fade with only a few washings. The problem: the pieces you wash less frequently (like dust ruffles and bumpers) will fade at different rates, spoiling the coordinated look you paid big money for. In case you're wondering how to determine whether the design is printed rather than stamped, printed fabrics have color that goes through the fabric to the other side. Stamped patterns are merely painted onto the top of the fabric.

3 MAKE SURE THE PIECES ARE SEWN WITH COTTON/POLY THREAD, NOT NYLON. Nylon threads will melt and break in the dryer, becoming a choking hazard. Once the thread is gone, the filling in bumpers and quilts bunches up.

4 CHECK FOR TIGHT AND SMOOTH STITCHING ON APPLIQUÉS. If you can see the edge of the fabric through the appliqué thread, the appliqué work is too skimpy. Poor quality appliqué work will probably unravel after only a few washings. We've seen some appliqués that were actually fraying in the store—check it before you buy.

5 HIGH THREAD-COUNT SHEETS. Unlike adult linens, most packages of baby bedding do not list the thread count. But, if you can count the individual threads when you hold a sheet up to the light, you know the thread count is too low. High thread-count sheets (200 threads per inch or more) are better since they are softer and smoother against baby's skin, last longer and wear better. Unfortunately, most affordable baby bedding has low thread counts (120 thread counts are common)—traditionally, it's the design (not the quality) that sells bedding in this business. Yet there are a few upstart brands (reviewed later) who are actually touting high thread counts for their sheets.

6 FEEL THE FILLING IN THE BUMPER PADS. If the filling feels gritty, it's not the best quality. Look for bumpers that are soft to touch (Dacron-brand filling is a good bet).

7 THE TIES THAT ATTACH THE BUMPER TO THE CRIB SHOULD BE NO LONGER THAN NINE INCHES IN LENGTH. Another tip: make sure the bumper has ties on both the top and bottom and are securely sewn.

8 THE DUST RUFFLE PLATFORM SHOULD BE OF GOOD QUALITY FABRIC—OR ELSE IT WILL TEAR. Longer, full ruffles are more preferable to shorter. As a side note, the dust ruffle is sometimes referred to as a crib skirt.

9 REMEMBER THAT CRIB SHEETS COME IN DIFFERENT SIZES— BASSINET/CRADLE, PORTABLE CRIB, AND FULL-SIZE CRIB. Always use the correct size sheet.

The Name Game: Reviews of Selected Manufacturers

Here are reviews of some of the brand names you'll encounter on your shopping adventures for baby bedding. You'll notice that we include the phone numbers and addresses of each manufacturer—this is so you can find a local dealer near you (most do not sell directly to the public, nor send catalogs to consumers). We rated the companies on overall quality, price, and creativity factors, based on an evaluation of sample items we viewed at retail stores. We'd love to hear from you—tell us what you think about different brands and how they held up in the real world by calling us at (303) 442-8792.

The Ratings

★★★★ EXCELLENT—*our top pick!*

★★★ GOOD— *above average quality, prices, and creativity.*

★★ FAIR—*could stand some improvement.*

★ POOR—*yuck! could stand some major improvement.*

Baby Gap ....★★ ¹/₂
Call (415) 952-4400 for a store near you. The Gap has had a hit with their Baby Gap clothing line, so it was no surprise that bedding would be next on their agenda. Baby Gap bedding is sold exclusively through Baby Gap and many Gap Kids stores and features a very limited selection of patterns. In fact, if you like blue, this is the bedding for you. On a recent visit to the Baby Gap on the Upper West Side of New York, we saw four different patterns of bedding in a chambray blue motif that mixed solids, stripes, checks and a cherry pattern. The overall look is very classy and each item (except for the Pro Fleece blankets) is 100% cotton. While we liked the quality of the items, we did notice there was a wide variation in the thread count of Baby Gap sheets. The solid chambray just had 130 threads per square inch, the ticking stripe was 160, the gingham had 180 and the cherry print came in at 205. Considering the prices (each pattern sheet is $24; the solid sheet is $16), we suggest going for the high thread (180+) count options. The other prices weren't bargains either— quilts $150 to $175, dust ruffles $42 and bumpers $68. Hence, a basic four-piece set (quilt, sheet, bumpers, dust ruffle) would run over $275. So, we have to give Baby Gap bedding a mixed review. While the patterns and quality (at least of the high thread count sheets) was good, the small selection and relatively high prices will limit the appeal of the line. As we went to press, we noticed some late-breaking color news at Baby Gap—they just came out with a sheet that's red.

Baby Guess .... ★★★★
Pour La Maison, Inc. 1426 S. Paloma St., Los Angeles, CA 90021; For a dealer near you, call (800) GUESS-HOME or (213) 745-1500. Baby Guess created quite a stir at a recent juvenile products convention when the company debuted their attractive, high-quality baby bedding. The eight collections

emphasize more adult looks with a mix of seersucker gingham, oxford stripes and chambray denim. One stand-out was the "Animal Attractions" pattern which featured black spots (tiger, cheetah and leopard) for a decidedly different nursery look. Similar to Baby Gap, Baby Guess also mixes and matches different patterns—their "Striped Patchwork" bedding incorporates stripes, checks and leaf patterns. Prices range from $275 to $300 for a four-piece set. While that ain't cheap, every thing is 100% cotton, pre-washed, and is made in the U.S. Best of all, the sheets feature 200 thread counts. Although the line is new, Baby Guess does offer a wide array of matching accessories such as mobiles and lamp shades. All in all, the Baby Guess line of baby bedding was very impressive.

Belinda Barton ....★★★ $^1/_2$
1625 Broadwaters Rd., Cutchogue, NY 11935 For a dealer near you, call (800) 556-5681 or (516) 734-2872. One of our favorite crib bedding designers has to be Belinda Barton of New York. Belinda was a design director for Ralph Lauren's home furnishings division before opening her own company in 1995 and she brings some of that Lauren-esque sophistication to her bedding line. We love the fresh feel of the designs. Stand-outs include seersucker ginghams in bright colors like Buttercup yellow and Petunia pink. New this year is a line of bright polka dot patterns and our favorite set, "Pocketful of Posies," a floral design in either blue or pink. The quality is very high—all items are 100% cotton, 200-thread count and some pieces are even made from Egyptian cotton. Unfortunately, the prices are high as well—a comforter is $120, a dust ruffle $140, bumpers $140 and sheets $45. Hence a four-piece set could run $400 or more. Yet, given the creative designs, ultra-high quality, unique fabrics (one Barton design has a diamond-weave pique finish), you may be able to justify the expense. Barton's bedding is available in 300 stores nationwide. If you like the designs but can't afford the prices, you might want to check out Redmon, reviewed later in this section. Barton has designed several patterns for Redmon in lower-price fabrics.

Brandee Danielle..★★ $^1/_2$
1711 McGaw, Irvine, CA 92714 For a dealer near you, call (800) 720-5656, (714) 752-2112. Despite it's feminine-sounding name, Brandee Danielle is one of the few makers that designs bedding with "boyish" themes. One pattern, "Dumpin' Dirt," even featured a series of construction equipment illustrations for the little handyman-to-be. Although Brandee Danielle does have a few pastel patterns, their specialty seems to be bright prints with male themes like "Sports Fan" and "Dune Buggy Baby." The bedding is all 100% cotton and most five

piece sets (including a pillow) run $250 to $300. As a side note, Brandee Danielle also makes car seat covers, stroller pads, and bedding for round cribs (which runs $600).

California Kids ....★★★ ¹/₂
621 Old Country Rd., San Carlos, CA 94070. For a dealer near you, call (800) 548-5214, (415) 637-9054. One of our favorite bedding lines, California Kids specializes in bright and upbeat looks. While there are a few baby-ish patterns, the bedding maker really shines with innovative designs like "Aspen." This mountain scene features deep purples, emerald greens and sapphire blues in a patchwork look. On a more whimsical note, the "Dippy Duck" bedding swims with a myriad of cartoon ducks on a dark blue background. The quality is excellent; everything is 100% cotton and made in California. Prices run $200 to $389 for a five-piece set (the average is about $300). With an amazing array of options (60+ patterns were available at last count), California Kids is available in specialty stores and upper-end departments stores. Available accessories include glider slip covers, wall hangings, lamp shades and fabric can be purchased by the yard. New this year at California Kids is "Nature's Wear," a collection of natural bedding made from 100% "green" cotton (no bleaches, starches, or other chemicals are used in its processing) and printed with low-impact dye. We saw this set at Nordstrom's for $370 for a five-piece set, which included an "Eco-Fleece" blanket made from 87% recycled plastic soda bottles.

Carousel Designs ....★★
4519 Bankhead Hwy., Douglasville, GA 30134. For a dealer near you, call (800) 662-2236 or (770) 949-2123. Atlanta-based Carousel Designs has been doing crib bedding in traditional motifs since 1986. "Conservative" is how we'd describe the very straight forward designs—you'll see solid primary colors in patchwork quilts and other very juvenile motifs (teddy bears, clowns, sailboats). The quality of the fabric is just average, which is somewhat disappointing when you consider a four-piece sells for $200 to $270. Among Carousel's better efforts is "Bright Floral," which features bold flowers accented with blue gingham ruffles. On the upside, Carousel does have a factory outlet in their Douglasville plant that is open to the public on Saturdays.

Cotton Tale ....★★★ ¹/₂
4030 Chandler Ave., Santa Ana, CA 92704. Call (800) 628-2621 or (714) 435-9558 for a dealer near you. What most impressed us about Cotton Tale was their originality. There are no licensed cartoon characters or trendy fabrics

like denim here. Instead, you'll see hand-painted looks in beautiful soft pastels, all made in the U.S. We loved the whimsical animal prints and the feminine touches in such patterns as "Baby's First Bouquet," with ribbon hearts and flowers. Best of all, Cotton Tale's prices are affordable—most range from $99 to $239 with an average of $140 for a five-piece set. And that's a good deal, considering almost all of the fabrics are 100% cotton. If we had to fault them for anything, it would have to be their applique work, which was just average on fabrics that are cotton/poly blends. New this year at Cotton Tale is a brushed cotton fabric in beautiful pastel hues. If you like their sponge-painted looks, you can even buy a kit that let's you sponge paint a wall border in your nursery. Cotton Tale bedding is available just about everywhere. . . we've even seen it in the JCPenney catalog and in Baby Superstore.

Glenna Jean ....★★
230 N. Sycamore St., Petersburg, VA 23803. For a dealer near you, call (800) 446-6018 or (804) 861-0687. We liked Glenna Jean's designs—as long as you stick with non-appliquéed patterns. The quality and sewing construction of the appliqués just wasn't very impressive. Glenna Jean is big on teddy bear designs, although most of the colors tend toward the darker side. One nice, non-appliquéed set featured a delicate floral pattern. The price: $99 for a quilt and bumper, $20 for the sheet, and $60 for the dust ruffle—not bad for the quality and design. Overall, a four-piece set from Glenna Jean runs $120 to $350. New this year is Glenna Jean's "denim lite" fabric—a pre-washed very soft fabric in several finishes (woven, printed and natural). Also new are matte lassé all-cotton coverlets as well as decorated covers for the Diaper Genie. Overall, the best bets in the Glenna Jean line are the 100% cotton patchwork and floral print designs (only certain collections of Glenna Jean's bedding are all-cotton).

Grey Fort Quilts ....★★ ¹/₂
For a brochure, call (800) 505-2660 or (519) 664-2130. A Canadian mother-to-be e-mailed us with her enthusiastic recommendation for this company. Ontario-based Grey Fort Quilts custom makes baby bedding, including bumpers, sheets, dust ruffles and, yes, quilts. We priced a log-cabin style quilt at just $70 Canadian—that works out to about $52 U.S., which is a great deal. The company will send you fabric swatches or you can use your own fabric.

House of Hatten .... ★★★
*301 Inner Loop Road, Georgetown, TX 78626. For a deal-
er near you, call (800) 5-HATTEN (542-8836) or (512)
819-9600.* House of Hatten makes beautiful appliquéed
and embroidered quilts. One of their best-sellers is "Home
Spun Charm," which features a patchwork quilt with
appliquéed baby animals on a chambray background with
red accents. Most quilts run $90 to $140.

House of Hatten's specialty is delicate embroidery on
either white fabric or pastel patchwork. While the quilts get
rave reviews, we heard mixed reviews on Hatten's other
products: the bumper pads and dust ruffles get lower
marks, thanks to cheaper construction.

On the plus side, all the fabric is 100% cotton and features high thread counts. All of the bedding is made in the
Philippines. Our recommendation: buy a quilt from House of
Hatten and forget the bumper pads and dust ruffle. You can
buy solid-color coordinating sets from other manufacturers.

Kidsline .... ★ ¹/₂
*151 W. 135th St., Los Angeles, CA 90061. Call (310) 660-
0110 for a dealer near you.* Kidsline's big license is the
"Rainbow Fish," a pastel bedding set inspired by the book of
the same name. This bedding sets the tone for the rest of
Kidsline's offerings, which use similar colors to achieve a
hand-painted/watercolor look. It's all very baby-ish—you'll
find lots of cutsey bears and baby animals in the line. For
example, "Save the Earth" features a seal, giraffe and pink
tiger on a teal chintz fabric. The quality was only OK for
prices that average $200 for a six-piece set—most of the fab-
rics are cotton/poly blends. On the plus side, Kidsline does
make some of the most affordable round crib bedding we
saw, with seven offerings that sell for $320 to $360.

Judi's .... ★ ¹/₂
*7733 East Gray Rd., Scottsdale, AZ 85260. For a dealer near
you, call (800) 421-9433 or (602) 991-5885.* Arizona-made
Judi's Originals bedding offers quite a few designs with three-
dimensional appliqué work. Unfortunately, in our opinion the
appliqué construction is very skimpy—you can see the fabric
through the stitching. We worry about its ability to hold up
after several washings. If you like Judi's bedding designs, consider sticking with non-appliquéed styles.

New this year at Judi's is licensed Mary Engelbreit bedding.
For those not familiar with her artwork, Engelbreit's designs
feature a retro 1940's look with three-dimensional fried egg
flowers (don't ask). An example of this bedding is the Love-A-
Bye's set in 100% cotton (a four piece set retails for $290). Also

new this year are day blankets, an optional accessory with every collection. These decorated flannel blankets are an example of the trend away from heavy comforters/quilts, responding to parents concerns about SIDS risk from soft bedding.

While most of Judi's bedding is in the affordable category ($150 to $200 for a four-piece set), the company has introduced several upper-end collections with impressive quality. We loved the new "Creme Brulee" line made of 100% Egyptian cotton with high thread counts. Cost: $250 for a four-piece set.

As you can see, the quality of Judy's Originals bedding is all over the board. If you stay with the 100% cotton collections (only 9 of 22 sets are 100% cotton) and avoid the appliqué work, you'll be happy.

Lambs & Ivy...★★★
5978 Bowcroft St., Los Angeles, CA 90016. For a dealer near you, call (800) 345-2627 or (310) 839-5155. This LA-based bedding company was founded in 1979 by Barbara Lainken and Cathy Ravdin. Their creative and affordable designs have generated legions of fans. One of Lambs & Ivy's all-time best-sellers is the "Paradise" line. This bright, cheerful print with appliquéed jungle animals runs $86 for the quilt, $78 for a headboard bumper, $44 for a dust ruffle, $20 for a sheet (these prices are from the JCPenney catalog). The tropical colors (purple, blue, and pink hues) are a nice contrast to traditional designs that either use black and white or muted pastels. Another popular line from Lambs & Ivy is "Country Noah," a biblical-theme fabric with a hand-painted look (retail: $199 for a five-piece set).

New this year at Lambs & Ivy is bedding with an "antique yesteryear" look. For example, the "Americana" set features a home-spun tattersall check fabric that echoes early-American hand-crafts. While we liked the style, we thought the colors (navy, camel and "cinnamon spice") were too dull. A better bet was the "Vintage Rose" line which featured appliquéed antique lace over a rose chintz fabric.

Lambs & Ivy recently launched "Bedtime Originals," a more affordable line of baby bedding available through "mass market" (read: discount) stores. All in all, we like Lambs & Ivy; the designs are well stitched and prices are reasonable.

Laura Ashley ....★★★
To find a store near you, call (800) 429-7678. In the first edition of our book, we weren't too thrilled with Laura Ashley's crib bedding. We found the styles boring (mostly muted pastels) and the prices high. Well, we're happy to report Ashley has added some pizzazz to their line. Now, you can choose from 35 different patterns. One that caught our eye was

"Fishes," a whimsical multi-color aquatic theme on a bright sapphire blue background. The quality is high—we saw 100% cotton fabrics, folded ruffles and other good construction qualities. Unfortunately, the prices are high as well. A quilt will set you back $98 to $108, as do the bumpers. A dust ruffle is $78, a fitted sheet runs $29, and a diaper stacker $34 to $40. On the upside, Ashley runs occasional sales (on our visit, they were offering a 20% to 30% discount). Ordering regular merchandise (if not in stock) takes two to four weeks, while custom orders take eight weeks. Fabric is available by the yard, as are coordinating lamps and bibs. Despite the high prices, we've upped Ashley's rating to reflect the positive feedback we've received about the bedding from readers of the first edition of this book.

Luv Stuff ....★★ ½
2809 Industrial Lane, Garland, TX 75041. Call (800) 835-BABY or (972) 278-BABY for a dealer near you. This high-end, all cotton bedding sells for $350 to $700, with an average four-piece set weighing in at $425. If you're still with us, we should note that Luv Stuff's claim to fame is their unique, hand-trimmed wall hangings. The Texas-based designer pairs plain fabric bedding with wild wall hangings in bright color combinations. An example: True Colors is a tour de force of contrasting plaid fabric and patchwork, swirled in electric yellows, blues and reds. Slightly more toned down is "Tropical II" which is a similar plaid pattern in deeper blue, green and pink hues. We liked Luv Stuff's high quality bedding, but we had a hard time swallowing those prices.

My Dog Spot .... ★★★
11588 Sorrento Valley Rd. #22, San Diego, CA 92121. For a dealer near you, call (619) 259-7200. Looking for something different? Check out My Dog Spot, a hilarious and funky collection of baby bedding that is anything but boring. Nine designs include our favorite, "Spot Visits the Northern Lights," with a 100% cotton quilt featuring the famous canine visiting a moose in Canada. Accessories include a coordinating "dog house" headboard bumper, dust ruffle, Spot or moose pillows, and more. Of course, you must pay for the privilege of visiting the Northern Lights with Spot. The quilt is a whopping $300, while the headboard bumper is $180, the ruffle is $80, and the sheets are $50 each. Ouch!

What makes My Dog Spot so unique is their fabrics. The Northern Lights pattern features a custom-dyed background made in Bali. Other patterns feature bright teal and pink patchwork (Spot Goes Underwater) or more muted desert hues (Spot Visits the Mojave). There's even a few raucous plaids (Spot Goes to Botswana) and wild checks (Spot Surfs Wailea).

New this year at Spot are coordinating art stencils and decor items like mirrors, painted floormats, clocks, shelves and book-ends. Of course, you can also buy the fabric by the yard.

So, who is Spot? According to company literature, he was born in San Diego in the summer of 1990, loves adventure, and "hates split pea soup." Spot bedding has been featured on TV shows like *Friends* and *Picket Fences*. All in all, Spot's creators Patti and Mike McDonald offer up some of the freshest and most innovative designs available in the juvenile bedding market today.

Nava's Designs ....★★ ¹/₂
16742 Stagg St. #106, Van Nuys, CA 91406. For a dealer near you, call (818) 988-9050. Want to spend a fortune on baby bedding? Check out Nava's Designs, a California-based bedding manufacturer that has sky-high prices. A typical example: a beautiful pattern like "Galaxy," which features stars, moons and swirls on a deep-blue background with striped ruffle. The price? Are you sitting down? How about a whopping $760 for a seven-piece set (quilt, ruffle, pillow, bumper, diaper stacker, stuffed animal, and sheet)? A major negative (besides the price): some designs don't wash well and may even have to be dry-cleaned (check the washing instructions carefully). On the upside, the fabrics are very heavy, high-quality cottons, and the stitching is excellent. Among the stand-outs in Nava's line are her floral prints, lushly rendered with large cabbage roses, delicate lace and shimmering rope piping. Nava is sold at many upper-end baby stores like Bellini (see review of this chain in the last chapter).

NoJo ....★★
Noel Joanna Inc., 22942 Arroyo Vista, Rancho Santa Margarita, CA 92688. For a dealer near you, call (800) 854-8760 or (714) 858-9717. Shirley Pepys founded NoJo in 1970 with just one product—a quilted infant carseat cover. Since then, NoJo has expanded into a wide range of bedding and nursery products. The company has shown remarkable marketing timing—their "Bright Dino" line of bedding was introduced years before Barney and *Jurassic Park* made dinosaurs a hot commodity. Prices are moderate: a three-piece set (quilt, bumper, sheet) is $159. The matching dust ruffle is $44. While we liked the bright pink and blue dinosaurs design, we did notice the fabric was a 50/50 poly/cotton blend.

In fact, that's probably the only disappointment with Nojo: most of their bedding is cotton/poly blends (only a handful of sets are 100% cotton). On the upside, Nojo does have several good licenses, including Paddington, Babar, and Spot the Dog. The company tries to do something for everyone. They make bedding in several prices ranges, from affordable (Nojo makes the mass-market Fisher Price bedding which runs $99 to $129 for a four-piece set), moderate ($149 to $199), to the upper-end ($200 to $249). On the pricier side, Nojo has "Stone Creek" (which is a Ralph Lauren-like plaid look), "New Naturals" (ivory on white designs with different textures) and "French Bebe," which featured a new cotton pique fabric in a plaid/navy Babar motif.

Another popular product by NoJo is their Baby Sling carrier. It retails for about $40 (more information on this and other carriers appears in Chapter 7). An additional interesting note: NoJo actually has a factory outlet store, which is rare in this business (see review in the outlet section of this chapter).

Oshkosh ....★★ $^1/_2$
Made by Marimac, 10340 Cote de Liesse, Suite 200, La Chime, Quebec Canada H8T1A3. Call (514) 422-1171 for a dealer near you. With the denim fad sweeping the baby bedding biz, was it any surprise that crib bedding by denim king Oshkosh would be far behind? The Wisconsin company famous for those too-cute overalls has licensed its "Baby B'Gosh" to Canada-based Marimac for a line of crib bedding that's surprisingly affordable. A three-piece set is $89 to $99 and a four-piece set is about $119 to $129. The most expensive design topped out at $199 for a five-piece set. This isn't a big line—we only saw eight collections, which mixed denim fabric with stripes, plaids and lace accents. While you might think Oshkosh's bedding would be a boy thing, there were quite a few feminine looks with frilly bows, lacy accents, etc. While the designs are good, the quality is only average—most of the bedding items are 50/50 cotton/poly blends, except for the denim (which is 100% cotton). The sheets have 160 thread counts, which is higher than some makers but below those of the better-made brands. The company did tell us they plan to introduce an all-cotton seersucker design later in 1997.

Patchkraft ....★★★
70 Outwater Lane, Garfield, NJ 07026. Call (800) 866-2229 or (201) 340-3300 for a dealer near you. If you want floral crib bedding, this company is probably a good bet—Patchkraft makes some of the best florals on the market today. We loved "Panache Fluer," a subtle mix of yellows, lavenders and blues with eyelet lace trim. If flowers aren't your game, another winner was "Twilight," whose celestial theme (moon, sun, stars) was set on a deep blue background. Watch the fabric content on this line; half the designs are made from 100% organic cotton. The rest are blends—at prices that run $300 to $350 for a four-piece set, that's a slight disappointment. Despite this, we

thought the construction and quality was above average. We also liked their nifty wall hangings and other accessories (lamp shades, canopies, blankets, etc.).

Pine Creek...★★★ $^1/_2$
PO Box 14, Aurora, OR 97002. Call (503) 266-6275 for a dealer near you. What's the most popular crib bedding in the Pacific Northwest? Yes, it's Pine Creek, the Oregon-based bedding maker that specializes in flannel baby linens. Now, at this point, you might be thinking "flannel? Are you nuts? Isn't that too hot?" Actually, Pine Creek uses *cotton* flannel, which is very soft yet still cool in the summer, thanks to its light weight and breathability. Hand-made of 100% cotton, Pine Creek's bedding features excellent quality. Our only disappointment: the company offers their famous flannels in just three plaid designs. While there is a new teddy bear flannel set with a white background, we'd like to see some more choices. If flannel isn't your cup of tea, Pine Creek does make regular, all-cotton bedding, in beautiful floral and patchwork motifs. Prices average $300 for a four-piece set, and some designs can reach $400. That ain't cheap, but the company has introduced a new line of mix-and-match solid-color flannels that start at $199 for a set. Pine Creek also sells round crib bedding, accessories like lamp shades and curtain valences, plus fabric is available by the yard. We also liked their flannel blankets, which are more useful (and safe) than a thick quilt. Even if you don't live in a cool/damp climate, this bedding would make an excellent choice for any nursery.

Quiltcraft Kids ....★★★
1233 Levee St., Dallas, TX 75207. For a dealer near you, call (800) 462-2805 or (214) 741-1662. Texas-based Quiltcraft Kids features good quality fabric, folded ruffles, and thick bumpers—at prices that are 15% to 20% less than comparable brands. We liked the American Gingham pattern the best; prices for this style ran $70 for a quilt, $70 for a bumper, $16 for sheets, and $35 for a dust ruffle. New this year are several interesting patterns, including "Collette" (a French country botanical theme) and "All Aboard" (a choo-choo theme in primary colors). While Quiltcraft Kids is on the mid to upper end of the price spectrum, they do provide good value for the dollar.

Quiltex ....★★
100 W. 33rd St., New York, NY 10001. For a dealer near you, call (800) 237-3636 or (212) 594-2205. Quiltex is famous for their Peanuts-inspired patterns, including the popular Snoopy Collection. "Country Snoopy" has bright, primary colors, while "Rainbow Snoopy" features subdued pastels.

Prices are moderate, with a quilt from this collection running $50 to $75 and sheets $18 to $20. Another popular Quiltex pattern is the Beatrix Potter collection. We saw a 5-piece set for $200 at LiL' Things; retail is $250 (the set includes headboard bumper, sheet, dust ruffle, diaper stacker, and quilt).

New this year at Quiltex are the Precious Moments and Cherished Teddies licenses. Fans of those characters will find a variety of styles in the requisite pastel hues. New Snoopy patterns this year include Camp Snoopy and Snoopy Golf, sport-themed bedding in primary colors.

The quality of the Quiltex designs we viewed is middle-of-the-road: some appliqué work leaves a bit to be desired, while other designs are merely stamped on the fabric. Make sure you check the stitching before you buy.

Red Calliope.. ★ $^{1}/_{2}$
711 W. Walnut St., Comptoneles, Los Angeles, CA 90220. For a dealer near you, call (800) 421-0526 or (310) 763-8100. Red Calliope is a division of Crown Crafts, the billion dollar bedding behemoth. As a result, Calliope's bedding designs are widely available and priced affordably; however, the quality isn't much to shout about. Most of Red Calliope's designs are cotton/poly blends and have patterns that are stamped into the fabric—as you know, we aren't big fans of stamped designs.

Fortunately, there are a few bright spots. Pooh, for one. To say that Calliope's Pooh bedding has been a run-away best-seller would be an understatement. Winnie the Pooh has been such a blockbuster for Calliope that the company has been very busy rolling out various Pooh spin-offs in several price points.

For the uninitiated, there are actually two types of Pooh bedding. Regular Pooh (sometimes called "Disney Pooh") is made by Calliope's Little Bedding subsidiary and features the bear as he looks in Disney cartoons. The seven collections of Disney Pooh are cotton/poly blends and priced for the "mass market" at $49 to $149 for a three-piece set (sheet, bumper and comforter).

On the upper-end is the "Classic Pooh" line, with designs from the original Pooh book by A. A. Milne. You can choose from six different Classic Pooh collections, which retail for $199 to $299 for a five-piece set (although this line is so popular that you can often find it on sale or discounted). New this year is "Mattellase Pooh" with upgraded fabric for $299 for a five piece set.

Pooh has been such a success for Calliope that you might forget they make other bedding designs. The company also holds the license for Royal Doulton's Bunnykins line as well as Baby Mickey (as in Mickey Mouse). New this year is the Patchwork Collection, which features 100% cotton fabric (about $199 retail for a five piece set).

While it's understandable why Pooh is so popular, the quality of the Pooh bedding is just not worth the price. If you want to do a Pooh theme, we suggest following the money-saving tip mentioned later in this chapter—decorate your baby's room with Pooh accessories and decor, but choose solid (non-Pooh) bedding. You can find 100% cotton sheets, blankets and other linen items in matching colors from a variety of sources.

Redmon..★★
PO Box 7, Peru, IN 46970. Call (317) 473-6683 for a dealer near you. If you liked Belinda Barton's bedding (reviewed earlier) but not the prices, consider Redmon. Barton has designed a couple of patterns for this Indiana company, which makes the bedding in poly/cotton blends to hit a lower price point. "Oh Buoy" features an all-over sail boat print on a bright blue background. The price: $130 for a three-piece set (quilt, bumper, sheet) or $159 for a four-piece (add a dust ruffle). Redmon also acquired some patterns from Clothworks, a defunct bedding maker with some interesting paisley print designs (now, that's a fabric you don't see in many nurseries). A four-piece set of "Precious Paisley" is $239. We loved this fabric's deep garnet and emerald tones. All in all, Redmon is a small player in the bedding market. Their 14 collections feature a mix of all-cotton and poly-cotton designs in the $119 to $289 price ranges for a four-piece set.

Sugar Plum ....★ ¹/₂
16585 C Von Karman, Suite 463, Irvine, CA 92714. Call (888) 600-6161 for a dealer near you. Say you want to decorate your baby's nursery in a Green Bay Packer theme—who do you call? Try Sugar Plum, a California-based company that has snagged the license for NFL bedding. At this writing, only 10 teams make up the collection (Bears, Bills, Cowboys, Dolphins, Eagles, 49er's, Packers, Raiders, Steelers, and Vikings). Sorry Jacksonville fans—you'll have to wait. Another bummer: the quality is merely average (all the fabrics are poly/cotton blends) and the prices are high. A five-piece set will run you $300. *Dead ball foul! Roughing the wallet!* Anyway, you can buy all those cute matching accessories, including mobiles, wall hangings, curtain valences and lamps that feature the team's mascot. Coming soon: NBA teams.

Sumersault ....★★★★
PO Box 269, Scarsdale, NY 10583. Call (800) 232-3006 or (201) 768-7890 for a dealer near you. Owner Patti Summergrade imports beautiful fabrics from Portugal and other European countries to create this very-adult bedding line.

We loved the plaids, which featured off-beat colors that match the richer wood tones popular for cribs in New England and the Northeast. A typical offering is "Hampton," which featured an aqua background and pale gold floral motif. Accented with ruffles of green, blue and gold, the look is quite sophisticated. Another stand-out was "Greenwich," a bow-tie patchwork quilt with denim and tartan plaids. Sumersault does few appliques and leaves most of the cutsey touches to optional wall-hangings. We liked the quality of Sumersault—most of the line is 100% cotton and one collection even boasts 200-thread count sheet. A four-piece set will run you $250 to $350.

Sweet Pea ....★★
PO Box 90756, Pasadena, CA 91109. Call (818) 578-0866 for a dealer near you. You gotta like Sweet Pea . . . their fun and funky fabrics are imported from places like the Vatican (which we didn't realize did anything other than Popes). Their 100% cotton bedding features a variety of very-adult finishes, including jacquards, satins and even crushed velvets. If you don't like the damask-woven fabric, consider a floral chintz that looks like Laura Ashley on acid. One impossibly over-the-top design featured mix-and-match cabbage roses, corded piping trim and ribbon accents. Unfortunately, the prices are also over-the-top: five piece sets *start* at $300 and can top $900. Ouch. While the quality is high, the prices are way out of the ballpark.

Other brands to consider: Simmons (the crib maker) also makes bedding, although none of the designs really caught our eye. *Riegel* (800) 845-3251 or (803) 275-2541 makes the Sesame Street "Fairy Tale" line featuring Big Bird and Elmo, although the quality of the bedding didn't impress us. It's aimed at the mass market discount stores. Also on a cartoon theme, *Dundee* (212) 556-6000 makes a series of "Disney Baby" bedding aimed at mass market discount stores.

Safe & Sound

While you might think to cover your outlets and hide that can of Raid, you might not automatically consider safety when selecting sheets, comforters, and bumpers. Yet, your baby will be spending more time with these products than any other. Here are several safety points to remember:

♣ *All linens should have a tag* indicating the manufacturer's name and address. That's the only way you would know if was recalled. You can also contact the manufacturer if you have a problem or question. While this is the law, some stores may sell discounted or imported linens that do not have tags.

License Translator
Who makes what brand of bedding

One of the hottest trends in crib bedding is licensed characters—just about every cartoon character imaginable has been licensed to one of the big bedding makers for use in juvenile bedding. But how can tell you tell who makes what? Here is a list of popular licensed characters and their bedding makers:

License	See bedding maker
Baby Mickey	Red Calliope
Barbar	Nojo
Beatrix Potter	Quiltex
Bunnykins	Red Calliope
Cherished Teddies	Quiltex
Mary Engelbreit	Judy's Originals
Paddington	Nojo
Precious Moments	Quiltex
Snoopy	Quiltex
Spot the Dog	Nojo
Winnie the Pooh	Red Calliope

♣ *Recent studies of Sudden Infant Death Syndrome* (SIDS, also known as crib death) have reported that there is an increased incidence of crib death when infants sleep on fluffy bedding, lambskins, or pillows. A pocket can form around the baby's face if she is placed face down in fluffy bedding, and she can slowly suffocate while breathing in her own carbon dioxide. The best advice: prop your infant on her side when she sleeps. And forget the lambskins and pillows.

♣ *Beware of ribbons or long fringe.* These are a possible choking hazard if they are not attached properly.

♣ *If you decide to buy bumper pads, go for ones with well-sewn ties at the top and bottom* (12 to 16 total). Ties should be no more than nine inches in length. Some bumpers just have top ties, enabling your baby to scoot under the bumper and get trapped. Some parents are abandoning bumper pads altogether because of safety concerns like this.

♣ *Never use an electric blanket or heating pad.* Babies can overheat, plus any moisture, such as urine, can cause electric shock.

♣ *Avoid blankets that use nylon (or fish-line type) thread.*
Nylon thread melts in the dryer and then breaks. These loose
threads can wrap around your baby's neck or break off and
become a choking hazard. Cotton thread is best.

Money Saving Secrets

1 IF YOU'RE ON A TIGHT BUDGET, GO FOR A GOOD
BLANKET AND A NICE SET OF HIGH THREAD-
COUNT SHEETS. What does that cost? A good cotton blanket runs $10 (even fancy Polartec ones are only
$25), while a fitted sheet runs $15 to $20. Forget all the
fancy items like pillow cases, window valances, diaper
stackers and dust ruffles. After all, your baby won't care if
she doesn't have perfectly coordinated accessories.

2 DON'T BUY A QUILT. Sure, they look pretty, but do you
really need one? Go for a nice cotton blanket, instead—
and save the $50 to $100. Better yet, hint to your friends that
you'd like receiving blankets as shower gifts.

3 INSTEAD OF EXPENSIVE WALL HANGINGS, DO IT YOURSELF.
Consider using stencils to give your baby's room a decorator border—craft stores like Michael's Arts & Crafts (call -
800-MICHAELS or 972-409-1300 for a store near you) are a
good source for such supplies. Or paint stars on the nursery
ceiling, so baby will have an interesting view. If you're handy
with a sewing machine (or have a friend or relative who is),
make a small quilted wall hanging yourself. There are dozens
of neat patterns available at fabric stores. Avoid expensive
wallpaper and other decorator accents for now. You can
always add them later if you like.

4 MAKE YOUR OWN SHEETS, DUST RUFFLES AND OTHER LINEN
ITEMS. A mom in Georgia called in this great tip on curtain valences—she bought an extra dust ruffle, sewed a curtain valence from the material and saved $70. Another twist
on this idea: buy an *adult bed size* dust ruffle in coordinating
fabric to make a curtain valence. All you need to do is remove
the ruffle from the fabric platform and sew a pocket along
one edge. I managed to do this simple procedure on my
sewing machine without killing myself, so it's quite possible
you could do it too. A good place for inspiration is your local
fabric store—most carry pattern books like Butterick,
Simplicity and McCalls, all of which have baby bedding patterns that are under $10. There are other pattern books you
can purchase that specialize in baby quilts—some of these
books also have patterns for other linen items like bumpers.

E-Mail from The Real World
Do-it-yourself baby bedding

 Our readers continue to e-mail us with do-it-yourself success stories with baby bedding. Here's a sampling:

Kasia Wilson of Seattle, Washington discovered a trick to make affordable crib sheets. Here is her tip:

"I saved a bundle on cribs sheets by making my own. You can get a pattern from any major company such as McCalls, Simplicity, etc. in local fabric stores. One full-size flat (adult) sheet makes two crib sheets. We bought several Ralph Lauren 200 thread count cotton sheets at a local outlet mall for under $10 each. Hence, the average cost per crib sheet worked out to about $4 . . . and that's for very high quality fabric. You also get many more colors to choose from."

Jennifer Klein of Boston sewed her son's entire bedding ensemble. Here's her story:

"For those so inclined, sewing one's own quilt, bumper and dust ruffle saves a heap of money. Many of the cotton fabrics being produced for quilters today are gorgeous, and perfect for bedding. Also, many better fabric/home decorating stores sell some of the fabrics used in popular bedding sets! I've also discovered quite a few catalogs sell crib sheets in bright colors that coordinate with just about any other fabric. Our bumper and dust ruffle have a royal blue mottled background with small gold stars scattered all over and yellow gold grosgrain ribbon ties. I bought royal blue and bright yellow crib sheets to coordinate. The quilt has an 18 pointed star on it in the six primary colors. All in all, I spent about $75 on materials for the bedding for my son's crib (quilt, bumper, and dust ruffle) and we have something that is perfect!"

Even if you buy good quality fabric at $6 per yard, your total savings will be 75% or more compared to "pre-made" items.

5 SHOP AT OUTLETS. Scattered across the country, we found a few outlets that discount baby linens. Among the better ones were House of Hatten and NoJo—see their reviews in the next section.

6 DON'T PICK AN OBSCURE BEDDING THEME. Sure, that "Exploding Kiwi Fruit" bedding theme is cute, but where will you find any matching accessories to decorate your baby's room? Chances are they'll only be available "exclusively" from the bedding's manufacturer—at exclusively high prices. A better bet is to choose a more common theme with lots of accessories (wall decor, lamps, rugs, etc.). The more plentiful the options, the lower the prices. Winnie the Pooh is a good example (see the box on "Pooh at a discount" later in this chapter), although you'll find quite a few accessories for other themes like Noah's Ark, teddy bears, rocking horses, etc.

7 GO FOR SOLID COLOR SHEETS AND USE THEMED ACCESSORIES. Just because you want to have a Beatrix Potter-themed nursery doesn't mean you have to buy Beatrix Potter *bedding*. A great money-saving strategy is to decorate the room in a certain theme but then use low-cost solid color sheets which match. Such bedding is available in a variety of colors—it won't take much effort to find matching sheets, blankets and other linen items.

8 DO IT BY MAIL. Later in this chapter, we'll go over the best mail order catalogs for baby bedding, plus reveal a "best buy" mail order source for name-brand linens. The savings can be as much as 50% off retail prices. Even simple items like crib sheets can be affordably mail ordered. One reader told us even LL Bean (800) 341-4341 sells crib sheets ($12 for a set of flannel sheets) at affordable price.

Best Buy

Baby Catalog of America

Call (800) PLAYPEN or (800-752-9736) or (203) 931-7760;
    Fax (203) 933-1147.
Internet: www.babycatalog.com/bca
Accept: all major credit cards
Order by mail or visit the Baby Club of America Warehouse Outlet,
719 Campbell Ave., West Haven, CT 06516.

How can you get name-brand bedding at a **BEST BUY** big discount ? Unfortunately, most catalogs sell bedding at full retail and baby stores are loathe to discount fancy brands.

Well, here's the good news: Baby Catalog of America is a one-stop source for brand new bedding, linen, decor and other accessories at prices 20% to 50% off retail. And we're not talking about just the low quality bedding brands either. The Baby Catalog of America sells bedding by Bedtime Originals, Brandee Danielle, California Baby, Carousel, Cotton Tale,

Forever Children, Glenna Jean, Judy's Originals, House of Hatten, KidsLine, Lambs & Ivy, Little Bedding, Nojo, Patchkraft, Red Calliope, Quiltcraft Kids, Quiltex, Simmons, Sumersault—and many more brands not listed here.

What about accessories? You can find all those lamps, wall decor, and other nursery items at good prices too. For example, you'll see a Classic Pooh Couristan Round Rug ($89.99, regularly $120), 100% cotton Pooh blankets in seven styles ($24.99, compare at $40) and much more. We also liked the Baby Catalog of America's selection of nursery decor, like "Stikarounds" wall stickers for $20 for a set of 45—compare that to the $30 price in the Right Start catalog for the same item. You can pick up 100% cotton crib blankets for $6.75, flannel crib sheets for $8, and a Nojo sheet saver for $13.66.

If those prices weren't low enough, the Baby Catalog of America will give you another 10% off each purchase if you buy an annual membership ($25). And you can save that much in one purchase when you notice the catalog also sells bassinets, changing tables, strollers, car seats, and high chairs—we'll talk more about their prices for those items later in this book.

Outlets

House of Hatten

Location: 3939 IH-35, Suite 725, San Marcos, TX.
(512) 392-8161.

Perhaps the only thing more beautiful than a great quilt is a great quilt on sale. That's why we love House of Hatten's fantastic outlet store in San Marcos, Texas—the only one like it in the country. You can find their quilts, as well as mobiles, bumper pads, dust ruffles, and sheets at 30% off retail. The store also sells their clothing line, which features smocked outfits for girls and boys (starting at 3-6 month sizes). Look for their sales near holidays for additional savings. The outlet offers mail-order service and ships nationwide. All items are discontinued, and some are imperfect or flawed.

Laura Ashley

Locations: Central Valley, New York (914) 928-4561, Woodbridge, Virginia (703) 494-3124; Myrtle Beach, South Carolina (803) 236-4244, Hilton Head, South Carolina (803) 837-2366, Orlando, Florida (407) 351-2785, St. Augustine, Florida 904-823-9533, Destin, FL (904) 654-2626, San Marcos, Texas (512) 396-5570, Lancaster, Pennsylvania (717) 397-7116, Jeffersonville, OH (614) 948-2016, Reading, Pennsylvania (610) 478-9604, Williamsburg, Iowa (319) 668-1555, Gilroy, CA (408) 848-5470, Osage Beach, MO (573) 348-1333.

The famous British designer has five outlets that occasionally get in baby bedding and clothing. The savings range from 20% to 50% off retail. We urge you to call before you visit since the selection may vary widely.

NoJo

Location: Rancho Santa Margarita, CA. (714) 858-9496. Fall in love with a NoJo pattern early in your pregnancy, only to discover later that it has been discontinued? Don't fret. Call the NoJo outlet store. This popular Orange County, California-based bedding manufacturer has a wonderful outlet that carries discontinued items and factory seconds—they even have items that are exclusively made for the outlet. Best of all, the savings is 20% to 60% off retail, with even bigger mark-downs during holiday sales. They even discount their famous Baby Sling to $29.90. Another plus: they take phone orders (and major credit cards) and ship nationwide! You can find crib bedding, lamps, wall boarders, fabric, car seat covers, head rests, and more at the store.

Quiltex

Location: 169 39th St., Brooklyn, NY (718) 788-3158.

Alert readers of our last edition pointed out the great bargains at the Quiltex factory outlet. And this is a real *factory* outlet (right on the floor of Quiltex's production facility in Brooklyn, NY). Andreana Doyle of Staten Island, NY e-mailed us with her bargain finds: a pram suit/snowsuit for $14 (compared to $25 at Burlington Coat Factory's Baby Depot), sweatshirt jackets embroidered with Peter Rabbet for $4 each and more. What makes this outlet so great is Quiltex's popular licenses—you'll find heavily discounted bedding, clothing and accessories from Beatrix Potter, Precious Moments and Snoopy. "Unbelievable bargain heaven" is how another parent describes the bargains and we agree. The outlet is only open weekdays from 8:30 am to 4:30 pm.

Have you found an outlet store for baby bedding that's not listed above? Call us at 303-442-8792 or e-mail at adfields@aol.com

Wastes of Money/Worthless Items

"I have a very limited budget for bedding, and I want to avoid spending money on stuff that I won't need. What are some items I should stay away from?"

It may be tempting to buy every new fad and matching accessory. And you'll get a lot of sales pressure at some

Winnie the Pooh at a discount

Who's the hottest bear in baby bedding? Why, it's Pooh, Winnie the Pooh to be exact. Sales of Pooh bedding have been off the charts for the past year and it seems like there's no stopping that silly old bear. But with the price for a basic four-piece set running close to $200, how can you get Pooh at a discount?

Unfortunately, there's only one company that makes Pooh crib bedding (Red Calliope/Little Bedding, reviewed earlier in this chapter), so you can't choose among several suppliers to get a better deal. On the upside, the bedding is widely available, so you can get it on sale (at places like JCPenney) or regularly discounted from a mail order source like Baby Catalog of America (800-PLAYPEN reviewed earlier in this chapter). The latter source discounts Pooh bedding at 30% to 50% off retail prices. If you purchase a $25 annual membership from Baby Catalog of America, you can save an additional 10%.

While many parents like Pooh, some told us they are less than thrilled with the quality of the Pooh bedding. Calliope's fabric in both the Classic Pooh and Disney Pooh lines is not 100% cotton and the thread counts are low. So what can you do? Here's an idea: who says you have to have Pooh *bedding* to do a Pooh-themed nursery?

Our advice is to buy solid color matching sheets and linen items and then accessorize with Pooh items. Fortunately, a myriad of companies make Pooh licensed accessories. For example, Michel & Co/Charpent (310) 390-7655 makes Pooh lamps, clocks and other accessories, Beacon (704) 686-3861 makes Pooh cotton blankets and throws, Couristan (800) 223-6186 makes hand-hooked Pooh-themed rugs, Sunworthy Wallcoverings (614) 297-6090 makes Pooh wall boards and wall paper and Gund (908) 248-1500 makes Pooh plush and soft toys.

stores to go for the entire "coordinated" look. Yet many bedding items are a complete waste of money—here's our list of the worst offenders:

1 DIAPER STACKER. This is basically a bag (in coordinating fabric, of course) used to store diapers—you hang it on

the side of your crib or changing table. Apparently, bedding makers must think stacking diapers on the shelf of your changing table or storing them in a drawer is a major etiquette breach. Take my word for it: babies are not worried if their diapers are out in plain sight. Save the $30 to $50 that bedding makers charge for diaper stackers and stack your own.

2 PILLOWS. We are constantly amazed at the number of bedding sets that include pillows or pillow cases. Are the bedding designers nuts, or what? Haven't they heard that it's dangerous to put your baby to sleep on a pillow? What a terrible safety hazard, not to mention a waste of your money. We don't even think a decorative pillow is a good idea. Forget the pillow and save $20 to $30.

3 SETS OF LINENS. Sets may include useless or under-used items like those listed above as well as dust ruffles and window valances. Another problem: sets are often a mixed bag when it comes to quality. Some items are good, while others are lacking. Many baby stores or even chains will sell bedding items a la carte. That way you can pick and choose just the items you need—at a substantial savings over the all-inclusive sets.

4 CANOPIES. Parents-to-be of girls are often pressured to buy frilly accessories like canopies. The emphasis is on giving her "everything" and achieving a "feminine" look for your nursery. Don't buy into it. The whole set-up for a canopy is going to be more expensive (you'll need a special crib, etc.)—it'll set you back $75 to $175 for the linens alone. And enclosing your baby's crib in a canopy won't do much for her visual stimulation or health (canopies are dust collectors).

5 ALL-WHITE LINENS. If you think of babies as pristine and unspoiled, you've never had to change a poopy diaper or clean spit-up from the front of an outfit. I'm amazed that anyone would consider all-white bedding, since keeping it clean will probably be a full-time job. Stick with colors, preferably bright ones. If you buy all-white linens and then have to go back to buy colored ones, you'll be out another $100 to $200.

6 TEETHING PADS FOR CRIB RAILS. Most new, name brand cribs will already have plastic teething guards on the side rails, so adding pads (cost: $20 extra) is redundant. One store owner pointed out that if your baby has nothing better to teeth on than the crib railing, he is spending too much time in the crib anyway.

7 HEADBOARD BUMPERS. Whatever side you come down on the bumper debate (some parents think they're a good safety item; others worry about the suffocation risk), there is a certain bumper that definitely is a waste of money—the headboard bumper. This bumper is designed to cover the entire headboard of the crib. Regular bumpers are just a six to nine-inch tall strip of padding that goes around the crib . . . and that's all you need if you want bumpers. Another good point: headboard bumpers are more expensive than regular bumpers, running another $25 to $75, depending on the maker.

Do It By Mail

Here's an overview of several catalogs that offer great deals on bedding and other layette items. For more information on these and other mail-order catalogs, see Chapter 11.

The Company Store.

To Order Call: (800) 285-3696; (800) 289-8508; Fax (608) 784-2366.
Shopping Hours: 24 hours a day, seven days a week.
Or write to: 500 Company Store Rd., La Crosse, WI 54601.
Credit Cards Accepted: MC, VISA, AMEX, Discover.

The Company Store manufactures their own down products, including comforters and pillows—plus they sell brand name and in-house bedding. They also offer down comforters in crib sizes priced at $55. Or you can order the same comforter with allergy-free "Primaloft" filling for the same price. Available in five colors, the comforters are covered in 232-thread-count cotton fabric—very high quality for the price. (Remember to never place baby face down in soft bedding). New this year at the Company Store are coordinated bedding sets (gingham checks in four colors) at reasonable prices. They also offer mattress pads, crib blankets (including a Polarfleece crib throw for $20), comforter covers, sheets and down-filled baby buntings.

Cuddledown of Maine

To Order Call: (800) 323-6793; Fax (207) 761-1948
Internet: www.cuddledown.com
Shopping Hours: 24 hours a day, seven days a week.
Or write to: 312 Canco Rd., PO Box 1910, Portland, ME 04104.
Credit Cards Accepted: MC, VISA, AMEX, Discover.

This catalog's specialty is hand-embroidered bedding. In a recent issue, we noticed a celestial theme (planets, clouds, cherubs) crib bedding design by Quail Hill Designs. At

$450 for a four-piece set, that's darn pricey. Even more expensive was a bedding design hand-made by the Shona tribe of Zimbabwe. A comforter cover, sheet, dust ruffle and bumper will run you $550.

Garnet Hill.

To Order Call: (800) 622-6216; Fax (603) 823-9578.
Shopping Hours: Monday-Friday 7:00 am-11:00 pm; Saturday and Sunday 10:00 am-6:00 pm Eastern Time.
Or write to: Garnet Hill, 262 Main St., Franconia, NH 03580.
Credit Cards Accepted: MC, VISA, AMEX, Discover.

If you want to spend the big bucks on bedding, check out Garnet Hill. This catalog makes a big deal out of its "natural fabric" offerings, and they do sell products we haven't seen elsewhere. They just offer them at a premium.

Garnet Hill sells both cotton and flannel bedding, available in separate pieces and in coordinated sets. For example, the patterned crib sheet sets are a whopping $48 to $54 and include a fitted sheet, flat sheet, and pillow case. Since you'll probably only use the fitted sheet, this seems like overkill. And you can't purchase the patterned pieces separately for some sets. Nevertheless, the designs are attractive, especially the "Cloud and Stars" pattern.

If you'd rather keep it plain, cotton flannel fitted sheets from Garnet Hill list at a hefty $20. The catalog's patchwork quilts are quite beautiful and cost $78. Cotton crib blankets are $42 to $75. New this year at Garnet Hill are quite a few more designs to choose from. We liked the cotton "percale" sheets (available separately or in sets). These woven sheets featured 200 to 220 thread counts for $20 to $27 per sheet (depending on the design).

JCPenney

To Order Call: (800) 222-6161. Ask for the "For Baby" catalog.
Shopping Hours: 24 hours a day, seven days a week.
Credit Cards Accepted: MC, VISA, JC Penney, AMEX, Discover.

JCPenny carries quite a wide range of name brand baby bedding from manufacturers like Quiltex (Beatrix Potter and Precious Moments), Cotton Tale, Nojo (Paddington), Lambs & Ivy (Country Noah), Judy's Originals, Glenna Jean and Red Calliope (Disney Pooh). While Penney's prices aren't always affordable (we compared some designs to other mail-order sources and found Penney's to be a few dollars higher), they do offer the most accessories we've ever found. For example, they carry every accessory available for the "Boynton for Babies" and "Beatrix Potter" lines. The catalog carries valances, wallpaper borders, mobiles, and wall hangings for these and other bedding designs. If you want a "complete look," give Penney's a call.

Kids Club

To Order Call: (800) 363-0500; Fax (216) 494-0265.
Shopping Hours: 24 hours a day, seven days a week.
Or write to: 7245 Whipple Ave. NW, North Canton, OH 44720.
Credit Cards Accepted: MC, VISA, Discover, AMEX.

We liked the bedding offerings in this affordable catalog. We saw several rich plaids in all-cotton fabrics—at $137 for a four-piece set, that's a good deal. A patchwork design with country motif was $189 for a set including quilt, bumper, dust ruffle and fitted crib sheet. Kid's Club also sells 100% cotton blankets ($16 to $25), sheet savers ($11.62 for a set of two) and other bedding accessories. Join the Kid's Club for an $18 annual fee and you get additional discounts and special deals.

Lands' End.

To Order Call: (800) 356-4444; Fax (800) 332-0103.
Shopping Hours: 24 hours a day, seven days a week.
Or write to: Lands' End Inc., 1 Lands' End Ln., Dodgeville, WI 53595.
Credit Cards Accepted: MC, VISA, AMEX, Discover.
Retail Outlets: They also have 11 outlet stores in Iowa, Illinois, and Wisconsin—call the number above for the nearest location to you.

The Lands' End "Coming Home" catalog offers a few bedding options for infants. The summer catalog features 200-thread count cotton crib sets, while the winter catalog typically carries cotton flannel crib sets. Choose from a solid color theme or three patterns.

We found the prices to be a good deal, given the quality. Solid color flannel sheets are $15, while the bumpers are $45 and the dust ruffle is $22. As mentioned earlier in this chapter, we liked the Lands' End "coverlets" (which are more substantial than a blanket but not as thick as a quilt/comforter) at $25 each. The Polartec blankets ($25) are also a good option for parents in cold climates.

While the patterns change each season, Land's End designs are whimsical without an overly commercial theme like Pooh or Mickey Mouse.

The Natural Baby Company

To Order Call: (609) 771-9233; Fax (609) 771-9342.
Shopping Hours: Monday through Saturday, 9am to 11pm Eastern.
   Sunday 9am to 6pm Eastern.
Or write to: 816 Silvia St. 800-BS, Trenton, NJ 08628.
Credit Cards Accepted: MC, VISA, Discover.
Outlet Store: This catalog has an outlet store in Princeton, NJ and also
has occasional sales at their headquarters location in Trenton. Call the
above number for more details.

As the name implies, this catalog has an ecological bent.
Their bedding features all-natural cotton blankets, sheets,
bumpers, quilts and dust ruffles. You can choose from several
colors, as well as an un-dyed "Green Cotton Flannel"—this
cotton is grown without pesticides and manufactured without
bleaches, dyes or other harmful chemicals. A quilt will set you
back $98, sheets are $14.50 and the dust ruffle is $48. While
we liked the Natural Baby Catalog overall, we have to flame
them for selling crib "futon" mattress and lamb skins. To sell
these soft-bedding products without any warning about the
possible risk of SIDS (Sudden Infant Death Syndrome) is darn
irresponsible. Shame on them.

One Step Ahead.

To Order Call: (800) 274-8440; (800) 950-5120; Fax (847) 615-7236.
Shopping Hours: 24 hours a day, seven days a week.
Or write to: One Step Ahead, 75 Albrecht Dr., Lake Bluff, IL 60044.
Credit Cards Accepted: MC, VISA, AMEX, Discover, Optima.

One Step Ahead offers a limited number of baby linen
options, including three baby quilts, which looked more like
lightweight coverlets than thick comforters. The 100% cotton
quilts have an heirloom look and cost $30 each.
We noticed that One Step Ahead also sells 100% cotton
sheets and receiving blankets. Sheets were priced at $15, and
thermal blankets were $10. What we liked best was One Step
Ahead's wide variety of colors—from bright hues like purple
and jade, to pastels like mint and periwinkle. New this year
are knitted cotton sheets and flannel sheets at $15 each.
As for bedding accessories, One Step Ahead carries sheet
protectors, crib rail pads, nursery decor and other items.

Orange Elephant.

To Order: (800) 467-5597 or (304) 744-9323; Fax (800) 329-6687
Shopping Hours: 9am to 9pm Eastern Time, seven days a week.
Or write to: 90 MacCorkle Ave. SW, South Charleston, WV 25303.
Credit Cards Accepted: MC, VISA, AMEX, Discover.
This general catalog carries quite a few bedding acces-

sories, including sheet savers ($15 for a set of two), crib rail guards, cotton blankets and more. There's even a set of basic bedding—the Oxford stripe pattern was $50 for a comforter or bumper, $20 for the sheet and $40 for the dust ruffle. The fabric was a cotton/poly blend.

Right Start Catalog.

To Order Call: (800) LITTLE-1 (800-548-8531); Fax (800) 762-5501.
Shopping Hours: 24 hours a day, seven days a week.
Or write to: 5334 Sterling Center Dr., Westlake Village, CA 91361.
Credit Cards Accepted: MC, VISA, AMEX, Discover.
Retail Outlets: The company also has 27 Right Start stores in 14 states, with more on tap for the coming year. Call the above number for the nearest location to you.

The Right Start doesn't showcase a huge amount of baby bedding, but it does carry the popular "Classic Pooh" from Red Calliope and several accessories. You can buy the four-piece "Pooh and his Hunny Pots" collection for $179, or the individual pieces a la carte. Five Pooh blankets are also available. The Right Start also carries a few bedding and decor accessories, including "Stikarounds" (decor appliques in such themes as Beatrix Potter), Crib Mates (sheet savers), padded crib rail guards and other items.

Schweitzer Linen

To Order: (800) 554-6367, (212) 249-8361; Fax (212) 737-6328
Shopping Hours: 10:00 am to 6:00 pm Monday-Friday (Eastern)
Or write to: 457 Columbus Ave., New York, NY 10024.
Credit Cards Accepted: MC, VISA, AMEX.
Retail Outlets: Three stores in the New York City area.

This upper-end linen catalog showcases unique designs and high-quality cotton fabrics. One stand-out was "Loveable II," which was made of 100% Italian cotton printed with tiny hearts in either pink, blue, yellow or green. A single fitted sheet will set you back $60, bumpers are $150, and a dust ruffle is $160. Schweitzer also sells crib blankets with appliquéed animals for $95. Fortunately, the catalog does run occasional sales. The issue we saw feature a 25% discount on all items.

Seventh Generation

To Order Call: (800) 456-1177; Fax (800) 456-1139.
Shopping Hours: 24 hours a day, seven days a week.
Or write to: One Mill St. Suite A26, Burlington, VT 05401.
Credit Cards Accepted: MC, VISA, Discover.
If you're concerned about the health aspect of typical crib

mattresses (yes, most are made of petrochemicals), then consider the "organic cotton crib mattress" from Seventh Generation. This eco-catalog sells the all-natural mattress, which features wool-wrapped batting and an organic cotton shell. Unfortunately, the mattress may cost more than your crib—at a whopping $650, it's quite a luxury. Seventh Generation also sells a selection of all-natural crib bedding made of organic cotton. Sheets run $48, duvet covers are $64, bumpers $138, and dust ruffles are $64.

THE BOTTOM LINE:
A Wrap-Up of Best Buy Picks

 For bedding, we thought the best brands were Baby Guess, Belinda Barton, California Kids, Cotton Tale, Pine Creek, and Sumersault. Of course, that's if you want to buy an entire set of bedding—we found that all baby really needs is a set of sheets and a good cotton blanket. Instead of spending $300 to $500 on a bedding set with ridiculous items like pillows and diaper stackers, use your creativity to decorate the nursery affordably and leave the crib simple.

Skip expensive wall hangings that can cost hundreds of dollars and use do-it-yourself stencils from arts and crafts stores for a decorative wall border. Instead of shelling out $300 on Classic Pooh bedding, buy solid color sheets and accessorize with affordable Pooh items like lamps, posters, rugs, etc.

Let's take a look at the savings:

Lands' End 100% cotton fitted sheets (three)	$45
Cotton coverlet blanket from Lands' End	$25
Miscellaneous (stencils, lamp, other decor)	$100
TOTAL	**$170**

If you live in a cold climate, you might want to get a Polar fleece blanket from a catalog like the Company Store for $20.

In contrast, if you go for a designer brand and buy all those silly extras like diaper stackers, you could be out as much as $750 on bedding alone—add in wall paper, accessories like wall hangings, matching lamps and you'll be out $1000 or more. So, the total savings from following the tips in this chapter could be as much as $800 to $900.

Now that your baby's room is outfitted, what about the baby? Flip to the next chapter to get the lowdown on those little clothes.

Chapter 4

The Reality Layette:
Little Clothes for Little Prices

What the heck is a "onesie"? How many clothes does your baby need? How come such little clothes have such big price tags? These and other mysteries are unraveled in this chapter as we take you on a guided tour of baby clothes land. We'll reveal our secret sources for finding name brand clothes at one-half to one-third off department store prices. Which brands are best? Check out our reviews and ratings of the best clothing brands for your baby and our nine tips from smart shoppers on getting the best deals. Next, read about the many outlets for children's apparel that have been popping up all over the country. At the end of this chapter, we'll even show you how to save big bucks on diapers.

Getting Started: When Do You Need This Stuff?

♣ **Baby Clothing.** You'll need basic baby clothing like t-shirts and sleepers as soon as you're ready to leave the hospital. Depending on the weather, you may need a bunting at that time as well.

You'll probably want to start stocking up on baby clothing around the seventh month of your pregnancy. It's important to have some basic items on hand (like sleepers or strechies) in case you deliver early; however, you may want to wait to do major baby clothes shopping until after any baby showers to see what clothing your friends and family give as gifts.

Be sure to keep a running list of your acquisitions so you won't buy too much of one item. Thanks to gifts and our own buying, we had about two thousand teeny, side-snap shirts by the time our baby was born. In the end, he didn't wear the shirts much (he grew out of the newborn sizes quickly and wasn't really wild about them anyway), and we ended up wasting the $20 we spent.

♣ **Diapers.** How many diapers do you need for starters? Are you sitting down? If you're going with disposables, we recommend 600. Yes, that's six packages of 100 diapers each (purchase them in your eighth month of pregnancy, just in case

Junior arrives early). You may think this is a lot, but believe us, we bought that much and we still had to do another diaper run by the time our son was a month old. Newborns go through many more diapers than older infants. Also, remember that as a new parent, you'll find yourself taking off diapers that turn out to be dry; then you can't really reuse them because the tabs don't stick as well. Or worse, you may change a diaper three times in a row because Junior wasn't really finished.

Now that you know how many diapers, what sizes should you buy? We recommend 100 newborn-size diapers and 500 "size one" (or Step 1) diapers. This assume an average-size baby (about seven pounds). But remember to keep the receipts—if your baby is larger, you might have to exchange the newborns for sizes one's (and some of the one's for two's).

If you plan to use a diaper service to supply cloth diapers, sign up in your eighth month. Some diaper services will give you an initial batch of diapers (so you're not without them when the baby comes home) and then await your call to start up regular service. If you plan to wash your own cloth diapers, buy two to five dozen diapers about two months before your due date. You'll also probably want to buy diaper covers (6 to 10) at that time.

Even if you plan to use disposable diaper, you should pick up one package of high-quality cloth diapers. Why? You'll need them as spit-up rags, spot cleaners and other assorted uses you'd never imagined before becoming a parent.

Sources:

There are seven basic sources for baby clothing and diapers:

 1 BABY SPECIALTY STORES. Specialty stores typically carry 100% cotton, high-quality clothes, but you won't usually find them affordably priced. While you may find attractive dressy clothes, playclothes are usually a better deal elsewhere. Because the stores themselves are usually small, selection is often limited.

As for diapers, most specialty shops don't carry disposables. If they do at all, it seems to be the new eco-diapers (Tushies is one brand). These are as much as *twice* as expensive as the major name brands. However, specialty shops do often carry a good selection of cloth diapers and diaper covers.

2 DISCOUNTERS/DEPARTMENT STORES. When it comes to basic sleepwear, your best bet may be discount chains like Toys R Us. T-shirts, booties, and such from brands like Carter's are just fine for the short time your baby will be wearing them. As for playclothes, which will get much more wear, we were less impressed with the polyester-blend clothes available from discounters like K-Mart and Target. Department stores are more likely to carry playclothes in the higher-quality, all-cotton brands we will recommend later in this chapter—and with frequent sales, department store prices can be relatively affordable.

While we had mixed feelings about discounters for baby clothes, they do have great buys on disposable diapers. You'll see later in this chapter that stores like Toys R Us are incredibly affordable compared to the place most folks buy diapers (grocery stores, of course). The discounters may even have promotional specials from time to time, and, to save even more money, you can utilize the many coupons you'll be getting in the mail. As far as cloth diaper supplies go, discounters typically have a limited selection.

3 BABY MEGA-STORES. Stores like LiL' Things and Babies R Us/Baby Superstore carry name brand clothing at incredibly low prices. For example, we saw such famous labels as Baby Guess and Esprit—at prices well below regular department store prices. They also carry basic items from brands like Carter's, Baby Grow, and Little Me. The best part: you'll find a huge selection.

As for diapers, Babies R Us/Baby Superstore and LiL' Things carry both disposable and cloth diapers, plus all the requisite accessories like wipes, diaper covers, pails, etc. The prices are very low, often 20% to 30% below grocery stores for name-brand disposable diapers.

4 WAREHOUSE CLUBS. Member-only warehouse clubs like Sam's and Price/Costco sell diapers at rock-bottom prices. The selection is often hit-or-miss—sometimes you'll see brand names like Huggies and Pampers; other times it may be off-brands. While you won't find the range of sizes that you'd see in grocery stores, the prices will be hard to beat. The downside? You have to buy them in "bulk," that is huge cases of multiple diaper packs that might require a fork lift to get home.

As a side note, we've even seen some baby clothes at warehouse clubs from time to time. We found very good quality blanket sleepers at Sam's for $8 each during one visit.

5 MAIL-ORDER. There are a zillion catalogs that offer clothing for infants. The choices can be quite overwhelming, and the prices can range from reasonable to ridiculous. It's undeniably a great way to shop when you have a newborn and just don't want to drag your baby out to the mall. Cloth diapers and diaper covers are often available through mail order. Later in this chapter, we'll highlight some of the better catalogs offering these products.

6 CONSIGNMENT OR THRIFT STORES. You might think of these stores as dingy shops with musty smells—purveyors of old, used clothes that aren't in great shape. Think again—many consignment stores today are bright and attractive, with name brand clothes at a fraction of the retail price. Yes, the clothes have been worn before, but most stores only stock high-quality brands that are in excellent condition. And stores that specialize in children's apparel are popping up everywhere, from Play it Again (718) 499-8589 in Brooklyn, New York, to Baby Bargains (602) 820-6406 in Phoenix, Arizona (no relation to this book, of course). Later in this chapter, we'll tell you how to find a consignment store near you.

7 GARAGE/YARD SALES. Check out the following box for tips on how to shop garage sales like the pros.

Garage & Yard Sales
Eight Tips to Get The Best Bargains

It's an American institution—the garage sale.

Sure you can save money at an outlet store or get a deal at a department store sale. But there's no comparing to the steals you can get at your neighbor's garage sale.

We love getting e-mail from readers who've found great deals at garage sales. We've heard about 25¢ stretchies, a snowsuit for $1, barely used high chairs for $5 and more. But getting the most out of garage sales requires some pre-planning. We interviewed a dozen parents who call themselves "garage sale experts" for their tips:

1 *Check the newspaper first.* Many folks advertise their garage sales a few days before the event—zero in on the ads that mention kids/baby items to keep from wasting time on sales that won't be fruitful.

2 *Get a good map of the area.* You've got to find obscure cul-de-sacs and hidden side streets.

3 *Start early.* The professional bargain hunters get going at the crack of dawn. If you wait until mid-day, all the good stuff will be gone. An even better bet: if you know the family, ask if you can drop by the day *before* the sale. That way you have a first shot before the competition arrives.

Baby Clothing

So you thought all the big-ticket items were taken care of when you bought the crib and other baby furniture? Ha! It's time to prepare for your baby's "layette," a French word that translated literally means "spending large sums of cash on baby clothes and other such items, as required by Federal Baby Law." But, of course, there are some creative (dare we say, sneaky?) ways of keeping your layette bills down.

At this point, you may be wondering just what does your baby need? Obviously it may be a few years before he or she wears your hand-me-downs. Sure you've seen those cute ruffly dresses and sailor suits in department stores—but what does your baby *really* wear everyday?

4 *Do the "box dive."* Many garage sale hosts will just dump kid's clothes into a big box, all jumbled together in different sizes, styles, etc. Figuring out how to get the best picks while three other moms are digging through the same box is a challenge. The best advice: familiarize yourself with the better name brands in this chapter and then pluck out the best bets as fast as possible. Then evaluate the clothes away from the melee.

5 *Concentrate on "family areas."* A mom here in Colorado told us she found garage sales in Boulder (a college town) were mostly students getting rid of stereos, clothes and other junk. A better bet was nearby Louisville, a suburban bedroom community with lots of growing families.

6 *Haggle.* Prices on big ticket items (that is, anything over $5) are usually negotiable.

7 *Don't buy a used crib or car seat.* Old cribs may not meet current safety standards. It's also difficult to get replacement parts for obscure brands. Car seats are also a second-hand no-no—you can't be sure it wasn't in an accident, weakening its safety and effectiveness.

8 *Be creative.* See a great stroller but hate the fabric? Remember that you can buy stroller seat covers from companies like Nojo (see a review of this company in the bedding chapter earlier in this book). For a small investment, you can rehabilitate a stroller into a showpiece.

Meet the layette, a collection of clothes and accessories that your baby will use daily. While your baby's birthday suit was free, outfitting him in something more "traditional" will cost some bucks. In fact, a recent study estimated that parents spend $12,000 on clothes for a child by the time he or she hits 18 years old—and that sounds like a conservative estimate to us. That translates into a 20 *billion* (yes, that's billion with a B) dollar business for children's clothing retailers. Follow our tips, and we estimate that you'll save 20% or more on your baby's wardrobe.

What Are You Buying?

Figuring out what your baby should wear is hardly intuitive to first-time parents. We had no earthly idea what type of (and how many) clothes a newborn needed, so we did what we normally do—we went to the bookstore to do research. We found three dozen books on "childcare and parenting"—with three dozen different lists of items that you *must* have for your baby and without which you're a very bad parent. Speaking of guilt, we also heard from relatives, who had their own opinions as to what was best for baby.

All of this begs the question: what do you *really* need? And how much? We learned that the answer to that last, age-old question was the age-old answer, "It depends." That's right, nobody really knows. In fact, we surveyed several department stores, interviewed dozens of parents, and consulted several "experts," only to find no consensus whatsoever. In order to better serve humanity, we have developed THE OFFICIAL FIELDS' LIST OF ALMOST EVERY ITEM YOU NEED FOR YOUR BABY IF YOU LIVE ON PLANET EARTH. We hope this stems the confusion.

Feel free to now ignore those lists of "suggested layette items" provided by retail stores. Many of the "suggestions" are self-serving, to say the least.

Of course, even when you decide what and how much to buy for your baby, you still need to know what *sizes* to buy. Fortunately, we have this covered, too. First, recognize that most baby clothes come in a range of sizes rather than one specific size ("newborn to 3 months" or "3-6 months"). *We recommend you buy "3-6 month" sizes (instead of newborn) so your child won't grow out of his clothes too quickly.* Stay away from newborn to three-month sizes. If you have a premature baby or an infant that is on the small side, we have identified a couple catalogs that specialize in preemie wear. And, if on the other hand, you deliver a 10-pounder, make sure you keep all receipts and packaging so you can exchange the clothes for larger sizes—you may find you're into six-month sizes by the time your baby hits one month old!

Remember, you can always buy more later if you need them. In fact, this is a good way to make use of those close friends and relatives who stop by and offer to "help" right after you've suffered through 36 hours of hard labor—send them to the store!

We should point out that this layette list is just to get you started. This supply should last for the first month or two of your baby's life. Also along these lines, we received a question from a mom-to-be who wondered, given these quantities, how often do we assume you'll do laundry. The answer is in the following box.

E-MAIL FROM THE REAL WORLD
How Much Laundry Will I Do?

Anna Balayn of Brooklyn, NY had a good question about layettes:

"You have a list of clothes a new baby needs, but you don't say how often I would need to do laundry if I go with the list. I work full time and would like to have enough for a week. Is the list too short for me?"

Our answer: there is no answer. Factors such as whether you use cloth or disposable diapers (cloth leaks more; hence more laundry) and how much your baby spits up will greatly determine the laundry load. Another factor: breast versus bottle feeding. Bottle-fed babies have fewer poops (and hence, less laundry from possible leaks). An "average" laundry cycle with our layette list would be every two to three days, assuming breast feeding, disposable diapers and an average amount of spit-up.

The "Baby Bargains" Layette

♣ *T-Shirts.* Oh sure, a t-shirt is a t-shirt, right? Not when it comes to baby t-shirts. These t-shirts could have side snaps, side ties, snaps at the crotch (also known as onesies or creepers) or over-the-head openings. If you have a child who is allergic to metal snaps (they leave a red ring on their skin), you might want to consider over the head or side tie t-shirts. As a side note, you have to wait until your baby's belly button falls off (don't ask; this usually happens in a week or two) until you can use the snap-at-the-crotch t-shirts.

By the way, is a onesie t-shirt an outfit or an undergarment? Answer: it's both. In the summer, you'll find onesies with printed patterns that are intended as outfits. In the winter, most stores just sell white onesies, intended as undergarments.

HOW MANY? T-shirts usually come in packs of three. Our recommendation is to buy two packages of three (or a total of six shirts) of the over-the-head variety. We also suggest buying one pack of side-snap shirts and one of side-tie shirts. This way, if your baby does have an allergy to the snaps, you have a backup. Later you'll find the snap-at-the-crouch t-shirts to be most convenient since they don't ride up under clothes.

♣ *Drawstring Gowns.* These are one-piece gowns with a drawstring or elastic at the bottom. They are used as sleeping garments in most cases, although we met one mom who used them when her baby had colic—the baby seemed to feel better when she had room to kick her feet. We've also heard from a few parents in hot climates who liked drawstring gowns for similar reasons; their baby seemed more comfortable.

The downsides? First, the drawstrings can be a serious choking and strangulation hazard so either remove them by the time your baby is 10 weeks old or buy gowns that have an elastic insert instead of string or ribbon. Another problem with drawstring gowns: your baby can't wear one and be put in a car seat, since it's difficult to buckle them in around the gown. HOW MANY? In our opinion, drawstring gowns are unnecessary. We never used them, and neither did many of the parents we interviewed. Therefore, we recommend buying none of these. However, if you want to give them a try, buy just one or two to see what your baby thinks.

♣ *Sleepers.* This is the real workhorse of your infant's wardrobe, since babies usually sleep most of the day in the first months. Also known as stretchies, sleepers are most commonly used as pajamas for infants. They have feet, are often made of flame-retardant cloth and snap up the front.

HOW MANY? Because of their heavy use, we recommend parents buy at least four to six sleepers.

♣ *Blanket Sleepers.* These are heavy-weight, footed one-piece garments. Used often in cool climates or when a baby is "cold natured," blanket sleepers usually have a zipper down the front.

HOW MANY? If you live in a cold climate or your baby is born in the winter, you may want to purchase one or two of these items. As an alternative to buying blanket sleepers, you could put a t-shirt on underneath her sleeper or stretchie for extra warmth.

 ♣ *Coveralls.* One-piece play outfits, coveralls (also known as rompers) are usually cotton or cotton/poly blends. Small sizes (under 6 months) may have feet, while larger sizes don't.

HOW MANY? Since these are really playclothes and small infants don't do a lot of playing, we recommend you only buy two to four coveralls for babies under four months of age. However, if your child will be going into daycare at an early age, you may need to start with four to six outfits.

 ♣ *Booties/socks.* These are necessary for outfits that don't have feet (like drawstring gowns and coveralls). As your child gets older (at about six months), look for the kind of socks that have rubber skids on the bottom (they keep baby from slipping when learning to walk).

HOW MANY? Three to four pairs are all you'll need at first, since your baby will probably be dressed in footed sleepers most of the time.

♣ *Sweaters.* What you think they are.

HOW MANY? Most parents will find one sweater is plenty (they're nice for holiday picture sessions). Avoid all-white sweaters, since they show dirt much faster.

 ♣ *Hats.* Believe it or not, you'll still want a light cap for your baby in the early months of life, even if you live in a hot climate. Babies lose a large amount of heat from their heads, so protecting them with a cap or bonnet is a good idea. And don't expect to go out for a walk in the park without the baby's sun hat either.

HOW MANY? A couple of hats would be a good idea—sun hats in summer, warmer caps for winter. We like the safari-style hats best (they have flaps to protect the ears and neck).

 ♣ *Snowsuit/bunting.* Similar to the type of fabric used for blanket sleepers, buntings also have hoods and covers for the hands. Most buntings are like a sack and don't have leg openings, while snowsuits do. Snowsuits can be used in a car seat, while buntings are a no-no. Both versions usually have zippered fronts.

How MANY? Only buy one of these if you live in a climate where you need it. Even with the Colorado winter, we got away with layering clothes on our baby, then wrapping him in a blanket for the walk out to a warmed-up car.

♣ *Kimonos.* Just like the adult version. Some are zippered sacks with a hood and terry-cloth lining. You use them after a bath.

How MANY? Are you kidding? What a joke! These items are one of our "wastes of money." We recommend you pass on the kimonos and instead invest in good quality towels.

♣ *Saque Sets.* Two-piece outfits with a shirt and diaper cover.

How MANY? Forget buying these as well. The shirt tends to ride up on your baby anyway.

♣ *Bibs.* These come in two versions, believe it or not. The little, tiny bibs are for the baby that drools the volume of Lake Michigan. The larger versions are used when you begin feeding her solid foods (about six months). Don't expect to be able to use the drool bibs later for feedings, unless you plan to change her carrot-stained outfit frequently.

How MANY? Drool bibs are rather useless—skip them. When you get into feeding solids, however, you'll need at least three or four large bibs. One option: plastic bibs for feeding so you can just sponge them off after a meal.

♣ *Washcloths and hooded towels.* OK, so these aren't actually clothes, but baby washcloths and hooded towels are a necessity. Why? Because they are small and easier to use, plus they're softer than adult towels and washcloths.

How MANY? At first, you'll probably need only three sets of towels and washcloths (you get one of each per set). But as baby gets older and dirtier, invest in a few more washcloths to spot clean during the day.

♣ *Receiving Blankets.* You'll need these small, cotton blankets for all kinds of uses: to swaddle the baby, as a play quilt, or even for an extra layer of warmth on a cold day.

How MANY? We believe you can never have too many of these blankets, but since you'll probably get a few as gifts, you'll only need to buy three or four yourself. A total of seven to eight is probably optimal.

What about the future? While our layette list only addresses clothes to buy for a newborn, you will want to plan for your child's future wardrobe as well. For the modern baby, it seems clothes come in two categories: playclothes (to be used in daycare situations) and dress-up clothes. Later in this chapter, we'll discuss more money-saving tips and review several brands of play and dress-up clothes.

Smart Shopper Tips
TIPS AND TRICKS TO GET THE BEST QUALITY

"I've received several outfits from friends for my daughter, but I'm not sure she'll like all the scratchy lace and the poly/cotton blends. What should she wear, and what can I buy that will last through dozens of washings?"

Generally, we recommend dressing your child for comfort. At the same time, you need clothes that can withstand frequent washings. With this in mind, here are our suggestions for finding the best clothing for babies.

1 SEE WHAT YOUR BABY LIKES BEFORE INVESTING IN MANY GARMENTS. Don't invest $90 in drawstring gowns, only to find the baby hates them.

2 WE GENERALLY RECOMMEND 100% COTTON CLOTHING. Babies are most comfortable in clothing that breathes.

3 TEST POLY/COTTON PLAYCLOTHES ON YOUR CHILD SPARINGLY WHEN SHE GETS OLDER (starting at 3-6 months) to see if she finds them uncomfortable.

4 IF YOU DISCOVER YOUR CHILD HAS AN ALLERGY TO METAL SNAPS (YOU'LL SEE RED RINGS ON HIS SKIN), CONSIDER ALTERNATIVES SUCH AS SHIRTS THAT HAVE TIES. Another option is a t-shirt that pulls on over the head. Unfortunately, many babies don't like having anything pulled over their heads. Another alternative for allergic babies: clothes with plastic snaps or zippers.

5 IN GENERAL, BETTER-MADE CLOTHES WILL HAVE THEIR SNAPS ON A REINFORCED FABRIC BAND. Snaps attached directly to the body of the fabric may tear the garment or rip off when changing.

6 IF YOU'RE BUYING 100% COTTON CLOTHING, MAKE SURE ITS PRE-SHRUNK. Some stores, like Gymboree (see review later in this chapter), guarantee that their clothes won't shrink. In other shops, you're on your own. Our advice: read the label. If it says "wash in cold water," assume the garment will shrink. On the other hand, care instructions that advise washing in warm water may indicate that the garment is already preshrunk.

7 GO FOR OUTFITS WITH SNAPS AND ZIPPERS ON BOTH LEGS, NOT JUST ONE. Dual-leg snaps or zippers make it much easier to change a diaper. Always check a garment for diaper accessibility—some brands actually have no snaps or zippers, meaning you would have to completely undress your baby for a diaper change! Another pet peeve: garments that have snaps up the back also make diaper changes a hassle.

8 BE AWARE THAT EACH COMPANY HAS ITS OWN WARPED IDEA ABOUT HOW TO SIZE BABY CLOTHES. See the following box on the next page for more details.

9 BEWARE OF APPLIQUÉS. Some appliqué work can be quite scratchy on the inside of the outfit (it rubs against baby's skin). Also, poor quality appliqué may unravel or fray after a couple washings.

The Name Game: Reviews of Selected Manufacturers

After each brand, we list the address and phone number of its corporate headquarters so you can contact them to find a dealer near you. In most cases, these companies do not sell directly to consumers—you must go through their retail dealers. The exception, of course, are manufacturers' outlets. We list the brands that have outlets later in this chapter, including the outlet's address and phone number.

There are over 700 stores that specialize in selling children's apparel—and that doesn't even count the department stores and discounters who also have baby clothing departments. As you visit these stores, here are some of the brands you'll encounter.

The Ratings

★★★★ EXCELLENT—*our top pick!*
  ★★★ GOOD—*above average quality, prices, and creativity.*
    ★★ FAIR—*could stand some improvement.*
      ★ POOR—*yuck! could stand some major improvement.*

Alexis ....★★★★
Manufactured by Warren Featherbone Co., PO Box 383, Gainesville, GA 30503. For a store near you, call (770) 535-3000. This is one of those amazing brands that lasts through

One Size Does Not Fit All

A six month-size t-shirt is a six-month-size t-shirt, right? Wrong. For some reason, baby clothing companies have yet to synchronize their watches when it comes to sizes. Hence, a clothing item that says "six-month size" from one manufacturer can be just the same dimensions as a "twelve-month size" from another. All this begs the question: how can you avoid widespread confusion? First, open packages to check out actual dimensions. Take your baby along and hold up items to her to gauge whether they'd fit. Second, note whether items are pre-shrunk—you'll probably have to ask the salesperson or catalog representative (if not, allow for shrinkage). Third, don't key on length from head to foot. Instead, focus on the length from neck to crotch—a common problem are items that seem roomy but are too tight in the crotch. Finally, forget age ranges and pay more attention to labels that specify an infant's size in weight and height, which are much more accurate. To show how widely sizing can vary, check out the following chart. *Parenting Magazine* compared "six-month" t-shirts from six major clothing makers (we've added dimensions from three popular catalogs, Hanna Anderson, Land's End and Talbot's Kids). Here's what these six-month t-shirts really translated to in terms of a baby's weight and height:

What a six month t-shirt really means

Maker	Weight	Height
Baby Gap	17-22 lbs.	26-29"
Carter's Layette	12-18 lbs.	25"
Gymboree	18-23 lbs.	26-29"
Hanna Anderson	14-21 lbs	26-30"
Healthtex	13.5-19 lbs.	24-27.5"
Land's End	14-18 lbs.	25-27"
Little Me	16-17 lbs.	27-28.5"
Oshkosh	16.5-18 lbs.	27-28.5"
Talbot's Kids	11-16 lbs.	24-27"

Here's another secret from the baby clothing trade: the more expensive the brand, the more roomy the clothes. Conversely, cheap items usually have the skimpiest sizing. What about the rule that you should just double your baby's age to find the right size (that is, buying twelve-month clothes for a six-month old?). That's bogus—as you can see, sizing is so all over the board that this rule just doesn't work.

several children. In fact, we bought a "previously worn" Alexis outfit from our local consignment shop, and it looked just like new. As for brand-new clothes, we saw an Alexis safari outfit, complete with khaki shorts with suspenders, animal-print shirt, and straw hat for just $25—not bad considering you get that cute hat. The quality is impeccable and worth the price, even at full retail.

Baby Dior ....★★
1590 Adamson Pkwy., Morrow, GA. (770) 961-8722. Manufactured by Carter's, Baby Dior is one of those upper-end lines that elicits many "oohs" and "aahs." We have mixed feelings about Baby Dior. On one hand, we like the quality of their towels and blankets, but their clothes aren't necessarily any better than more affordable brands. For example, we purchased a Baby Dior terry sleeper that snagged badly in the wash and pilled up just as much as the less expensive Carter's sleepers. If you plan to buy any Baby Dior designs, try to catch them on sale or at the many Carter's outlet stores across the U.S. (later in this chapter, we'll review the Carter's outlets). In addition, be careful to check for crotch snaps—some Baby Dior designs lack diaper accessibility.

Baby Gap...★★★$^{1}/_{2}$
For a store near you, call (415) 952-4400. This is probably one of our favorite clothing brands. An off-shoot of the Gap label, Baby Gap clothes are available at regular Gap stores and at the smaller Gap Kids and Baby Gap shops. The Baby Gap label encompasses everything from coveralls to leggings to socks—and even sunglasses, hats, and shoes. On a recent visit to a Gap Kids, we noticed a cute shorts coverall outfit with a red checkered background (like a picnic tablecloth), covered with various condiments like catsup bottles, watermelon slices, and hot dogs. Cost: $15. Plain purple leggings were $12.50, and a beautiful cardigan sweatshirt with an appliquéed yellow pear was $18. New this year at Baby Gap is a layette line with newborn-size clothing, hats, socks and more. All in all, the prices are a mixed bag—basic items like shoes and t-shirts are affordable while fancier stuff (sweaters, embroidered jackets) can get pricey. Fortunately, Baby Gap's frequent sales (especially at the end of seasons) produce bargains at 25% to 50% off. The quality is very good (most styles are 100% cotton) and the items stand up well after multiple washings. We also like their salespeople, who aren't as obnoxious as other chains and seem knowledgeable about sizing and product questions. One even offered to call another store to get an out-of-stock size in an item we wanted. While Gap stores that sell Baby Gap clothing are all over the U.S., they are more numerous in the eastern states.

Carter's .... ★★★
1509 Adamson Pkwy., Morrow, GA 30260. For a store near you, call (770) 961-8722. We often hear from moms that Carter's is "a good brand for baby to spit up on"—and that's a compliment. Their affordable, all purpose playclothes are especially nice as "daycare wear" and for other uses when an expensive outfit would be overkill. We've seen Carter's just about everywhere, from department stores to baby specialty shops, outlets to discounters. Prices are always affordable, even when you don't find Carter's on sale. For example, we saw Carter's sleepers regularly priced at $20 on sale for $15.99. If you like Carter's, you'll also find **Baby Gro** (made by Kleinert's, Inc., 112 W. 34th St., Suite 1714, New York, NY 10120; 212-736-7030) interesting, another all-purpose brand name similar in quality and price. We saw one of their sleepers (in a simple design) for $17. Carter's has a large number of outlet stores, which we'll review later in this chapter.

Flapdoodles ....★★ ¹/₂
Delaware Industrial Park, Neward, DE 19713. For a store near you, call (302) 731-9793. Flapdoodles specializes in 100% cotton, pre-shrunk playclothes. We liked the reinforced crotches and the easy-to-use large buttons. We do have one bone to pick with this designer, however: we bought a Flapdoodles shorts outfit ($25) that was designed in such a way that it made diaper changes an Olympic sport. Why? While the outfit had snaps, you couldn't entirely unsnap it because of fabric bands around each leg. The upshot: diaper changes were hell. On the bright side, Flapdoodles has two outlets, which we'll review later in this chapter.

Gerber ....★
531 S. Main St., Greenville, SC 29601. For a store near you, call (864) 240-2840. We just don't get it. Why take a well-respected (or at least well-known) name like Gerber and slap it on a cheap line of baby clothing? We just didn't like their clothing, which tends toward synthetic fabrics (or blends) with styling that's just plain boring. They should stick to food. While we wouldn't buy most Gerber items, their t-shirts and washcloths are affordable and widely available.

Good Lad of Philadelphia ....★★★ ¹/₂
431 E. Tioga St. Philadelphia, PA 19134. For a store near you, call (215) 739-0200. If you're seeking outfits for dressier occasions (or even for an outing of miniature golf), you won't find a better designer than Good Lad of Philadelphia. We were impressed with their high quality and (relatively) affordable dress outfits, which often include accessories like hats

and suspenders. For example, one outfit that caught our attention was a girl's sailor dress with a navy blue and white sailboat print for $28—and that included a cute hat. Another big plus: their tags offer some of the most detailed sizing information we've seen. Good Lad designs are also available through several catalogs, including Olsen's Mill Direct (800) 537-4979.

Gymboree ....★★¹/₂
700 Airport Blvd., Suite 200, Burlingame, CA 94010. For a store near you, call (800) 990-5060 or (415) 579-0600. An off-shoot of the famous play classes that go by the same name, Gymboree stores market their own brand of high-quality baby and children's clothes. We visited a local store and found a wide selection of coordinating clothes for both boys and girls. The sizes are color coded (with age, height, and weight) and the fabrics are 100% cotton. Instead of dividing the clothes into boys and girls sections, Gymboree separates the primary color patterns from the pastel designs. For babies, we saw a cotton knit animal print one-piece outfit for $25 and thick receiving blankets for $26. For girls, leggings are most popular ($16). A coordinating A-line jumper is $28. We liked their overall outfits ($24 for the overalls, $17 for the shirt), and they even have coordinating socks, hats, shoes, sunglasses, and purses. The designs are a refreshing change from the standard fare.

While we liked Gymboree, we have to admit the chain is an acquired taste. Some parents we interviewed love it (one mom said their clothes were sized perfectly for her tall/skinny baby), while others think the bold color palette is way too loud. One mom we spoke to took Gymboree's sales staff to task for being too pushy, "always pressuring you to put together a coordinating 12 piece outfit." Another parent said the prices were too expensive and thought their sales were too infrequent.

If there isn't a Gymboree near you now, there probably will be one soon. The chain currently has about 350 stores and is opening 50 to 75 more each year. While you might expect this chain to have outlets in such populous states as Texas and California, they also have stores in states like Delaware, New Mexico, and Alabama (call the above number for the nearest location). Another interesting fact: Gymboree guarantees that their clothing will not shrink or fade—so even though it isn't cheap, you know it will last.

Health-Tex by Triboro .... ★★
172 S. Broadway, White Plains, NY 10605. For a store near you, call (914) 428-7551. Health-Tex is a "bread and butter

brand" of kids clothing—basic playclothes that are priced affordably and that you won't mind your child destroying at daycare. A big plus is Health-Tex's excellent sizing information, clearly displayed on each tag. The only downside: many of the designs are poly/cotton blends, so if you prefer 100% cotton, check the label.

Le Top ....★★ $1/_2$
Made by CK Enterprises. 2975 Technology Ct., Richmond, CA 94806. For a store near you, call (800) 333-2257 or (510) 222-0477. Widely available in department stores nationwide, Le Top specializes in 100% cotton designs that feature bright and colorful whimsical prints and large button detailing. We bought several Le Top outfits and really like them—our baby is very comfortable, and the prices didn't dent our wallet. For example, a shorts jumper and shirt outfit runs about $25. While we liked Le Top, another mom we interviewed didn't totally share our enthusiasm. She complained that Le Top's clothes aren't pre-shrunk. Her advice: be careful to buy a big enough size. She made the mistake of buying her daughter's usual size in a Le Top outfit—only then to have the outfit shrink so much that it became unwearable.

Little Me ....★★★★
Made by the Schwab Company, Upper Potomac Industrial Park, Cumberland, MD. For a store near you, call (301)729-1188. Little Me is a wonderful brand of playclothes that feature great appliqués, all-cotton and poly-cotton blends, and great prices. How great? All cotton onesies run about $10—that's about 50% less than Gymboree. Sizing is clear—each outfit comes with an easy-to-read tag that helps you select the right size. Best of all, Little Me is widely available in just about every size, including preemies. We've bought several Little Me outfits, including an adorable pale yellow creeper with matching booties and embroidered ducks for $25. We can't say enough nice things about Little Me—they wash well and are a very good value.

OshKosh/Baby B'Gosh ....★★★★
112-T Otter Ave., PO Box 300, Oshkosh, WI 54901. For a store near you, call (414) 231-8800. Who hasn't seen a baby in those adorable denim overalls and thought, "Isn't that cute?" Okay, so we broke down and bought our son an Oshkosh overall outfit that makes him look like a little Iowa farmer—perfect for those grandparent photo-ops. Of course, OshKosh makes more than those famous overalls. The designer's label also adorns sweatsuits, pants, t-shirts, socks, shoes, coats, and hats—all with that too-cute OshKosh B'Gosh name.

The overalls are all cotton in most cases, but, unfortunately, the shirts that coordinate are often poly cotton blends. Our advice: simply buy the overalls without the coordinating tops. Cost: An overall set with poly/cotton t-shirt was $37. Just buying a pair of overalls was $18. Cotton onesie t-shirts were $8. By the way, we should mention that OshKosh also has a layette line for infants, called Baby B'Gosh. They offer sleepwear, socks, and onesies. Even though the suggested retail prices for OshKosh items are somewhat high, we never buy this brand at full price—you can almost always find OshKosh on sale at a department store or discounted at one of their numerous outlets (reviewed later in this chapter). In addition, OshKosh is also available through several mail-order catalogs like Olsen's Mill Direct (800-537-4979).

Patsy Aiken Designs ....★★★★
4812 Hargrove Rd., Raleigh, NC 27604. For a store near you, call (919) 872-8789. This designer is one of our favorites for dressy kids clothes. Patsy Aiken makes the most beautiful, appliquéed, 100% cotton designs on the market. They also wash well and may even last through several children. Although they can be very expensive (a shorts outfit can cost $40), Patsy Aiken's clothes are worth the money. They also make a great gift item (hint, hint, Grandma). If you live in Raleigh, check out Aiken's "attic sales:" four times a year, the company opens up an outlet store with tremendous 50%-off bargains on overstock and exclusive items. Call the above number to get on their mailing list.

Other great brands. Seattle-based ***Sisters 3*** (call 800-51-TEDDY or 206-284-3404 for a store near you) makes the "Teddy Toes" blanket with feet. This soft fleece item is breathable, warmer than wool and absorbs little water. At $44.95, it may not seem cheap, but the blanket works from newborn to 18 months. We can't say enough about "Teddy Toes"—it's perfect to bundle up baby in an infant car seat for those cold winter days, but you can also use it in strollers, back packs and swings. Available in specialty stores, department stores like Nordstrom's or directly from the company (800) 51-TEDDY.

The ***Sweet Potatoes*** factory outlet in Berkeley CA (510) 527-5852 sells samples, returns and overstock items from the all-cotton brand. Even if you can't make it to the outlet, check out this brand in regular stores—their whimsical and colorful designs are worth the money at full price. Call (510) 527-7633 for a store near you.

If you're looking for baby clothes made from "organic cotton," check out ***Earthlings*** (call 805-646-2601 for a store near you). The brand makes coveralls, playsuits, hats and snap-at-the-crotch t-shirts. Prices are rather expensive—a dress can cost $42, a footed overall $32. Available in Nordstrom's, Macy's and specialty stores, plus the One Step Ahead catalog (800) 274-8440. If you have an infant with allergy sensitivity, check out *Jake N Me* (call 970-352-8802, internet: www.frii. com/~jakenme). This brand features 100% cotton clothes made exclusively to address the concerns of allergy-sensitive infants.

If just plain cotton will do, we found two other all-cotton brands that were good in quality and construction: *Mother-Maid* (770) 479-7558 and *Mini Classics* (imported by Impact Imports International 201-569-7357) are two brands worth checking out. In Canada, there's *Baby's Own* by St. Lawrence Textiles. For flame-retardant all-cotton pajamas, the "Skivvydoodles" brand by *My Boy Sam* (860) 210-0005 is a good choice to consider.

Our Picks: Brand Recommendations

What clothing brands are best? Well, there is no one correct answer. An outfit that's perfect for day care (that is, to be trashed in Junior's first painting experiment) is different than an outfit for a weekend outing with friends. And dress-up occasions may require an entire different set of clothing criteria. Hence, we've divided our clothing brand recommendations into three areas: good (day care), better (weekend wear) and best (special occasions). While some brands make goods in two or even three categories, here's how we see it:

| Good | For everyday comfort (and day-care situations), basic brands like Carter's, Little Me, Health Tex, Osh Kosh are your best bets. Even Carter's sister brand Baby Dior at sale/outlet prices would work in this case. We also like the basics (when on sale) at Baby Gap for day-care wardrobes. As for catalogs, After the Stork, Playclothes and Chock are good mail-order sources. Another good choice: the basic items in Biobottoms will also do the trick.

| Better | What if you have a miniature golf outing planned with friends? Or a visit to Grandma's house? The brands of better-made casual wear we like best include Alexis, Baby Gap, Flapdoodles, Good Lad of Philadelphia, Gymboree, and Le Top. Baby Guess (especially items on sale at their outlet stores) is a good bet as well. For catalogs, we like the clothes in Hanna Anderson and Talbot's Kids as good brands, as well as the better items in Biobottoms.

| Best | Holidays and other special occasions call for special outfits. We like the brands of Patsy Aiken, Good Lad of Philadelphia, and the fancier items in Gymboree

line. As for catalogs, check out Storybook Heirlooms and Wooden Solider.

Note: For more on these brands, check out the Name Game earlier in this chapter. See "Do it By Mail" for more information on the catalogs mentioned above.

Safe & Sound

 Should your baby's sleepwear (that is, the items he'll wear almost non-stop for the first several months of life) be flame retardant? What the heck does "flame retardant" mean anyway?

According to the Consumer Product Safety Commission (CPSC), items made of flame retardant fabric will not burn under a direct flame. Huh? Doesn't "flame retardant" mean it won't catch fire at all? No—that's a common myth among parents who think such clothes are a Superman-style second skin that will protect baby against any and all fire hazards.

Prior to 1996, the CPSC mandated that an item labeled as sleepwear be made of "flame retardant fabric." More often than not, that meant polyester. While there are a few companies that make cotton sleepwear that is chemically treated to be fire retardant, the prices of such items were so high that the de facto standard for baby's sleepwear was polyester.

Then the government changed its mind. The CPSC noticed that many parents were rebelling against the rules and putting their babies in all-cotton items at bed-time. After an investigation, the CPSC revised the rules to more closely fit reality.

First, pajamas for babies nine months and under were totally exempt from the flame-retardancy rules. Why? Since these babies aren't mobile, the odds they'll come in contact with a fire hazard that would catch their clothes on fire is slim. What if the whole house catches fire? Well, the smoke is much more dangerous than the flames—hence, a good smoke detector in the nursery and every other major room of your house is a much better investment than fire retardant clothes.

What about sleepwear for older babies? Well, the government admits that "close-fitting" all-cotton items don't pose a risk either. Only flowing night gowns or pajamas that are loose-fitting must meet the flame retardancy rules today.

If you still want to go with "flame retardant" baby items, there are a couple of options beyond polyester. The Land's End catalog now sells "Polar Fleece" pajamas for babies and young children. The fabric, while polyester, is specially woven to breathe and be more comfortable. Another option: some catalogs listed later in this chapter sell cotton clothes treated to be flame retardant.

Finally, one final myth to dispel on this topic: does washing flame-retardant clothing reduce its ability to retard flames? Nope—fabrics like polyester are naturally flame retardant (that is, there is no magic chemical they've been doused with that can wash out in the laundry). What about those expensive treated all-cotton clothes? We don't think that's a problem either. While we haven't seen any much evidence to the contrary, we think those companies that sell these pricey items would be drummed out of business in a heartbeat if the flame-retardancy of their clothes suddenly disappeared after a few spins in the rinse cycle.

There is one exception to the laundry rule: if you do choose to buy flame-retardant clothing, be sure to avoid washing such clothing in soap flakes. Soap flakes actually add a flammable chemical residue to the clothes. Instead, we recommend you use regular power or liquid laundry detergent.

What about other safety hazards with children's clothing? Here are a few more to consider:

♣ *Check for loose strings.* These could become a choking hazard, or the strings could be wrapped around fingers or toes, cutting off circulation. Be careful about appliqués as well. "Heat-welded" plastic appliqués on clothes can come off and cause choking. Poorly sewn appliqués can also be a hazard.

♣ *Avoid outfits with easy-to-detach, decorative buttons or bows*—these may also be a choking hazard. If you have any doubts, cut the decorations off.

♣ *With drawstring gowns, remove the strings or buy gowns with elastic on the bottom instead.* Another good idea: remove the drawstrings from the hoods of coats or sweatshirts with hoods. In recent years, many manufacturers have voluntarily eliminated such drawstrings. Hence, today this might be more of an issue with hand-me-downs or clothes bought from second-hand shops.

Money Saving Secrets

1 WAIT UNTIL AFTER SHOWERS AND PARTIES TO PURCHASE CLOTHES. Clothing is a popular gift item, and you may not need to buy much yourself.

2 STICK WITH BASICS—T-SHIRTS, SLEEPERS, CAPS, SOCKS AND BLANKETS. For the first month or more, that's all you need since you won't be taking Junior to the opera.

3 TAKE ADVANTAGE OF BABY REGISTRIES. Many baby stores offer this service, which helps avoid duplicate shower

gifts or too many of one item. This saves you time (and money) in exchanging gifts.

4 GO FOR THE SALES! The baby department in most department stores is definitely SALE LAND. At one chain we researched, the baby section has at least some items that are on sale every week! Big baby sales occur throughout the year, but especially in January. You can often snag bargains at up to 50% off the retail price. Another tip: consider buying for the future during end-of-season sales. If you're pregnant during the fall, for example, shop the end-of-summer sales for next summer's baby clothes.

5 CHOOSE QUALITY OVER LOW PRICE FOR PLAYCLOTHES AND BASICS. Sure that 100% polyester outfit is 20% cheaper than the cotton alternative. HOWEVER, beware of the revenge of the washing machine! You don't realize how many times you'll be doing laundry—that play outfit may get washed every couple of days. Cheap polyester clothes pill or fuzz up and look like crap after just a few washings—making you more likely to chuck them. Quality clothes have longer lives, making them less expensive over time. The key to quality is thicker or more heavyweight 100% cotton fabric, well-sewn seams and appliqués, and snaps on a reinforced fabric band.

6 FOR SLEEPWEAR, GO FOR THE AFFORDABLE BRANDS. Let's get real here: babies pee and poop in their sleepers. Hence, fancy designer sleepers are a money-waster. A friend of ours who lives in Texas uses affordable all-cotton onesies as sleepwear in the hot summer months. For the winter here in Colorado, we use thermal underwear—for example, Chock catalog (800) 222-0020 sells Carter's two-piece cotton, thermal knit long underwear for $8.25.

7 CAN'T RETURN IT? Did you get gifts of clothing you don't want but can't return to a local store? Consign it at a local thrift store. We took a basketful of clothes that we couldn't use or didn't like and placed them on consignment. We made $40 in store credit or cash to buy what we really needed.

8 SPEAKING OF CONSIGNMENT STORES, HERE IS A WONDERFUL WAY TO SAVE MONEY: Buy barely used, consigned clothing for your baby. We found outfits ranging from $5 to $7 from high quality designers like Alexis. How can you find a consignment or thrift shop in your area specializing in high-quality children's clothes? Besides looking in the phone book, you could write to the National Association of Resale & Thrift Shops, 20331 Mack Ave., Detroit, MI 48236, Attention:

Children's Resources. Send a self-addressed, stamped envelope, and they'll mail you back a list! If you have any questions, you can call the association at (800) 544-0751

9 CHECK OUT DISCOUNTERS. In the past, discount stores like Target, Wal-Mart and Marshalls typically carried cheap baby clothes that were mostly polyester. Well, there's good news for bargain shoppers: in recent years, these chains have beefed up their offerings, adding more all-cotton clothes and even some brand names. For basic items like t-shirts and play-clothes that will be trashed at day care, these stores are good bets. As a side note, even the baby mega stores like Babies R Us/Baby Superstore (and their sister chain, Kids R Us) and LiL' Things (reviewed in-depth in Chapter 2) have also added all-cotton outfits to their clothing selections.

10 DON'T FORGET ABOUT CHARITY SALES. Readers tells us they've found great deals on baby clothes and equipment at church-sponsored charity sales. Essentially, these sales are like large garage/yard sales where multiple families donate kids' items as a fund-raiser for a church or other charity.

E-MAIL FROM THE REAL WORLD
Second-hand bargains easy to find

 Shelley Bayer of Connecticut raved about Once Upon A Child, a nationwide chain of consignment stores with 100+ stores (call 614-791-0000 for a location near you).

"We have two of these consignment stores in Connecticut and I love them! The clothes and toys are of great quality and very affordable. The good thing about these stores is that when you take something in to be sold, they pay you cash. You do not have wait for something to be sold and keep checking your account like a traditional consignment shop."

One caution about second-hand stores—if you buy an item like a stroller or high chair at a consignment shop, you may not be able to get replacement parts. One mom told us she got a great deal on a stroller that was missing a front bar . . . that is, it was a great deal until she discovered the model was discontinued and she couldn't get a replacement part from the manufacturer.

Outlets

There's been a huge explosion in the number of outlet stores over the last few years—and children's clothing stores haven't been left out of the boom. Indeed, as we were doing research for this section, we heard from many manufacturers that they had even more outlets on the drawing board. Therefore, if you don't see your town listed below, call the numbers provided to see if they've opened any new outlets. Also, outlet locations open and close frequently—always call before you go.

There is one publication that lists nearly every outlet store in the U.S.—Outlet Bound magazine, which is published by Outlet Marketing Group ($7.95 plus $3.50 shipping, 800-336-8853). The magazine contains detailed maps noting outlet centers for all areas of the U.S. and Canada, as well as store listings for each outlet center. We liked the index that lists all the manufacturers, and they even have a few coupons in the back. The publication also has an excellent web site (www.outletbound.com) with the most up-to-date info on outlets in the U.S. and Canada.

Baby Guess

Locations: Eight outlets, under the names Baby Guess/Guess Kids. Gilroy, CA; Los Angeles, CA; Hilton Head, SC; Sunrise, FL; Orlando, FL; Philadelphia, PA; Jeffersonville, OH; Price William, Va. To find the location near you, call (800) 228-4644 or (213) 892-1289.

Baby Guess is famous for their funky/casual look, with acid-washed overalls and other playclothes for babies and children. Their eight outlets feature savings of 50% to 60%. While some of the garments have flaws, most are first quality. Sizing runs from six months up to youth sizes. A salesperson at one of the stores told us they tend to get their stock about a month or so after it hits the retail stores. We should note that Baby Guess asked us not to write about their outlet stores since "that's not something we want to promote." So just pretend that you didn't get this information from our book. Or better yet, tell them you did.

Carter's

Locations: Over 100 outlets.
Call (770) 961-8722 for the location nearest you.

It shows you how widespread the outlet craze is when you realize that Carter's (the famous brand that also makes Baby Dior) has over 100 outlets in the U.S. That's, right, 100. If you don't have one near you, you probably live in Bolivia.

We visited a Carter's outlet and found a huge selection of infant clothes, bedding, and accessories. Terry-cloth sleepers, originally $20, were available for only $15.99. Baby Dior clothes were also available, although they are about 10% more than comparable Carter's designs. One Dior outfit that caught our eye was a footed sleeper with embroidered bunnies on the yoke and a knit, spread collar. Cost: $17.99, regularly $26.

Be sure to look for Dior receiving blankets and towels while you're there as well. The Carter's outlets don't always have these in stock, but on one visit we found a few for 25% off the retail price. The extra thick receiving blankets are especially good buys.

As for baby bedding, we noted the outlet sells quilts, bumpers, and pillows as well as fitted bassinet sheets and towels at low prices.

If you think those deals are great, check out the outlet's yearly clearance sale in January when they knock an additional 25% to 30% off their already discounted prices. A store manager at the Carter's outlet we visited said that they also have various items on sale every month. Regardless of what they have on sale, the Carter's outlets sell only first quality goods—no seconds or rejects.

Esprit

Locations: Eight locations, with more to come. Dallas, TX; San Marcos, TX; San Francisco, CA (415) 957-2540; Colorado; Maine; Michigan; New York; Vermont. Call (415) 648-6900 for the location nearest you.

Not all of the Esprit outlets carry children's clothing, but those that do have sizes from 12 months through youth sizes. The designs include dresses, pant suits, and shorts. The prices are 30% to 70% off, and they sell only first quality overruns—no seconds. Call the outlet nearest you to see if it carries Esprit's children's line.

Flapdoodles

Locations: Lancaster/York, PA (717) 390-7073, as well as New York state, Florida and Gilroy, CA. New stores scheduled for Florida, Colorado, and Missouri. Call their corporate headquarters at (302) 731-9793 for the locations.

The 100%-cotton designs from Flapdoodles are a great value even at retail, but you can actually find the clothes at 20% to 40% off retail in their outlet stores. With first quality merchandise and sizes from six months up to youth size 14, Flapdoodles outlets are worth a peek for long-lasting, high-quality playclothes.

Florence Eiseman

Locations: Michigan City, IN (219) 879-1767 and Lancaster/York, PA (717) 295-9809.

Florence Eiseman's children's clothing designs are carried at Neiman Marcus, Saks, and Nordstroms, just to name a few places . . . so you can imagine they aren't exactly cheap. That's why a visit to one of their two outlets may be worth the effort.

The outlet store carries infant through youth sizes, with some layette designs as small as newborn. Florence Eiseman specializes in party dresses and swimwear, but this designer also carries casual outfits as well. The savings at the outlet stores are an impressive 30% to 40% off retail—all of it first-quality merchandise.

Hanna Anderson

Locations: Outlets Stores: Lake Oswego, OR (503) 697-1953 ; Michigan City, IN (219) 872-3183; Portsmouth, NH (603) 433-6642.

If you like Hanna Anderson's catalog, you love their outlet stores, which feature overstock, returned items and factory seconds. For more information on Hanna Anderson, see "Do It By Mail" later in this chapter.

Hartstrings

Locations: Strafford, PA (610) 971-9400, Redding, PA (610) 376-8808.

Hartstrings' outlet stores specialize in first-quality apparel for infants, boys, and girls and even have some mother/child outfits. Infant sizes start at three months and go up to 24 months. The savings range from 30% to 50%.

Health-Tex

Locations: 45 outlets. Call (610) 378-0408 for the location near you.

Health-Tex children's clothing is owned by Vanity Fair Corporation, which also produces such famous brands as Lee jeans, Wrangler, and Jansen. The company operates nearly four dozen outlets under the names VF Factory Outlet or Outlet Marketplace. They sell first-quality merchandise; most are discontinued items. VF Outlets discounts 50% everyday, while Outlet Marketplace sells at 30% to 70% off retail. Both outlet chains sell the Health-Tex brand.

Baby on vacation

Just because you're a parent doesn't mean you'll never take a vacation again. Yet, how do you travel with baby . . . or more importantly, with all baby's stuff? Well, the good news is you don't have to lug all that baby equipment with you on the plane (or in the car). Baby's Away (800) 571-0077 rents everything you need at many resort and vacation spots in the U.S. and Canada. You can rent cribs, strollers, high chairs, safety gates, potty seats, toys and more at reasonable rates ($3 to $9 per day or $18 to $54 a week).

Nathan J

Location: Huntington Beach, CA (714) 843-0611.

You might see Nathan J's all-cotton, high-quality baby clothing in such fancy department stores as Bloomingdales, Neiman Marcus and Nordstroms. But if you want it at 30% to 60% off, you'll have to go to their one and only outlet in Huntington Beach, California. Attached to their corporate headquarters, the Nathan J outlet sells first-quality overruns from previous seasons. You'll find layette items, dresses, rompers, underwear, booties, hats, receiving blankets, saque sets, and more. Among Nathan J's biggest hits this year is the licensed Classic Winnie the Pooh infant all-cotton clothing, which is sold in 3000 specialty stores (in addition to the department stores mentioned above). Look for discount coupons (good for 10% or 25% off purchases) in *Orange County Parenting* magazine and the book: *Parenting—The Guide 1997* , a Southern California guide to discounts, special offers and other parenting info (call 714-550-1240 for more information on this publication).

OshKosh

Locations: 125+ outlets. Call (414) 231-8800 for the nearest location.

OshKosh, the maker of all those cute little overalls worn by just about every kid, sells their clothes direct at over 125 outlet stores. With prices that are 30% to 40% off retail, buying these playclothes staples is even easier on the pocketbook.

We visited our local OshKosh store and found outfits from infant sizes up to children's size 7. They split the store up by gender, as well as by size. Infant and toddler clothes are usually in the back of the store.

Surfing the web for baby clothes

The Internet has evolved into a great place to shop for baby clothes, especially obscure high-quality brands that have limited distribution. Take "Baby Armadillo," for instance. We've received several notes from readers who've raved about this wonderful clothing line. But how can you find a brand that has limited distribution? Sure, you can call every baby shop in town, but who has the time? We have a better solution: surf the net. A case in point: soon after we posted a mention about Baby Armadillo on our web page, an internet site called Little Prince and Princess (http://home1.gte.net/lpp) e-mailed us to say they carried the brand among other high-quality lines like Mother Maid. The lesson: check the Web to track down great baby clothes.

So, how are the prices? The famous denim overalls (regularly $18.50) were marked down to $14.80. A girl's skirted overall was a mere $13.35. Coordinating shirts were $8, and sweats were $8.75 for pants and $9.75 for shirts.

The outlet also carries OshKosh shoes, socks, hats, and even stuffed bears dressed in overalls and engineer hats. Seasonal ensembles are available, including shorts outfits in the summer and snowsuits ($42) in the winter. Some clothes are irregulars, so inspect the garments carefully before you buy.

Pattycakes

Locations: 2669 Santa Rosa Ave., Santa Rosa, CA. (707) 543-8543.

Pattycakes' outlet store offers their creative children's apparel at 50% to 80% off the retail price. Sold in high-end department stores and boutiques, Pattycakes concentrates on casual playwear in bright prints and pastels. Sizes start at three months and go up to size 10. Although generally first-quality, current merchandise, the outlet does have one rack of seconds in the store. Another plus: they take additional markdowns from time to time, so the savings you find may be even better.

Peaches & Cream

Locations: 131 W. 33rd St, New York City (212) 239-4660.

A reader in New York City discovered this great outlet— in her words, "a terrific line of baby and children's clothing at very affordable prices."

Schwab Factory Outlet (Little Me clothing)

Locations: Cumberland, MD. (301) 722-5636.

While we like the Little Me brand, we have to give thumbs down to the obnoxious service at their outlet store, the Schwab Factory Outlet in Cumberland, MD (Schwab is Little Me's parent company). The "helpful" salesperson who answered the phone couldn't tell us their address, didn't know what highway they are located on, and generally had the IQ of a house plant. Combine this with the fact that the discounts are a meager 10% to 20% off retail, and you may want to only visit this outlet if you happen to be in the neighborhood.

Sir Alec

Locations: 5541 Lovers Lane, Dallas, TX. (214) 654-0226.
103 E. Virginia St., Suite 107, McKinney, TX. (972) 562-8990.
2482 Bolsover, Houston, TX. (713) 520-1015.

Sir Alec makes beautiful, handmade dress clothes for babies and children. If you walked into one of the exclusive boutiques that sells this brand, you'd pay $55 to $100 for the fancy 100% cotton outfits. However, we found a Sir Alec outlet where you can get the same adorable clothes for just $28 to $70—those prices are on average 30% below retail. And additional clearance sales can bring the total savings to as much as 70%. With three outlets in Texas (Dallas, McKinney and Houston), Sir Alec takes great care of its clothes—all outfits are hung in plastic bags to keep them looking brand-new. Most of the designs are one piece jumpers and bubbles. Sizes start at three months for girls, six months for boys.

On a recent visit, we bought an outfit with butter-yellow corduroy short pants that buttoned to a cotton-pique white shirt (complete with Peter Pan collar and blue piping accents). Originally, this was $62. We paid $16. We took this outfit on talkshows to show off an example of great outlet bargains and most folks couldn't believe it! If you live in or near Dallas or Houston (or are planning a trip to Texas), we definitely recommend Sir Alec.

Storybook Heirlooms

Locations: Gilroy, CA (408) 842-3880.

If you've ever received Storybook Heirlooms' catalog, you probably know that they have very fancy and very expensive children's clothing. Thankfully, they also have a factory outlet in Gilroy, California to help you save a little money. The outlet sells most items shown in their catalog, including last season's merchandise, left-overs in sizes, and even current merchandise. They offer a 25% discount off their catalog prices, plus clearance sales with discounts as low as 70% off retail. Sizes start at 12 months and range up to youth size 14.

Did you discover an outlet that you'd like to share with our readers? Call us at 303-442-8792 or e-mail adfields@aol.com.

Wastes of Money

Waste of Money #1

CLOTHING THAT LEADS TO DIAPER CHANGING GYMNASTICS

"My aunt sent me an adorable outfit for my little girl. The only problem: it snaps up the back making diaper changes a real pain. In fact, I don't dress her in it often because it's so inconvenient. Shouldn't clothing like this be outlawed?"

It's pretty obvious that some designers of baby clothing have never had children of their own. What else could explain outfits that snap up the back, have super tiny head, leg and arm openings, and snaps in inconvenient places (or worse, no snaps at all)? One mother we spoke with was furious about outfits that have snaps only down one leg, requiring her baby to be a contortionist to get into and out of the outfit.

Our advice: stay away from outfits that don't have easy access to the diaper. Look instead for snaps or zippers down the front of the outfit or on the crotch. If your baby doesn't like having things pulled over his head, look for shirts with wide, stretchie necklines.

Waste of Money #2

THE FUZZ FACTOR

"My friend's daughter has several outfits that aren't very old but are already pilling and fuzzing. They look awful and my friend is thinking of throwing them out. What causes this?"

Your friend has managed to have a close encounter with that miracle fabric known as polyester. Synthetics such as polyester will often pill or fuzz, making your baby look a little rag-tag. Of course, this is less of a concern with sleepwear—some parents believe the flame retardancy of the fabric outweighs the garment's appearance.

However, when you're talking about a play outfit, we recommend sticking to all-cotton clothes. They wash better, usually last longer, and generally look nicer—not to mention that they feel better to your baby. Cotton allergies are rare, unlike sensitivities to the chemicals used to make synthetic fabrics. You will pay more for all-cotton clothing, but in this case, the extra expense is worth it. Remember, just because you find the cheapest price on a polyester outfit doesn't mean you're getting a bargain. The best deal is not wasting money on outfits that you have to throw away after two washings.

Waste of Money #3

DO I REALLY NEED THESE?

"My mother bought me a zillion drawstring gowns before my baby was born, and I haven't used a single one. What the heck are they for?"

"The list of layette items recommended by my local department store includes something called a saque set. I've never seen one, and no one seems to know what they are. Do I really need one?"

"A kimono with matching towel and washcloth seems like a neat baby gift for my pregnant friend. But another friend told me it probably wouldn't get used. What do you think?"

All of these items come under the heading "Do I Really Need These?" Heck, we didn't even know what some of these were when we were shopping for our baby's layette. For example, what in the world is a saque set? Well, it turns out it's just a two-piece outfit with a shirt and diaper cover. Although they sound rather benign, saque sets are a waste of money. Whenever you pick up a baby under the arms, it's a sure bet her clothes will ride up. In order to avoid having to constantly pull down the baby's shirt, most parents find they use one-piece garments much more often than two-piece ones.

As for drawstring gowns, the jury is still out on whether these items are useful. These seem kind of silly, but a parent we interviewed did mention that she used the gowns when her baby had colic. She believed that the extra room in the gown made her baby more comfortable. The choice is up to you; however, we definitely recommend buying only a few to start with so you don't sink too much money into such a questionable purchase.

There is no question in our minds about the usefulness of a baby kimono, however. Don't buy it. For a baby who will only wear it for a few minutes after a bath, it seems like the quintessential waste of your money. Instead, invest in some good quality towels and washcloths and forget those cute (but useless) kimonos.

Waste of Money #4

COVERING UP THOSE LITTLE PIGGIES

"I was looking at shoes for my baby the other day, and I saw a $35 pair of Baby Air Jordans at the store! This must be highway robbery! I can't believe babies' shoes are so expensive. Are they worth it?"

Developmentally, babies don't need shoes until after they become quite proficient at walking. In fact, it's better for their muscle development to go barefoot or wear socks. While those expensive Baby Air Jordans might look cute, they're really a waste of time and money.

One mother we interviewed insisted her daughter wear shoes whenever they went out. If you, too, feel uncomfortable if your child goes shoe-less, at least look for shoes that have the most flexible soles. You'll also want fabrics that breathe and stretch, like canvas and leather—stay away from vinyl shoes. The best brands we found: "Padders" soft-sided shoes (available from the One Step Ahead catalog, 800-274-8440) run $10 and have non-skid soles. Another good brand: Storkenworks (available from the Natural Baby Catalog, 609-771-9233) cost $19.95 and are soft shoes made of natural leather. Booties and moccasins are available from many catalogs and retail stores. The best moccasins we found are from Herb Farm Moccasins (call 970-641-6758 or write to 6752 County Rd. 763. Gunnison, CO 81230.). Prices range from $23 for infants to $27 for one year olds if you order directly from the company. Sheepskin in-soles are $4 extra.

What about shoes for one or two year olds? We've found great deals at Target, whose wide selection of sizes and offerings were impressive. Another good source: Gap Kids/Baby Gap. Their affordable line of tennis shoes are very good quality. Parents have also told us they've also had success with Baby Superstore's in-house brand. If none of these stores are convenient, consider mail-order—the After the Stork catalog (see review later in this chapter) has a special catalog with reasonably priced shoes.

Waste of Money #5
To Drool or Not to Drool

"I received a few bibs from my mother-in-law as gifts. I know my baby won't need them until she's at least four to six months old when I start feeding her solids. Plus, they seem so small!"

What you actually got as a gift from your mother-in-law was a supply of drool bibs. Drool bibs are tiny bibs intended for small infants who start teething and hence drool all over everything. Our opinion: they're pretty useless, even if you use them for their intended purpose. When we decided we needed a few bibs for drooling, we got larger, more absorbent versions that we could reuse later when we started feeding solids to our baby.

When you do buy bibs, stay away from the ones that tie. Bibs that snap or have Velcro are much easier to get on and off. Also, stay away from the super-size vinyl bibs that cover your baby's arms. We've been told that babies can get too hot in them. However, we do recommend you buy a few regular-style vinyl bibs for travel. You can wash them off much more easily than the standard terry-cloth bibs. As for sources of bibs, many of the catalogs we review in this book carry such items.

Waste of Money #6
The Dreft Syndrome

"I see ads in parenting magazines that say an infant's clothes should be washed in special laundry detergent. Is this true?"

No, not in our opinion. We call it the "Dreft Syndrome" (after the laundry soap that claims it's better for infant clothes)—parents, typically first-timers, think if they don't wash Junior's clothes separately with expensive special soap, something bad will happen. Hogwash. Unless you have the rare child who suffers from skin allergies (and chance are, you don't), just throw baby's clothes in with the rest of the wash. And use regular laundry soap. If you're worried about perfumes or dyes, use one of the "clear" detergents free of such additives. Washing your baby's clothes separately in special soap is not only expensive, but you'll have to do much more laundry, since you can't throw the items in with your regular laundry.

Do it by Mail

After the Stork.

To Order Call: (800) 333-5437 or (505) 867-7168;
Fax (505) 867-7101.
Shopping Hours: 24 hours a day, seven days a week.
Or write to: After the Stork, 1501 12 St. NW, PO Box 44321, Rio Rancho, NM 87174.
Internet: www.AftertheStork.com
Credit Cards Accepted: MC, VISA, AMEX, Discover.

 After the Stork is one catalog that actually offers great prices on kids' cotton clothing. While they may not be fancy, the clothes in here are good, well-made basics, like the $20.50 henley coverall we saw (sizes 6 months up to 4T). This is a perfect staple for your kid's closet.

After the Stork offers a layette section with baby basics like striped coveralls, printed onesies, caps and jackets. Another good point to remember: each After the Stork catalog usually features a few sale items for even bigger discounts.

As a side note, After the Stork occasionally comes out with limited edition specialty catalogs. For example, their "Little Feet" catalog features a wide variety of shoes, from water sandals to hiking books to dress shoes.

Biobottoms.

To Order Call: (800) 766-1254 (U.S. and Canada) or (707) 778-7945 or fax (707) 778-0619.
Shopping Hours: Monday-Friday 5 am-9 pm; Saturday 6 am-6 pm; Sunday 8 am-4 pm Pacific Time.
Or write to: Biobottoms, PO Box 6009, Petaluma, CA 94955.
Internet: www.biobottoms.com/
Credit Cards Accepted: MC, VISA, AMEX, Discover.

This California-based catalog started out selling "lamb-soft wool" diaper covers called Biobottoms for babies in cloth diapers. Along the way, they branched out into colorful, 100% cotton clothing in bold patterns and bright colors.

The bulk of the Biobottoms catalog showcases their cheerful, fun clothing. Check out the layette pages for babies and toddlers and you'll find dresses with leggings, "tummy toppers" (onesies), baby sweaters, caps pants and coveralls. The patterns and colors are whimsical and bright including a cute boys onesie with plane patch and matching star covered pants ($24).

We purchased clothes for our baby from Biobottoms and found them to be well made and long lasting. The clothes didn't shrink or fade after many washings, and our son found them very comfortable. The prices aren't exactly a bargain, but the fun designs and high quality make them worth the purchase price.

Children's Wear Digest

To Order Call: (800) 242-5437; Fax (800) 863-3395.
Shopping Hours: 24 hours a day, seven days a week.
Or write to: Children's Wear Digest, 3607 Mayland Ct., Richmond, VA 23233.
Credit Cards Accepted: MC, VISA, AMEX, Discover.

If you're looking for name brands, check out Children's Wear Digest, a catalog that features clothes in sizes 12 months to 14 for both boys and girls.

In a recent catalog, we saw clothes by Sweet Potatoes, Avery Kids, Mulberribush, Funtasia, Kitestrings, Flapdoodles, EIEIO, and Sarah's Prints. One neat design was a "moon romper" made from all-organic cotton by Green Babies for $34. We also liked their coordinating outfits for both a baby and toddler—for example, a blue check jumpsuit with blueberry motif ($34) matched a blueberry t-shirt and plaid skirt combo for $42.

Children's Wear Digest doesn't offer much of a discount off regular retail, but it does have a selection of sale clothes from time to time with savings of 15% to 25%. Otherwise, prices were about regular retail.

One negative: the catalog's poor organization means you have search each page to find clothes for babies. Sections organized by age would be more helpful. Nevertheless, the majority of clothes are 100% cotton and many designs come with coordinating accessories for a complete look.

Chock

To Order Call: (800) 222-0020; or (212) 473-1929;
Fax (212) 473-6273.
Shopping Hours: Sunday-Thursday 9:30 am to 5:30 pm Eastern.
Or write to: Chock, 74 Orchard St., New York, NY 10002.
Credit Cards Accepted: MC, VISA, Discover.
Retail store: 74 Orchard St., New York, NY 10002.

This small, black and white catalog focuses on basics at very good prices. You'll see name brands like Gerber and Carter's, plus a good selection of t-shirts, caps, booties, gowns, sleepers, towels and washcloths. Best of all, the prices are discounted about 25% off the manufacturer's suggested list prices. For example, a footed sleeper (called a bodysuit) is $7.25, compared to $9.50 list. Another plus for Chock: they always stock a supply of all-year-round merchandise, especially out-of-season items.

Hanna Anderson.

To Order Call: (800) 222-0544; Fax (503) 321-5289.
Shopping Hours: 5 am to 9 pm Pacific Time, seven
days a week. They have an automated order system after hours to
take your order.
Or write to: 1010 NW Flanders, Portland, OR, 97209.
Credit Cards Accepted: MC, VISA, AMEX, Discover.
Retail Stores: 125 Westchester Ave., Suite 3370, White Plains, NY
10601; (914) 684-2410 and 327 NW Tenth Ave., Portland, OR
97209; (503) 321-5275.
Outlets Stores: Lake Oswego, OR (503) 697-1953 ; Michigan City,
IN (219) 827-3183; and Portsmouth, NH (603) 433-6642.

Hanna Anderson says it offers "Swedish quality" 100%
cotton clothes. Unfortunately, Swedish quality is going to set
you back some big bucks.

For example, a simple coverall with zippered front was a
whopping $30. While Anderson's clothing features cute pat-
terns and attractive colors, it's hard to imagine outfitting your
baby's wardrobe at those prices.

These aren't clothes you'd have your baby trash at daycare—Hanna Anderson's outfits are more suitable for
weekend wear or going to Grandma's house. One note of
caution: while the quality is very high, some items have difficult diaper access (or none at all). On the upside, the catalog does have a unique charity program called
"Hannadowns." You send in used Anderson clothes, they
donate them to charity and give you a 20% credit for
future purchases. Call the catalog for more details.

Lands' End

To Order Call: (800) 734-5437,(800) 356-4444; Fax (800) 332-0103.
Internet: www.landsend.com
Shopping Hours: 24 hours a day, seven days a week.
Or write to: 1 Lands' End Ln., Dodgeville, WI 53595.
Credit Cards Accepted: MC, VISA, AMEX, Discover.
Discount Outlets: They also have a dozen or so outlet stores in Iowa,
Illinois and Wisconsin—call the number above for the nearest location.

New this year in the Lands' End children's catalog is a complete layette line—and it's darn cute. The clothes feature 100%
cotton "interlock knit," which the catalog claims gets softer
with every washing and doesn't pill. Choose from playsuits,
reversibles cardigans, onesies, pants, and side-snap t-shirts—all
in sizes three to 12 months. We love the colors, which included
such options as "rosebud." "ice blue" and "sun-washed yellow." Especially cute were the playsuits with matching cap
($25); most items were $12 to $26. For older babies, Lands'
End all-cotton playcothes range from size 6 months to 4T.

Don't look for fancy dress clothes from this catalog; instead the catalog specializes in casual playwear basics.

Olsen's Mill Direct.

To Order Call: (800) 537-4979, (414) 426-6360 or
Fax (414) 426-6369
Shopping Hours: 7:00 am to 11:00 pm Central Time.
Or write to: Olsen's Mill Direct, 1641 S. Main St,
Oshkosh, WI 54901.
Credit Cards Accepted: MC, VISA, Discover.

One of the best organized catalogs we've seen, Olsen's Mill Direct offers an attractive selection of such famous brands as Good Lad of Philadelphia, OshKosh, and more.

Another plus: the catalog has large photos of the clothes, so you can see what you're getting. For example, a beautiful, bold-patterned set of outfits by Good Lad included a girl's red flannel dress ($32-$36), boy's suspendered overalls ($37-$40), and red corduroy bib overalls with a bear print and matching shirt ($41).

We found the prices similar to retail list prices you'd see in stores and most items are 100% cotton.

Patagonia Kids

To Order Call: (800) 638-6464; Fax (800) 543-5522.
Shopping Hours: Monday-Friday 6 am- 6 pm Pacific; Saturday 8 am- 4 pm Mountain Time.
Or write to: 8550 White Fir St., PO Box 32050, Reno, NV 89533.
Credit Cards Accepted: MC, VISA, AMEX, Discover.

Outdoor enthusiasts all over the country swear by Patagonia's scientifically engineered clothes and outerwear. They make clothing for skiing, mountain climbing, and kayaking—and for kids. That's right, Patagonia has a just-for-kids catalog of outdoor wear.

In their recent 30-page kids catalog, we found five pages of clothes for babies and toddlers. They offer synchilla (synthetic pile) clothes like cardigans ($46), coveralls ($45), and baby buntings ($62). We bought our baby a bunting from Patagonia and found that it had some cool features. For example, with a flick of its zipper, it converts from a sack to an outfit with two leg openings, making it more convenient for use with a car seat. It also has a neck to knee zipper (speeding up diaper changes), flipper hands, and a hood. When your baby's bundled up in this, you can bet she won't get cold.

Other gear for tots includes two-piece sets of capilene long underwear ($32), an insulated snowsuit ($145) as well as interesting accessories like "Baby Pita Pocket" mittens ($16) and assorted shoes, hats and booties.

Although the selection of infant clothing from Patagonia is limited, the cold weather gear is unlike that from any other manufacturer.

Playclothes.

To Order Call: (800) 362-7529; (800) 222-7725;
    Fax (913) 752-1095.
Shopping Hours: 24 hours a day, seven days a week.
Or write to: Playclothes, PO Box 29137, Overland Park, KS 66201.
Credit Cards Accepted: MC, VISA, AMEX, Discover.

As the name implies, Playclothes focuses on affordable, attractive, and comfortable clothing in bright, bold patterns. For example, we saw an outrageously colorful coverall covered with jungle animals that cost only $18. This 100% cotton outfit also had a matching baseball cap for $6.

Sizes start at 12 months and go up to girl's size 14 and boy's size 16. Infant clothes were scattered throughout the catalog rather than grouped into one section.

Glancing through a recent catalog, we especially liked the bright animal prints and cheerful florals (giant strawberries and sunflowers were standouts). The catalog even showcased licensed sports apparel, like a Florida Marlins romper with matching hat for $25. Other teams include Colorado Rockies, New York Yankees, and Atlanta Braves—what! No Mets? Despite this transgression, we give Playclothes two thumbs up.

Talbot's Kids

To Order Call: (800) 543-7123 (U.S. and Canada) or
(617) 740-8888; Fax (800) 438-9443.
Shopping Hours: 24 hours a day, 7 days a week.
Or write to: Talbot's Kids, 175 Beal St., Hingham, MA 02043.
Credit Cards Accepted: MC, VISA, AMEX.
Retail stores: 57 stores—call the above number for the nearest location.

Talbot's splashes its bright colors on both layette items for infants (three months to 12 months) and toddlers (six months to 4T sizes). For baby, the catalog features a good selection of t-shirts, gowns, caps, booties and blankets. Prices, as you might expect, are moderate to expensive. We saw a cotton-footed coverall for $22, cotton t-shirts with crotch snaps for $12 (or two for $20). Other stand-outs include a few dress-up outfits in bold hues like hot pink or bright purple. Nearly all items are 100% cotton.

That Lucky Child

To Order Call: (800) 755-4852 or (410) 876-9071.
Shopping Hours: 24 hours a day, seven days a week.
Or write to: PO Box 245, Hunt Valley, MD 21030.
Credit Cards Accepted: MC, VISA.

That Lucky Child clothing catalog was inspired by the birth of the owners' daughter. Born prematurely at 24 weeks and weighing only one pound, four ounces, their daughter first wore Cabbage Patch doll clothes. In an effort to improve the options available for parents of preemies, they started That Lucky Child.

The catalog offers a nice selection of clothes, from sleepwear to playclothes to dressy christening outfits—all in preemie to newborn sizes. For example, stretchies in several different prints, some with embroidery and lace accents, cost $12.95 to $18.95. 100% cotton rompers were priced at $17.95 each, and adorable three-piece outfits of overalls, cap, and shirt were $23.95. New this year is a preemie bunting for $40. Brand names from That Lucky Child include Little Me and Something Precious.

Basic clothing items are available, such as Carter's t-shirts, drawstring gowns, and flannel pajamas just for preemies. That Lucky Child also carries a number of books on premature babies, breastfeeding, and infant massage. Good books to consider include *Newborn Intensive Care: What Every Parent Needs to Know* ($26) and a title for siblings, *No Bigger Than My Teddy Bear* by Valerie Pankow for $4.95.

Another suggestion for preemie clothes: a reader suggests the Preemie Store in Orange County, California. They also have a mail order catalog with special deals for parents of multiples; call (800) O-SO-TINY for more info.

Wooden Soldier

To Order Call: (800) 375-6002 or (603) 356-7041;
   Fax (603) 356-3530.
Shopping Hours: Monday-Friday 8:30 am to midnight
Saturday and Sunday 8:30 am to 9 pm Eastern Time.
Or write to: The Wooden Soldier, PO Box 800,
North Conway, NH 03860.
Credit Cards Accepted: MC, VISA, AMEX, Discover.

If you really need a formal outfit for your child, Wooden Soldier has the most expansive selection of children's formalwear we've ever seen. Unfortunately, the prices are quite high. For example, we noted a girl's dress outfit of red velvet with organdy collar decorated with lace for a whopping $64 to $79. For the young man, a red velvet shortall with ivory shirt was $52 to $58.

New this year is a wider selection of casual outfits. For example, we noticed a periwinkle jumpsuit with Scottie Dog buttons for $36—it even has a matching hat ($18.50). The catalog has quite a few matching accessories to complete the look.

Unfortunately, the prices in Wooden Soldier were disappointing. We saw the same red and white stripe cotton dress in both Wooden Solider and Children's Wear Digest (reviewed earlier in this chapter). Wooden Soldier marked the item at $38; Children's Wear Digest sold it at $28.

Another mail order catalog. Warner Bros. Studio Store (800)223-6524 has a mail-order catalog with four pages of "baby wear." We saw terry cloth coveralls, sweatsuits, denim overalls, and bodysuits—all emblazoned with such Looney Tunes characters as Tweety, Bugs Bunny and the Tasmanian Devil. A sample price: $26 for the denim overalls.

Diapers

The great diaper debate still rages on: should you use cloth or disposable? One on side are environmentalists, who claim cloth is better for the planet. On the other hand, those disposable diapers are darn convenient.

Considering the average baby will go through 2300 diaper changes in the first year of life, this isn't a moot issue. And that statistic is for disposable diapers—cloth diapers require even more changes. We took a fresh look at the diaper debate when we appeared on the *Today Show* in 1996—here's a rundown of the pros and cons with cloth and disposable diapers.

Cloth. Prior to the 1960's, this was the only diaper option available to parents. Today, folks who choose cloth do so for environmental reasons. They point out that 19 billion disposable diapers (that's three million tons) are sent to landfills each year. If that weren't enough eco-damage, another 82,000 tons of plastic and 1.8 million tons of wood pulp (250,000 trees) are consumed to make disposables each year. Cloth diapers, on the other hand, are recyclable and reusable. Your city's municipal sewage system handles the solid waste.

Parents with the best of eco-intentions, however, often get frustrated with cloth diapers. The biggest problem: leaks. Cloth diapers can't hold a candle to today's super-absorbent disposable diapers. As a result, you'll be doing extra laundry even if you hire a commercial diaper service. Add in the time needed to do extra diaper changes (cloth requires twice as many changes as disposables) and you've got a significant time investment here.

Of course, there's another reason why cloth diapers aren't very popular today—most day care centers don't allow them.

Disposables. Disposable diapers were first introduced in 1961 and now hold an amazing lead over cloth diapers—about 95% of all households that use diapers go for disposables. Today's diapers have super-absorbent gels that greatly reduce diaper rash (although in some ways, there is a downside to this—the diapers work so well, it takes longer to toilet train children today. Why? Kids who sit in a soggy cloth diaper are more likely to use the potty quicker than those who use those super-efficient disposables).

Besides the eco-arguments about disposables, there is one other disadvantage—higher trash costs. In some communities, the more trash you put out, the higher the bill. Hence, using disposable diapers may result in slightly higher garbage expenses.

The eco-bottom line: it's hard to convince an ardent environmentalist that disposable diapers aren't evil incarnate. But let's look at this issue in perspective—yes, all those disposable diapers are sent to landfills each year, but by weight it's only 1.5% to 2% of landfill volume. Compare that to newspapers (which account for 40% of trash volume) and you see it's small potatoes. Yes, it may take a disposable diaper 500 years to decompose in a landfill, but cloth diapers have environmental costs too—all that water, heavy chemicals and energy used to dry and deliver diapers takes its toll too. Chlorine bleach used to sanitize diapers may be released into our environment through water treatment systems.

As a result, we've come to this conclusion: from an environmental view, it depends on where you live. In arid parts of this country where water is scarce and landfill space is abundant, disposable diapers may make a better eco-choice. In other parts of the U.S., the situation is reversed—there's plenty of water but not much landfill space. The conclusion if you live there: cloth diapers may make more environmental sense.

The financial bottom line: Surprisingly, there is no clear winner when you factor financial costs into this equation.

Cloth diapers may seem cheap at first, but consider the hidden costs. Besides the diapers themselves ($100 for the basic varieties; $200 to $300 for the fancy diaper systems), you also have to buy diaper *covers*. Since you need to buy five or so covers in each size as your baby grows, you're talking $300 to $500 in additional expense.

What about laundry? Well, washing your own cloth diapers at home may be the most economical way to go, but most folks don't have the time or energy. Instead, most parents use a cloth diaper service. In a recent cost survey of such services across the U.S., we discovered that most cost $500 to

$725 a year. While each service does supply you with diapers (relieving you of that expense), you're still on the hook for the diaper covers. So, the total financial damage for cloth diapers (using a cloth diaper service) for one year is $800 to $1200.

By contrast, let's take a look at disposables. If you buy disposable diapers from the most expensive source in town (typically, a grocery store), you'd spend about $550 to $600 for the first year. Yet, we've found discount sources (mentioned later in this chapter) that sell disposables in bulk at a discount. By shopping at these sources, we figure you'd spend $450 to $500 per year.

The bottom line: the cheapest way to go is cloth diapers laundered at home. The next best bet is disposables. Finally, cloth diapers from a diaper service are the most expensive.

Our Picks: Brand Recommendations

We have to admit that our non-scientific diaper test was probably biased since we have a boy. Our son had an uncanny way of leaking from some of the best diapers in this world. We did learn eventually that if you fold down the front of the diaper to form a little pocket, you'll have fewer leaks. Luckily, girls don't tend to "shoot off" upwards and therefore have few leaks from the top of the diaper. One mother did mention that her daughter had a tendency to "blow out" the back of her diapers during bowel movements. (And you thought being a parent was just deciding what cute clothes your baby should wear).

Here's an overview of the best brands for disposable diapers:

The two most popular diaper brands are **Huggies** and **Pampers**. For some reason, we've noticed that parents of boys prefer Huggies and parents of girls like Pampers. We're not sure why this is—perhaps the leak protection of Huggies is better for boys, while parents of girls have no problem with Pamper' slightly different design.

Nonetheless, we're big fans of Huggies (but, of course, we've got two boys). The brand makes two types of diapers: regular Huggies and Huggies Supreme. The latter feature a cloth-like outter cover and Velcro closures . . . and cost about 25% more than the regular Huggies. At first we thought these more expensive Huggies were merely a gimmick. Yet, after experimenting with both types, we've come to the conclusion that the Supremes are actually an improvement. The Velcro tabs make it easier to check if a diaper needs changing—the regular diapers use standard sticky tabs that can't be re-sealed after opening. Another plus: you can close the Velcro tabs even if you have lotion on your hands (the lotion removes the stickiness of standard tabs).

The soft, outer cover of the Huggies Supreme is a plus with

new infants, whose belly button area may still be sensitive while healing. All this is not to say regular Huggies are inferior—the company has made steady improvements to this line as well. Today, regular Huggies have a cloth-like outer cover (although not as soft as Huggies Supreme) and are super-thin. Unlike the bulky disposable diapers of years past, all Huggies today have super-absorbent acrylic gels which suck up moisture (in years past, wood pulp was used).

Pampers recently announced it was eliminating gender-specific diapers—now all sizes will be unisex (Huggies still makes different varieties for girls and boys). The sizing of Pampers is somewhat different than Huggies—parents with smaller babies tell us Huggies newborns fit better, since they are smaller (that is, thinner and narrower) than Pampers.

The same company that makes Pampers also makes *Luv's*, which is a lower-price brand. We gave Luv's a try and liked them . . . we couldn't really tell any difference between them and Pampers.

If you're looking to a more environmentally-friendly alternative to traditional disposable diapers, *Tushies* (to find a dealer near you, call 203-454-8831) is one possibility. These diapers are made of natural ingredients (no chemicals) with a filling that's 30% cotton and 70% wood pulp. We gave them a test drive and didn't like them. While the leak control was about the same as traditional diapers, the Tushies were more bulky and less convenient to use. The stiffer materials made it somewhat difficult to close. And Tushies are very expensive—about twice as much as Huggies or Pampers.

If you really want to save money, consider *store brands*. Chains like Target, Toys R Us and Wal-Mart and many grocery stores have their own in-house brands of diapers which they sell at deep discounts. Even LiL' Things and Baby Superstore carry their own brands of diapers. At Baby Superstore, we noticed the in-store brand was 23% cheaper than Huggies or Pampers. You might think these cheap diapers are inferior, but think again—we've heard from many parents who've used these generic diapers and been very happy. That makes us wonder if the big manufacturers who make the expensive brands also churn out similar diapers for the store brands. Do they merely slap fancy names and packing on the same diapers and charge a premium?

While store-brand diapers are great, wipes are another story. We found the cheap generic wipes to be inferior to name brands. With less water and thinner construction, the several brands of store brand wipes we sampled were losers. Our favorite brand is *Baby Fresh*, although other parents we interviewed swear by Huggies' wipes. A great money-saver is Suave—their wipes are 20% less than Baby Fresh.

The bottom line on diapers: we recommend you buy a 100 or so Huggies Supremes to use for your baby's first few weeks and then switch to the lower price regular Huggies or store brands.

Money Saving Secrets

1 BUY IN BULK. Don't buy those little packs of 20 diapers—look for the 80 or 100 count packs instead. You'll find the price *per diaper* goes down when you buy larger packs.

2 GO FOR WAREHOUSE CLUBS. Both Sam's and Price/Costco wholesale clubs sell diapers at incredibly low prices. At Sam's, we found a 160-count package of Pampers Phase 1 for $27.99. And Price/Costco sells a 100-count package of Huggies Step 1 for just $15. We also found great deals on wipes at the wholesale clubs. Sam's had a package of 336-count Baby Fresh Wipes for $7.83. A store brand with 462 wipes was just $6.97.

3 BUY STORE BRANDS. As mentioned earlier in this chapter in brand reviews, many parents find store brand diapers to be equal to the name brands. And the prices can't be beat—many are 20% to 30% cheaper than name brands. Chains like Target, Wal-Mart, and Toys R Us carry in-house diaper brands, as do many grocery stores. Heck, even Sam's wholesale club stocked a generic brand of diapers that was 26% cheaper than name brands.

4 CONSIDER TOYS R US. Sure, you may not have a whole-sale club nearby, but you're bound to be close to a Toys R Us. And we found them to be a great source for affordable name-brand diapers. Both Pampers and Huggies were $7.67 for a 50-count package. The Toys R Us store brand was even cheaper, at $6.99 for 54 diapers. If you like Luvs, you'll love the price: $6.77 for 54-count package. Don't forget to check the front of the store for copies of Toys R Us's latest catalog. Occasionally, they offer in-store coupons for additional dia-per savings—you can even combine these with manufacturer's coupons for double savings.

5 WHEN YOUR BABY IS NEARING A TRANSITION POINT, DON'T STOCK UP. Quick growing babies may move into another size faster than you think, leaving you with an excess supply of too-small diapers.

6 DON'T BUY DIAPERS IN GROCERY STORES. We compared prices at grocery stores and usually found them to be

I Dream of the Diaper Genie

Excuse us for a moment while we wax rhapsodic about the Diaper Genie, the neatest invention for parents since the baby-sitter. This sleek white plastic can has done what years of diaper pails have failed to do: taken the stink out of stinky diapers.

Here's how it works: you pop in a disposable diaper and give the lid a twist. That's it! No brain damage! The Diaper Genie seals the diaper in air-tight, deodorized plastic and stores it in the container base. There are no batteries or motorized parts to worry about: just hit a lever on the base and a chain of sealed diapers emerges for easy disposal (the container holds up to 20 diapers). Best of all, there's no smell and no deodorant cartridges to replace.

The Diaper Genie retails for $40, but we've seen it as low as $19.95 in the Baby Superstore and $25 to $30 in other stores. And then you've got to buy the refill canisters that hold the plastic wrap—these retail for $7, but you can find them for $5 at Toys R Us and just $3.97 from the Baby Catalog of America (800-752-9736).

Now, one of those refill canisters wraps 150 to 180 diapers—or about 10 days to two weeks worth of diapers. So, if you use the Diaper Genie for a year, your total cost would be about $150 (including the cost of the Genie itself). That isn't cheap and probably explains the resistance of some parents to the Diaper Genie, who don't want to part with that much cash to keep their nursery odor-free. (One money-saving tip: use the Genie only for the stinky diapers. Put the other diapers in the regular trash—that will save you some in refill purchases).

Despite the cost, we've used the contraption for a while now and think it is worth it. It's relatively easy to use, although it does take a little getting used to. The process of emptying the diapers is relatively straightforward (you twist a cutter on top and the chain of diapers that look like sausages plops out the end), but the switching of canisters is a little more complicated. It takes a few times before you'll get the hang of it, but since you'll be changing as many as 100 diapers a week in the beginning, you'll adjust pretty fast.

New for 1997, the Diaper Genie will introduce a revised version that corrects some of the original Genie's shortcomings. First, the Diaper Genie will have a wider opening to stuff those super-soaked and larger-size diapers. The new design also lets you dispose of a diaper with one hand (the old one required two hands) and is larger (holding 25 diapers instead of just 20). The new Diaper Genie will use a different refill package, so make sure you get the right size when re-stocking. Expect the price to rise about $3, although the product is so popular (some two million have been sold) that it's bound to remain priced about where it is today.

Even if you don't buy a Diaper Genie, you'll need some type of diaper pail (which run $10 to $25). And, in the fancy models, every three months you still have to replace those charcoal filters that keep the odors down (at a cost of $4 to $5 each).

The Diaper Genie's success has spawned knock-offs—both Safety 1st and Fisher Price have introduced "odor free" diaper pails that use regular kitchen garbage bags (no expensive refills to buy). While we've heard from parents who've used these alternatives with success, we still give the edge to the Diaper Genie in odor removal. So, we give the Diaper Genie a big "thumbs up." It's not cheap, but the convenience factor is hard to beat. (For a store near you that carries the Diaper Genie, call 330-626-4490.)

The diapers available through Natural Baby Co. are not the usual square cloth diapers you see in stores. No, these have a unique hourglass shape that doesn't require any fancy folding. All this doesn't come cheap. The prices range from $20 to $33 per dozen, depending on the style.

The Natural Baby Co. sells Nikky diaper covers, in either cotton or wool. Cotton runs $20, while wool is $25. A third style of Nikky diaper cover (with 80% cotton and 20% polyester) costs $15 each. The catalog also offers its own brand of waterproof nylon diaper covers for only $5 each. New this year in the catalog are diaper covers in "fun prints" for $10.30 each and Ruez'M Diapers, a 100% cotton flannel diaper with a waterproof layer sandwiched inside. Unlike other all-in-one diapers, this one doesn't have a plastic outside. Cost: $11.50 each (or $74 for a set of six).

The Nurtured Baby

To Order: (800) 462-2293 or (919) 747-7785.
Or write to: Route 2, Box 327, Walstonburg, NC 27888.
Credit Cards Accepted: MC, VISA.

The Nurtured Baby sells their own "Cotton-Baby" diaper system. They claim its energy efficient design enables quick drying (only 25 minutes in the dryer). Cost: $45 to $62 for a box with six to eight diapers. The catalog sells two diaper covers and the Bravado maternity bra (reviewed in chapter 5).

THE BOTTOM LINE:
A Wrap-Up of Our Best Buy Picks

 In summary, we recommend you buy the following layette items for your baby:

Quantity	Item	Cost
6	T-shirts/onesies (over the head)	$22
6	T-shirts (side snap or side tie)	$25
4-6	Sleepers	$64-$96
1	Blanket Sleeper*	$10
2-4	Coveralls	$40-$80
3-4	Booties/socks	$12-$16
1	Sweater	$16
2	Hats (safari and caps)	$30
1	Snowsuit/bunting*	$20
4	Large bibs (for feeding)	$24
3 sets	Wash clothes and towels	$30
7-8	Receiving blankets	$42-$48

TOTAL		**$340 to $422**

* If you live in a cold climate.

Chapter 5

Maternity/Nursing Clothes & Feeding Baby

L ove 'em or hate 'em, every mother-to-be needs maternity wear at some point in her pregnancy. Still, you don't have to break the bank to get comfortable, and, yes, fashionable maternity clothes. In this chapter, we tell you which sources sell all-cotton, casual clothes at unbelievably low prices. Then, we'll review the top maternity chains and reveal our list of top wastes of money. You'll learn which outlet stores offer tremendous savings on career wear. Finally, learn all about breastfeeding, including five sources for help, and the low-down on which breast pumps work best.

Maternity & Nursing Clothes

Getting Started:

 It may seem obvious that you'll need to buy maternity clothes when you get pregnant, but the irony is you don't actually need all of them immediately. The first thing you'll notice is the need for a new bra. At least, that was my first clue that my body was changing. Breast changes occur as early as the first month, and you may find yourself going through several different sizes along the way.

Next, your belly will begin to "swell." Yes, the baby is making its presence known by making you feel a bit bigger around the middle. Not only may you find that you need to buy larger panties, but you may also find that skirts and pants feel tight as early as your second or third month. Maternity clothes at this point may seem like overkill, but some women do begin to "show" enough that they find it necessary to head out to the maternity shop.

If you have decided to breastfeed (more on this later in this chapter), you'll need to consider what type of nursing bras you'll want. Buy two or three in your eighth month so you'll be prepared. You may find it necessary to buy more nursing bras after the baby is born, but this will get you started. As for other nursing clothes, you may or may not find these worth the money. Don't go out and buy a whole new wardrobe right off the bat. Some woman find nursing shirts and tops to be helpful while others manage quite well with regular clothes. More on this topic later in the book.

Sources

1 MATERNITY WEAR CHAINS. Not surprisingly, there are quite a few nationwide maternity clothing chains. Visit any mall and you'll likely see the names Pea in the Pod, MothersWork, Pageboy, Mimi Maternity, and Motherhood, to mention a few. More on these chains later in the chapter.

2 MOM AND POP MATERNITY SHOPS. These small, independent stores sell a wide variety of maternity clothes, from affordable weekend wear to high-priced career wear. Some baby specialty stores carry maternity wear as well. The chief advantage to the smaller stores is personalized service—we usually found salespeople who were knowledgeable about the different brands. In addition, these stores may offer other services; for example, some rent formal wear for special occasions, saving you big bucks. Of course, you will pay for the extra service with higher prices. Whether you want all that service is a personal decision.

3 CONSIGNMENT STORES. Many consignment or thrift stores that specialize in children's clothing may also have a rack of maternity clothes. In visits to several such stores, we found some incredible bargains (at least 50% off retail) on maternity clothes that were in good to excellent condition. Of course, the selection varies widely, but we strongly advise you check out any second-hand stores in your area.

4 DISCOUNTERS. When we talk about discounters, we're referring to chains like Target and K-Mart. Now, let's be honest here. When we think of good places to buy clothes, those chains may not first come to mind. Yet, you'll be surprised about their maternity clothes, especially the casual wear. Later, we'll tell you about the incredible prices on these all-cotton clothes.

5 DEPARTMENT STORES. Most folks think of their local department store first when looking for maternity clothes. And many department stores do carry maternity fashions. The big disadvantage: the selection is usually rather small. This means you'll often find unattractive jumpers in abundance and very little in the way of fashionable clothing. Even worse, maternity clothes almost never go on sale.

6 MAIL ORDER. Even if you don't have any big-time maternity chains nearby, you can still buy the clothes they sell. Many chains offer a mail-order service (later in this chapter, we'll give you more details). We also found several mail-order catalogs that specialize in maternity clothes. In the "Do It By Mail" section of this chapter, we'll give you the run-down on these options.

7 NON-MATERNITY STORES. Here's a great way to save money: buy large clothes from non-maternity stores. Chains that specialize in "woman's-size" clothing and the like often have prices that are way below the maternity shops. Sales are more numerous here, too.

8 YOUR HUSBAND'S CLOSET. What's a good source for over-sized shirts and baggy sweaters? Look no further than the other side of your closet, where your husband's clothes can often double as maternity wear.

What Are You Buying?

 What will you need when you get pregnant? There is no shortage of advice on this topic, especially from the folks trying to sell you stuff. But here's what real moms advise you buy:

♣ *Maternity Bras.* Maternity bras are available just about everywhere, from specialty maternity shops to department stores, mail-order catalogs and discount chains. More on this topic in the follow box "News from Down Under: Maternity Bras for the Real World."

HOW MANY? Two in each size as your bustline expands. I found that I went through three different sizes during my pregnancy, and buying two in each size allowed me to wear one while the other was washed.

♣ *Sleep Bras.* What do you need a bra to sleep in for, you ask? Well, some women find it more comfortable to have a little support at night as their breasts change. Toward the end of pregnancy, some women also start to leak breast milk (to be technical, this is actually colostrum). And once the baby arrives, a sleeping bra (cost, about $10) will keep those breast pads in place at night (to keep you from leaking when you inadvertently roll onto your stomach—yes, there will come a day when you can do that again). Some woman just need light support, while others find a full-featured bra a necessity.

HOW MANY? Two sleep bras are enough—one to wear, one to wash.

News from Down Under
Maternity Bras for the Real World

What makes a great maternity bra? Consider the following points while shopping:

♣ *Support—part I.* How much support do you need? Some women we interviewed liked the heavy-duty construction of some maternity bras. For others, that was overkill.

♣ *Support—part II.* Once you decide how much support you need, consider the *type* of support you like. The basic choice: underwire bras versus those that use fabric bands and panels. Some moms-to-be liked stretchy knit fabric while others preferred stiffer, woven fabric.

♣ *Appearance.* Let's be honest: some maternity bras can be darn ugly. And what about the bras that claim they'll grow with you during your pregnancy? Forget it—expect to go through several sizes as the months roll along.

♣ *Price.* Yes, the best maternity bras can be pricey. But I've found it doesn't pay to scrimp on underwear like bras and panties. Save money on other items in your maternity wardrobe and invest in comfortable undergarments.

♣ *Underpants.* There two schools of thought when it comes to underpants. Traditional maternity underwear goes over your tummy, while bikini-style briefs are worn under the belly. Some women like the traditional maternity briefs, while others find bikini-style underwear more comfortable. Whichever style you choose, be sure to look for all-cotton fabric, wide waist bands and good construction—repeated washings take their toll on cheap undies. See "Our Picks: Brand Recommendations" later in this section for the best bets.

How many? I don't like to do lots of laundry, so I bought eight pairs. Since you may be wearing them even after your baby is born for a few weeks, get some that will last.

♣ *Nursing Bras.* What's the difference between a nursing bra and a maternity bra? Nursing bras have special flaps that fold down to give baby easy access to the breast. If you plan to nurse, you should probably buy at least two during your eighth month (they cost about $20 to $35 each). Why then? Theoretically, your breast size won't change much once your baby is born and your milk comes in. I'd suggest buying one with a little larger cup size (than your eighth month size) so you can compensate for the engorgement phase. You can always buy more later and, if your size changes once the baby is born, you won't have invested too much in the wrong size. If you want more advice on nursing bras, you can call Playtex (800-537-9955) for a free guide.

How MANY? Buy two to three bras in your eighth month. After the baby is born, you may want to buy a couple more. Another good tip: buy two to three pairs of breast pads (to prevent leaks) before the baby is born.

♣ *Career Clothing.* Our best advice about career clothing for the pregnant mom is to stick with basics. Buy yourself a coordinating outfit with a skirt, jacket, and pair of pants and then accessorize.

Now, we know what you're saying. You'd love to follow this advice, but you don't want to wear the same old thing several times a week—even if it is accessorized. I don't blame you. So, go for a couple dresses and sweaters too. The good news is you don't have to pay full price. We've got several money-saving tips and even an outlet or two coming up later in this chapter.

At some point, you'll notice that regular clothes just don't fit well, and the maternity buying will begin. When this occurs is different for every woman. Some moms-to-be begin to show as early as three months, while others can wait it out until as late as six months. But don't wait until you begin to look like a sausage to shop around. It's always best to scope out the bargains early, so you won't be tempted to buy outfits at the convenient (and high-priced) specialty store out of desperation.

♣ *Casual clothes.* Your best bet here is to stick with knit leggings or sweat pants and big tops. You don't necessarily have to buy these from maternity stores. In fact, later in this chapter, we'll talk about less-expensive alternatives. If you're pregnant in the summer, dresses can be a cooler alternatives to pants and shorts.

♣ *Dress or formal clothes.* Forget them unless you plan to have a full social calendar or have many social engagements associated with your job. Usually, you can find a local store that rents maternity formal wear for the one or two occasions when you might need it.

Smart Shopper Tips

Smart Shopper Tip #1
Battling Your Wacky Thermostat

"It's early in my pregnancy, and I'm finding that the polyester-blend blouses that I wear to work have become very uncomfortable. I'm starting to shop for maternity clothes—what should I look for that will be more comfortable?"

It's a fact of life for us pregnant folks—your body's thermostat has gone berserk. Thanks to those pregnancy hormones, it may be hard to regulate your body's temperature. And those polyester-blend clothes may not be so comfortable anymore.

Our advice: stick with natural fabrics as much as possible, especially cotton. Unfortunately, a lot of lower-priced maternity clothing is made of polyester/cotton blend fabrics. To make matters worse, you may also find that your feet swell and are uncomfortable as your pregnancy progresses. As a result, wear shoes that have low heels for maximum comfort.

Smart Shopper Tip #2
Seasons Change

"Help! My baby is due in October, but I still need maternity clothes for the hot summer months! How can I buy my maternity wardrobe without investing a fortune?"

Unless you live in a place with endless summer, most woman have to buy maternity clothes that will span both warm and cold seasons. The best bet are items that work both in either winter or summer—for example, light-weight long-sleeve shirts can be rolled up in the summer. Leggings can work in both spring and fall. Another tip: layer clothes to ward off cold. Instead of buying expensive sweaters, wear a couple of shirts for warmth.

Our Picks: Brand Recommendations for Maternity Undergarments

Thank goodness for e-mail. Here at the home office in Boulder, CO our e-mail (adfields@aol.com) has overflowed with great suggestions from readers on maternity undergarments.

God bless Canada—those Maple Leaf-heads make the best maternity bra in the world. Toronto-based *Bravado Designs* (for a brochure, call 800-590-7802 or 416-466-8652) makes a maternity/nursing bra of the same name that's just incredible. "A godsend!" raved one reader. "It's built like a sports bra with no underwire and supports better than any other bra

I've tried . . . and this is my third pregnancy!" The Bravado bra comes in three support levels, sizes up to 42-46 with an F-G cup and a couple of wonderful colors/patterns. Available via mail order, the bra costs $29-$31 U.S. (or $32 to $35 Canadian). Another plus: the Bravado salespeople are knowledgeable and quite helpful with sizing questions.

The *Natural Baby Catalog* (800) 388-2229 sells an "awesome" maternity bra, says another reader. The all-cotton bra has five hooks in back and off-sizes that fit ("just try finding a 38-40 B bra that doesn't have a cup that looks like a D," she says). Available in underwire and plain with cup sizes up to H. Cost: $22 to $30.

Readers of our first edition gave a thumbs up to "Strap Relief" from the *Clotilde* catalog (800) 772-2891. These add-on cushion pads slip around your too-narrow bra straps to spread out the pressure. No sewing is required; it costs just $5.52 per pair.

One Hanes Place (800) 300-2600 is a great catalog with 50% off bargains on maternity bras, panties and hose (more on this later in this chapter). Readers rave about this catalog, which features name brands like Playtex and L'Eggs.

Looking for maternity shorts/tights for working out? The catalog *Title Nine Sports* (510) 655-5999 offers some answers. Tights are $39 and shorts $34—each has a belly band for extra support. Regular "multi-sport" shorts are also in the catalog for $34 with a four-inch waistband that rides under the tummy.

Large-size maternity undergarments can be darn difficult to find. Our readers suggest the *Bust Stop* in Tulsa, OK (800) 858-3887, *Cameo Coutures* in Dallas, TX (214) 631-4860, *Decent Exposures* in Seattle, WA (800) 524-4949, *Extra Emphasis* (916) 581-0848, and *Lady Grace Intimate Apparel* of Malden, MA (800) 922-0504. Of course, the JCPenney catalog (reviewed later in this chapter) is another source for large-size maternity fashions. If you're on the Internet, check out the news group "soc.support.fat-acceptance"—this group posts a monthly FAQ (frequently asked questions) with sources for large-size maternity fashions, both in the U.S. and Canada.

What about underwear? The best I found were *Japanese Weekend* (800) 808-0555, a brand available in stores and via mail order (see review later in this chapter). Their "OK" bikini-style underwear boasts 100% thick cotton fabric and an extra-wide waistband that cradles your belly. Although they aren't cheap (three for $26), I found them incredibly comfortable *and* durable, standing up to repeated washings better than other brands.

The Name Game: Reviews of Selected Maternity Stores

 Usually this section is intended to acquaint you with the clothing name brands you'll see in local stores. When it comes to maternity wear, however, the biggest players are actually the stores themselves. National chains like MothersWork and Dan Howard have their own store brands. Here's a wrap-up of what's available. We've also included Japanese Weekend, which is a maternity brand sold in department and specialty stores and via mail order.

The Ratings

★★★★ EXCELLENT—*our top pick!*
   ★★★ GOOD—*above average quality, prices, and creativity.*
      ★★ FAIR—*could stand some improvement.*
         ★ POOR—*yuck! could stand some major improvement.*

Dan Howard ....★★
Call (312) 263-6700 to find a store near you or (800) 966-6847 for a catalog. A manufacturer of maternity career, dress and casual fashions, Dan Howard sells its clothes in 90 locations that they call "factory outlets." Yet our sharp-eyed readers noticed the prices weren't anything special. Dan Howard marks all their clothes with tags that compare their prices to "suggested retail," yet the latter prices seemed inflated to us. Nevertheless, the quality of the clothes is OK; besides career clothing, we noticed leggings, bike shorts, undergarments and even bathing suits.

Japanese Weekend. .... ★★★★
To find a store near you that carries this brand of clothing, call (800) 808-0555, (415) 621-0555, or write to 22 Isis St., San Francisco, CA 94103. You can also ask for a catalog. Japanese Weekend is a line of women's maternity clothing that emphasizes comfort. They are best known for their unusual "OK" belly-banded pants, which have a waistband that circles under your expanding tummy for support (rather than cutting across it).

In recent years, Japanese Weekend has expanded its line beyond pants to include jumpers, tops, catsuits, nightgowns, and skirts. We really like the simple, comfortable style of the clothes and highly recommend them. For once, a company has created all-cotton clothing for moms-to-be, avoiding the all too common polyester blends.

One nice plus: Japanese Weekend will send you a list of

stores that carry their clothes (call the above number for more information). In addition, the designer has a company store in San Francisco (415-989-6667).

Mothercare...★★★
Over 120 stores. Call (312) 263-6700 for a store near you.
Mothercare Maternity stores offer medium-priced maternity clothing with a wide selection of casual and work clothes. For example, we saw a blue and white check trapeze shirt for $42, paired with matching blue stirrup pants for $24. Considering that we've seen leggings and stirrups for as much as $50 in other maternity shops, Mothercare is a bit easier on the pocketbook.

Dresses and suits are also available. If you're looking for a high-style pant suit, we noticed a teal outfit with gold-button detailing for only $64. A rayon floral print dress was only $69. Undergarments and swim suits are also reasonably priced.

As an interesting side note, Mothercare is owned by the same parent company that operates Dan Howard (reviewed earlier).

Motherhood ....★★$^{1}/_{2}$
For a store near you call (800) 825-2268. Yet another national chain of maternity shops (owned by MothersWork, see review below) with a mix of weekend casual and workday suits. The standouts? A beautiful silk print blouse accented with pearl buttons ($62) and a coordinating slip skirt ($36). Once again, we were not impressed with the hefty price tags. At least the fabrics were mostly natural, and the designs put comfort first.

MothersWork ....★★$^{1}/_{2}$
1309 Noble St., Philadelphia, PA 19123. Call (800) 825-2268 or (215) 625-9259 for a store location or a catalog.
MothersWork dominates the retail maternity market with hundreds of stores, which go under names like "Pea in the Pod," "Mimi Maternity," and "Maternity Works," as well as their own name.

Each store carries a similar mix of casual and career wear, albeit at different price levels. MothersWork's eponymous stores seem to have more emphasis on casual clothing, while Pea in the Pod carries more career outfits and other items like bathing suits. Mimi Maternity is the company's "upper-end" concept—you'll see this name in upscale malls and the merchandise boasts higher prices to match the digs.

No matter which MothersWork chain you're in, there is one constant—high prices. For example, you can buy a navy jacket from MothersWork for $148, a pleated slip skirt ($68), or a straight slip skirt ($58). Other pieces include a coordinating floral dress ($138) or jumper ($114). At Pea in the Pod, we noticed a double-breasted, six-button rayon dress in periwinkle blue for $200 and a silk suit with skirt and jacket ran $284. Heck, a simple all-cotton t-shirt at Mimi Maternity tops $40. Ouch.

On the upside, the quality is generally good—most items are 100% cotton and stylish. What about the service? Well, it's a mixed bag. We found generally helpful salespeople at most MothersWork stores, yet the folks at Pea in the Pod can get a little pushy. Like static cling, one saleswoman followed me around and asked one too many questions about my pregnancy. As soon as you walk in, it takes less than five seconds for someone to offer you spring water—a contrived, albeit nice, gesture.

Wastes of Money

Waste of Money #1
MATERNITY BRA BLUES

"My old bras are getting very tight. I recently went to my local department store to check out larger sizes. The salesperson suggested I purchase a maternity bra because it would offer more comfort and support. Should I buy a regular bra in a larger size or plunk down the money for a maternity bra? When I saw the $28 price tag on the maternity bra, I wasn't sure it was worth it."

We've heard from quite a few readers who've complained the expensive maternity bras they've bought were very uncomfortable and/or fell apart after just a few washings. Our best advice: try on the bra before purchase and stick to the better brands. Compared to regular bras, the best maternity bras have thicker straps, more give on the sides and more hook and eye closures in back (so the bra can grow with you). Most of all, the bra should be comfortable and have no scratchy lace or detailing. I've had luck with the Olga "Christina" maternity bras (sold in department stores) and the Bravado bra, mentioned earlier in this chapter.

Waste of Money #2
ORANGE YOU GOING TO WEAR HOSE?

"Have you seen the horrendous colors available in maternity hose? I can't wear those orange things to work!"

Don't. You don't have to buy ugly maternity hose—those thick, itchy horrors only sold in four shades of orange (Ugly, Sheer Ugly, Super-Duper Ugly, and Son of Ugly). Maternity hose must have been invented by a third world country looking for a new torture device; now, it takes its rightful place next to the bridesmaid's dress as one of the most dreaded apparel items for women.

Fortunately, there is some good news on this front. The One Hanes Place catalog (800) 300-2600 carries L'Eggs Sheer Energy and Playtex maternity panty hose in several colors besides orange. Best of all, the prices are great. The "slightly imperfect" hosiery goes for about $3 per pair.

If you'd prefer a fancier brand, we found Hue (made by Leslie Fay Co.; call 212-947-3666 for a store near you) comes in several attractive colors and retails for $14 a pair.

What about large-size panty hose? A mother-to-be in Georgia e-mailed us a recommendation for "Just My Size." This special line for larger-size woman is manufactured by L'eggs and sold for half the price of "official preggo" pantyhose, she said.

Of course, there is another solution to the maternity hose dilemma: don't buy them. With a few modifications, you may be able to wear regular hose during your pregnancy. Try rolling the waistband down under your tummy. It works, believe me. When I was six months pregnant and invited to a formal occasion, I wore regular hose in that manner and had no problem. Or you may find that cutting the waistband of your hose gives you some breathing room for a few months. If you wear only long skirts and dresses, knee-hi hose are an option; no one will know you're not wearing full hose. Some women swear by self-supporting stockings, the kind with rubber-like grippers around the bands. While a few pregnant moms find them uncomfortable (check with your doctor if you have concerns about blood circulation in your legs), this tip worked for others we interviewed.

Waste of Money #3

OVER THE SHOULDER TUMMY HOLDER

"I keep seeing those 'belly bras' advertised as the best option for a pregnant mom. What are they for and are they worth buying?"

Belly bras were invented to provide additional support for your back during your pregnancy. One style envelops your whole torso and looks like a tight-fitting tank top. No one can argue that, in many cases, the strain of carrying a baby and the additional weight that goes with it is tough even on women in great physical shape. So, if you find your back, hips, and/or legs are giving you trouble, consider buying a belly bra or support panty.

However, in our research, we noticed most moms don't seem to need or want a belly bra. The price for one of these puppies can range from $35 to an incredible $55. The bottom line: hold off buying a belly bra or support panty until you see how your body reacts to your pregnancy. Also, check with your doctor to see if she has any suggestions for back, hip, and leg problems.

Waste of Money #4
OVEREXPOSED NURSING GOWNS/TOPS

"I plan to nurse my baby and all my friends say I should buy nursing gowns for night feedings. Problem is, I've tried on a few and even though the slits are hidden, I still feel exposed. Not to mention they're the ugliest things I've ever seen. Can't I just wear a regular gown that buttons down the front?"

"I refuse to buy those awful nursing tops! Not only are they ugly, but those weird looking panels are like wearing a neon sign that says 'BREASTFEEDING MOM AHEAD'!"

Of course you can. And considering how expensive nursing gowns can be ($35 to $50 each), buying a regular button-up nightshirt or gown will certainly save you a few bucks. Every mother we interviewed about nursing gowns had the same complaint. There isn't a delicate way to put this: it's not easy to get a breast out of one of those teenie-weenie slits. Did the person who designed these ever breastfeed a baby? I always felt uncovered whenever I wore a nursing gown, like one gust of wind would have turned me into a poster child for a nudist magazine.

And can we talk about nursing shirts with those "convenient button flaps for discreet breastfeeding"? Convenient, my fanny. There's so much work involved in lifting the flap up, unbuttoning it, and getting your baby positioned that you might as well forget it. My advice: stick with shirts you can pull up or unbutton down the front. These are just as discreet, easier to work with, and (best of all) you don't have to add some expensive nursing shirts (at $30 to $50 each) to your wardrobe.

Money-Saving Secrets

1 CONSIDER BUYING "PLUS" (LARGE LADIES) SIZES FROM A REGULAR STORE. Thankfully, fashion styles of late include leggings and oversized tops and sweaters. This makes pregnancy a lot easier since you can buy the same styles in larger ladies' sizes to cover your belly without compromising your fashion sense or investing in expensive and often shoddily made maternity clothes. We found the same fashions in large-ladies' stores for 20% to 35% less than maternity shops (and even more during sales).

One drawback to this strategy: by the end of your pregnancy, your hemlines may start to look a little "high-low"—your expanding belly will raise the hemline in front. This may be especially pronounced with skirts and dresses. Of course, that's the advantage of buying maternity clothes: the designers compensate with more fabric in front to balance the hem line. Nonetheless, we found that many moms we interviewed were able to get away with large-lady fashions for much (if not all) of their pregnancy. And how much money can you save? We priced a pair of cotton-blend leggings from Mimi Maternity at $44. Meanwhile, we found that Eddie Bauer carries cotton/spandex leggings for only $24 to $30—and we'd hardly call Eddie Bauer a cheap source for clothes. And Eddie Bauer sells leggings through their catalog in petites, talls, extra large, and extra, extra large sizes.

2 DON'T OVER-BUY BRAS. As your pregnancy progresses, your bra size is going to change at least a couple times. Running out to buy five new bras when you hit a new cup size is probably foolish—in another month, all those bras may not fit. The best advice: buy the bare minimum (two or three).

3 DON'T SKIMP ON MATERNITY BRAS AND UNDERWEAR. Take some of the money you save from other parts of this book and invest in good maternity underwear. Yes, you can find cheap underwear for $3 pair at discount stores, but don't be penny-wise and pound foolish. We found the cheap stuff is very uncomfortable and falls apart, forcing you to go back and buy more. Investing in better-quality bras and underwear also makes sense if you plan to have more than one child—you can actually wear it again for subsequent pregnancies.

4 CONSIDER TARGET, MERVYNS, K-MART FOR CASUAL CLOTHES. Okay, I admit that I don't normally shop at K-Mart or Target for clothes. But I was surprised to discover both chains carry casual maternity clothes in 100% cotton at very affordable prices. Let's repeat that—they have 100% cotton t-shirts, shorts, pants, and more at prices you won't believe. Most of these clothes are in basic solid colors—sorry, no fancy prints. At Target, for example, I found cotton chambray maternity shirts and shorts at just $10 each. At $20 per outfit, you can't beat it. We found 100% cotton maternity shirts in K-Mart for just $8.98. Hello? Try to find that price at a chain maternity store.

While Target and K-Mart don't carry any career wear (as you might expect), you'll save so much on casual/weekend clothes that you'll be ecstatic anyway. Witness this example. At A Pea in the Pod, we found a cotton knit tank top and shorts outfit in solid yellow. The price: a heart-stopping $82. A similar all-cotton tank top/shorts outfit from Target was $20. Whip out a calculator, and you'll note the savings is an amazing 75%. Need we say more?

E-MAIL FROM THE REAL WORLD
Two thumbs up for Eddie Bauer

 Annie M. of Brooklyn, NY found great deals at Eddie Bauer on clothes that can work as maternity fashions:

"Eddie Bauer is my salvation. I'd marry the man if I weren't so damn fond of my husband. The XL and XXL leggings are $24 to $30 and they last and last. The shirts are all available in petite through XXL sizes, the lengths are good for short or tall people, and they have many styles that are suitable for late in pregnancy without looking 'smocky.' I also know that I'll be able to wear most of the stuff again and again after I have the baby. Eddie Bauer's generously cut sundresses wear wonderfully and are accommodating me beautifully into my sixth month (with lots of room to grow). And another plus: they also have great sales!"

5 RENT EVENING WEAR—DON'T BUY. We found that many maternity stores rent evening wear. For example, a local shop we visited had an entire rack of rental formalwear. An off-white lace dress (perfect for attending a wedding) rented for just $50. Compare that with the purchase price of $175. Since you most likely would need the dress for a one-time wearing, the savings of renting versus buying would be $125.

6 CHECK OUT CONSIGNMENT STORES. You can find "gently worn" career and casual maternity clothes for 40% to 70% off the original retail! Many consignment or second-hand stores carry only designer-label clothing in good to excellent condition. If you don't want to buy used garments, consider recouping some of your investment in maternity clothes by consigning them after the baby is born. You can usually find listings for these stores in the phone book. (Don't forget to look under children's clothes as well. Some consignment stores that carry baby furniture and clothes also have a significant stock of maternity wear.)

7 FIND AN OUTLET. Check out the next section of this chapter for the low-down on maternity clothes outlets.

8 Get the One hanes place catalog. This is our favorite catalog (800) 300-2600 for maternity hose, Playtex nursing bras, and maternity briefs. Some items are "slightly imperfect," but we couldn't find any visible flaws. Best of all, prices are 40% or more below retail.

9 Be creative. Raid your husband's closet for over-sized shirts and sweat pants. One mom we interviewed found a creative use for her pre-pregnancy leggings. She simply wore them backwards! The roomier backside gave her space for her expanding tummy.

Outlets

MothersWork/Maternity Works

Locations: 35 outlets. For location info, call (215) 625-9259.

The offspring of the catalog and retail stores of the same name (see our review in "Do It By Mail" later in the chapter), MothersWork/Maternity Works outlets have started springing up in outlet malls across the country. On a recent visit, the outlet featured markdowns from 20% to 75% on the same top-quality designs you see in the catalog or the retail stores.

For example, we noticed a cotton knit jumper at MothersWork for $59 that was regularly priced at $98. Knit stirrup pants were on sale for $39, almost 20% off the regular price of $48. A suit jacket was priced at a mere $39 (regularly $158), and the matching skirt was only $29 (regularly $58). That's right, you could pick up this whole outfit for just $68, instead of the $226 retail price. The outlet also carried a decent selection of party dresses, undergarments, and casual wear.

Mothertime

Location: Secaucus, NJ (201) 392-1237.

Even though Mothertime is the retail division of Dan Howard Maternity, the chain has its own outlet store in Secaucus, New Jersey. In addition to carrying casual and career maternity clothes, Mothercare also sells children's clothing (from newborn to 24 months). The discounts are rather slim, however, averaging about 20% off retail.

Motherwear

Location: Northampton, MA (413) 586-2175.

The Motherwear catalog has a factory outlet that is open

just Fridays and Saturdays. They sell seconds, overstock and discontinued items. "Great bargains—worth the trip," says a reader who visited the outlet.

Do it By Mail

Garnet Hill.

To Order Call: (800) 622-6216, (603) 823-5545; Fax (603) 823-9578.
Shopping Hours: Monday-Friday 7 am-2 am; Saturday and Sunday 9 am-11 pm Eastern Time.
Or write to: Garnet Hill, Box 262 Main St., Franconia, NH 03580.
Credit Cards Accepted: MC, VISA, AMEX, Discover.

 Unfortunately, Garnet Hill is a good example of how expensive maternity clothes can get. Sample impressions from a recent catalog: a white cotton maternity shirt was a whopping $68. We also saw leggings for $56, a jumper for $118, and a velour dress for $78.

Well, at least the clothes are stylish. While we like Garnet Hill's contemporary and fresh designs (they sell only natural fabrics), their casual wear is overpriced. On the upside, they do occasionally offer a discount for new customers. And look for sale catalogs—those $56 leggings were last seen selling for $24.

JCPenney.

To Order Call: (800) 222-6161. Ask for "Maternity Collection" catalog.
Shopping Hours: 24 hours a day, seven days a week.
Credit Cards Accepted: MC, VISA, JCPenney, AMEX, Discover.

JCPenney offers a free "mini-catalog" called "Maternity Collection." A recent edition featured 36 pages of maternity clothes, plus a small selection of nursery items.

Perhaps the best aspect of Penney's offerings is their wide range of sizes—you can find petites, talls and woman's sizes. It's darn near impossible to find "womens sizes" in maternity wear today, but Penney's carries up to size 26w.

What most impressed us about Penney's maternity catalog was their career clothes. For example, we saw a "three-piece wardrobe" suit (v-neck top with gold buttons, matching skirt and pants) for just $60 to $65. This acetate/rayon outfit was available in every conceivable size, including "women's petites." Another stand-out: Penney's "Dividends 4 You," a complete wardrobe of five pieces (pullover jumper, tunic, skirt, t-shirt and leggings) in cotton/lycra spandex for $99.

While most of the career wear are blends of rayon and polyester, Penney's casual maternity clothes feature more all-cotton fabrics. We saw a wide array of cotton maternity shirts ($20 to $35) and jeans ($22 to $27), as well as denim dresses and jumpers. A selection of nightgowns, swim suits, lingerie, and hose round out the offerings in this catalog.

MothersWork/Motherhood

Call: (800) 825-2268 or (215) 625-9259; Fax (215) 440-9845.
Shopping Hours: 24 hours a day, seven days a week.
Or write to: MothersWork, 456 N. 5th St., Philadelphia, PA 19123.
Credit Cards Accepted: MC, VISA, AMEX.

The maternity retail behemoth MothersWork has a mail-order division that puts out catalogs under the names "Motherswork" and "Motherhood." Both are quite similar in terms of selection and pricing—each focuses on career clothing, although you'll also see a smattering of casual and evening wear as well. A recent catalog featured a long-sleeve empire dress in black and white checks for $49. We liked the navy suit jacket and skirt combo for $70. As for more casual offerings, the catalog had cotton long-sleeve t-shirts ($17), cotton lycra jumpsuits ($38) and stone-washed jeans ($28).

In our last edition, we complained that MothersWork/Motherhood's prices were too high. Well, there is some good news to report on this front: their most recent catalogs seem to have more down-to-earth pricing.

Nursing fashions in Canada: The Toronto-based Breast is Best catalog sells a wide variety of nursing tops, blouses and dresses. For a free catalog and fabric swatches, call (416) 461-3890.

Maternity Wear for Grown-Ups

Tired of t-shirts emblazoned with the word "baby" and an arrow pointing down to your tummy? Seen one too many cute denim overall outfits? Then have we found the designer for you: Lauren Sara M.

You've probably seen designer Lauren Sara's clothes on such famous celebrity moms-to-be as Paula Zahn and Demi Moore. Lauren told us she was inspired to design the line after a wealthy New York socialite (who was five months pregnant) hired her to design an evening gown. The dress was a smashing success, and Lauren set out to design a line of maternity wear with style. The collection includes career wear like suits (jackets run $320 to $385, and skirts and pants cost $150 to $225), daytime dresses ($250), and even a few evening gowns (about $500). Sure, the prices aren't cheap, but we challenge you to find a more fashionable alternative. Lauren Sara M is available via mail order only; call (212) 730-0007 for a catalog.

For the sew-it-yourself crowd, we noticed Lauren Sara M's maternity designs are in the Vogue pattern books (in fabric stores nationwide). We saw three patterns in the most recent book, including a short-sleeve evening dress ($22) and a two-piece jacket/dress top and skirt combo for $22.50.

E-MAIL FROM THE REAL WORLD
Stay fit with pregnancy workout videos

Margaret Griffin e-mailed us with her opinions of several popular workout videos tailored for the pregnant woman. Here are her thoughts:

"As a former certified aerobics instructor, I have been trying out the video workouts for pregnancy. I have only found three videos available in my local stores, but I wanted to rate them for your readers.

"Buns of Steel 8 Pregnancy Workout with Madeleine Lewis gets my top rating. Madeleine Lewis has excellent cueing, so the workout is easy to follow. Your heart rate and perceived exertion are both used to monitor your exertion. There is an informative introduction. And I really like the fact that the toning segment utilizes a chair to help you keep your balance, which can be off a little during pregnancy. Most of the toning segment is done standing. This is a safe, effective workout led by a very capable instructor and I highly recommend it.

"A middle rating goes to *Denise Austin's Pregnancy Plus Workout*. Denise has a good information segment during which she actually interviews a physician. She also provides heart rate checks during the workout. However, there are a couple of things about this workout that I don't particularly like. First, during the workout, there are times when safety information is provided regarding a particular move. This is fine and good, but instead of telling you to continue the movement and/or providing a picture-in-a-picture format, they actually change the screen to show the safety information and then cut back into the workout in progress. Surprise! You were supposed to keep doing the movement. Second, Denise Austin is a popular instructor, but I personally find that her cueing is not as sharp as I prefer and sometimes she seems to be a little off-beat with the music. My suggestion is get this video to use in addition to other videos if you are the type who gets easily bored with one workout.

"The video I recommend that you skip altogether is the *Redbook Pregnancy Workout* led by Diane Gausepohl. I have nothing positive to say regarding this workout. I did the workout once and immediately retired the tape. The instructor has poor cueing skills and does not keep time with the music well at all. This makes the workout hard to follow. My husband was actually laughing at the instruction, it was so poor. I also don't like the fact that it includes toning exercises that can be done (and are demonstrated) lying on your back. We all know that by the fifth month of pregnancy, the weight of the uterus can restrict the blood flow in the inferior vena cava, so you should not lie flat on your back. Even though these exercises can be modified I think it is better to avoid the temptation altogether. There are plenty of other toning exercises that are effective that do not require you to lie on your back at all. My advice is to skip this video altogether."

Breastfeeding

Suppose we told you that you could take a miracle pill during pregnancy that would do amazing things for your baby.

What things? How about a higher IQ? Yes, this miracle drug would do that, as well as lessen your child's chance of respiratory and gastrointestinal infections. The same pill would mean fewer and less severe allergies, and your baby would have better jaw and teeth development. Speech problems and ear infections in childhood? This pill would help eliminate them, as well as provide protection from illnesses like rubella, chicken pox, bronchitis, and polio. If that weren't enough, taking this pill would even reduce the chance your child would be obese as an adult. Not only would this miracle pill do all that for your baby, but it would also lower the chance of breast cancer and heart disease in you, the mother.

Surprise! There is no pill that does all that! But there is something you can do for your baby that does everything described above and more: breastfeeding.

Certainly, comparing breastfeeding to taking a pill during pregnancy isn't entirely fair. While breastfeeding may seem intuitive to some women, most have to work to get it right—and those first few days can seem like hell. So, it's important to know how to find help. This section will provide you with tips and tricks to successfully breastfeed, including a list of products and organizations that can make the process easier.

What if you can't or don't want to breastfeed your baby? If you're adopting a baby or have a medical/work situation that precludes breastfeeding, there's no choice. For such parents, we've also included a part in this section on infant formula, bottle systems and other necessary accessories.

Breastfeed Your Baby and Save $500

Since this is a book on a bargains, we'd be remiss in not mentioning the tremendous amount of money you can save if you breastfeed rather than use formula. Just think about it: no bottles, no expensive formula to prepare, no special insulated carriers to keep bottles warm, etc.

So, how much money would you save? Obviously, the biggest money-saver would be not having to buy formula. Even if you were to use the less expensive powder, you would still have to spend nearly $8 per 16-ounce can. (For reference, we used our local grocery store's price of $7.79 per can as a price point.) Since each can makes 116 ounces of formula when mixed with water, the cost per ounce of formula is about 7¢.

That doesn't sound too bad, does it? Unless you factor in that a baby will down 32 ounces of formula per day by 12 weeks of age. Your cost per day would be $2.15. Assuming you breastfeed for the first six months, you would save a grand total of $387. Not only is breastfeeding better for your baby's health, it is much kinder to your wallet.

To be fair, there are some optional expenses that might go along with breastfeeding. The biggest dollar item: if you work outside the home, you might decide to rent or buy a piston electric breast pump. The cost? About $50 per month to rent or $200 to buy.

If $387 doesn't sound like a lot of money, consider the savings if you had to buy formula in the concentrated liquid form instead of the cheaper powder. A 13-ounce can of Similac liquid concentrate costs about $2.30 at a grocery store and makes just 26 ounces of formula. The bottom line: you could spend over $500 on formula for your baby in the first six months alone! And that doesn't even include the cost of bottles, sterilizers and other accessories. Even if you ignore the fantastic health benefits from breastfeeding your baby, it's hard to argue against the money it saves.

What's a Breastfeeding Mom's Biggest Misconception?

"I'M NOT MAKING ENOUGH MILK"

In some ways, a mom who feeds her baby formula has it easy. She measures out a certain amount of formula and can see her baby's progress as she empties the bottle. Breastfeeding, however, is based a little more on faith. You can't see how much milk you have, nor can you tell how much milk your baby has consumed. The truth is most women make plenty of milk. The nagging fear that your baby isn't eating enough is often just that: a fear.

To be frank, however, we should note that in a small number of cases mothers may not have enough milk to breastfeed their babies. According to a report in the *Wall Street Journal*, "insufficient-milk syndrome may occur as much as 5% of the time, affecting about 200,000 mothers a year in the U.S. Some physicians say certain breasts are structurally incapable of producing enough milk; in addition, women who have had breast surgery are at risk. Some infants, meanwhile, are incapable of learning how to breast-feed."

The result: mothers with the best of intentions can actually starve their babies. Two infant deaths caused by insufficient-milk syndrome were reported in a recent year. Since the signs of dehydration can be subtle, the best advice may be to see your doctor immediately if your think your baby is not getting enough milk in the first few days. Of course, failing to breastfeed your baby does not mean that you're a failure as a mother.

Fortunately, this syndrome is quite rare. Most women have no problem producing enough milk for their baby. The biggest obstacle to breastfeeding may be mental. Many moms start out with the best of intentions, only to abandon breast-feeding because of lack of support or self-confidence. The next part of this chapter addresses this problem.

Sources: Where to Find Help

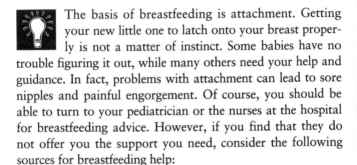 The basis of breastfeeding is attachment. Getting your new little one to latch onto your breast proper-ly is not a matter of instinct. Some babies have no trouble figuring it out, while many others need your help and guidance. In fact, problems with attachment can lead to sore nipples and painful engorgement. Of course, you should be able to turn to your pediatrician or the nurses at the hospital for breastfeeding advice. However, if you find that they do not offer you the support you need, consider the following sources for breastfeeding help:

1 La Leche League (800-LA LECHE). Started over 35 years ago by a group of moms in Chicago, La Leche League has traditionally been the most vocal supporter of breastfeeding in this country. You've got to imagine the amount of chutzpah these women had to have had in order to promote breastfeeding at a time when it wasn't fashionable (to say the least).

In recent years, La Leche has established branches in many communities, providing support groups for new moms inter-ested in trying to nurse their children. They also offer a cata-log full of books and videotapes on nursing, as well as other child care topics. Their famous book *The Womanly Art of Breastfeeding* is the bible for huge numbers of breastfeeding advocates.

Although we admire the work La Leche League has done to help nursing mothers and to change society's attitudes toward them, we disagree with some of the group's tenets. For example, their approach toward parenting includes an unhealthy dose of negativism when it comes to working moms. Let's get real, folks. Most moms today have to work outside the home, at least part-time—to have such a presti-gious organization as La Leche promoting a traditional stay-at-home role model is anachronistic.

Of course, this is a minor point of disagreement. All in all, La Leche provides an important service and, coupled with their support groups and catalog of publications, is a valuable resource for nursing mothers.

2 NURSING MOTHERS' COUNCIL (408-272-1448). Similar in mission to La Leche League, the Nursing Mothers' Council differs on one point: the group emphasizes working moms and their unique needs and problems.

3 LACTATION CONSULTANTS. Lactation consultants are usually nurses who specialize in breastfeeding education and problem solving. You can find them through your pediatrician, hospital, or the International Lactation Consultants Association (312) 541-1710. Members of this group must pass a written exam, complete 2500 hours of clinical practice and 30 hours of continuing education before they can be certified. At our local hospital, resident lactation consultants are available to answer questions by phone at no charge. If a problem persists, you can set up an in-person consultation for a minimal fee (about $40 to $90 per hour, although your health insurance provider may pick up the tab).

Unfortunately, the availability of lactation consultants seems to vary from region to region. Our research shows that, in general, hospitals in the western U.S. are more likely to offer support services, such as on-staff lactation consultants. Back east, however, the effort to support breastfeeding seems spotty. Our advice: call area hospitals before you give birth to determine the availability of breastfeeding support.

4 HOSPITALS. Look for a hospital in your area that has breastfeeding-friendly policies. What are these? Hospitals that allow 24-hour rooming in (where your baby can stay with you instead of in a nursery) and breastfeeding on demand are best. Pro-nursing hospitals do not supplement babies with a bottle and don't push free formula samples. Their nurses will also respect your wishes concerning pacifier usage, which is important if you are concerned about nipple confusion.

5 BOOKS. Although they aren't a substitute for support from your doctor, hospital, and family, many books provide plenty of information and encouragement. Check the La Leche League catalog for sources.

6 THE INTERNET. We found several great sites with breastfeeding information and tips. Our favorite was Medela (www.medela.com), which is a leading manufacturer of breast pumps. Medela's site features extensive information resources and articles on breastfeeding, as well as advice on how to choose the right breastpump. Of course, you can also get info on Medela's breast pumps and other products, find a dealer near you and more.

The catalog Bosom Buddies (www.bosombuddies.com

or call 914-338-2038) has a web site with a good selection of breastfeeding articles, product information and links to other breastfeeding sites on the web.

If that weren't enough, there's even a news group dedicated to the subject: misc.kids.breastfeeding. Moms post questions, swap stories and trade information about which products work best.

Smart Shopper Tips

Smart Shopper Tip #1
PUMPED UP

"My husband and I would really like to go out to dinner sometime before our daughter is 15 years old. I've been looking at different breastpumps—which really works best?"

Expressing milk is a science in itself. You'll notice a wide variety of pumps, from manual pumps that cost a few dollars to huge, piston electric pumps that run into the hundreds of dollars (you can rent or buy these). Here's a rundown of the four options:

♣ *Manual Expression:* There are several good breastfeeding books that describe how to express milk manually. Most women find that the amount of milk expressed, compared to the time and trouble involved, hardly makes it worth using this method. A few women (we think they are modern miracle workers) can manage to express enough for an occasional bottle; for the majority of women, however, using a breastpump is a more practical alternative.

♣ *Manual Pumps:* Non-electric, hand-held pumps create suction by squeezing on a handle. While they're cheap, manual pumps are also the least efficient—you simply can't duplicate your baby's sucking action by hand. Therefore, these pumps are best for moms who only need an occasional bottle or who need to relieve engorgement. We've seen an Evenflo manual pump (Natural Mother Breast Pump Kit) in stores like Target and Toys R Us for $19 to $22.

Recommendation: Egnell's Mother's Touch One-Handed Breast Pump ($26-$30). It's easier to use and is available through La Leche League's catalog (800) LA-LECHE, or call the company at (800) 323-8750 or (847) 639-2900 for a store that carries the pump. Another brand to look for at your local baby store is the Medela Manualectric Breast Pump/Feeding System ($24.95, call 800-435-8316 or 815-363-1246 for a dealer near you).

♣ *Mini-Electrics:* I bought one of these, and it was probably a waste of money. I thought these battery-operated breast-pumps would be good for expressing an occasional bottle. Unfortunately, the sucking action is so weak that I quickly discovered it took twenty minutes *per side* to express a significant amount of milk. And doing so was not very comfortable, to say the least. Why is it so slow? Most models only cycle nine to fifteen times per minute—compare that to a baby who sucks the equivalent of 50 cycles per minute! Some of the most inefficient mini-electric breastpumps just so happen to be manufactured by formula makers (like Gerber). Coincidence? We wonder.

Recommendation: The Medela Mini Electric (about $70 to $80 retail) is one of the few battery operated breastpumps that actually operates at 50 cycles per minute. Call Medela at (800) 435-8316 for the store nearest you. Sure, you can find other mini-electrics for $30 to $50 at discount and drug stores, but be sure to check the cycles per minute before you buy.

♣ *Piston Electric Pumps:* The Mercedes Benz of breast-pumps—we can't sing the praises of the piston electric pumps enough. In just ten to twenty minutes, you can pump *both* breasts. And they are much more comfortable than mini-electrics. In fact, at first I didn't think the piston electric pump I rented was working well because it was *so* comfortable. The bottom line: there is no better option for a working woman who wants to provide her baby with breast milk.

Today, you have two options when it comes to these pumps: rent a hospital-grade pump or buy a high-end retail double-pump. As for rental, a wide variety of sources rent breast-pumps on a daily, weekly or monthly basis. We called a lactation consultant at a local hospital who gave us a list that included maternity stores, small private companies, and home-care outfits. Another possibility is to call La Leche League (see number earlier in this chapter) or other lactation support groups for a referral to a company that rents piston electric pumps.

What does it cost to rent a hospital-grade pump? One company we surveyed rented pumps for $60 for one month or $45 per month if you rent for two or more months. In general, we found rental charges ranged from $1 to $2.60 per day, with the lower rates for longer rentals. You'll also have to buy a kit of the collection bottles, shields, and tubes (this runs about $30 to $35). Medela's Lactina Select (800) 435-8316, White River Concepts Model 9050 (800) 824-6351 and Egnell Elite (800) 323-8750 are all hospital grade pumps available for rental.

If you don't want to rent, you can buy—two companies make retail electric pumps that you can purchase. The best choice is the Medela "Pump In Style," which retails for $200 but is discounted through the Baby Catalog of America (800) PLAYPEN. I used this pump for my second child and was impressed—it's a fully automatic double pump that uses diaphragm action to best simulate a baby's sucking motion. Best of all, it's portable (about seven pounds) and is hidden in an attractive black leather bag for discretion.

A good second choice is the "Double Up" from Natural Choice (call 800-528-8887 for a dealer near you). It's less expensive ($120 to $140), but is only semi-automatic—you control the pump rate by lifting a finger over a hole. The package includes the pump, a collection kit, instruction video and pump tote.

Recommendation: Before you invest in a retail high-end pump like the Pump In Style or Double Up, *rent* a hospital-grade pump first for a week or two (or a month). After you decide you're serious about pumping and you're comfortable with the double-pumping action, *then* consider buying one of your own. Given the hefty retail prices, it makes sense to buy only if you plan to pump for several months or have a second child.

There are a couple disadvantages to these retail pumps. Some woman find the sucking action weaker than hospital-grade pumps—hence, it may take longer to pump. I've used both the Medela hospital-grade pump and the Pump In Style and while I definitely like the Pump In Style, the hospital-grade pump was more comfortable to use. On the other hand, the portability of the retail pumps may outweigh any of their disadvantages. Hospital grade pumps are bulky and can weigh over 20 lbs.

Smart Shopper Tip #2

NIPPLE CONFUSION?

"When I check the catalogs and look in baby stores, I see bottles with all different shaped nipples. Which one is best for my baby? How do I avoid nipple confusion?"

Nipple confusion occurs when a baby learns to suck one way at the breast and another way from a bottle. This happens because the "human breast milk delivery system" (i.e., the breast and nipple) forces babies to keep their sucking action forward in their mouth. The result: they have to work harder to get milk from a breast than from a conventional baby bottle.

So, what bottle and nipple do the experts recommend? Playtex Nursers. That's right, Playtex offers a nipple that helps keep your baby's sucking in the natural position. Longer bottle nipples push the sucking action farther back into the baby's mouth, so when you switch baby back to the breast, she might get confused and frustrated. The medical specialists we interviewed also prefer Playtex Nursers because they encourage better oral motor skills.

What about pacifiers? Some experts say early use of pacifiers might interfere with breastfeeding. The best advice: wait until lactation is firmly established before introducing a pacifier. Which type of pacifier is best? There are two types—regular pacifiers have round nipples, while "orthodontic" pacifiers have flat nipples. There's no consensus as to which type is best—consult with your pediatrician for more advice on this topic.

Waste of Money

EVEN COWS OPT FOR THE ELECTRIC KIND
"I'll be going back to work a couple of months after my baby is born. My co-worker who breastfeeds her baby thinks manual and mini-electrics breastpumps are a total waste of money. What do you think?"

While they may be useful to relieve engorgement, manual pumps aren't very practical for long-term pumping when you're at work. They are very slow, which makes it hard to get much milk. Mini-electric breastpumps are better but are really best only for occasional use—for example, expressing a small amount of milk to mix with cereal for a baby that's learning to eat solids. Mini-electrics do extract more milk but may be painful and still too slow.

Your best bet if you plan to do some serious pumping is to rent a piston electric pump. These monsters maintain a high rate of extraction with amazing comfort. A lactation consultant we interviewed said piston electric pumps can empty both breasts in about 10 to 15 minutes—contrast that with 20 to 30 minutes for mini-electrics and 45 minutes to an hour for manual pumps.

Introduce the Bottle Early

If you plan to introduce a bottle to your baby so you can go out on the town or back to work, do it between the third and sixth week of age. Most parenting books tell you about this, *but* they don't stress how important it is to keep giving a bottle regularly—perhaps two or three feedings per week. In our case, we didn't give a bottle consistently, and by the time our son was about four months old, he absolutely refused to take a bottle at all. Oops! That made going out to dinner and a movie alone a lot tougher. A word to the wise: keep up the occasional bottle.

Breastfeeding in Public: Exposing Yourself for Onlookers' Fun and Your Baby's Heath

Here's a controversial topic to discuss around the office water cooler: breastfeeding in public. Since our society tends to see a woman's breasts as sexual objects rather than as utilitarian milk delivery systems, we often run into disapproval of breastfeeding, especially in public. Ironically, this is one of the chief advantages of breastfeeding—it's very portable. No hauling and cleaning bottles, mixing and warming formula, and your child gets nourishment exactly when he wants it.

Amazingly, some parts of this country still manage to equate breastfeeding in public with indecent exposure. Florida just recently repealed a law forbidding public breastfeeding after several woman were cited by the "breast" police for whipping it out at a local mall. It's hard to believe that until just recently laws in this country branded one of life's most basic needs—eating—as illegal. You can call your local La Leche League or other breastfeeding sources to find out if your city or state still has laws like these. If they do, consider getting involved in trying to get them repealed. For example, Austin, Texas, managed to pass an ordinance allowing breastfeeding in public after moms let their feelings be known.

The irony is that breastfeeding in public involves very little flashing of flesh. As an admitted public breastfeeder, I can attest to the fact that it can be done discreetly. Here are some suggestions:

1 IF THE THOUGHT OF BREASTFEEDING IN PUBLIC IS NOT YOUR CUP OF TEA, CONSIDER BRINGING A BOTTLE OF EXPRESSED MILK WITH YOU. We know one couple who did this and never seemed to have a problem.

2 USE THE SHAWL METHOD. Many women breastfeed in public with a shawl or blanket covering the baby and breasts. While this works well, you must start practicing this early and often with your baby. Otherwise, you'll find that as she gets more alert and interested in her surroundings, she won't stay under the shawl. We saw one (called a Nursing Bib) for $19.95 in the One Step Ahead catalog (800) 247-8440.

3 FIND ALL THE CONVENIENT REST ROOM LOUNGES IN YOUR TOWN. Whenever we visit the local mall, I nurse in one of the big department store's lounge areas. This is a great way to meet other breastfeeding moms as well. Of course, not every public rest room features a lounge with couches or comfy chairs, but it's worth seeking out the ones that do. We applaud stores like LiL' Things and Baby Superstore for having "family restrooms" with glider-rockers and changing tables for easy nursing.

Another creative alternative: stores will usually let you use a dressing room to breastfeed. Of course, some stores are not as "breastfeeding friendly" as others. New York City, for example, has 10 million people and about seven public rest rooms. In such places, I've even breastfed in a chair strategically placed facing a wall or corner in the back of a store. Not the best view, but it gets the job done.

4 YOUR CAR. My son knows the back of both of our cars extremely well now. I found it easier and more comfortable to feed him there, especially when he started to become distracted in restaurants and stores. The car holds no fascination for him, so he tends to concentrate on eating instead of checking out the scenery. I suggest you keep some magazines in the car since you may get bored.

Formula

Is there any difference between brands of formula? According to our research, the answer is no. Almost all the commercially available baby formula sold in the U.S. and Canada contain the same ingredients . . . the only difference is the color of the label on the outside of the can.

How can you save money? First, stay away from the pre-mixed liquid (formula comes in two varieties: power, which you mix with water, and the ready-to-pour liquid). As you might guess, liquid formula costs several times more than the powder version. Guess what type formula companies gives out as freebies in doctor's offices and hospitals? Yes, it's often the liquid stuff. These companies know babies get hooked on the particular taste of the expensive stuff, making it hard (if not impossible) to switch to the powder form later. Sneaky, eh?

If you can find free samples of powder formula, go for it. One reader in Arizona said she got several free cases from her doctor, who simply requested more freebies from the formula makers.

Coupons are another bargain tactic. The largest formula makers each have coupon programs—call to be added to their mailing lists. Similac has the "Welcome Addition Club" (800) 227-5767, and Enfamil has "Family Beginnings" (800) 472-1000.

Another money-saving strategy: shop around. Readers of our first edition noticed that formula prices varied widely, sometimes even at different locations of the same chain. In Chicago, a reader said they found at some stores, Toys R Us charged $1.20 less *per can* for the same Similac with Iron ready-to-feed formula. "They actually have a price check book at the registers with the codes for each store in the Chicagoland area," the reader said. "At our last visit, we saved $13.20 for two cases (about 30% of the cost), just by mentioning we wanted to pay the lower price."

Another reader noticed a similar price discrepancy at Wal-Mart stores in Florida. When she priced Carnation Good Start powder formula, she found one Wal-Mart that marked it at $6.61 per can. Another Wal-Mart (about 20 miles from the first location) sells the same can for $3.68! When the reader inquired about the price discrepancy, a customer service clerk admitted that each store independently sets the price for such items, based on nearby competition. That's a good lesson—many chains in more rural or poorer locations (with no nearby competition) often mark prices higher than urban stores.

Formula for disaster
Confusing cans confront soy users

Soy formula now accounts for 15% of the infant formula market. Yet, a case of mistaken identity has lead some parents to nearly starve their infants. Apparently, parents mistakenly thought they were feeding their babies soy formula, when in fact they were using soy *milk*. The problem: soy milk is missing important nutrients and vitamins found in soy formula. As a result, babies fed soy milk were malnourished and some required hospitalization. Adding to the confusion, soy milk is often sold in cans that look very similar to soy formula. The government has asked soy milk makers to put warning labels on their products, but some have still not complied. If you choose soy formula, be careful to choose the right can at the grocery store.

Bottles

What's the best bottle for baby? To be honest, we've tried out several different brands and haven't seen much of a difference. Perhaps our baby is a genetically-predisposed bargain lover, but he seemed just fine on the affordable disposable brands like Playtex, Gerber and Evenflo.

That isn't to say premium, reusable bottle brands like *Avent* don't have their advantages. The company claims its nipples are clinically proven to reduce colic, the endless crying that some infants develop around one month of age. Avent says its nipples are better since their shape mimics the breast—and many parents consider Avent superior to the competition, according to our surveys.

Unfortunately, Avent isn't cheap. Their products cost about twice as much as other less-expensive bottles and nipples. Until recently, the company only made reusable bottles, missing out on the one-third of the market that prefers the convenience of disposable nursers. Well, there's good news to report: Avent's has just introduced a new disposable bottle that includes their famous nipple and storage bags that clip on the bottle.

Among the more hip new products on the bottle front are the "angled nursers." *Johnson & Johnson's* "Health Flow" started the trend, which purportedly keeps baby from gulping too much air and is easier for parents to monitor the amount of liquid baby's consumed. Evenflo has introduced a similar product and several other companies have knocked-off the Health Flow in the past year.

If you're looking for an innovative on-the-go bottle, check out Colorado-based *UMIX*. Their new "shake and go" bottle

Baby Formula Manufacturers:
Modern Convenience or Sinister Conspiracy?

We got an interesting package in the mail the other day. It was from Enfamil, one of the country's largest formula makers. This wasn't any special treatment because we had authored this book. Nope, it appears to be standard practice. What was inside this special delivery? A case of six cans of formula and, get this, a pamphlet with tips on *breastfeeding*. We were appalled. It was sort of like Marlboro sending us a booklet on how to quit smoking—along with a case of cigarettes.

We've got nothing against formula, per se. Sure, we're firm believers in breastfeeding, but we realize there are times when formula is the only option. Woman who can't breastfeed or parents who adopt obviously have no other choice. What really bothers us is not formula itself, but the way formula companies *market* their product. In a word, it's shameful.

If you knew what was going on behind the scenes in the formula war, it might make you sick. Among the more interesting activities we discovered: formula makers shower hospitals with all kinds of gifts and free samples—all in the hope that the nurses will pass the word to you and other new mothers. One company offers gift incentives to nurses who hand out the most formula packets to new moms. Another firm has even shamelessly produced a video on breastfeeding, with a plug for their formula tactfully inserted at the end. Hospitals get the video free of charge and send one home with each new mom.

You can always spot the new parents when they check out of a maternity ward—they're the ones weighed down with free diaper bags, rattles, and toys, all emblazoned with the fancy logos of the formula makers.

All this makes us think, what kind of message are they trying to send? Sure, you should breastfeed, but if it seems too challenging, we want to make sure a convenient can of formula is never that far away. One of our favorite examples of this duplicity was a rattle we received as a gift, once again at the hospital. Emblazoned with the name Enfamil, it featured a picture of a rabbit feeding its baby with a *bottle*! We don't know about you, but we haven't seen any rabbits in the Wild Kingdom who bottlefeed their young.

Consider a recent advertising campaign for Carnation's Good Start formula: a new mom looks into the camera and says something like "Remember, breast milk is best, but Carnation's Good Start is made to be gentle for your baby." Sort of like a beer company saying "Don't drink and drive, BUT if you're going to get sloshed, make it a Spuds Beer."

Frankly, we think the baby formula companies are taking advantage of new mothers, plying us poor souls (who are already short of sleep) with slick pitches for "convenient" solutions to our babies' feeding problems.

Adding insult to injury, several of the formula makers just pleaded guilty to price-fixing charges. If you've wondered why most formula is marked at about the same price in many stores, it's apparently no accident.

What's our solution to this marketing muddle? Ban direct advertising of formula to consumers. That's what several European countries have done, with no adverse consequences to mothers or babies. A couple of major formula makers (namely, Mead/Johnson and Ross) already restrict their marketing to the medical community, and they don't seem the worse for it. We'd also like to see an end to the promotional freebies that hospitals give out—and strict enforcement of anti-price-fixing laws to keep formula companies from gouging consumers.

Formula companies aren't run by dummies. They realize that when a breastfeeding mother switches to formula within her baby's first year, odds are she will have to continue formula feeding for the rest of that first year. Contrast that with the fact that moms who never breastfeed often switch to whole cow's milk after just six months. Hence, it's more lucrative for these companies to target breastfeeding moms, since getting them to switch racks up bigger profits in the long run.

Considering the overwhelming evidence that breastfeeding is infinitely better for babies, it is time this country took a hard look at regulating the out-of-control marketing of baby formula.

keeps powdered formula and water stored separately until baby is hungry. Align the chambers with a simple motion, give it a shake and the bottle is ready. For a store near you that carries UMIX, call (719) 532-9942 (internet: www.umix.com).

As for all the other necessary accessories reusable bottles require, check out Baby Catalog of America (800) PLAYPEN. We noticed the catalog carried bottle warmers, electric steam sterilizers, bottle gift sets and other accessories at discount prices. They also carry the full Avent line. Another neat product: "The Bottle Burper" from Tender Moments (800) 699-BURP, which eliminates air from disposable bottles (which can contribute to colic). It's dishwasher safe, fits most disposable bottles and is available from Baby Catalog of America or in stores like Baby Depot, Baby Superstore, Toys R Us and more. Cost: $1.50 to $2 each.

THE BOTTOM LINE:
A Wrap-Up of Our Best Buy Picks

For career and casual maternity clothes, we thought the best deals were from the JCPenney catalog. Compared to retail maternity chains (where one suit can run $200 to $300), you can buy your entire wardrobe from Penney's for a song.

If your place of work allows more casual dress, check out the prices at large ladies stores. A simple pair of leggings that could cost $45 to $50 at a maternity shop are only $30 or less at "regular" stores. Another good idea: borrow from your husband's closet—shirts, sweat pants and sweatshirts are all items that can do double-duty as maternity clothes.

For weekend wear, we couldn't find a better deal than the 100% cotton shirts and shorts at discounters like Target and K-Mart. Prices are as little as $8.98 per shirt—compare that to the $40 price tag at maternity chain stores for a simple cotton shirt.

Invited to a wedding? Rent that dress from a maternity store and save $100 or more. In fact, if you follow all our tips on maternity wear, bras, and underwear, you'll save $700 or more. Here's the breakdown:

1. Career Wear $180
JCPenney's maternity catalog features a three-piece "maternity suit" (jacket, skirt and pants) for just $60. Buy two of these in different colors, add one nice dress (another $60) and you're set.

2. Casual Clothes $100
Five outfits of 100% cotton t-shirts and shorts/pants from

Target or K-Mart run $100. Or check out JCPenney's "Dividends 4 You" maternity ensemble. For $99, you get a cotton lycra jumper, tunic, skirt, leggings and t-shirt. Another plus: all Penney's clothes are also available in woman's sizes.

3. Underwear $200 to $300

The One Hanes Place catalog features great deals on maternity underwear—$11 for a nursing bra, $3.50 for maternity panties, and $3 for a pair of maternity hose. On the other hand, we strongly suggest investing in top-quality underwear for comfort and sanity purposes. For example, a Bravado bra is $31 and Japanese Weekend "OK" bikini maternity underwear are three for $26. Either way, you need eight pairs of maternity underwear, plus six bras, including regular/nursing and sleep bras.

Total damage: $480 to $580. If you think that's too much money for clothes you'll only wear for a few months, consider the cost if you outfit yourself at full-retail maternity shops. The same selection of outfits would run $1200 to $1400.

If you plan to breastfeed, we strongly recommend either renting a piston electric pump (about $45 per month) or purchasing the Medela Pump In Style (about $200). The other pumps (manual or mini-electrics) are inefficient and a waste of money, except for very occasional uses.

We found all major brands of formula to be virtually identical—except for the price. Like diapers, this item is most expensive in grocery stores . . . and least expensive in discount stores like Wal-Mart.

Questions or comments? Did you discover a bargain you'd like to share? Call the authors at (303) 442-8792 or e-mail adfields@aol.com! Updates to this book are posted at *www.windsorpeak.com*

Chapter 6

Around the House: Monitors, High Chairs, Swings & More

What's a "Flatobearius"? Which baby monitor looks like a space ship? Why do baby foods look like a sinister science experiment gone wrong? In this chapter, we explore everything for baby that's around the house. From a basic list of toys to which baby monitors are best, we'll give you tricks and tips to saving money. You'll learn seven safety tips for toys and which new brand of baby food is sweeping the country. Finally, we've got reviews of the best high chairs, a new swing that's pretty cool, and even tips for making sure pet and baby get along.

Getting Started: When Do You Need This Stuff?

 The good news is you don't need all this stuff right away. While you'll probably purchase a monitor before the baby is born, other items like high chairs, activity seats, and even bathtime products aren't necessary immediately (you'll give the baby sponge baths for the first few weeks, until the belly button area heals).While you may not need some items immediately, it still may be more convenient to shop for home and bath items before the baby is born. In each section of this chapter, we'll be more specific about when you need certain items.

What Are You Buying?

 Here is a selection of items that you can use when your baby is three to six months of age. Of course, these ideas are merely suggestions—none of these items are "mandatory." We've divided them into three categories: bath-time, the baby's room and toys.

Bath

1 TOYS/BOOKS. What fun is it taking a bath without toys? Many stores sell inexpensive plastic tub toys, but you

can also use other items like stacking cups in the tub as well. And don't forget about tub safety items, which can also double as toys. For example, Safety 1st (800) 739-7233 makes a *"Bath Pal Thermometer,"* a yellow duck or tug boat with attached thermometer (to make sure the water isn't too hot) for $3. *Tubbly Bubbly* by Kel-Gar (214) 250-3838 is an elephant or hippo spout cover that protects against scalding. In fact, Kel-Gar makes an entire line of innovative bath toys and accessories.

2 TOILETRIES. Basic baby shampoo like the famous brand made by Johnson & Johnson works just fine, and you'll probably need some lotion as well. The best tip: first try lotion that is unscented in case your baby has any allergies. Also, never use talcum powder on your baby—it's a health hazard. If you need to use a absorbent powder, good old corn starch will do the trick.

What about those natural baby products that are all the rage, like Mustela or the Mama Toto line from the Body Shop? We got a gift basket for our baby of the Body Shop's expensive potions, and—sorry, all you granola heads out there—we didn't like them. The shampoo dried out our baby's hair so much he had scratching fits. Another negative: they don't have a no-tears formula, which is no fun whatsoever. We suppose the biggest advantage of these products is that they don't contain mineral oil and petroleum by-products. Also, most don't have perfumes, but then, many regular products now come in unscented versions. The bottom line: it's your comfort level. If you want to try them out without making a big investment, ask for them as a shower gift.

3 THE MEDICINE CABINET. In Chapter 8, we discuss what you need in your baby's medicine cabinet.

Baby's Room

1 A DIAPER PAIL. As you know, we're big fans of the *Diaper Genie* (reviewed earlier in Chapter 4). If the idea of buying refill packages sounds too expensive, however, both Safety 1st and Fisher Price make "odor free" diaper pails that use regular kitchen trash bags. Parents tell us these work fine, but we still think the Diaper Genie does the best job of eliminating odors. Of course, different folks have different tolerances for this—some readers of our last edition said they merely used a regular trash can with a lid and took out the trash each day.

2 MONITOR. Later in this chapter, we have a special section devoted to monitors, including some creative

money-saving tips. Of course, if you have a small house or apartment, you may not even need a baby monitor.

3 THE CHANGING AREA. The well-stocked changing area features much more than just diapers. Nope, you need wipes and lots of them. Our favorite brand is ***Baby Fresh*** (about $4 for a 126-count box at Toys R Us). Store brands of wipes are cheaper, but are of inferior quality—they're thinner, less absorbent, etc. Other mothers we've interviewed like ***Huggies Wipes*** ($3.69 for a 120-count box at Toys R Us). We stocked up with ten boxes of wipes before the baby was born and soon found ourselves at the store to buy more. Why? Inexperienced parents can go through four or five wipes per diaper change. Most brands come in scented and unscented versions and some have aloe or lotion.

We should note that we've heard from some thrifty parents who've made their own diaper wipes—they use old wash-cloths or cut-up old cloth diapers and warm water.

Now that you've got the poop on wipes (sorry), here's another item to consider: a diaper-wipe warmer. Ever change a baby's diaper with a cold wipe at three in the morning? If so, you'd fork over the $25 for one of these devices, which wrap around the wipe box and warm it to a toasty 99 degrees. The ***Comfy Wipe Warmer*** features a machine-washable, quilted cover that attaches to wipe boxes with Velcro. Retail is $24.99, but we found it for as little as $19.50 on sale. Another good brand is ***Dex*** (for a store near you, call 800-546-1996 or 707-748-4199), which makes a wipe warmer for about the same prices as Comfy. We tried out both the Comfy and Dex wipe warm-ers and give the edge to Dex—their product kept the wipes warmer and fit the box better.

Other products to consider for the diaper changing station include diaper covers (if you're using cloth), diaper rash oint-ment (A & D, Desitin, etc.), lotion or cream, cotton swabs, petroleum jelly (for rectal thermometers) and rubbing alcohol to care for the belly button area. Another excellent product to consider: ***BabySmart's*** (800) 756-5590 or (908) 766-4900 wipes and diaper holders. Made of lucite, each clips on to the edge of your changing table. The wipes holder is about $7 and the diaper holder is $16.

4 PORTABLE CRIBS/PLAYPENS. While this item doesn't nec-essary go in your baby's room, many folks have found portable cribs/playpens to be indispensable in other parts of the house (or when visiting grandma's). Later in this chap-ter, we have a special section devoted to this topic.

Toys

1 STACKING CUPS. Once your baby starts to reach for objects, a nice set of stacking cups can supply endless hours of fun—although we had second thoughts about whether we'd later regret teaching our son to knock over objects. Sage insight or the ramblings of a first-time parent? Anyway, you can find a set of stacking cups at grocery stores, toy stores and chains like Toys R Us. Cost: about $5. Speaking of affordable toys, we also liked the *Lamaze* line of baby toys by Learning Curve (800) 704-8697 (internet: www.learning-toys.com). These fun developmental toys (categorized by age) include a puzzle ball, soft stacking rings and more.

2 MOBILE FOR CRIB. Sure, a mobile sounds like the perfect accessory for any crib, but how do you choose one? Here's our best advice: look at it from underneath. It's surprising to see the number of flat two-dimensional mobiles out there—get underneath them and look from the baby's perspective and what do you see? Nothing—the objects seem to disappear! The best mobiles are more three-dimensional. Our favorite brand: *Dakin by Applause* (call 800-777-6990 for a dealer near you). Their colorful and fun mobiles retail for $50 to $60 and are widely available. We liked the Panda Bear/Stars mobile the best. Another, less expensive brand of mobile we liked was made by Dolly (call 800-758-7520 for a dealer near you). At only $20, the three-dimensional design was a great buy. New this year is the *Fisher Price "Magic Motion"* mobile ($25) which features beads and butterflies that swirl around a rotating ring and mirror. Best of all, unlike other mobiles that have to be removed from the crib when baby starts to sit up, this one is safe for use up to 24 months and even later detaches from its base to become a musical floor toy.

3 ACTIVITY CENTER/BUSY BOX. Ah, the old stand-by. This venerable toy (about $15) features various spinning balls, bells, phone dialer, squeakers, etc.—all attached to molded plastic. One famous brand is the *Fisher Price Activity Center*, which has been around since 1973. While the current version features bright, primary colors, we've seen older ones in consignment stores dating back to the '70s—in such baby-friendly colors as avocado green and harvest gold. We wonder if playing with toys in such colors contributed to the warped sensibilities of Generation X. Just a thought.

On a more practical note, the Fisher Price Activity Center (like other toys) has a strap that enables you to attach it to the crib. We found two problems with this: first, it's hard to do, since the crib's bumper pads may be in the way. Also, such crib toys make it difficult to put the baby down to sleep—any time you touch the crib, the toy makes a sound, and the baby might wake up. Our advice: plan on using "noisy" toys outside the crib.

4 ACTIVITY GYM. Among our favorites is the *Gymfinity* by Today's Kids. What most impressed us about the Gymfinity is its versatility. First, it's an infant toy bar, which dangles high-contrast toys for the baby to play with from underneath. Then, it converts to a toddler play table, with puzzle pieces, interlocking gears, and other fun activities for kids through age three. The only drawback to the Gymfinity: its hefty retail price ($45.95) is somewhat hard to swallow. The best price we saw: $37.99 from the Baby Catalog of America (1-800-PLAY-PEN). Even when you factor in the shipping and handling at $6.95, you still come out somewhat ahead. We should also note we've seen the Gymfinity on special at local stores from time to time for as little as $30. Another company that makes a similar product is the Gymini by Tiny Love. The *"Gymini Activity Arch"* (about $30) can either be attached over the crib (for babies under five months) or to the side of the crib for older babies. The company also makes the *"Gymini 3-D Activity Gym"* which is an activity blanket and toy bar in one ($45). Both of these products are also available at a discount from the Baby Catalog of America.

5 ACTIVITY SEAT/BOUNCER WITH TOY BAR. An activity seat (also called a bouncer) provides a comfy place for baby while you eat dinner, and the toy bar adds some mild amusement. The *Playtime Bouncer Seat with Toy Bar* by Summer runs about $50 retail. Optional accessories include matching canopy (about $15) and head rest ($12). Another parent told they couldn't live with their *Fisher Price "Soothing Bouncer Seat"* (about $27 to $35). The seat has a batter-powdered vibrator (sort of like baby version of "Magic Fingers") that simulates a car side. Here's another money-saving tip: turn your infant car seat into an activity center with an attachable toy bar. Children on the Go (for a dealer near you, call 847-537-3797) makes a toy bar with rattles and spinning toys for just $10 to $15. Two elastic straps attach to any brand infant carrier and the product is available in primary colors or black and white. Another plus: your baby is safer in an infant car seat carrier than in other activity seats, thanks to that industrial-strength harness safety system.

6 TAPE PLAYER. Gotta have something to play those Raffi tapes on. Actually, there is quite a selection of

musical tapes for babies that are less irritating than you might think. (Check out the Music for Little People catalog, 800-727-2233, reviewed in Chapter 10). Look for a tape player designed specifically for use with small children. Such products have child-safe battery compartments and simple controls. Most of the "general" baby catalogs mentioned in this book carry a tape player or two for about $20.

7 SELECTION OF BOOKS. As book authors, we'd be remiss if we didn't recommend that you buy lots of books for your baby. Visit your local bookstore, and you'll find stiff board books (easier for young hands to turn or, at least, not destroy) as well as squishy cloth books. There are even books made of vinyl to make bathtime more fun. Although you can find such books at general bookstores, many towns have bookstores that specialize in children's books; look under "bookstores" in the phone book to find one near you. Used bookstores are another excellent source as are book sales at libraries and other charity events.

8 FLATOBEARIUS. Our hip California cousins Ken and Elizabeth Troy turned us on to this adorable line of small stuffed animal rattles. *"Flatobearius"* is a flat, squishy bear rattle, part of the "Flato" series from North American Bear Co. (to find a dealer near you, call 800-682-3427 or 312-329-0020). Once you get hooked, you'll have to acquire the entire collection of animal rattles—flatopup, flatjack (a rabbit), and squishy fish to name a few. The small flato rattles are about $9 to $12 (not cheap, but worth it), and they even have a couple of larger versions that cost $25 to $55.

Discovery Toys

When our son Jack was born, we received a box of Discovery Toys as a gift and were quite impressed. The line of developmental toys, books and games (sold through local representatives; call 800-426-4777 in the U.S. or 800-267-0477 in Canada for more information) are featured in an 80+ page catalog that relates how items develop certain skills. You'll find toys that teach "thinking/learning," "creativity," "senses and perception" and more—the catalog features little symbols to point out the skills each item promotes.

Safe & Sound for Toys

 Walk through any toy store and the sheer variety will boggle your mind. Buying toys for a newborn infant requires more careful planning than for older children. Here are seven tips to keep your baby safe and sound:

1 MAKE SURE STUFFED ANIMALS HAVE SEWN EYES. A popular gift from friends and relatives, stuffed animals can be a hazard if you don't take a few precautions. Buttons or other materials for eyes that could be removed by the baby present a choking hazard—make sure you give the stuffed animal the once over before putting it in the crib.

2 BEWARE OF RIBBONS. Another common decoration on stuffed animals, remove any ribbons before giving the toy to your baby.

3 MAKE SURE TOYS HAVE NO STRINGS LONGER THAN 12 INCHES—another easily avoided strangulation hazard.

4 WOODEN TOYS SHOULD HAVE NON-TOXIC FINISHES. If in doubt, don't give such toys to your baby. The toy's packaging should specify the type of finish.

5 BATTERY COMPARTMENTS SHOULD HAVE A SCREW CLOSURE. Tape players (and other battery-operated toys) should not give your baby easy access to batteries—a compartment that requires a screw driver to open is a wise precaution.

6 BE CAREFUL OF CRIB TOYS. Some of these toys are designed to attach to the top or sides of the crib. The best advice: remove them after the baby is finished playing with them. Don't leave the baby to play with crib toys unsupervised, especially once she begins to pull or sit up.

7 DO NOT USE WALKERS. And if you get one as a gift, take it back to the store and exchange it for something that isn't a death trap. Exactly what are these invitations to disaster? A walker suspends your baby above the floor, enabling him or her to "walk" by rolling around on wheels. The only problem: babies tend to "walk" right into walls, down staircases, and into other brain damage-causing obstacles. It's a scandal that walkers haven't been banned by the Consumer Products Safety Commission. How many injuries are caused by these things? Are you sitting down? 25,000 a year! Why juvenile products manufacturers continue churning out these death traps is beyond us.

What are the alternatives to walkers? Several companies are marketing "stationary activity centers" that provide all the fun with none of the injury. One of the best is the Exersaucer by Evenflo—babies can bounce, rock, stand, sit, and play, thanks to a rotating seat that has three height adjustments. The only disadvantages: it's bulky (you need a pretty big area to set it up), and it's expensive—$50 to $70 retail. Fortunately, there are several versions of the Exersaucer with different prices and you can often find it on sale at places like Toys R Us.

The Excersaucer has been such a hit that other companies have rushed into the "stationary activity center" market. Among the better offerings is Baby Trend's "Play in Place" Excerciser, Graco's "Stationary Entertainer with Bouncer" and Summer's "Play it Safe" with a seat that both bounces and swivels. Each of these products retails for $80 to $100, but we found them in Baby Catalog of America (800) PLAYPEN for just $60 to $63.

Money-Saving Secrets

1 CHILDREN'S BOOK CLUBS OFFER BIG SAVINGS. For example, we joined the Dr. Seuss book club and received eight hardcover books for $1.99. You agree to buy eight more at $4.99 per book—a 28% savings off the retail price. The bottom line: you get 16 books for about $3.50 per book (including shipping); they even throw in a free stand. And we're talking all the classics, like "Green Eggs and Ham." Write to Dr. Seuss and His Friends, the Beginning Readers' Program, Grolier Books, Sherman Turnpike, Danbury, CT 06814, for more information. As mentioned earlier in this chapter, library sales and used bookstores are also great sources for children's books at low prices.

2 SHOP AT BABY MEGA-STORES. For the best prices on monitors, toys, high chairs, and just about everything else you need around the house, check out the prices of those baby mega-stores like LiL' Things (817) 649-6100, Baby Superstore (864) 962-9292 and Baby Depot (609) 386-3314. We found their prices to be 20% to 30% less than specialty shops—and even less than traditional discounters like Wal-Mart and K-Mart. Best of all, they have the best name brands, which you can't find at the discount stores. (The exception to this rule: Target, which has beefed up its name-brand offerings for baby equipment at good prices).

3 CHECK OUT TOYS R US. They don't always have the lowest price, but we like Toys R Us for their selection. Sure, you'd expect lots of toys, but we were surprised by the wide

assortment of items like baby monitors and swings. Best of all, they tend to keep everything in stock, so you can get it and go. Unfortunately, the service (or lack thereof) means you're pretty much on your own. Nonetheless, if you know what you're looking for, it's hard to beat Toys R Us.

4 DON'T FORGET CONSIGNMENT STORES. A great item to find at second-hand stores specializing in children's clothing and products: mobiles. Most aren't handled by babies so they're in excellent condition—at prices that are typically 50% or more off retail. We found quite a few in our local baby consignment store for $10 to $20; compare that to the $50 retail price these fetch at specialty stores. Since you tend to use a mobile for such a short period of time, you can then re-consign it at the shop and get some money back! Of course, these stores sell much more than mobiles—you can pick up toys, high chairs, and, of course, clothes at tremendous savings. Check your phone book under "Consignment" or "Thrift Stores"; many also list under "Clothes & Accessories—Infant & Child—Retail." Another great source for bargains: garage sales. Refer back to Chapter 4 for more tips on shopping garage/yard sales.

5 GO FOR REFILLABLE PACKAGES. Take diaper wipes, for example. You can often buy refillable packages of wipes to fit into those plastic boxes. The savings: about 20% off the cost of buying a new box. And you save another plastic box from the landfill.

6 GET A PRICE QUOTE FROM THE BABY CATALOG OF AMERICA. The catalog (which can be ordered by calling 800-752-9736) has fantastic prices on high chairs, toys, swings, and even baby monitors. They also carry items that aren't in the catalog; call to see if they carry the brand you're looking for.

7 CHECK OUT SUAVE BABY CARE PRODUCTS. Helene Curtis recently introduced an entire line of baby care products under their Suave brand name—and the prices are amazing. In Celina, Ohio, a Wal-Mart store sells Suave baby wipes for just $1.87 (80-count box). Compare that to Baby Fresh at $2.37 for the same quantity—a 20% savings! You can also find great deals on Suave baby lotion, shampoos, and powders. Our slogan on baby care products is "never pay retail." Savvy shoppers avoid grocery stores for these items and instead shop discounters like Wal-Mart, K-Mart, Target, and Drug Emporium—even warehouse clubs like Sam's Club and Price/Costco will carry some baby care basics.

8 REUSE THAT MOBILE. Safety experts say crib mobiles should be removed when baby starts to sit up. Why? Those strings can be a strangulation hazard. But that doesn't mean you have to consign the mobile to a garage sale. Instead, reuse it—we hung ours over the changing table to entertain baby during those zillion diaper changes.

Wastes of Money

1 FANCY TOYS. We interviewed one couple who bought a fancy set of expensive toys for their infant daughter, only to be dismayed that she didn't want to play with them. What did baby really like to play with? Their keys. The lesson: sometimes it's the simple, inexpensive things in life that are the most fun.

2 FANCY BOOKS. Walk through any children's section in your local bookstore and you'll see a zillion children's books, all lavishly illustrated and beautifully packaged. And do you know what most babies want to do with books? Eat them. We liked the suggestion that one mom discovered when it came to books: many popular hardcover children's books come in softcover or paperback versions, at substantially lower prices. That way if Junior decides his favorite book looks like lunch one day, you're not out as much money. Board books (and even cloth books) are good to chew on too.

3 FANCY BURP PADS. Do you really need to spend $5 on a burp pad—a scientifically designed piece of cloth for you to put on your shoulder to keep spit-up off your clothes when Junior burps? No, just put a cloth diaper on your shoulder (average price 50¢ or less) and save the money.

4 BLACK AND WHITE MOBILES. Yes, they are all the rage today. True, your baby is attracted to high-contrast black and white images in the first four months, and such mobiles may be quite fascinating. But $20-$40 seems like a lot of money to be spent on an item that's used for just four months. We liked the money-saving suggestion from one dad we interviewed: he drew patterns with a black pen on white index cards and then attached the cards to a regular color mobile. The baby liked the improved version just fine, and the parents saved $20 to $40. (One safety tip: make sure the cards are attached firmly to the mobile. And, as always, remove all mobiles from the crib after five months when your baby sits up). Another money-saving tip: forget the mobile altogether. Some parents we interviewed said their baby got along fine without one.

5 BABY BATH TUB. Save the $15 to $25 that these tubs cost and just give your baby a bath in the kitchen sink. Or bring the baby into the bathtub with you. Not everyone agrees with this tip, however. One reader of our last edition wrote that she tried giving her baby a bath in the kitchen sink and found it awkward. She couldn't both hold the baby and wash him at the same time. That's true—it's best to have two people to do the job (one to hold the baby, the other to wash). If you're find yourself bathing baby alone, a baby bath tub may not be a bad investment (buy one second-hand or at a garage sale if you can). Another solution: the Comfy-Bear Foam Bath Cushion (available in Baby Catalog of America 800-PLAYPEN) is a $5 two-inch thick foam cushion that supports baby while you bathe her in the sink or tub.

Monitors

For her first nine months, your baby is tethered to you via the umbilical cord. After that, it's the baby monitor that becomes your surrogate umbilical cord—enabling you to work in the garden, wander about the house, and do many things that other, childless human beings do, while still keeping tabs on a sleeping baby. Hence, this is a pretty important piece of equipment you'll use every day—a good one will make your life easier and a bad one will be a never-ending source of irritation.

Smart Shopper Tips for Monitors

Smart Shopper Tip #1
BUGGING YOUR HOUSE

"My neighbor and I both have babies and baby monitors. No matter what we do, I can still pick up my neighbor's monitor on my receiver. Can they hear our conversations too?"

You better bet. Let's consider what a baby monitor really is: a radio transmitter. The base unit is the transmitter and the receiver is, well, a receiver. So anyone with another baby monitor can pick up your monitor—not just the sound of your baby crying, but also any conversations you have with your mate about diaper changing technique.

You'll notice that many monitors have two channels "to reduce interference," and some even have high and low range settings—do they help reduce interference eavesdropping? No, not in our opinion. In densely populated areas, you can still have problems.

We should note that you can also pick up baby monitors

on many cordless phones—even police scanners can pick up signals as far as one or two miles away. The best advice: remember that your house (or at least, your baby's room) is bugged. If you want to protect your privacy, don't have any sensitive conversations within earshot of the baby monitor. You never know who might be listening.

Another solution: some new baby monitors work on the 900 Mhz frequency. While it doesn't preclude eavesdropping, the 900 Mhz baby monitors may be a better bet to avoid static and interference from other radio sources.

Smart Shopper Tip #2
BATTERY WOES

"Boy, we should have bought stock in Duracell when our baby was born! We go through dozens of batteries each month to feed our very hungry baby monitor."

Most baby monitors have the option of running on batteries or on regular current (by plugging it into a wall outlet). Our advice: use the wall outlet as often as possible. Batteries don't last long (maybe a day or two with constant use) in baby monitors. You can buy another AC adapter from a source like Radio Shack for $10 or less—you can leave one AC adapter in your bedroom and have another one available in a different part of the house.

What about those rechargeable batteries? They're more hassle than they're worth—you have to change (and recharge) them so often, it's not worth the savings. We haven't experimented yet with the new alkaline rechargeable batteries, but several readers tell us they're better than the nickel rechargeables.

Another solution: several new baby monitors (reviewed later in this chapter) feature rechargeable receivers! You'll never buy a set of batteries for these units.

Smart Shopper Tip #3
CORDLESS COMPATIBILITY

"We have a cordless phone and a baby monitor. Boy, it took us two weeks to figure out how to use both without having a nervous breakdown."

If we could take a rocket launcher and zap one person in this world, it would have to be the idiot who decided that baby monitors and cordless phones should share the same radio frequency. What were they thinking? Gee, let's take two people who are already dangerously short of sleep and make them real frustrated!

After hours of experimentation, we have several tips. First, make sure your cordless phone has the ability to switch among 10 channels to find the clearest reception. If you don't have this feature, you may find your phone and monitor are always in conflict, no matter how times you flip that "Channel A or B" switch on the baby monitor.

Another tip: consider buying one of those new cordless phones that work on the 900 Mhz frequency—then you'll be assured there won't be any interference since they won't share the same frequency. (For techno-heads out there, most cordless phones and baby monitors work on the 46 to 49 Mhz radio frequency). The only disadvantage to this tip is that the new 900 Mhz cordless phones can be pricey—as much as twice the cost of regular cordless phones.

Always keep the receipt for any baby monitor you buy—you may have to take it back and exchange it for another brand if you find the interference is too much for you. It sure would be nice if manufacturers of cordless phones and baby monitors would label their products with the radio frequency they use, so you could spot conflicts before they happen.

Smart Shopper Tip #4
THE ONE-WAY DILEMMA

"Our baby monitor is nice, but it would be great to be able to buzz my husband so he could bring me something to drink while I'm feeding the baby. Are there any monitors out there that let you communicate two ways?"

Nope, not that we found in our research. To get two-way communication, you need to buy an intercom. We decided it was worth the investment after we got tired of shouting back and forth between the baby's room and our living room.

Radio Shack sells a basic intercom for about $40—you can "call" the other unit and have two-way conversations. Most also have a "lock" feature that you can leave on to listen to the baby when he's sleeping. Of course, the only disadvantage to intercoms is that they aren't portable; most must be plugged into a wall outlet. Another advantage to intercoms: you can always deploy the unit to another part of your house after you're done monitoring the baby.

The Name Game: Reviews of Selected Manufacturers

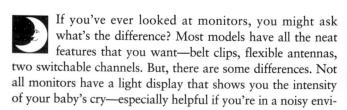 If you've ever looked at monitors, you might ask what's the difference? Most models have all the neat features that you want—belt clips, flexible antennas, two switchable channels. But, there are some differences. Not all monitors have a light display that shows you the intensity of your baby's cry—especially helpful if you're in a noisy envi-

ronment and can't hear the monitor. Some new models have rechargeable batteries, work on the clearer 900 Mhz frequency, have hidden antennas and more.

By the way, most of these monitors are available at Toys R Us, where we found the best selection and lowest prices. Use the phone numbers listed below to call to find a dealer near you (most manufacturers don't sell directly to the public).

The Ratings

★★★★ EXCELLENT— our top pick!
★★★ GOOD—above average quality, prices, and creativity.
★★ FAIR—could stand some improvement.
★ POOR—yuck! could stand some major improvement.

First Years ....★★★★
To find a dealer near you, call (800) 225-0382 or (508) 588-1220. If we had to give an award for the most innovative baby monitors on the market, it would have to go to First Years—their products have more features at better prices than most competitors. Their "Crisp and Clear" monitor ($50, new for 1997) features rechargeable batteries, 900 Mhz frequency for better reception and a sound/light display. Best of all, the receiver has an all-but-non-existent antenna. We tested an early version of this monitor (the Rechargeable monitor with sound-activated lights, $40) and were impressed. It worked well and we loved the lack of antenna—it looked like a small pager attached to your belt. Our only complaint: the unit wasn't as sensitive as the Fisher Price Sound N Lights and sometimes static interfered with reception. These problems may be solved with the new Crisp and Clear's 900 Mhz frequency.

Fisher Price ....★★★★
To find a dealer near you, call (800) 828-4000 or (716) 687-3000. The "Sound 'N Lights" monitor is our favorite—it's got everything you want at a decent price (about $40). The variable light display is great. The unit also features "high/low range selector for added privacy," a belt clip, and more. We've used this product extensively and found it is the most sensitive monitor available on the market today (not counting the new 900 Mhz monitors, which we haven't tested yet). Besides the Sound N Lights monitor, Fisher Price also makes a rechargeable model (the Cordless Nursery Monitor) and a basic unit without the light feature (the Super-Sensitive Nursery Monitor).

Gerry ....★★
*To find a dealer near you, call (800) 525-2472 or (303) 457-
0926.* Gerry's "Range Check" monitor ($40) does have a
unique feature—it sports a button on the parent's receiver
that lets you check to make sure you haven't strayed too far
from the transmitter. The unit features a round antenna for
portability and has a sound/light display. Gerry's "Clear
Choice" monitor has rechargeable batteries and a sound/light
display, but is so bulky that we wonder how useful it is. A
better designed unit may be the Gerry "Lights, Sound,
Action" monitor featuring a compact receiver with a "fold
and lock" antenna and "fiber optic sound lights that are easy
to see." While we liked Gerry's offerings, the company suffered a public relations black eye recently when they had to
recall a million monitors whose improper wiring caused at
least one fire. While the recalled monitors were made in 1988
to 1990 and are no longer on the market, this gaffe has made
us pause in recommending Gerry's monitors.

Safety 1st ....★
*To find a dealer near you, call (800) 962-7233 or (617)
964-7744.* We got a Safety 1st monitor as a gift and used it
for about a week before we couldn't resist the urge to
smash it into electronic pulp. Why? The monitor didn't
have a continuous transmission system; when the baby
would cry, it would trip the monitor, which would turn on
with a loud BRAAPPP! It sounded like a CB radio from
hell, but much more obnoxious. We could only take so
much torture before we permanently unplugged it. To be
nice, we should note that Safety 1st has come out with new
models that fix this problem and now have "continuous
transmission." The line's least expensive offering is a basic
model (The Lightweight Cordless Nursery Monitor) with
no lights or other special doo-dads. If you want a rechargeable monitor, Safety 1st has a new model which does that—
plus, it has a sound/light display and even monitors the
baby's room temperature. Safety 1st also makes a 900 Mhz
monitor (the SuperSound 900, $60) and a Deluxe Musical
Nursery Monitor ($35), which has a sound-activated sys-
tem that "responds to baby's sounds with one of four pre-
selected soothing tunes to generally lull a child back to
sleep." While we appreciate Safety 1st's attempt at innovation in this category, our experience with Safety 1st has left
such a bitter aftertaste that we just can't recommend their
baby monitors. The sensitivity of their new models is still
suspect—parents tell us other brands pick up subtle sounds
(coughs, sneezes) much better.

Do you need a baby surveillance camera?

It may sound Orwellian, but there are several companies that offer *video* nursery monitors. Smart Choice (800) 444-6278 or (972) 280-9380, Fisher Price and Safety 1st offer a way for you to both hear *and* see your child. Each has a wireless camera that sends a black and white picture (with sound) to a parent's monitor in another room. Unfortunately, these baby surveillance cameras come with a hefty price tag—Safety 1st's monitor is about $200; Fisher Price and Smart Choice's Baby Cam are about $300. So, are they worth it? Well, we tested a Smart Choice Baby Cam and thought it worked OK. A low-light sensor lets you see grainy pictures at night (*Consumer Reports* says that Fisher Price's camera worked somewhat better in low-light situations than the Baby Cam, though). For most parents, however, a video monitor is probably overkill. We found we could tell whether our child really needed us based on his different cries—no picture was necessary. While it was nice to see whether baby was standing up in the crib (and having a full-blown fit) or merely crying themselves to sleep, we wonder if this product is really necessary. Another bummer: we found the wireless camera interfered with our home security system (apparently they transmit on similar frequencies). On the upside, you can always move the camera outside as a video front door monitor later in life. And parents who have pools or kids with medical problems that need constant monitoring might find video monitors to be helpful.

Sony ....★★½

Like most gadgets that Sony sells, their "Baby Call" monitor is an attractive unit but grossly overpriced. We liked the rounded antenna (on both the transmitter and receiver), but it's missing a sound-activated light display. And the price (about $45 to $50) is too much for us to handle. We should note, however, that we did find it at the Baby Superstore for $39.

Other Brands. *Graco* (800) 345-4109, (610) 286-5951, the juvenile products giant best known for strollers and playpens, will debut its first baby monitor in 1997. The company claims its "Ultra Monitor" will utilize new technology to eliminate interference and feature a sound/lights display. We saw a prototype of the monitor when it was displayed at a juvenile products show and thought it looked OK. It didn't seem particularly innovative (no rechargeable batteries or hidden antenna). Whether it really offers an improvement over existing monitors or is just a "me-too" product remains to be seen.

Pet Meets Baby

If you already have a dog and are now expecting a baby, you're probably wondering how your "best friend" is going to react to the new family addition. Doubtless you've heard stories about how a dog became so jealous of its new "sibling" that the dog had to be given away. How can you avoid this situation?

Here are seven tips on smoothing the transition.

1 IF THE DOG HASN'T BEEN OBEDIENCE TRAINED, DO IT NOW. Even if you feel confident that your dog is well trained, a refresher course can't hurt.

2 DON'T OVERCOMPENSATE. You may start feeling guilty while you're pregnant because you won't be able to spend as much time with Fido after the baby comes. So what mistake do expectant parents make? They overcompensate and give the dog extra attention before the baby arrives. Do this and then the dog *really* misses you and resents the new baby. While it might seem counter-intuitive, gradually give your best friend less attention so he or she can adjust before baby comes.

3 IF YOUR DOG HAS NEVER BEEN AROUND BABIES AND SMALL CHILDREN, now is the time to introduce him—before your baby is born.

4 CONSIDER BUYING A BABY DOLL. Why? If you practice loving and attending to a baby doll for a few weeks prior to your baby's actual arrival, your dog can begin to get used to you paying attention to small bundles wrapped up in blankets. We did this, and our dog ZuZu got over her curiosity about it quickly. By the time the baby arrived, she didn't much care what we were carrying around (as long as it didn't smell like doggie biscuits!).

5 BEFORE THE BABY COMES HOME FROM THE HOSPITAL, have a friend or relative bring home a blanket or piece of clothing the new baby has slept on or worn in the hospital. This helps the dog get used to the smell of the new addition before you bring on the actual baby. We put a blanket the baby slept on in our dog's kennel, and we really think it helped smooth the transition.

6 STRATEGIES FOR BRINGING BABY HOME. Make sure your dog is under control when you first come home with your new baby (on a leash or under voice command). Greet your four-legged friend first, *without* the baby. This allows your dog to release some of his excitement and jumping (remember he hasn't seen you for a few days), without you worrying about the dog harming a baby in your arms. Next, Dad should hold the dog by

the collar or leash while Mom shows Fido the baby. Give your dog time to sniff a little, but don't let the dog turn the situation into a lick-fest. If everything looks OK, you can release the dog.

7 NEVER LEAVE THE DOG ALONE WITH THE BABY—especially if the dog has shown any signs of jealousy toward your child. Don't allow the dog to sleep under the crib (there have been incidents of dogs standing up and pushing the mattress off its supports, causing the mattress to crash to the floor).

Always supervise how your baby plays with the dog. For example, now that our son is older, he finds our Dalmatian very interesting. However, he tends to pull on her ears and tail whenever he gets a hold of them. So, we constantly encourage gentle petting and discourage grabbing.

What about cats?

Cats have recently surpassed dogs in popularity as America's favorite domestic pet. So as not to slight those cat lovers out there, here are three pieces of advice.

1 BEFORE YOU GET PREGNANT, HAVE YOUR CAT TESTED FOR TOXOPLASMOSIS, a disease that is caused by a parasitic organism that is transmitted to humans from cat feces. Toxoplasmosis is dangerous and may cause the fetus to become seriously ill or die.

If your cat is infected, have it boarded at a kennel or have someone take care of it for the period of infection (usually about six weeks). It's also best not to get pregnant during this time. You can avoid getting the infection yourself by having someone else clean out your cat's litter box. If you keep your cat indoors and he or she doesn't catch mice or birds outside, chances are the cat won't be infected (outdoor cats are more likely to be exposed to toxoplasmosis). Consult your doctor and your cat's veterinarian if you have any questions about this serious problem.

2 INTRODUCE YOUR CAT TO THE BABY SLOWLY. Similar to the way you would introduce a dog to your new baby, keep an eye on your cat's reactions. Don't leave your cat alone with the baby if you suspect any jealousy. Most cats will ignore the new addition with their usual aplomb.

3 CONSIDER USING A NET OVER YOUR BABY'S CRIB. Cats love to sleep in warm places and might decide to take up residence with your bundle of joy. Many of the safety catalogs we mention in Chapter 8 have crib nets and other items. Another idea: train your cat where *not* to go by using sticky tape on such items as the crib, changing table, etc.

Baby Food

At the tender age of four to six months, you and your baby will depart on a magical journey to a new place filled with exciting adventures and never-before-seen wonders. Yes, you've entered the SOLID FOOD ZONE.

Fasten your seat belts and get ready for a fun ride. As your tour guide, we would like to give a few pointers to make your stay a bit more enjoyable. Let's take stock:

Smart Shopper Tips on Mealtime Accessories

Smart Shopper Tip #1
TRACKING DOWN UFFOS (UNIDENTIFIABLE FLYING FOOD OBJECTS)

"We fed our baby rice cereal for the first time. It was really cute, except for the part when the baby picked up the bowl and flung it across the kitchen! Should we have bought some special stuff for this occasion?"

Well, unless you want your kitchen to be redecorated in Early Baby Food, we do have a few suggestions. First, a bowl with a bottom that suctions to the table is a great way to avoid flying saucers. Plastic spoons that have a round handle are nice, especially since baby can't stick the spoon handle in her eye (yes, that does happen—babies do try to feed themselves even at a young age). Spoons with rubber coatings are also nice; they don't transfer the heat or cold of the food to the baby's mouth and are easier on his gums. One of our favorite spoons is Munchin's "Soft Bite Safety Spoon" (call 800-344-2229 or 818-893-5000 to find a dealer near you). This spoon uses new technology to change color when baby's food is too hot (105 degrees or warmer). Neato!

Smart Shopper Tip #2
AVOIDING MEALTIME BATHS

"Our baby loves to drink from a cup, except for one small problem. Most of the liquid ends up on her, instead of in her. Any tips?"

Cups with weighted bottoms (about $5) help young infants to get the hang of this drinking thing. A sipping spout provides an interim learning step between bottle and regular cup. When your baby's older, we've found clear plastic cups to be helpful. Why? Your baby can see out the bottom and not feel like someone has turned out the lights.

No-spill cups are a godsend—Playtex (203) 341-4000 pioneered this category with a cup that doesn't leak when tipped over. While Playtex's cup is nice, it does have one drawback: the lid contains springs that make it difficult to clean. Other companies have solved this problem with better designs. For example, First Years' "Tumble Mates Spill-Proof Cup" is dishwasher safe and cleans easily (it has no springs).

The Name Game: Reviews of Selected Manufacturers

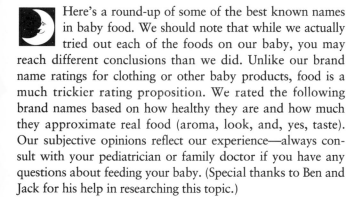 Here's a round-up of some of the best known names in baby food. We should note that while we actually tried out each of the foods on our baby, you may reach different conclusions than we did. Unlike our brand name ratings for clothing or other baby products, food is a much trickier rating proposition. We rated the following brand names based on how healthy they are and how much they approximate real food (aroma, look, and, yes, taste). Our subjective opinions reflect our experience—always consult with your pediatrician or family doctor if you have any questions about feeding your baby. (Special thanks to Ben and Jack for his help in researching this topic.)

The Ratings

★★★★ EXCELLENT—*our top pick!*
  ★★★ GOOD—*above average quality, prices, and creativity.*
    ★★ FAIR—*could stand some improvement.*
      ★ POOR—*yuck! could stand some major improvement.*

Earth's Best ....★★★1/2
(800) 442-4221. Internet: www.earthsbest.com If you're looking for jarred baby food but don't like brands that add sugar, salt, and other additives, then you've got to try Earth's Best. This company has a complete line of "natural" baby foods—all vegetables and grains are certified to be organically grown (no pesticides are used), and meats are raised without antibiotics or steroids. Earth's Best foods have no added sugars, salt, or modified food starches, plus they use whole grains (the only baby food to do so). Unfortunately, it isn't cheap— about twice as much as Gerber charges for a four-ounce jar. We tried Earth's Best and were generally pleased. Our only complaint: they tend to do a lot of "combo" foods, like the Vegetable Turkey Dinner with carrots, apples, turkey, and barley flour. The problem is you are supposed to introduce new foods to baby one food at a time. If the baby had an allergic reaction, was it the carrots or the turkey? Also, some of the dinners have corn, a highly allergenic food that is not

supposed to be introduced until your baby is 12 months old. Despite this problem and the lack of single food options, we really like Earth's Best—a much-needed natural alternative to the standard fare that babies have been fed for far too many years. A side note: Earth's Best, which started in Vermont and cultivated it's natural image in a move to Boulder, CO, was sold in 1996 to Heinz, one of the baby food giants. Heinz promises it will keep Earth's Best as an all-natural brand . . . but we'll be watching to make sure the standards don't slip. Heinz will be expanding Earth's Best distribution, which just reaches half of all mainstream grocery stores.

Gerber ....★
Dominating the baby food business with a whopping 70% market share (that's right, three out of every four baby food jars sold sport that familiar label), Gerber sure has come a long way from its humble beginnings. Back in 1907, Joseph Gerber (whose trade was canning) mashed up peas for his daughter, following the suggestion of a family doctor. We imagine those peas looked quite different from Gerber's peas today. Now, thanks to scientific progress, Gerber's peas are put through such a rigorous canning process that they don't even look like peas . . . instead more like green slime. And it's not just the look, have you actually smelled or tasted any of Gerber's offerings? Yuck. Sure it's cheap (about 30¢ for a 2 1/2 ounce jar of Gerber 1st Foods), but we just can't feed our baby this stuff with a clear conscience. On the upside, Gerber offers parents one key advantage: choice. The line boasts an amazing 200 different flavors. And we have to give Gerber credit: in 1996, the company announced it would respond to parents' concerns and reformulate it's baby food to eliminate starches, sugars and other fillers. Whether that will make Gerber's peas look more like the real thing remains to be seen.

Growing Healthy ....★★★★
2905 Northwest Blvd. #250, Plymouth, MN 55441. (800) 755-4999 or (612) 557-6088. Hands down, our pick for the best baby food is Growing Healthy, a fantastic line of frozen, all-natural baby food. Yes, you read right—it's frozen. Each package contains two individual trays that can be popped into the microwave to thaw. Best of all, it looks and tastes like real food . . . the carrots have a real orange color, the applesauce tastes like, well, applesauce. How do they do it? Well, they start with all-natural ingredients, don't add empty fillers and then "gently simmer and freeze" to retain "more of the nutrients and a delicious taste." Our baby just loves this stuff. We do wish there were more varieties, though. Growing Healthy divides its foods into three categories (strained fruits and cereals, strained

vegetables, and dinners) and has just 21 varieties total. As you might expect, it costs more than the jarred stuff, but we think it's worth it. The fruits run 79¢ for two, two-ounce servings, the veggies cost 91¢, and the dinners cost $1.30.

Perhaps the worst thing we can say about Growing Healthy is that it just isn't available in many places yet. Besides their home base of Minneapolis/St. Paul, the food is available in some stores in the Northeast, the Midwest (specifically, Chicago and parts of Wisconsin), Dallas, Denver and Arizona. That's it. Our advice: ask your grocer to get it in and make sure to check the freezer section— Growing Healthy is often separated from the rest of the other jarred baby foods since it is frozen.

If you can't find in stores, there is another option: The One Step Ahead catalog (800) 274-8440 will ship it directly to your home! Their "Growing Healthy" Club ships you a "master case" of 72 trays of baby food every three weeks (or as often as you wish). You choose the varieties and One Step Ahead ships it to you via second-day express delivery. Cost: $45.50, including shipping. If you're turned off by jarred baby food and are looking for a more healthy option, we can't recommend Growing Healthy highly enough.

Other Brands We Discovered. There are two other brands of baby food that are available regionally: Beech-Nut and Heinz. ***Beech-Nut*** says it doesn't add fillers (starches and sugars) to its 120 flavors, making it one of the few national brands not to so. Priced similar to Gerber, this baby food is only available in Florida, Ohio, Illinois, New York and California.

Heinz is probably the best bargain amongst the national baby food brands. A recent price survey revealed Heinz's baby food is typically 10% to 20% cheaper than Gerber. The company has more success selling baby food abroad then here in the U.S.—it's only available in the Southeastern and Central parts of the U.S. Another bummer: Heinz adds sugars and starches to many its foods. On the upside, Heinz recently announced it was reformulating some its products to eliminate the additives.

A reader called to tell us that the Amway catalog sells a natural brand of baby food called *J. R. Woods* with no added sugars or starches—we've yet to hear from any other parents with positive or negative experiences with this brand, though.

Have you found a brand of baby food that you (and your baby) just love? Since many brands are produced by small, regional manufacturers, we found tracking them down to be difficult. As a result, we'd love to hear from you if you've discovered a great brand. Call us at (303) 442-8792 to spread the word.

Safe & Sound

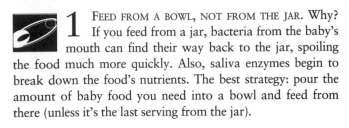 **1** FEED FROM A BOWL, NOT FROM THE JAR. Why? If you feed from a jar, bacteria from the baby's mouth can find their way back to the jar, spoiling the food much more quickly. Also, saliva enzymes begin to break down the food's nutrients. The best strategy: pour the amount of baby food you need into a bowl and feed from there (unless it's the last serving from the jar).

2 DON'T STORE FOOD IN PLASTIC BAGS. If you leave plastic bags on the baby's high chair, they can be a suffocation hazard. A better solution: store left-over food in small, plastic containers.

3 DO A TASTE TEST. Make sure it isn't too hot, too cold, or spoiled.

4 CHECK FOR EXPIRATION DATES. Gerber's jarred food looks like it would last through the next Ice Age, but check that expiration date. Most unopened baby food is only good for a year or two. Use opened jars within two to three days.

Money-Saving Tips

1 MAKE YOUR OWN. Let's be honest: baby food like mushed bananas is really just . . . mushed bananas. You can easily whip up this stuff with that common kitchen helper, the food processor. Many parents skip baby food altogether and make their own. One tip: make up a big batch at one time and freeze the left-overs in ice cube trays. Check the library for cookbooks that provide tips on making baby food at home.

2 BELIEVE IT OR NOT, TOYS R US SELLS BABY FOOD. If you think your grocery store is gouging you on the price of baby food, you might want to check out the prices at Toys R Us. We found Gerber 1st Foods in a four-pack of 2.5 ounce jars for $1.13—that works out to about 28¢ per jar or about 5% to 10% less than grocery store prices. Toys R Us also sells four-packs of assorted dinners from Gerber's 2nd and 3rd Food collections. If that weren't enough, you can also buy a case of Gerber formula (a dozen 13-ounce cans of concentrated liquid) for just $23.88—that's only $1.99 per can!

3 COUPONS! COUPONS! COUPONS! Yes, we've seen quite a few cents-off and buy-one-get-one-free coupons on baby food and formula—not just in the Sunday paper but

E-MAIL FROM THE REAL WORLD
Making your own baby food isn't time consuming

 A mom in New Mexico told us she found making her own baby food isn't as difficult as it sounds:

"My husband and I watch what we eat, so we definitely watch what our baby eats. One of the things I do is buy organic carrots, quick boil them, throw them in a blender and then freeze them in an ice cube tray. Once they are frozen, I separate the cubes into freezer baggies (they would get freezer burn if left in the ice tray). When mealtime arrives, I just throw them in the microwave. Organic carrots taste great! This whole process might sound complicated, but it only takes me about 20 minutes to do, and then another five to ten minutes to put the cubes in baggies."

also through the mail. Our advice: don't toss that junk mail until you've made sure you're not trashing valuable baby food coupons. Another coupon trick: look for "bounce-back" coupons. Those are the coupons put in the packages of baby food to encourage you to bounce back to the store and buy more.

4 BUY HEINZ. As noted above, Heinz baby food is often priced 10% to 20% below the competition. The only drawback: it isn't available everywhere. Heinz is mostly sold only in the Southeastern and Central U.S. Another problem: Heinz also has more starches and fillers (like sugar) than other brands. Hence, you're saving money, but giving your baby less protein, minerals and vitamins with each spoonful. Yet, if that doesn't bother you and the cheapest deal is your primary concern, try Heinz.

5 SUBSTITUTE COMPARABLE ADULT FOODS. What's the difference between adult applesauce and baby applesauce? Not much, except for the fact that applesauce in a jar with a cute baby on it costs several times more than the adult version. While the adult applesauce isn't fortified with extra vitamins, it probably doesn't matter. Baby will get these nutrients from other foods. Another rip-off: the "next step" foods for older babies. Gerber loves to tout it's special meals for older babies in its "Graduates" line. What's the point? When baby is ready to eat pasta, just serve him small bites of the adult stuff.

6 GO FOR THE BETTER QUALITY. That's a strange money-saving tip, isn't it? Doesn't better quality baby food (Growing Healthy or brands with fewer fillers) cost more? Yes, but look at it this way—the average baby eats 600 jars of baby food until they "graduate" to adult foods. Sounds like a lot of money, eh? Well, that only works out to $100 or so in total expenditures. Hence, if you go for the better-quality food and spend, say, 20% more, you're only out another $20. Therefore it might be better to spend the small additional dollars to give baby better-quality food.

High Chairs

As soon as Junior starts to eat solid food, you'll need this quintessential piece of baby furniture—the high chair. Surprisingly, this seemingly innocuous product generates nearly 9000 injuries each year. Hence, in this section, we'll look at how to buy a safe high chair and provide tips for proper use. And, as always, we'll give you some money-saving tips and a review of some of the most popular brands out there today.

Smart Shopper Tips for High Chairs

Smart Shopper Tip #1
HIGH CHAIR BASICS 101

"My mother insists I buy a high chair that looks like Captain Kirk's chair from Star Trek. I prefer something simpler, but every chair I see in the stores has to have some high-tech gimmick, converting into a toaster and so on. What's really important?"

Basically, the most important thing to look for in a high chair is one that doesn't tip over—the cause of many high chair injuries. The best chairs have a wide base. Another important item to check in the store is the tray release. Many brands advertise "one hand release," but the ease with which the tray really releases varies from maker to maker. Another wise tip: make sure the tray mechanism can't pinch your baby's fingers.

Beyond the basics, the hot trend in high chairs is convertibility—models that transform into hook-on seats, youth chairs, and even a table and chair set (sorry, no toasters, yet). The big decision you'll have to make: do you want a high chair that is height-adjustable? Without this feature, you'll spend $50 to $60. Chairs that adjust run $65 to $150. Is it worth it? We think so—you can adjust it to different table heights, using it in the standard position when the baby is young and then lowering it to table height as a youth chair when she gets older. If this feature is important to you, go for a chair that is fully height adjustable (not just a couple of preset positions).

Washability is another key feature to look for—make sure the high chair you buy has a removable washable seat cover OR a seat made of vinyl that you can sponge clean.

Smart Shopper Tip #2
TRAY CHIC AND OTHER RESTAURANT TIPS

"We have a great high chair at home, but we're always appalled at the lack of safe high chairs at restaurants. Our favorite cafe has a high chair that must date back to 1952—no straps, a metal tray with sharp edges, and a hard seat with no cushion. Are these people nuts or what?"

We think so. Restaurateurs must search obscure third world countries to find the world's most hazardous high chairs. The biggest problem? No straps, enabling babies to slide out of the chair, submarine-style. The solution? When the baby is young, keep them in their infant carseat; the safe harness keeps baby secure. When your baby is older (and if you eat out a lot), you may want to invest in a portable booster seat. The Evenflo Snack & Play II ($30, 800-837-9201) turns any chair into a high chair, with three height levels and a deep tray with anti-splash sides. Another solution might be Safety 1st's Compact Folding Booster Seat ($25), which folds up to half-size for portability. And if your favorite restaurant has a high chair with no straps, consider bringing your own: the Perfectly Safe catalog (800) 837-KIDS sells a high chair safety strap for $7.

The Name Game: Reviews of Selected Manufacturers

 Many high-tech high chairs feature height adjustments and extra-large feeding trays. While most are made of plastic and metal, there are still fans out there who like traditional wood chairs. In the southern U.S., wood chairs by Simmons and Child Craft (yes, they're the same names you saw in Chapter 2 in the crib reviews) still sell well, despite their lack of fancy features (you can't adjust the height, they doesn't fold up, etc.). Contrast that with upscale baby stores in East Coast cities where they can't keep foreign-made brands like Peg Perego in stock. In order to make everyone happy, here's a round-up of the different brands you'll encounter on your high-chair shopping excursion:

The Ratings

★★★★ EXCELLENT—*our top pick!*
  ★★★ GOOD—*above average quality, prices, and creativity.*
   ★★ FAIR—*could stand some improvement.*
    ★ POOR—*yuck! could stand some major improvement.*

Baby Trend .... ★★★★
1928 W. Holt Ave., Pomona, CA 91768. For a dealer near you, call (800) 328-7363 or (909) 469-1188. Internet: www.babynet.com Our pick as one of the best high chairs available today is the Home and Roam LX by Baby Trend. We like the thickly padded seat, extra-wide tray, and six-position height adjustment. It also has a two-position reclining seat for infant feeding and casters for easy maneuvering. The Home & Roam's big claim to fame is it's convertibility—the seat detaches and becomes a hook-on chair for Grandma's house or restaurants. To be honest, we didn't use this feature much . . . the chair is simply too bulky to take to restaurants and Grandma didn't have the right kind of table to hook it to. Nonetheless, we still liked Home & Roam. The one-handed tray release worked fine (it could be a little easier to release) and the height adjustments are easy to do. Available in white or a series of prints, the price is $100—not cheap, but it is some $50 less than our other top-rated high chair, Peg Perego's Prima Poppa (reviewed later). If you want to spend

---

Living the High Life

Hook-on chairs and booster seats are close relatives to the familiar high chair. Depending on your needs, each can serve a purpose. Hook-on chairs do exactly what they say—hook onto a table. While some have trays, most do not, and that is probably their biggest disadvantage: baby eats (or spills and throws food) on your table instead of hers. At least they're cheap: about $25 to $40 at most stores. Best use: if your favorite restaurants don't have high chairs (or don't have safe ones) or if you plan to do some road trips with Junior.

Booster seats are more useful. With or without an attached tray, most strap to a chair or can be used on the floor. We use ours at Grandma's house, which spares us the chore of dragging along a high chair or hook-on chair. It's also convenient to do evening feedings in a booster seat in the baby's room, instead of dragging everyone to the kitchen. And you can't beat the price: $18 to $30 at most stores. One of the better brands is the Evenflo Snack and Play, which comes in two models (one with a cushion, one with out). Their theme is "the neat little eat seat" that turns most any chair into a high chair. The Snack and Play features an adjustable tray and seat—pretty neat.

---

less money, Baby Trend does make a basic high chair model with a machine washable seat pad, six height adjustments and wheels. Compared to the Home & Roam, it doesn't have the extra padded seat, nor does it have a one-hand tray release or reclining seat feature.

Cosco ....★★
2525 State St., Columbus, IN 47201. Call (812) 372-0141 for a dealer near you (or 514-323-5701 for a dealer in Canada). Internet: www.coscoinc.com The "Rise & Dine" is Cosco's major high chair offering—it has three height adjustments, four recline positions, one-hand tray release and locking casters. It's unique "rotating t-bar" feature provides easy access and security from sub-marining. Our biggest complaints with the Rise & Dine: first, the padding is skimpy for a chair that retails for $60 to $70. Second, it's ugly. While the chair design itself is OK, the seat-cushion patterns are dated, to say the least.

Evenflo ....★★★
1801 Commerce Dr., Piqua, OH 45356. For a dealer near you, call (800) 837-9201 or (513) 773-3971. Evenflo's most interesting high chair is the "Phases," a molded plastic unit which has four uses: first, it can be an "infant feeding seat" that holds the On My Way infant car seat (which is not included). Then it becomes a regular high chair with two height positions and three tray adjustments. Take the tray off and the Phases becomes a booster chair. Finally, the unit converts to a table and chair. For $80 to $90, that's a good deal. What the downside? Well, it doesn't have casters, so you can't roll it around the kitchen. Also, the vinyl seat padding is somewhat skimpy, the tray lacks a one-handed release and the limited number of height adjustments may not work for some people. Nonetheless, the Phases high chair is a decent value, if you don't need all the bells and whistles of fancier high chairs. As a side note, Evenflo does make a "traditional" high chair, the "Right Height." This $70 high chair features a one-handed tray release, six height adjustments, casters for mobility and thicker seat padding. It's a nice chair, if not somewhat behind the times—the Right Height doesn't have a reclining seat for infant feeding, nor does it offer a bar to keep the baby from sliding out under the tray (only a strap holds baby in).

Fisher Price ....★★
636 Girard Ave., East Aurora, NY 14052. For a dealer near you, call (800) 828-4000 or (716) 687-3000. Fisher Price's "Adjustable High Chair" does have one unique feature: it's wide tray features a splash guard to keep food off baby. Well, that's a novel concept—most splash guards on high chairs are

aimed at keeping food/juice from spilling off the *side* of the tray. While we appreciate Fisher Price's attempt at innovation, as parents we'd like to say this concept won't work in the real world. As anyone knows who's tried to feed a baby, no splash guard will keep them from wearing most of their food. Anyway, we were little disappointed with Fisher's Price's high chair. Considering it's a "new" model, the chair lacks several important features—it doesn't have casters, the seat doesn't recline (for infant feeding) and there's no safety bar to keep baby from sliding out under the tray. While it's nice to have the six height adjustments and one-handed tray release, Fisher Price has some way to go before it reaches the high chair big leagues.

Gerry ....★★$^1/2$
12520 Grant Dr., Denver, CO 80241. For a dealer near you, call (800) 525-2472 or (303) 457-0926. One of the first com-

---

Baby Tenda's "safety" seminar: Anatomy of a Hard Sell

We got an interesting invitation in the mail the other day—a company called "Baby Tenda" invited us to a free safety seminar at a local hotel. Our curiosity piqued, we joined a couple dozen other expectant parents on a Saturday afternoon to learn their expert safety tips.

What followed was a good lesson for all parents—beware of companies that want to exploit parents' fears of their children being injured in order to sell their expensive safety "solutions." Sure enough, there was safety information dispensed at the seminar. The speaker started his talk with horrific tales of how many children are injured and killed each year. The culprit? Cheap juvenile equipment products like high chairs and cribs, he claimed. It was quite a performance—the speaker entranced the crowd with endless statistics on kids getting hurt and then demonstrated hazards with sample products form major manufacturers.

The seminar then segued into a thinly veiled pitch for their products: the Baby Tenda high chair/feeding table and crib. The speaker (read: salesperson) spent what seemed like an eternity trying to establish the company's credibility, claiming Baby Tenda has been in business for 60 years and only sells its products to hospitals and other commercial institutions. We can see why—these products are too ugly and far too expensive to sell in retail stores.

How expensive? The pitchman claimed their crib retailed for $725 . . . but is available for you today at the special price of $489! And the high chair/feeding table (which converts into a walker, swing, etc.)? It "regularly" sells for $450, but we'll give you a special deal at $298!

We found Baby Tenda's sales pitch to be disgusting. They used misleading statistics and outright lies to scare parents into

panies that made a high chair that converts to a play table and chairs was Gerry. Their "Play Top" high chair features a wrap-around seat pad and one-hand tray release. Pull the chair out of the base, flip the base over and it becomes a play table and chair. Compared to Evenflo's Phases, the Play Top does have a couple of advantages—first, it's less expensive (about $70-$75). Second, it's made out of wood, not molded plastic. On the other hand, it does not have any height adjustments. That inflexibility will rankle some parents whose kitchen tables are too tall or short to fit the Play Top. The Play Top's chair also doesn't recline, making it difficult to use an infant feeding station. Gerry also makes three more traditional high chairs, including the "Adjust a Height" ($65) with six height positions and a one-hand tray release. Oddly enough, none of these models has casters, which is pretty much a standard feature for most high chairs in this price range.

---

thinking they were putting their children in imminent danger if they used store-bought high chairs or cribs. Many of the statistics and "props" used to demonstrate hazards were as much as 20 years old and long since removed from the market. Even more reprehensible were claims that certain popular juvenile products were about to be recalled. Specifically, Baby Tenda claimed the Evenflo Exersaucer was "unsafe and will be off the market in six months," an accusation that Evenflo strongly denies.

The fact that Baby Tenda had to use such bogus assertions raised our suspicions about whether they were telling the truth about their own products. Sadly, the high pressure sales tactics did win over some parents at the seminar we attended—they forked over nearly $800 for Baby Tenda's products. Since then, we've heard from other parents who've attended Baby Tenda's "safety seminars," purchased the products and then suffered a case of "buyer's remorse." Did they spend too much, they ask?

Yes, in our opinion. While we see nothing wrong per se with Baby Tenda's "feeding table" (besides the fact it's god-awful ugly), you should note it costs nearly *twice* as much as our top recommended high chair, the very well-made Prima Poppa from Peg Perego. (At some seminars, the price for the feeding table is $400, but you get a free car seat with your purchase. Whoopee). There's nothing wrong with the crib either—and yes, Baby Tenda, throws in a mattress and two sheets. But you can find all this for much less than the $500 or so Baby Tenda asks.

So, we say watch out for Baby Tenda, who also markets their products under the names "Baby Sitter" and "Babyhood." We found their "safety seminar" to be bogus, their high pressure sales tactics reprehensible and their products to be grossly overpriced.

Graco ....★★
Rt. 23, Main St., Elverson, PA 19520. For a dealer near you, call (800) 345-4109, (610) 286-5951. Graco will debut a new high chair this year that will feature several height adjustments and a safety bar to keep Junior from sliding out from under the tray. The price: $49 to $59, which makes it one of the more affordable high chairs to sport those features. Graco also makes a more expensive version of this chair with a reclining seat (for infant feeding) at $79 to $89. While Graco is a price leader in this category, the quality is only average.

Peg Perego .... ★★★★
3625 Independence Dr., Ft. Wayne, IN 46808. For a dealer near you, call (219) 482-8191. Peg Perego has hit a home-run with their "Prima Poppa" high chair. Sure, it does what most high chairs do—it has seven height adjustments, four seat-recline positions, casters for mobility, and a spacious tray with one-handed release. But the Prima Poppa does one trick no other full-feature high chair does—it folds up! With a couple of quick motions, the chair folds up to a mere 11" in width for storage, a boon for families with small kitchens or eating areas. The downside? It ain't cheap—the Prima Poppa retails for $200, but we've seen it for $150 at LiL' Things (see Chapter 2) and in the Baby Catalog of America (800) PLAYPEN. Considering the quality and reputation of Perego high chairs, however, we think it's worth it. The only disappointment is the chair doesn't have a safety bar to keep baby from sliding out under the tray (there is a crotch strap, though). Nonetheless, this is probably the best high chair money can buy. If the Prima Poppa's too much for you, we should note that Peg Perego also makes a less-expensive high chair, the Bravo. This excellent high chair features the same tray as the Prima Poppa, a thickly padded seat, six height adjustments, and casters. For $120 to $130, it's a good second choice if you don't need the folding capability of the Prima Poppa.

Playskool ....★
108 Fairway Ct., North Vale, NJ 07647. For a dealer near you, call (800) 777-0371 or (201) 767-0900. When Playskool's 1-2-3 high chair was released a couple of years ago, it was a big hit. The Consumer Products Safety Commission even gave the chair for an award for its safety bar, which keeps babies from sliding out from under the tray. Unfortunately, the 1-2-3 then suffered through a public relations black-eye when it had to be recalled for a base problem (which was corrected). Then it was recalled again in 1997—the culprit this time was the aforementioned "safety" bar. Turns out that it can crack or break off, "which

may allow a child who is not secured with the high chair's seat belt to fall from the chair and be injured," says a press release from the Consumer Products Safety Commission. Playskool received hundreds of complaints about this problem and 40 reports of injuries to children falling from the 1-2-3. While Playskool fixed the problem with 1-2-3's made after June 1996 (and offered a free replacement safety bar to existing owners), that's one too many recalls for us. Yet, despite the chair's safety record, it's still a hot seller. At a retail price of $70 to $80, it's one of the few lower-price chairs to feature a reclining seat. Despite this innovation, there is one glaring flaw in the 1-2-3— when you tilt back the seat, the tray also tilts up, rendering it useless. New this year, Playskool has added an interesting feature to the 1-2-3: a tray with "Microban" antibacterial protection. The company says this germ-fighting technology "inhibits a broad range of bacteria, mold, mildew, fungus from growing on the surface of the tray." Silly us, but we always just washed off the tray after each use.

Other Brands We Encountered. If you're looking for a high chair that needs to fit into a small space, Italian-made *Chicco's* (for a dealer near you, call 800-521-2234, 612-545-2303) metal high chairs might do the trick. The "Spazio" ($100-$120) is a bare-bones model that folds-up for storage. Chicco's "Lift" high chair has more features, including a six-position height adjustment and casters. At $160, it's pricey considering the somewhat skimpy seat cushions and the lack of a one-handed tray release.

Another Italian-made high chair is the *Brevi* Maxi Chair (marketed in the U.S. by C&T International, 201-461-9444). The model features a two-position seat recline, eight height adjustments, one-handed tray release, thickly padded seat, and casters. To be honest, we didn't think this high chair was worth it's hefty price tag ($120 to $140). Its base isn't as wide as similar priced Peg Perego or Baby Trend Home & Roam— as a result, it seemed less stable. Also, we thought the tray wasn't was big as the competition either.

Our Picks: Brand Recommendations

Here is our round-up of the best high chair bets. All the prices quoted below are from the Baby Catalog of America (800) PLAYPEN. Most of these models are widely available in stores like Toys R Us, Babies R Us/Baby Superstore, LiL' things and other baby stores

| Good | If you don't need all the bells and whistles of those fancy high chairs, we like the Evenflo "Phases" as a good entry-level high chair that won't end up in a basement

after baby outgrows it. At $80, you get a high chair that easily converts to a play table and chair.

| Better | The Baby Trend "Home & Roam" ($100) is an excellent full-feature chair at a price that won't break the bank. Compared to lower-price high chairs, you get a model with casters, multi-height positions, thickly padded cushions and more. Another good bet is the Peg Perego "Bravo," which has similar features at $126.

| Best | Is there any contest? Peg Perego's "Prima Poppa" runs away with the crown. Not only does this high chair do it all, it also folds up for compact storage. At $150, it's a pricey investment, but the sleek design and quality construction make it worth it.

Safe and Sound

Considering the number of injuries caused by high chairs, it's important to understand the safety basics when it comes to these products. Here's the scoop:

♣ *Most injuries occur when babies are not strapped into their chairs.* Sadly, four to five deaths occur each year when babies "submarine" under the tray. Other babies are injured when they tip over the chair by pushing against the wall. Make sure your high chair is not placed near a wall or object that the baby might be able to push off on.

♣ *The safety standards for high chairs are voluntary.* In a recent report, Consumer Reports claimed that not all high chairs meet these voluntary standards. Perhaps the safest bet: look for JPMA-certified high chairs. The JPMA requires a battery of safety tests, including checks for stability, a locking device to prevent folding, a secure restraining system, no sharp edges, and so on.

♣ *Inspect the seat—is it well upholstered?* Make sure it won't tear or puncture.

♣ *Look for stability.* It's basic physics: the wider the base, the more stable the chair.

♣ *Carefully inspect the restraining system.* Belts should hold the baby so she can't stand or slide out under the tray. Straps around the hips and between the legs do the trick.

♣ *Some high chairs offer different height positions,* including a reclining position that supposedly makes it easier to feed a young infant. The problem? Feeding a baby solid foods in a reclining position is a choking hazard.

Swings

You can't talk to new parents without hearing the heated debate on swings, those battery-operated or wind-up surrogate parents. Some think they're a god-send, soothing a fussy baby when nothing else seems to work. Cynics refer to them as "neglect-o-matics," sinister devices that can become far too addictive for a society that thinks parenting is like microwaving—the quicker, the better.

Whatever side you come down on, we do have a few shopping tips. First, forget the wind-up models. Sure, you'll save about $20 and some batteries but don't believe those claims that they swing by themselves for 15 minutes. Instead, go for a basic battery operated swing. Most run about $70 to $90, and we found stores like Toys R Us have a pretty decent selection. You might be able to steal a deal on a swing at a second-hand baby store; we saw swings in decent shape for as little as $20 in such places.

Remember to observe safety warnings about swings, which are close to the top 10 most dangerous products as far as injuries go. You must always stay with your baby, use the safety belt, and stop using the swing once your baby reaches the weight limit (about 25 pounds in most cases). Always remember that a swing is not a baby-sitter.

The coolest swing we saw was the *Graco Advantage*. It does away with the overhead bar (which you always hit your baby's head on no matter how careful you are). Battery-operated, the swing has a flip-open tray, adjustable reclining seat, and thick padding. At $100 retail, it ain't cheap—but we've seen it for $65 in the Baby Catalog of America (800-PLAYPEN) as well as on sale in stores like Toys R Us and Baby Superstore.

Playpens

The portable playpen has been so popular in recent years that many parents consider it a necessity. Compared to the old wooden playpens of years past, today's playpens are made of metal and nylon mesh, fold compactly for portability and feature such handy features as bassinets, canopies, wheels and more.

While several companies make portable-playpens, the two best brands are *Graco* and *Evenflo*. Each offers a basic no-frills playpen (about $70) and others with more accessories ($90 to $110). If you plan to use your playpen outside, consider Graco's "Made in the Shade" Pack N Play—this deluxe version features large wheels, zippered side mesh for ventilation and an aluminized canopy that helps cut down on heat inside the playpen. Cost: $110. Of course, Graco also makes simpler models with fewer bells and whistles. We have a Pack N Play with the bassinet feature ($90) here in our home office and it works well.

Evenflo makes a couple different portable play yards. The "Happy Cabana" features a canopy, bassinet attachment, roll down shade, large wheels, toy bag and Evenflo's "roll and go" system, which lets you wheel a folded up playpen like a piece of carry-on luggage. Price: about $100. Simpler versions of Evenflo's playpens (called "Happy Campers") omit the bassinet, toy bag and wheels.

We've seen portable playpens on sale at Target and other discounters, but you can find them just about everywhere.

THE BOTTOM LINE:
A Wrap-Up of our Best Buy Picks

In the nursery, we highly recommend the Diaper Genie "diaper disposal system" and wipes by Baby Fresh and Suave. Discount stores like Toys R Us had the best deals on wipes, but don't go for the generic ones—we found them inferior in quality to the name brands.

The best toys for infants include a basic set of stacking cups ($5), an activity center ($15), and a play center ($30). An activity/bouncer seat with a toy bar is a good idea, with prices ranging from $30 to $50. If you're using an infant car seat, consider a toy bar for about $10.

Of course, our favorite stuffed animal/rattle is the Flatobearius line—at $9 to $12, they make affordable gifts. As for where to shop, the best deals on toys and books are often found at garage sales and second-hand stores.

Baby monitors have come a long way in recent years. Look for models with rechargeable batteries, 900 Mhz frequencies for clearer transmission and compact design for easier carrying. The best brands are Fisher Price and First Years.

What about baby food? If you're on a tight budget and/or have the time, consider making your own. If convenience is more important but you still want that fresh taste, go for Earth's Best or Growing Healthy. Finally, if you don't care about organic baby food and just want the cheapest stuff, try Heinz.

The best high chairs are from Baby Trend and Peg Perego ($100 to $150), although Evenflo's Phases is an affordable alternative ($80) that converts to a table and chair.

Questions or comments? Did you discover a bargain you'd like to share? Call the authors at (303) 442-8792 or e-mail adfields@aol.com! Updates to this book are posted at *www.windsorpeak.com*

Chapter 7

Places to Go! Car Seats, Strollers, Carriers & More

How can you get a Century car seat for free? You'll learn this and other tips on how to make your baby portable—from infant car seats to strollers, carriers to diaper bags. And what do you put in that diaper bag anyway? We've got nine suggestions, plus advice on dining out with baby. This chapter also features in-depth brand reviews of the best strollers, including which names are high-quality and which wish they were.

Getting Started: When Do You Need This?

You can't leave the hospital without a car seat. By law, all states require children to be restrained in a car seat. You'll want to get this item early (in your sixth to eighth month of pregnancy) so you can practice wedging it into the back seat.

What about all those other items that make baby portable? While you don't need a stroller, diaper bag or carrier immediately, most parents purchase them before baby arrives anyway. Some stroller models must be special-ordered, requiring a lead time of two to four weeks.

Sources to Find Car Seats & Strollers

 1 MASS MERCHANDISERS. Car seats have become a loss-leader for many discount stores. Chains like Target and Toys R Us sell these items at small mark-ups in hopes you'll spend money elsewhere in the store. As for strollers, these stores typically sell only inexpensive, umbrella-type strollers. Toys R Us has a little wider selection, with some strollers topping $100.

2 BABY SPECIALTY STORES. Independent juvenile retailers have all but abandoned car seats to the chains. With the exception of premium brands like Britax, you'll only see a few scattered offerings here. On the other hand, most specialty

stores stock a wide variety of strollers. Typically you'll see all the upper-end brand names—at upper-end prices.

3 BABY MEGA-STORES. Chains like LiL' Things and Babies R Us/Baby Superstore (see Chapter 2) combine the best of both worlds: high-quality brands at lower prices. Each carries just about every car seat known to man. The only drawback: when it comes to strollers, some stores don't stock the entire line. Instead, you may find just one or two models represented. Another disadvantage: discount chains have limited fabric choices. Car seat and stroller makers offer wider fabric options to independent juvenile stores.

4 MAIL ORDER. Yes, you can buy a car seat or stroller through the mail. Later in this chapter, we'll discuss one catalog that sells premium brand names at discount prices.

Car Seats

Here's an overview of what to look for and how to save money.

Smart Shopper Tips

Smart Shopper Tip #1
INFANT CAR SEATS: ARE THEY WORTH IT?

"Are infant car seats a waste of money? Since you can only use them until the baby reaches 20 pounds, it seems like a lot of money for such a short period of time."

Children's car seats come in two flavors: "infant" and "convertible." Infant car seats are just that—they're designed to be used with infants up to 20 lbs. or so. Convertible car seats can be used for both infants *and* older children. For babies under 20 lbs, convertible car seats face the rear of the car. When your baby passes that weight mark, you can turn the car seat around and face the baby forward. Most convertible car seats can hold a child up to 40 lbs.

So does it make more sense buying *one* convertible car seat, skipping the infant car seat? Nope. Safety experts say it's best for babies under 20 lbs. to be in an infant car seat—they're built to better accommodate a smaller body and baby travels in a semi-reclined position, which better supports their head and neck. Furthermore, most babies don't reach the 20-pound mark until about six to 12 months—and that can be a very long period of time if you don't have an infant car seat.

Why? First, it's helpful to understand that an infant car

seat is more than just a car seat—it's also an infant carrier when detached from its base. Big deal, you might say? Well, since most infants spend much of their time sleeping (and often fall asleep in the car), this is a big deal. By detaching the carrier from the auto base, you don't have to wake the baby when you leave the car. Buy a convertible car seat, and you'll have to unbuckle the baby and move her into another type of carrier (and most likely wake her in the process). Take it from us: let sleeping babies lie and spend the additional $50 to $70 for an infant car seat, even if you just use it for six months.

Smart Shopper Tip #2
ONE SIZE DOES NOT FIT ALL
"My friend has a car seat that just doesn't fit very well into her car. Do car seat manufacturers put out any literature that tells you which car seat fits best in which cars?"

Nope. You're on your own since car seat manufacturers take a "one-size-fits-all" attitude about their product. Since the backseats of cars can vary widely from model to model, you can bet that not every car seat will fit like a glove. The best advice: keep the receipt and check the store's return policy. Right after you buy the car seat, set it up in your backseat. If it doesn't fit, take it back. Never buy a car seat from a store that has a no-returns policy.

Smart Shopper Tip #3
HOLDING YOUR BABY BACK: SAFETY HARNESS ADVICE
"Which safety harness works best—the five-point, bar-shield, or T-shield?

The consensus of the safety experts we consulted seems to be that the five-point harness is best, although this may be because there is more testing information available on this design than on the alternatives. The jury is still out on the bar-shield and T-shield designs (which lower over the baby's head).

Let's be honest, however: the five-point harness is the *least convenient* to use. You have to put each strap around baby's arms, find the lower buckle (which always seems to disappear under their rump) and then snap them in. Bar-shields and t-shields slip over the baby's head in one motion and are easier to buckle in.

So, what's the best solution? We still say go with the five-point harness. First, small infants don't fit well into a bar-shield or t-shield car seat. Second, some bar-shield car seats don't adjust to accommodate growing children. And even those expensive models that feature adjustable shields only adjust so much—if your child grows quickly, they still might outgrow the car seat. The result? You'll have to move them into a booster seat (making an extra purchase) sooner than you need to.

The fact that the five-point harness is inconvenient is just tough. Remember, it's the safest design on the market today. And sometimes as a parent you have to do what's best for your child, even if that makes your life less convenient.

Here are seven more shopping tips for car seats:

♣ *How easily does it recline?* Some convertible car seats have a lever in front that makes the seat recline (nice for a sleeping baby). Unfortunately, not all car seats recline equally—some levers are more difficult to work than others. Check it out in the store before you buy.

♣ *Check the belt adjustments.* You don't merely adjust the car seat's belts when your baby grows—if you put Junior in a coat, you'll need to loosen the belts. As a result, it's important to check how easily the belts adjust. The majority of car seats have belts that adjust manually, although exactly how this works varies from maker to maker. The best car seats let you adjust the belts from the front. Those models that require you to access the back of the seat to adjust the belts are more hassle. As a side note: a few car seats have belts that adjust automatically—like a car's regular seat belts, these restraints automatically retract for a snug fit.

♣ *Are the instructions in Greek?* Before you buy the car seat, take a minute to look at the set-up and use instructions. Make sure you can make sense of the seat's documentation. Another tip: if possible, ask the store for any installation tips and advice.

♣ *Is the pad cover machine-washable?* You'd think this would be a "no brainer," but a surprising number of seats have covers that aren't removable or machine washable. Considering how grimy these covers can get, it's smart to look for this feature.

♣ *Does the seat need to be installed with each use?* The best car seats are "permanently" installed in your car. When you put baby in, all you do is buckle them in the seat's harness system. Yet some infant car seats and even a few convertible models need to be installed with each use—that means you have to belt the thing in every time you use it. Suffice to say, that's a major drawback.

♣ *Watch out for hot buckles.* Some inexpensive car seats have exposed metal buckles and hardware. In the hot sun, these buckles can get toasty and possibly burn a child.

♣ *If the baby comes early, many hospitals rent car seats at affordable rates.* You can rent one for a few days until you get your own.

Safe & Sound

1 NEVER BUY A USED CAR SEAT. You don't know what happened to the car seat—if it was in an accident (even a minor one), the car seat may be unsafe. What about a hand-me-down? Make sure it has never been in an accident—and confirm that the seat has not been recalled (see phone number below for the National Highway Traffic Safety Administration). Safety seats made before 1981 may not meet current safety standards (unfortunately, most seats aren't stamped with their year of manufacture, so this may be difficult to determine). The bottom line: risky hand-me-downs aren't worth it. A brand new car seat (which starts at $50) isn't that huge of an investment to insure your child's safety. If you follow our money-saving tip later in this chapter, you can even get a brand-new, name-brand car seat for free.

2 READ THE DIRECTIONS VERY CAREFULLY. Many car accidents end in tragedy because the car seat was used improperly. If you have any questions about the directions, call the company or return the car seat for a model that is easier to use. Another tip: read your car's owner's manual for any special installation instructions (especially if a supplemental attachment is need). Consult with your auto dealer if you have any additional questions.

What's the number-one problem with mis-installed car seats? The locking clip, perhaps the most misunderstood part of your child's car seat. When you install a car seat in a vehicle with a retractable seat belt, you must use a locking clip to insure the seat belt holds the seat in place in case of an accident. Without it, the seat could become a projectile, injuring or killing your child. After you install the car seat, you attach the locking clip on the belt next to the latch (see your car seat's instructions for more information).

Make sure the safety seat is held firmly against the back of the car seat and doesn't wobble from side to side (or front to back). Later in this chapter, we'll review a new car seat that has a built-in locking clip.

3 USE YOUR CAR SEAT. Don't make the mistake of being in a hurry and forgetting to (or just not wanting to) attach the restraints. Many parents merely put their child in the seat without hooking up the harness. It is *more* dangerous to leave your child in a car seat unrestrained by the safety harness than it is to put him or her in a regular seat belt. If your child is under 20 lbs., make sure that she are facing the rear of the vehicle.

4 PUT THE CAR SEAT IN THE BACK SEAT. Air bags and car seats don't mix—several reports of injuries and deaths have been attributed to passenger side air bags that deployed when a car seat was in the front seat. As a result, the safest place for kids is the backseat. And what the safest part of the backseat? Safety experts say it's the middle. The only problem with that advice is that some cars have a raised hump in the middle of the backseat that makes it difficult/impossible to safely install a car seat. Another problem: safety seats are best held against the car's back seat by a three-point belt—and most middle seats just have a two-point belt.

5 BUY ANOTHER LOCKING CLIP. If you rent a car, most rental agencies will also rent you a car seat so you don't have to lug your own on the plane. What's the problem? Most forget to give you a locking clip (see above for an explanation). As a result, we suggest buying an extra locking clip (available for a few dollars at most stores) and taking it with you whenever you travel.

6 REGISTER YOUR SEAT. Don't forget to send the registration card for the car seat back to the manufacturer. That's the only way you'll be notified of any recalls or problems that may be discovered in the future.

7 BEWARE OF CONFLICTING ADVICE. Here's a dilemma faced by many parents: at what point is your child ready to graduate from an infant car seat to a "convertible" forward-facing car seat? If you're using just a convertible car seat, when do you turn it around? Most car seat makers tell parents the weight limit for infant seats or rear-facing convertible seats is 20 pounds (although that can vary by product). What makes this confusing is conflicting advice that some safety groups put out . . . one says a child should be both 20 pounds AND one year of age before graduating to a forward-facing seat. But, what if you have a big baby who hits 24 pounds at seven months of age? If your baby can hold his head up, does that mean he can sit in a forward-facing seat, no matter what his age or weight? Our advice is to adhere to the seat's instructions. The key criteria is the weight limit (that's what manufacturers crash test for), though one maker (Evenflo) also has a maximum length for an infant using their On My Way infant seat.

Recalls

The National Highway Traffic Safety Administration has a toll-free hot-line to check for recalls or to report a safety problem. Call (800) 424-9393 or (202) 366-0123—you can have a list of recalled car seats automatically faxed to you at no charge. The NHTSA, which has a web site at www.nhtsa.gov, can also send you a list of which cars seats fit your make and model vehicle. Note that this is a different governmental agency than the Consumer Product Safety Commission, which regulates and recalls other juvenile products. (For Canadian recalls and safety seat rules, see the special section at the end of this book for more info).

Are lax U.S. safety standards for car seats putting your baby at risk?
The saga of the Century 590 exposes troubling questions

The bombshell dropped in September 1995. That was the month *Consumer Report's* issue on children's safety seats hit the stands, complete with allegations that several popular models failed its crash tests. Among the failures was the Century 590, the U.S.'s top-selling infant car seat made by one of the country's largest manufacturers of such seats.

Unfortunately, the controversy didn't stop there: Century disputed the findings and refused to recall the seat, which was also part of their popular "4-in-1" stroller/car seat combo product. In 1997, the company quietly phased out the 590, replacing it with the Smart Fit (which subsequently did pass *Consumer Report's* crash tests).

How could this happen? Doesn't the government crash tests these seats to make sure they're safe? Why did Century not recall the seat, disputing the findings in the *Consumer Reports* article? And even more important: why are there so many safety problems in children's car seats, prompting 236 product recalls since 1988 alone? When you add it up, over 18 *million* car seats have been involved in recalls since 1981. (As a side note, Century leads the recall race, with a whopping 95 product recalls in the past nine years).

After the Century/*Consumer Reports* fracas, we launched an investigation into when and how car seats are tested in the U.S. and Canada. The result: we were shocked to find a surprisingly lax system that pales in comparison to European safety standards. Parents who trust the government and these companies to make sure they're children are safe when traveling by car are being betrayed. Here's what we found:

In 1996, the National Highway Traffic Safety Administration (NHTSA) toughened safety standards for car seats. The government required a 20 pound-dummy to be used in crash tests of infant car seats and rear-facing convertible seats. In the past, only a 17.5 pound dummy was used. While that sounds like a minor difference, it apparently tripped up Century. Their 590 infant car seat (whose package said it was safe for babies up to 20 lbs.) passed with the lighter dummy, but failed with the 20-pound dummy. In *Consumer Reports* test, which simulated a 30 mph head-on crash, the force of impact separated the carrier from the base. The result: your baby could go flying in an accident. *Consumer Reports* found the seat was safe when used *without* the base, but that dramatically cut down on the product's convenience (which Century touted as a major selling feature).

The failure of this seat made national headlines—and rightly so. Each year, 700 children die in car crashes (it's the leading cause of death for children under five) and another 60,000 to 70,000 are injured. Even more troubling is the series of recalls that have plagued children safety seats. If the U.S. is supposed to have the world's best safety standards and laws, how can all these accidents and recalls still happen?

The answer: the U.S. (and Canada) have loopholes in their child safety seat laws big enough to drive a truck through. And the saga of Century's 590 car seat perfectly illustrates exactly how these loopholes can be disastrous— *Consumer Reports* notes several class action lawsuits have been filed against Century, with at least one case of the 590 failing in an accident since their report.

Our investigation turned up troubling revelations about the U.S. and Canada's safety standards in three areas: *who* tests the seats, *when* they are tested and *how* the safety standards are much weaker than those in Europe.

Who. As a parent, you might assume that the government tests all safety to seats to make sure they're safe.

Wrong.

It's a little known fact of the car seat business—the U.S. and Canada rely on car seat manufacturers to test their own products. This program, known as "self-certification," puts the burden of testing for compliance with safety standards solely on the company. Why does the U.S. do this? Theoretically, self-certification means less bureaucracy and more of an opportunity for product innovation—companies can move quicker to bring a product to market, without having to wait for some government body to give the seat a "seal of approval."

While the government *sets* the safety standards, surprisingly they let companies interpret their own crash test results to determine whether the seats meet those rules. And that can lead to abuse—while you'd hope companies would have nothing to gain by putting out an unsafe car seat that leads to death and injury, some may be more ethically challenged.

We should point out that the U.S. government does occasionally tests seats itself . . .but the key word in that sentence is "occasionally." Neither the U.S. nor Canada regularly test new or existing seats each year to see if they meet current standards. And that's what probably happened in the case of the several-year-old Century 590—it's obvious the government watchdog was asleep at the switch.

How does the U.S./Canadian system compare with Europe? Most European countries require car seats to pass government-sponsored tests before they can be sold to the public. These tests are done by a third-party company, which certifies that the seats meet the safety criteria. The result: a more objective and dispassionate process that insures safety seats meet guidelines. Unlike the U.S., European car seat makers are not allowed to interpret their own crash test results.

When. You'd think the government would require car seat makers to not only make sure their *new* seats are safe, but also continuously test *older* existing models to make sure there are no production problems. But, once again, you'd be wrong.

It doesn't take a rocket scientist to realize that a glitch in production of any product can lead to problems. Yet, once again, the U.S. and Canadian governments have failed parents—neither clearly defines the required level of what is called "compliance of production" testing. Should companies crash test every 5000th seat made? 10,000th? 20,000th? Not only does the government not set this standard, but it also lets companies keep their own internal standards secret. Sure, most major car seat manufacturers probably crash test a certain number of their car seats from time to time, but by not forcing companies to make these numbers public, consumers are left in the dark as to which companies are more rigorous than others. The mere requirement of companies to disclose this data would probably encourage more safety testing.

European countries, by contrast, require all car seat makers to test (at least) each 5000th car seat made. And that crash test must be done with a third-party test company or an in-house program that is certified by the government. In addition, some countries go one step further—they themselves do testing on a one year or six-month cycle. The bottom line: any fault in production of a car seat is discovered much quicker than in the U.S. or Canada.

All these requirements have encouraged European car seat makers to be more forthcoming with their own safety programs. Britax (reviewed later in this chapter) says it crash tests every 2500th car seat made in both the U.S. and Europe.

For the record, Century maintained that its own safety tests of the 590 indicated the seat was safe. Yet, it was the *company* who did the testing, not the government. Century (like all other U.S. car seat makers) does not publicly disclose their "compliance of production" testing levels.

How. Even more troubling than the lax standards of who tests car seats and when they are tested are the test standards *themselves*—in our opinion, they are grossly insufficient. Here is a run-down of what's wrong:

♣ **Unrealistic test conditions.** The U.S. and Canadian safety standards use a flat bench to test car seats. That bench is equipped with a two-point belt that lacks buckle hardware and emerges from the seat "bite" (the crease where the seat and back meet). Notice anything wrong here? Most cars today don't have flat back seat benches with two point belts—instead, most models have bucket seats with *three-point belts*. And most cars have seat belts that are anchored well forward of the seat bite. As a result: a safety seat that passes a U.S. crash test may fail in real cars in the real world. Parents probably already notice this problem in a small way—with many safety seats, the car's safety belts loosen during travel, even if the seat is installed properly with a locking clip. The European safety standards address these problems by having a more realistic test bench, complete with forward anchored safety belts and other refinements. Europe also tests car seats with three-point seat belts, not two.

♣ **Side impact padding.** The U.S. and Canadian safety standards just address head-on crashes. Yet automobile accidents in the real world involve side-impact crashes and roll-overs. Europe has recognized this problem by requiring all car seats to have side-impact protection (basically extra padding). In contrast, the NHSTA is silent on this issue and most car seats sold in North America do not have this protection.

♣ **More dummies.** Europe requires car seat makers to use a more comprehensive set of test dummies, in a variety of weights. European car seats are tested with *six* dummies that weigh the same as a newborn, nine-month old, a one and a half year old, a three-year-old, six year old and ten year old. By contrast, the U.S. just requires three crash test dummies (a nine-month old, a three year old and a six year old).

♣ **No locking clip.** It's the most misunderstood and misused piece of car seat equipment—the dreaded locking clip. This little piece of metal "locks" the seat belt, keeping the car seat secure in the case of an accident. Safety checks done by police departments consistently uncover parents who either mis-install the locking clip . . . or simply don't use one at all. Without a locking clip, a safety seat isn't safe at all.

Europe has banned the locking clip. Instead, European

car seats use a "locking clamp," which is built into the seat and much easier to use. We've seen demonstrations of car seats with such systems and believe they better anchor the safety seat to the car.

Each of these testing deficiencies probably contributed to the woes of the Century 590. How the seat passed the company's tests yet failed *Consumer Reports'* tests is still a mystery, as is decision not recall the seat (as we noted earlier, the company is no stranger to car seat recalls). There is one possible explanation, however: in 1995, Century was readying a new car seat model (the Smart Fit) to be released in mid 1996. If Century recalled the 590, it would have gone nearly a year with no infant car seat model with base to sell before the Smart Fit was ready. Whether Century was convinced that its car seat was truly safe or it merely wanted to sell through the inventory of 590's stacked up in its warehouse is left for one to wonder. (Our request for Century to comment on this matter went unanswered).

All of Century's denials still ring hollow to us. The fact remains: Century continued to sell the Century 590 well into 1997, despite the fact they were informed in July 1995 that the seat failed *Consumer Reports* crash tests with a 20 lb. dummy. While other car seat makers recalled their products in the wake of failing CR's tests, Century refused. Worse yet, the government took no action to remedy the situation.

So what can you do as a parent? Well, first, make sure your car seat is installed correctly. Honestly, not all car seats work well with all cars. Those models with wide bases (of which there are many) may not fit cars with bucket or contoured seats. Return any seat that doesn't work and search for one that fits. Second, stay up on recalls and the latest crash tests—*Consumer Reports* provides a critical safety valve for a flawed testing system.

Third, consider a car seat that meets both the U.S. and European safety standards. Despite our criticism, we realize the U.S. safety standards aren't totally bankrupt. The U.S. requires car seats to be tested for "head accelerations" (that is, the impact of a crash on a child's head). Europe just tests for "chest accelerations." Another plus for the U.S.: we have an informal safety standard for cars with shorter belt lengths, common in some models today.

Hence, a car seat that can pass both the U.S. *and* the European tests is probably the best bet. As a result, our top recommendation for a forward-facing car seat (the Britax Freeway, see review later in this chapter) meets this criteria.

The Name Game: Reviews of Selected Manufacturers

The Ratings

★★★★ EXCELLENT—*our top pick!*
 ★★★ GOOD—*above average quality, prices, and creativity.*
  ★★ FAIR—*could stand some improvement.*
   ★ POOR—*yuck! could stand some major improvement.*

Britax...★★★★
*460 Greenway Industrial Dr., Ft. Mill SC 29715.
For a dealer near you, call (888) 4-BRITAX or (803)*
802-2022. Britax is our pick as one of the best new car seats on the market today. The largest manufacturer of child safety seats in Europe and Australia, Britax came to the U.S. in 1996, shipping its car seats from their factory in South Carolina. What makes Britax's car seats so great? First, they meet *both* the U.S. and European standards for safety (earlier in this chapter, we discuss how Europe's car seat rules are better in some ways than U.S. regulations). Second, we liked the car seat's innovative design and safety features. For example, Britax's flagship car seat, "The Freeway" has a patented "lock-off" clamp that securely attaches the seat to the car's belt. As a result, the Freeway doesn't require a locking clip, that often misunderstood and mis-installed piece of equipment that every other car seat maker requires. Of course, there are some downsides to Britax's Freeway—it only works in a forward-facing position and is intended for children 20 to 40 lbs. Unlike competitors' "convertible" car seats, the Freeway can't be used in a rear-facing position for infants under 20 lbs. Yet, if you plan to use a separate infant car seat (as per our recommendation), this drawback doesn't matter. Another bummer: the Freeway is only sold in specialty stores and isn't cheap. The basic version (which features a full recline and sculpted base) retails for $169 to $189, making it the priciest car seat on the market. Britax also offers a more plush version of the Freeway (the SE, for "shower edition" as in a baby shower gift), which features extra padding, matching sunshade, and pillow for $199. New for 1997, Britax plans to introduce an infant seat called the "Rock A Tot," which will sell for $79 to $89. We saw a prototype of this product at a trade show and, while we noted it's roomier than other infant seats, it does have one limitation—it doesn't have an auto base for quick release. As a result, you'll have to buckle in the seat each time you use it, a major disadvantage in our opinion. Also coming out in mid-1997: a convertible

car seat called the "Elite," which Britax says can be used rear-facing with infants up to 30 lbs. and forward-facing up to 50 lbs—in all, the company says you can use it for children five months to six years of age. Pricing info on this model wasn't available at press time.

Century..★★*¹*/2
9600 Valley View Rd., Macedonia, OH 44056. For a dealer near you, call (216) 468-2000. You can't go car seat shopping without seeing this brand name—Century is the market-leader in both infant and convertible car seats. Yet, that tenure has been bumpy as of late. In a high profile report that generated wide media attention, *Consumer Reports* declared Century's top-selling 590 infant car seat to be unsafe when used with its base. Century vigorously denied the accusations, although they quietly discontinued the seat in 1997. (For the record, Century's car seats have been involved in 95 recalls since 1988). See the article earlier in this chapter for more on this controversy. Meanwhile, here's an overview of Century's current offerings:

Infant car seats. Century has replaced the ill-fated 590 infant car seat with two options: the Smart Fit and the Assura. The Smart Fit ($65 to $70) features a sculptured "All Ways" handle for easily carrying and a contoured base Century claims will better fit cars with bucket seats. The Assura is a scaled down version of the Smart Fit and costs less. The Assura 565 ($40 to $45) is just a seat (no base). Hence you have to buckle in the seat each time you use it, which is very inconvenient in our opinion. The Assura Premiere ($50 to $60) uses the same Smart Fit base and hence is probably a better bet than the 565. What's the difference between the Assura Premier and Smart Fit? While both have a level indicator to make sure the seat's in right, the Smart Fit has that special handle, more plush fabric and a two-piece harness tie (the Assura's harness goes over the baby's head). As a side note, *Consumer Reports* has crash tested both the Assura and Smart Fit car seats and declared them safe.

Convertible car seats. Century offers an amazing number of choices in this category. On the low end, the no frills STE car seats are good buys. The 1000 STE ($50 to $60) was top-rated in *Consumer Reports* and is available essentially for free from Midas (more on this later). The other STE car seats ($50 to $80) offer more plush fabrics in both five-point (1500 STE), T-shield (2000 STE) and bar-shield (3000 STE) versions. The top-of-the line 3500 STE features a bar shield with a "Room to Grow" feature—four adjustments to accommodate larger children. On the upper end, Century offers its "Smart Move" car seats in both five-point and bar-shield versions. This pricey car seat ($150 retail, $100 to $130 in stores like LiL' Things, Babies R Us/Baby Superstore and the Baby Catalog of America 800-PLAYPEN) offers a full recline for infants that "rotates instantly and automatically to an upright protective position in the event of a frontal collision." The super plush car seat is lined with foam for extra comfort. Another unique feature: the Smart Move is one of the few convertible car seats with rear-facing use up to 30 lbs for infants (most car seats must be turned around after 20 lbs). For some reason, Century must have decided it didn't have enough car seats and hence will introduce a third line in mid 1997—the "Ovation" car seats will be priced between the STE and Smart Move lines. Ovation car seats will have more features and plusher fabrics than the STE's, plus will be available in three versions: five-point ($79), t-bar ($89) and bar shield ($89). Each will have a one-hand recline lever, adjustable t-shields and a contoured base the company claims will better fit cars with bucket seats. So what to we think of Century overall? Well, we give the company high marks for innovation—they really are trying to make their car seats easier to use. The fabric choices are excellent and the prices for most offerings (except the Smart Move) are moderate. Yet, we're troubled by the high number of recalls that Century has suffered. True, some of these recalls involve minor issues like incorrect labeling, but other seats have suffered problem latches, harness, buckles or outright failure in crash tests. Since the company is the leading U.S. manufacturer of car seats, one would assume it would have more recalls than others, but this is still unsettling.

Cosco ....★★
2525 State St., Columbus, IN 47201. Call (812) 372-0141 for a dealer near you (or 514-323-5701 for a dealer in Canada). Internet: www.coscoinc.com Cosco, which is owned by Canadian conglomerate Dorel Industries, makes several car seats that are widely available in both the U.S. and Canada. What makes Coscos seats unique their "auto tighten" belt systems. Instead of manually tightening (or loosening) the belts every time you put baby into the car seat, the belts on some Cosco models automatically retract for a secure fit, sort of like a car's regular seat belts. Why the other major car seat makers (that is, Century and Evenflo) haven't thought of this yet is beyond us. Here's an overview:

Infant car seats. Like Century, Cosco makes infant car seats in two flavors: one with a fancy handle and one without. The "Turnabout" ($60) features a handle grip that rotates 360 degrees into any position and then locks in place. Our only complaint: one version of the Turnabout (the 02-764) has a canopy that wraps around the handle, making it difficult or impossible to carry the handle under your arm. Oddly enough, this mistake isn't in repeated three other versions of the Turnabout. Another oddity: Cosco's Auto Reel belt tightening system (described above) is only available on two of the Turnabouts (the 02-760 and the 02-766). If you want this feature, make sure you shop carefully. (As a side note, Cosco also makes a plain car seat without the fancy handle—the "Arriva" also lacks the Auto Reel feature). Parents of twins or premature babies, take note: Cosco is one of very few manufacturers to make a "travel bed." For babies that need to travel laying down, the Cosco "Dream Ride" is about $90.

Convertible car seats. Cosco has a dozen or so car seats, but only their "Olympian" car seats feature the "Auto Retract" harness system. Unfortunately, this upper-end model only comes in t-shield and bar-shield versions—no five point. All Olympians have the option of an extra infant cushion insert and harness covers. Of course, Cosco does make less-expensive car seats too—the entry-level Touriva ($50 to $90) comes in both basic and "deluxe" padding and the Regal Ride, which features even more deluxe padding. Both the Touriva and Regal Ride come in five-point, t-shield and bar-shield versions. All in all, we have to give Cosco a mixed rating. While we liked the auto-retract harness systems, their car seats lack features common with the competition. For example, even their most expensive convertible car seats don't recline, a very handy feature for sleeping infants. Also we've heard little feedback from parents about the quality and durability of these car seats; Cosco seems to been more successful in Canada than the U.S.

Evenflo .... ★★ *1/2*
1801 Commerce Dr., Piqua, OH 45356. For a dealer near you, call (800) 837-9201 or (513) 773-3971. In Canada, PO Box 1598, Brantford, Ontario, N3T 5V7. (905) 337-2229.
Next to Century, Evenflo has the country's second best-selling line of car seats. Here's an overview:

Infant car seats. Our top recommendation for infant car seats has to go to Evenflo's On My Way 207 ($55 to $65). Its excellent design and unique S-shaped handle give it an edge on the competition. Our favorite feature is a notch in the back of the seat that allows it to easily fit into shopping cars . . . and those wooden restaurant high chairs without having to turn them over. Our only complaints about the On My Way: it weighs about four pounds more than Century's Smart Fit and the wide base may not fit into some cars' back seats. Nevertheless, we've used an On My Way for our second child and have been very happy. Evenflo even sells the auto base separately so you can use it in a second car ($20 through the Baby Catalog of America 800-PLAYPEN). We should note that Evenflo also sells two other less fancy infant car seats: the Travel Tandem looks similar to the On My Way, except it has less plush fabric and lacks the s-shaped handle. Evenflo's Joy Ride is essentially the Travel Tandem without a base. Hence you have to buckle in the seat each time you use it in a car.

Convertible car seats. While we liked Evenflo's infant car seats, we're less enthused by their convertible models. The problem: they're overpriced and the belts are cheap—after repeated use, they twist and become difficult to adjust. At least that's what happened on our Evenflo Ultara V. While this seat has plush fabric and a five-point harness system, we were disappointed in the belts, especially for a seat that sells for $80 to $100. Anyway, like Century, Evenflo sells car seat models in several price ranges. The entry-level Scout ($50 to $65) has basic fabric and comes in five-point and t-shield versions. The Champion and Trooper car seats ($60 to $80) have plusher fabric and bar shields (although only the Trooper has a shield that adjusts as your child grows). On the upper-end, Evenflo's Ultara car seats have a three-position recline and come in either bar shield or five-point versions. The Ultara I ($90 to $100) is a bar-shield, while the Ultara V ($80 to $100) is a five-point harness. Each Ultara has a "Premier" option which includes an extra insert cushion for infants and a removable pillow for toddlers. New in the Evenflo line is their ultra-plush "Medallion" car seat (about $100). This model features a "seat within a seat" for infants and comes in both five-point and adjustable bar-shield versions. Overall, we have to give Evenflo a mixed review. Thumbs up for the infant car seats, thumbs down for the convertible models.

Guardian ....★★★
Made by Early Development, 6135 Park South Dr., Suite 420, NC 28210. For a dealer near you, call (704) 643-8400. One of the things we like best in the baby business is how a company with a good idea can hit a home run. Such is the case with the Guardian car seats, whose innovative designs have parents buzzing and the competition scrambling. What's all the fuss about? Consider their "Folder Car Seat"—it's the first convertible car seat to fold up for travel or storage. That's right, it easily opens and closes and has a carrying handle. The Folder has a three-position recline, plush fabric and comes in either five-point, t-shield and bar-shield versions. You also have a choice of manual or automatic belt adjustments, which we thought was a great feature. And the price? The Folder Plus five-point with automatic belt adjustment is just $120 to $150 in stores (or try the Kids Club catalog 800-363-0500), priced about the same as other upper-end car seats.

So, should you rush right out and buy one? Well, hold it. Most people don't really need the fold-up feature. We can think of a couple uses—if you live on the upper west side of Manhattan and want a portable car seat to use in taxis, the

Guardian is a good bet. Some parents also like the Guardian for day care drop-offs—instead of having two car seats, you simply fold-up the Guardian and leave it at day-care for the spouse who picks up baby. But let's get real: you could buy two (or three) basic car seats for the price of one Guardian, so why lug it around? Speaking of which, this thing ain't exactly light—it weighs in at close to 20 lbs., making it a schlep for all but the most fit parents.

Perhaps a better bet would be the little-noticed Guardian "Comfort Plus" car seat. It has all the features of the Folder (plush fabric, auto belt adjustments, three position recline) but doesn't fold up. A five-point Comfort (which also comes in t-shield or bar-shield versions) costs $90 to $120, making it a very good deal. Guardian also makes a cheaper version of this seat called the "Express" which omits the recline feature. One note of caution: our only hesitation about Guardian's car seats is the fact that they've yet to be crash-tested by *Consumer Reports* as of this writing. CR tests about once a year and tends to be somewhat behind the times in terms of new models like the Guardian. We'd like to see a car seat pass CR's tests before we give it our full recommendation (check out our web page at *www.windsorpeak.com* for the latest news on this and other car seat topics).

Other brands to consider: Fisher Price (800) 828-4000 or (716) 687-3000 has been out of the car seat business for a couple of years, after a string of embarrassing recalls forced the company to withdraw from the market. Well, Fisher Price is giving it another try in 1997, introducing a new convertible car seat that will reportedly use a tether strap that is permanently mounted to a car's back seat. While details and pricing were sketchy at press time, we hear Fisher Price will team up with Goodyear locations to have the tether straps installed free in cars.

Renolux (954) 987-6262 is a French brand of car seats that won fans for their innovative design and ease of use. Yet, the company withdrew from the U.S. market in 1994, after suffering a string of 15 recalls (crash test failures and other glitches). Well, the company's U.S. distributor is trying again, promising to bring back the car seats in 1997. The only problem is this is the same distributor that also promised Renolux car seats would be out in 1996. The year came and went with no car sets, so we'll have to see whether they can get their act together.

We thought ***Gerry's*** car seats were rather ho-hum. There was nothing innovative about their infant car seat (the "Secure Ride", $40 to $60), except that it's handle can be locked in place to make the seat a rocker. Their "One Click" convertible car seat ($80 to $100) does have one interesting feature: a one-step locking movement that automatically adjusts the seat's belts. Unfortunately, this feature is only available on a bar-shield harness system. Gerry does sell a plain five-point convertible car seat (the "Pro-Tech"), but it doesn't recline and has a manual belt adjustment.

Another also-ran in the car seat business is *Kolcraft* (773) 247-4494. Their infant car seats ("Travel-About" and "Infant Rider") feature a "smart handle" that has a pivoting foam grip. In a way, this is a copy of Evenflo's On My Way, yet the special handle sits quite high on the bar. Translation: in order to carry the seat and keep it from hitting the ground, you'd better be tall. Kolcraft's convertible car seats are heavy on the bar shield models—out of their three models, only one is a five-point. Only the more expensive "Secure Fit" features an adjustable bar shield. There was nothing special about these car seat designs or functionality (except they all have a two-position recline).

In contrast to the me-too offerings of Gerry and Kolcraft, the *Sit N Stroll* ($140) from Safeline Corporation (800) 829-1625, (303) 757-2400 has won a small but loyal fan base for its innovative car seat/stroller. With one flick of the hand, this convertible car seat converts into a stroller. Like some kind of Batmobile, a handle pops up from the back and wheels appear from the bottom—pressto! You've got a stroller without having to remove baby from the seat.

We've seen a few parents wheel this thing around, and though it looks somewhat strange, they told us they've been happy with its operation. We have some doubts, however. First, unlike the four-in-one car seat/stroller combos reviewed later in this chapter, the Sit N Stroll's use as a stroller is quite limited—it doesn't have a full basket (only a small storage compartment) or a canopy (a "sunshade" is an option). We'd prefer a seat that reclines (it doesn't), has a five-point harness system (the Sit N Stroll has a four-point) and you've got to belt the seat in each time you use it in a car—even if you don't take it along as a stroller. Not only is installation a hassle, but the Sit N Stroll's wide base may also not fit some vehicles with short safety belts or contoured seats. Plus, lifting the 14-pound car seat with a full-size child out of a car to put on the ground is quite a workout. So, we're not sure we can wholeheartedly recommend this seat. On the other hand, we did hear from a flight attendant who loved her Sit N Stroll—it wheels down those narrow plane aisles and is a FAA-certified flight seat. So, it's a mixed bag for the Sit N Stroll. While we salute the maker for their innovation, the product's drawbacks may limit its appeal.

Our Picks: Brand Recommendations

Infant car seats

Good Let's be honest: if you're on a super-tight budget, consider not buying an infant car seat at all. A good five-point, convertible car seat (see below for recommendations) will work for both infants and children. Of course, if you think you can spare $40 to $50, you could get a no-frills infant car seat. The Century Assura 565 is a good example—sure, you don't get any fancy handles or padding, but it works and is safe.

Better We like the Century Smart Fit ($55 to $65) as a good second bet. If you have a car with deep bucket seats, this infant seat's sculpted base might fit your car better. Another plus: this is the lightest infant car seat among the more premium brands, weighing some four pounds less than the Evenflo "On My Way."

Best Despite the fact it weighs more than the Century's Smart Fit, our top nod goes to Evenflo's "On My Way" car seat ($55 to $65). We love the S-shaped handle and special notch on the carrier that fits easily into shopping carts, restaurant high chairs and more. Evenflo also sells the On My Way Travel System, which combines the car seat and a decent stroller, which we'll recommend as our top "combo model" later in this chapter.

Convertible car seats.

Good For a decent, no-frills car seat, we recommend the Century 1000 STE, which is available essentially for free from Midas (more on this later). Even at retail ($50 to $70), it's a good deal. This five-point model has decent padding and is easy to use.

Better The Guardian Comfort Plus is an excellent buy: plush fabric, automatic belt adjustments and a three-position recline. The seat sells for $90 to $120, but Guardian also makes less expensive version (the Express) which omits the recline feature.

Best If you can afford it, our top-of-the-line recommendation is Britax's Freeway. While it doesn't have the automatic belt adjustments of the Guardian, it does have a full recline. And the safety features (especially the locking clamp) can't be beat. At $169 to $189, it's quite an investment.

Car Seat Recalls

Here's a fascinating report you can get on your fax machine. Call the National Highway Transportation Safety Administration at 800-424-9393 and select report 51. In short order, your fax machine will spit out *eight* pages of car seat recalls since 1988. Such recalls occur for both minor reasons (labeling, etc.) and major gaffes (crash test failures, defective latches, and so on). You'll note some companies are more recall-prone than others. Here's a break-down of the recalls by company:

Company	# of car seat recalls since 1988
Century	95
Evenflo	56
Kolcraft	25
Fisher Price	16
Cosco	11
Gerry	3
Others*	30

*Note: of the 236 recalls, 30 were attributed to companies that are now out of business or withdrawn from the market.

Money-Saving Secrets

1 GET A CAR SEAT FOR FREE! Midas Muffler and Brake Shops offer a great deal—a basic Century car seat (model #STE-1000) for free. How does this deal work? Midas sells you the seat at the wholesale price of $42. Then, when your baby outgrows the seat, you take it back to Midas and they give you a $42 certificate for auto repairs. The bottom line: you get a car seat for free! Even if you decide not use the certificate, a car seat at the wholesale price of $42 is a pretty good deal in itself (this seat retails for $50 to $70). We commend Midas for this program (called "Project Safe Baby"), which the company launched to encourage more parents to put their babies in car seats.

2 CHECK WITH YOUR HEALTH INSURANCE CARRIER. Some of these companies offer free car seats (or a car seat at a greatly reduced price) for expectant parents who attend a safety seminar. One parent told us members of the USAA insurance company can purchase up to three Century car seats for just $35 each.

3 EXPENSIVE MODELS AREN'T NECESSARILY BETTER. We bought a $100 car seat and another one that was just $50. Sure the $100 one had thicker padding and fancy fabric, but surprisingly we found the cheaper model easier to use—the seat belt slid easier under the base, it was less bulky, and the straps were easier to adjust. The bottom line: price doesn't always indicate which seat is easiest to use.

4 CHECK OUT TOYS R US. Unlike other juvenile product categories, Toys R Us has most of the premium brands (including Century and Evenflo) at prices that are hard to beat. Infant car seats start at $45, and regular car seats run $50 to $100—about 10% to 20% lower than the prices at baby specialty stores. Even better: wait for a sale. Toys R Us has a "Baby Month" sale in the spring when they knock even more off their prices. Another great place for car seat deals: Baby Depot, part of the Burlington Coat Factory (609) 386-3314. They have incredible prices on name-brand car seats. We also like Target, which sells a good selection of name brands at low prices.

Strollers

Baby stores offer a bewildering array of strollers for parents. Do you want the model that converts from a car seat to a stroller? What about a stroller that would work for a quick trip to the mall? Or do you want a stroller for jogging? Hiking trails? The urban jungle of New York City or Boston?

And what about all the different brand names? Will a basic brand found at a discount store work? Or do you need a higher-quality brand from Japan or Europe? What about strollers with anti-lock brakes and air bags? (Just kidding on that last one).

We hope this section takes some of the mystery out of the stroller buying process. First, we'll look at the six different types of strollers on the market today. Next, we'll zero in on features and help you decided what's important and what's not. Then, it's brand ratings and our picks as the best recommendations for different lifestyles. Finally, we'll go over several safety tips, money-saving hints, wastes of money and a couple of mail-order catalogs that sell strollers.

What Are You Buying?

There are six types of strollers you can buy:

 ♣ *Umbrella stroller.* The name comes from the appearance of the stroller when it's folded, similar to an umbrella.

WHAT'S COOL: They're lightweight and cheap—that is, low price (about $25 to $35). We should note that a few European-made brands (Maclaren and Peg Perego) make a couple of pricey umbrella strollers that sell for $150 to $200.

WHAT'S NOT: They're cheap—that is, low quality (well, with the exception of the Maclaren and Peg Perego's). You typically don't get any fancy features like canopies, storage baskets, reclining seats, and so on. Another problem: most umbrella strollers have hammock-style seats with little head support, so they won't work well for babies under six months of age.

♣ *Carriage/strollers.* A carriage (also called a pram) is like a bed on wheels—most are similar in style to a bassinet. Since this feature is most useful when a baby is young (and less helpful when baby is older), most companies make carriages that convert to strollers.

WHAT'S COOL: If your baby is sleepy, she can lie down. Most combo carriage/strollers have lots of high-end features like reversible handles or seats (so you can push the stroller and see your baby at the same time).

WHAT'S NOT: Hefty weight (not easy to transport or set up) and hefty price tags. Another negative: most have fixed front wheels, which makes maneuvering difficult on quick trips. Some carriage/stroller models can top $300 and $400.

♣ *Lightweight strollers.* These strollers are our top recommendation: they're basically souped-up umbrella strollers with lots of convenience features and not a lot of weight.

WHAT'S COOL: Most offer easy set-up and fold-down; some even fold up similar to umbrella strollers. An amazing number of features (canopies, storage baskets, high-quality wheels) at amazingly light weights (some as light as seven pounds).

WHAT'S NOT: Can be expensive—most high-quality brands run $200 to $300. Some models are so popular, you might have to wait for delivery.

♣ *Jogging strollers.* These strollers feature three big wheels and lightweight frames—perfect for jogging or walking on rough dirt roads.

WHAT'S COOL: How many other strollers can do 15 mph on a jogging trail? Some even have brakes, and the best fold up for easy storage in the trunk.

WHAT'S NOT: They can be darn expensive, topping $200 or even $300. Jogging strollers are a single-purpose item—thanks to their sheer bulk and a lack of steering, you can't use one in a mall or other location.

♣ *All-terrain.* The baby equivalent of four-wheel drive sport-utility vehicles, these strollers are pitched to parents who want to go hiking or other outdoor adventures.

WHAT'S COOL: Big knobby tires and high clearances work better on gravel trails (or roads) than standard strollers. All-terrain strollers still have convenience features (baskets, canopies, etc.), yet don't cost as much jogging strollers (most are under $100). Besides, they look macho.

WHAT'S NOT: A few models have fixed front wheels, making them a hassle to use—when you want to turn the stroller, you have to lift the entire front half off the ground. Even if the front wheels swivel, the larger wheels make the stroller less maneuverable in tight spaces.

♣ *Combo car seats/strollers.* It's the current rage among stroller makers—models that combine infant car seats and strollers. Century kicked off this craze in 1994 with their "4-in-1" model that featured four uses (infant carrier, infant car seat, carriage and toddler stroller).

WHAT'S COOL: Great convenience—you can take the infant car seat out of the car and then snap it into the stroller frame. Voila! Instant baby carriage, complete with canopy and basket. Later, you can use the stroller as, well, just a stroller.

WHAT'S NOT: High price—many of these units can top $150. And what do you get for the money? Well, the infant car seat is nice (which would cost you $50 to $60 anyway), but the strollers themselves are rather cheap. These aren't the high quality brands that you'll read about later in this chapter—most combo units feature heavy strollers that don't fold compactly and lack durability. For example, the original Century 4-in-1 (now discounted to $90 to $100 in some stores) features a very cheap toddler stroller. And you have to use tools to convert the unit from its carriage use to the stroller (a big hassle). Since then, manufacturers have refined the concept and some models require no "conversion" to go from carriage to stroller.

Smart Shopper Tips

Smart Shopper Tip #1
GIVE IT A TEST DRIVE

"My friend was thinking of buying a stroller from a catalog. Should you really buy a stroller without seeing it first in a store?"

Always try before you buy. Most stores have at least one stroller set up as a floor model. Give it a whirl, practice folding it up, and check the steering. Once you've tried it out, shop for price through mail-order sources. Ask a retailer if they will meet or beat prices quoted to you by catalogs (many quietly do so).

Smart Shopper Tip #2
WHAT FEATURES ARE REALLY IMPORTANT?

"Let's cut through the clutter here. Do I really need a stroller that has deluxe shock absorbers and four wheel drive? What features are really important?"

Walk into any baby store and you'll encounter a blizzard of strollers. Do you want a stroller with a reversible handle? Full boot and retractable canopy? What the heck is a boot, anyway? Here's a look at the features common to most strollers available today:

Features for baby:

♣ *Reclining seat.* Since babies under six months of age sleep most of the time and can't hold their heads up, strollers that have seats that recline are a plus. Yet, how much each stroller reclines varies by model. Some have full reclines, a few recline part of the way (120 degrees) and some don't recline at all.

♣ *Front bar.* As a safety precaution, many strollers have a front bar that keeps baby secure (though you should always use the stroller's safety belt). Better strollers have a bar that's padded and removable. Why removable? Later, when your baby gets to toddlerhood, you may need to remove the bar to make it easier for the older child to access the stroller.

♣ *Seat padding.* You'll find every possible padding option out there, from bare-bones models with a single piece of fabric as a baby's seat to strollers with deluxe-quilted padding made from fine fabrics. Some strollers have cardboard platforms as seat area's (these can be uncomfortable for long rides) and other models have fabric that isn't removable nor machine washable (a big no-no).

♣ *Shock absorbers.* Yes, a few strollers do have wheels equipped with shock absorbers for a smoother ride. We're unsure how effective this feature really is—it's not like you could wheel baby over potholes without them waking up. On the other hand, if you live in a neighborhood with uneven or rough sidewalks, it might be worth a look.

♣ *Weather protection.* If you want, you can buy a stroller that's outfitted for battle with Mother Nature. The options include retractable hoods/canopies and "boots" (which protect a child's feet) to block out wind, rain or cold. Fabrics play a role here too—some strollers feature quilted hoods to keep baby warm and others claim they are water repellent. While a boot is truly an option some may not need, hoods/canopies are rather important, even if just to keep the sun out of baby's eyes. Some strollers just have a canopy (or "sunshade") that partially covers baby, while other models have a full hood that can completely cover the stroller. Look for canopies that have "peak-a-boo" windows that let you see baby even when closed.

Features for parents:

♣ *Storage baskets.* Many strollers have deep, under-seat baskets for storage of coats, purses, bags, etc. Yet, the amount of storage can vary sharply from model to model. Inexpensive umbrella strollers may have no basket at all, while models from Japanese makers like Combi and Aprica have tiny baskets. American-made strollers (Graco, etc.) typically have the most storage.

♣ *Removable seat cushion for washing.* Let's be honest: strollers can get gross. Crushed-in cookies, spilt juice and the usual grime can make a stroller a mobile dirt-fest. Some strollers have removable seat cushions that are machine washable—other models let you remove all of the fabric for a washing. Watch out for those models with non-removable fabric/seat cushions—while you can clean these strollers in one of those manual car washes (with a high-pressure hose), it's definitely less convenient (especially in the winter).

♣ *Lockable wheels.* Some strollers have front wheels that can be locked in a forward position—this enables you to more quickly push the stroller in a straight line.

♣ *Wheel size.* You'll see just about every conceivable size wheel out there on strollers today. As you might guess, the smaller wheels are good for maneuverability, but larger wheels handle rough sidewalks (or gravel paths) much better.

♣ *Handle.* This is an important area to consider—the best strollers feature a "reversible" handle. Why would you want that? By reversing the handle, you can push the stroller while the baby faces you (better for small infants). Later, you can reverse the handle so an older child can look out while being pushed from behind. Another important factor: consider the handle *height*. Some handles have adjustable heights to better accommodate taller parents (more on this later). One stroller maker (Aprica) makes a "one-touch fold" handle. Hit a button on the stroller and it can be folded up with one motion.

♣ *Compact fold.* Some strollers fold compactly and can fit in a narrow trunk or airline overhead cabin, which is great if you plan to do much traveling. Not only should you consider how compactly a stroller folds, but also how it folds in general. The best strollers fold with just one or two quick motions; others require you to hit 17 levers and latches.

♣ *Durability.* Should you go for a lower-price stroller or a fancier European brand? Let's be honest: the lower-priced strollers (say, under $200) have nowhere near the durability as the models that cost $200 to $400. Levers that break, reclining seats which stop reclining and other glitches can make you hate a cheap stroller mighty quick. Yet, some parents don't need a stroller that will make it through the next world war. If all you do is a couple of quick trips to the mall every week or so, then a less expensive stroller will probably be fine. Yet, if you plan to use the stroller for more than one child, live an tough urban environment with rough sidewalks, or plan extensive outdoor adventures with baby, then invest in a better stroller. Later in this chapter, we'll go over specific models and give you brand recommendations for certain lifestyles.

♣ *Overall weight.* Yes, it's a dilemma: the more feature-laden the stroller, the more the weight. And, the super light-weight strollers are often quite expensive. Yet it doesn't take lugging a 30-pound stroller in and out of a car trunk more than a few times to justify the expense of a lighter-weight design. Carefully consider a stroller's weight before purchase. Some parents end up with two strollers—a lightweight/umbrella-type stroller for quick trips (or air travel) and then a more feature-laden model for extensive outdoor outings.

Smart Shopper Tip #3
THE CADILLAC OR FORD ESCORT DILEMMA
"This is nuts! I see cheap umbrella strollers that sell for $30 on one hand and then fancy designer brands for $300 on the other. Do I really need to spend a fortune on a stroller?"

Whether you drive a Cadillac or Ford Escort, you'll still get to your destination. And that fact pretty much applies to strollers too—most function well enough to get you and baby from point A to point B.

So, should you buy the cheapest stroller you can find? Well, no. There *is* a significant difference in quality between a cheap $30 umbrella stroller and a name brand that costs $100, $200 or more. Unless you want the endless headaches of a cheap stroller (wheels that break, parts that fall off), it's important to invest in a stroller that will make it through the long haul.

The real question is: do you need a fancy stroller loaded with features or will a simple model do? To answer that, you need to consider *how* you will use the stroller. Do you live in the suburbs and just need the stroller once a week for a quick spin at the mall? Or do you live an urban environment where a stroller is your primary vehicle, taking all the abuse that a big city can dish out? Climate plays another factor—in the Northeast, strollers have to be winterized to handle the cold and snow. Meanwhile, in Southern California, full canopies are helpful for shading baby's eyes from late afternoon sunshine.

Figuring out how different stroller options fit your lifestyle/climate is the key to stroller happiness. Later in this chapter, we'll recommend several specific strollers for certain lifestyles and climates.

Smart Shopper Tip #4
TOO TALL FOR THEIR OWN GOOD

"I love our stroller, but my husband hates it. He's six feet tall and has to stoop over to push it. Even worse, when he walks, he hits the back of the stroller with his feet."

Strollers are made for women of average height. What's that? About 5'6" to 5'8". If you (or your spouse) are taller than that, you'll find certain stroller models will be a pain to use.

This is probably one of the biggest complaints we get from parents about strollers. Unfortunately, just a few stroller models have height-adjustment handles that let a six-foot tall person comfortably push a stroller without stooping over or hitting the stroller with their feet. One smart shopping tip: if you have a tall spouse, make sure you take him or her stroller shopping with you. Checking out handle heights in person before you buy is the only way to avoid this problem.

The Name Game: Reviews of Selected Manufacturers

Here's a wrap-up of many of the stroller brands on the market today. We evaluated strollers based on hands-on inspections, interviews with recent parents, as well as conversations with juvenile product retailers. For us, the most important attribute for strollers was convenience and durability (not to mention safety). Of course, price to value (as reflected in the number of features) was an important factor as well. The prices quote here are "suggested retail." Of course, many of these prices are less at discount stores and mail-order catalogs.

The Ratings

★★★★ EXCELLENT—*our top pick!*
 ★★★ GOOD—*above average quality, prices, and creativity.*
  ★★ FAIR—*could stand some improvement.*
   ★ POOR—*yuck! could stand some major improvement.*

Aprica ....★★★★
1200 Howell Ave., Anaheim, CA 92805. For a dealer near you, call (310) 639-6387 or (201) 883-9800. Aprica (pronounced Ah-pree-cah) has been making strollers for 45 years—and has apparently figured out how to do it right. The Japanese brand is famous for lightweight strollers (one tips the scales at a mere 7 lbs.). Most models that are jam-packed with features like an "independent shock absorbing system," a triple-layered head support, and tires with a lifetime guarantee (sorry, no air bags yet). Our favorite Aprica feature: the "one touch" open/close handles which fold (or unfold) a stroller with a simple "click."
The models. Aprica divides its line into two categories: Prestige (pricey, lightweight aluminum frame strollers) and Royale (less expensive, heavier steel-frame strollers). In the Prestige line, the top-of-the line "Windsor Elite" model features the one-touch open/close, plush padding, triple-padded head support, zip-off boot and pop-up head protection. This model (which is based on the old Prima stroller) also has a height adjustable handle and weighs just 13.5 pounds. Price: $450. If you want an even lighter-weight stroller that folds compact, consider the "Super Zap," which weighs a mere 10 lbs. Although it doesn't have as many features as the Windsor Elite, the Super Zap does have a fully reclining seat, one-touch fold, and a height-adjustable handle (which is a new feature this year). A Super Zap LX runs $300, while the Super Zap EP (which includes a full-length boot) is $325. Two other Prestige models include the Super Mini ($400, which is the same as the Super Zap but includes a reversible handle) and the Flash ($230, a seven-pound stroller with one-touch open/close).
 Realizing those prices are hard to swallow, Aprica recently introduced a lower-price line (Royale) that is made from heavier steel frames. Of course, "heavy" is a relative term—many of these strollers are still much lighter than the competition and, as such, great buys. Basically, the Royale models are based on similar Prestige strollers—the Quantum Royale ($260, 16 lbs.) is similar to the Windsor Elite (but no boot), the Calais Royale ($200, 14 lbs.) is the same as the Super Zap (but no height-adjustable handle or boot), and the Spring Royale ($200, 9 lbs.) is similar to the Flash. The entry-level "Escort" will also weigh 9 lbs. but won't have a reclining seat or safety bar. It will retail

for about $100. We should also point out that Aprica makes the only a tandem stroller (Prestige Embrace) on the market with a reversible handle. It runs about $500.

Our view. Let's be honest: these are great strollers, but the prices are way too high. The new Royale line will certainly help correct this problem, but Aprica remains a brand that few can afford. Nonetheless, if you want to make the investment, the quality and durability of the brand is good. Our only complaint: the storage baskets are skimpy.

Century ....★★
9600 Valley View Rd., Macedonia, OH 44056. For a dealer near you, call (216) 468-2000. Century shook up the stroller world when they introduced the "4-in-1" system a few years ago. By combining an infant car seat and a stroller, Century essentially created an affordable carriage system for the masses. Since then, they've refined the concept and introduced several spin-offs. Of course, Century makes other strollers, from basic umbrella models to all-terrain models. Here's a wrap-up.
The models. All the Century 4-in-1's now use the Smart Fit infant car seat (the 590 has since been phased out). You can still buy the "original 4-in-1" ($100 to $120) but it only comes with a cheap stroller that doesn't recline, plus you need tools to convert it to a stroller . A better bet is the "4-in-1 Pro-Sport" ($150) which includes a nicer stroller that reclines and has a "suspension" system for a smoother ride. New this year, Century will introduce the "4-in-1 TraveLite" that will also feature a reclining stroller, requires no tools for conversion and will be priced between the original and Pro-Sport models. If an all-terrain stroller is what you want, consider the "Adventure", which features oversized swivel weeks that lock for off-road trips. It has a reclining seat, multiple storage areas, and machine washable fabric.
Our view. While we applaud Century for their innovation with the 4-in-1, other manufacturers (specifically, Evenflo) have improved the concept in both design and features. Century's strollers are just average in quality and durability.

Chicco ....★1/2
Distributed by Regalo, 5740 Wayzata Blvd., Minneapolis, MN 55416. For a dealer near you, call (800) 521-2234 or (612) 545-2303. Chicco (pronounced kee-ko) has a 50-year history as one of Europe's leading juvenile products makers. However, the Italian brand has struggled here in the U.S. Its schizophrenic distribution strategy (you can find Chicco in both discount outlets like Baby Superstore and fancy specialty stores) led the company to sack its U.S. distributor and tap Regalo, an unknown Minneapolis start-up with little

experience in the juvenile products business. Whether this will help kick-start Chicco's U.S. sales remains to be seen.

The models. Chicco offers everything from a lightweight umbrella strollers to chrome-frame European-style prams with bassinets (a la Emmaljunga, see review later). The top-of-the-line Belle Epoque is a chrome frame, 32 lb. monster with big wheels and comes complete with both bassinet and stroller. Price: $600. If that's too much, more traditional strollers with reclining seats (the Magic or Mondia) weigh 22-25 lbs. and sell for $390 to $430. On the low-end, Chicco's umbrella strollers (the Baby Fly 5, $160, 11.5 lbs and Clik Clak Super, $250, 16 lbs.) feature fully-reclining seats, storage baskets and washable seat pads.

Our view. How do you say "overpriced"in Italian? Chicco's lack of success in the U.S. can be directly attributed to its very high prices. While the quality is OK, you can find a similar Italian-made stroller at a lower price from Peg Perego (see review later). Another negative: we don't like Chicco's U.S. distributor's pricing policies. Regalo is attempting to set up a U.S. dealer network in which certain stores are granted exclusives on Chicco strollers. Why? To keep prices high, in our opinion. Oddly enough, we should also note that Regalo will be marketing their own brand of strollers. The Taiwanese strollers will include carriage models, tandems and all-terrain "outdoor discovery" strollers. We saw prototypes at a recent show and weren't that impressed. The models were not terribly innovative and the prices ($220 to $270) quite high.

Combi ....★★★★

199 Easy St., Carol Stream, IL 60188. For a dealer near you, call (800) 752-6624, (800) 992-6624, (630) 871-0404. Like Aprica, Combi is a Japanese brand that specializes in high-quality, lightweight strollers. And, also like Aprica, Combi is rolling out a new steel frame line of its strollers that will be lower in price (and somewhat heavier in weight). Yet, Combi does have one advantage—its prices were already below Aprica and hence Combi's new strollers will be even better buys. Let's break it down:

Models. Combi's most successful model must be the "Savvy," a terrific 7 lbs. stroller this is among the lightest weight strollers on the market. Since it only partially reclines, this stroller is probably best for babies six months or older. The compact-folding Savvy comes in two versions: the Z ($250, which has removable, washable seat cushions) and the IV ($215, which doesn't). We've got to hand it to Combi—they have some of the wildest fabric patterns on the market today, including a snazzy leopard print for the Savvy Z. If you're looking for a more full-feature stroller, the 16 lb. "Spirit" includes a reversible handle, three-position reclining seat, one-touch foot release to open and close, plush fabric and a height adjustable handle. Price: $350, which includes a boot. The "Legacy" ($400) is essentially the same as the Spirit, except for more plush fabric. Combi also makes the "Cambridge," a budget version of the Spirit that weighs slightly more (18 lbs.) but costs about $250 (which includes a boot). If that weren't enough, Combi also makes the lightest weight tandem stroller on the market, the Twin Spin ($400)—at 20 lbs., it features a full reclining rear seat and height adjustable handle. A slightly more plush version of this tandem stroller with upgraded fabric (the Twin Star, $460) is also available.

The biggest news at Combi this year is their introduction of lower-price steel frame strollers to be sold in discount stores and baby mega-stores. For example, the compact-folding "Gem" is basically the same as the Savvy, yet weighs 11.5 pounds. The 17.5 lb. "Kidsport" includes more features, including a reclining seat. Perhaps the best new model, however, is the 22 lb. "Dynasty." This upgraded version of the Kidsport includes double-quilted fabric, a fully closing canopy, reversible seat (that makes the stroller into a carriage) and full boot. While prices haven't been set at press time, we expect these three models to retail for $100 to $150, with some stores discounting them below $100.

Our view. Combi is one of our favorite strollers; we own a Savvy as a "second stroller" and have been very happy. The light weight is a great plus for a suburban lifestyles (that is, hauling in and out of a trunk). Combi's quality and durability is excellent. Our only complaint: skimpy baskets. Most Combi's could stand to have their baskets enlarged—fortunately, the new Kidsport and Dynasty models include bigger storage. And its those new, steel-frame models that could take the market by storm. While regular Combi's aren't cheap, you can find them at discount outlets like the Burlington Coat Factory's Baby Depot and mail order catalogs for much less.

Cosco ....★★
2525 State St., Columbus, IN 47201. Call (812) 372-0141 for a dealer near you (or 514-323-5701 for a dealer in Canada). Internet: www.coscoinc.com Long an also-ran in the U.S stroller market, Cosco (owned by Canadian conglomerate Dorel) has recently introduced several new stroller models that are both innovative and affordable. All these models are built in a Chinese factory that is part-owned by Combi, which might explain the cutting-edge design (each model has a contoured arc frame) and up-to-date fashion fabrics (navy blue or hunter green pindots). While we liked these strollers, it remains to be seen whether they can lift Cosco above a crowded marketplace. Here's an overview:

The models. In 1996, Cosco introduced the "Rock N Roller" stroller which rocks *or* glides to soothe a fussy baby—pretty neat. The original Rock N Roller ($89) had a large basket and a full reclining seat that also reversed (so you can see a younger infant while pushing). In 1997, Cosco will debut a "Deluxe" Rock N Roller that will feature a bigger seat, boot and shock absorbers. Also new are two combo car seat/stroller models—the Rock N Roller car/seat stroller ($140), which combines their Turnabout infant car seat with a Rock N Roller stroller) and the "Voyager" ($80, which uses their Arriva car seat and a more plain stroller). While we liked this 4-in-1 model, the real show stopper in 1997 will be a low-price tandem stroller (the "Two Ways") that has a reversible front seat, so the children can face one another. This model features deluxe quilted hoods, full reclining seats, shock absorbers and more—for $120, it's a steal.

Our view. We have to give it to Cosco—unlike other juvenile product giants who churn out look-alike products year after year, this company is really trying to do something innovative. Their new strollers (which sport great features like huge baskets) have piqued our curiosity; but, will do they do the same for parents? To be honest, it will be tough road. For years, Cosco was known for low-price (and cheap quality) strollers. Whether these new models will turn this image around remains to be seen (since they are so new, we've yet to receive significant feedback from parents).

Emmaljunga ....★★¹/₂
Imported by Bandaks-Emmaljunga, 632 Aero Way, Escondido, CA 92029. For a dealer near you, call (800) 232-4411 or (619) 739-8911. Snob appeal, anyone? Made in Sweden, the 70-year-old Emmaljunga line (pronounced Emma-young-ah) features strollers that are built like a '57 Chevy—big, boxy, and with lots of heavy bagmetal. With prices that start at $225, many Emmaljunga models can top $300 and even $400. For that money, you'd expect top-of-the-line features and Emmaljunga doesn't disappoint: oversized polypropylene tires with steel rims for any terrain, shock absorbers, a five-point safety harness, exterior fabrics treated with Scotchgard, and interior linings treated with an anti-microbial finish to prevent mold.

The models. Emmaljunga's top-seller is the "Viking," which is a good example of the line. Built on a steel chrome chassis, the Viking features a full boot and three-position reclining seat, which can be locked into the chassis facing forward or backward (like a carriage). At 34 lbs. and $350, it's a heavy investment. Emmaljunga also sells a "Viking Plus" ($450) which includes a bassinet with wind guard. The rest of Emmaljunga's line features similar strollers with different fabric choices. New to the line are lighter weight models with less features, including the Malibu ($225, 19 lbs., no reclining seat) and the Rio ($270, 29 lbs., with a seat that reclines). If money is no object, Emmaljunga's top-of-the-line model ($550) is an aluminum chassis stroller with matching bassinet.

Our view. We're not sure what the appeal of Emmaljunga stroller is—do parents like the quality and features of a true European-style pram? Or is it merely the sight of a shiny chrome stroller that will impress their friends? On a more realistic note, the drawbacks of Emmaljunga strollers limit their practicality. For example, all models feature fixed front wheels. While that's nice for walking in a straight line, the strollers can't weave in and out of traffic. And the limited maneuverability is complicated by the strollers' heavy weight (many are over 30 lbs.), which will make it difficult to lug in and out of a trunk. As a result, Emmaljunga strollers are really a niche product. If you do serious walking (or slow jogging) on paved or light gravel surfaces, a high-quality Emmaljunga won't disappoint.

Evenflo ....★★¹/₂
1801 Commerce Dr., Piqua, OH 45356. For a dealer near you, call (800) 837-9201 or (513) 773-3971. In Canada, PO Box 1598, Brantford, Ontario, N3T 5V7. (519) 756-0210. As you read earlier in this chapter, Evenflo makes our top-recommended infant car seat, the On My Way. Well, the company has taken this car seat and combined it with a stroller to make the On My Way Travel system.

The models. The On My Way Travel system ($150) is our pick as one of the best combo units on the market today. Yes, Evenflo shamelessly copied the concept from Century, but they went one step further—they improved it. Not only is the car seat better (the On My Way has an easy-to-carry s-shaped handle), but the stroller has better features than the Century. You can convert the unit from carriage to stroller without any tools and the Travel System's stroller has a large canopy—when combined with the canopy on the infant car seat, you can completely shield the baby from the weather. The stroller has a huge storage basket and reclining seat, and removable washable pad. Evenflo also makes a less-expensive version of this model which incorporates the Joy Ride car seat (which doesn't have an auto base or the s-shaped handle) and a simpler stroller that doesn't recline. The Joy Ride Travel System costs about a $100. Of course, Evenflo makes many other stroller models, including a new all-terrain stroller called the "Tri-Wheel." As the name implies, this stroller has three wheels and looks like a jogging stroller with knobby wheels. Other features include a two-position height adjustable handle, a compact fold, multi-position reclining seat, and retractable canopy.

Our view. We own an On My Way Travel System and, while we love it, we're the first to admit it has some flaws. First, don't get any delusions about the stroller. While it does have nice features, the quality and durability isn't anywhere near some of the top brands reviewed in this section. For example, one of the stroller's wheels wobbles and its overall weight (of both the car seat and the stroller) is tiresome. If you buy this system, you'll probably want a second stroller that's lighter and folds more compactly.

Graco ....★¹/₂

Rt. 23, Main St., Elverson, PA 19520. For a dealer near you, call (800) 345-4109, (610) 286-5951. Graco is a great example of what's right (and wrong) with American-made strollers today. The company (a division of Rubbermaid) is probably the market-leader in strollers, with affordable models that are packed with features like oversized baskets. You'll find Graco at chains and discount stores like Target, Toys R Us, Babies R Us/Baby Superstore and more. Graco's line is too numerous for us to describe here, so here's a quick look at the best offerings (in our opinion, of course):

The models. Our favorite Graco stroller has to be the LiteRider ($79 at discount stores). It's lightweight, has a reclining seat, an easy fold, attractive fabric (it comes in navy blue) and a huge storage basket. We've heard very good feedback on this stroller from parents, who like its convenience and low price. If you want a more full-feature model, Graco offers the Seville ($130, 31 lbs.) which has a height-adjustable and reversible handle, three-position reclining seat and large storage basket. A more plush version of this stroller (the Marquis, $150, 32 lbs.) features a full boot and quilted canopy. Graco's tandems are also affordably priced, with the Duo LTD II at $140. We should also mention Graco's all-terrain models. The company helped pioneer this category in 1995 when they debuted with the "Navigator," ($90 to $100) a garish yellow stroller with big knobby tires and high clearance. The only problem with that model was the fact its front wheels were fixed (and hence didn't maneuver well). Graco fixed that problem with a new version with swiveling front wheels—this model is called the "Outrider" ($100 to $110).

Our view. The adage "you get what you pay for" unfortunately applies to Graco. Sure, they're affordable and packed with goodies. That's the good news. The bad news: Graco strollers suffer from far too many quality problems. Yes, they are $100 or $200 less than similar European or Japanese brands, but these strollers just aren't as durable—levers break, reclining seats stop reclining, retractable canopies stop retracting, etc. That's probably why we see many parents who used a Graco for their first child buy a better brand for child #2. Another bummer: these strollers are far too heavy. Many full-feature Graco models tip the scales at over 30 lbs., which may have you cursing the thing in a parking lot. Yet, if all you need is a very light-duty stroller that doesn't have to survive more than one child, a Graco is not a bad choice. The LiteRider would make a good budget stroller for a quick trips to the mall and several parents we interviewed like the Navigator for easy hiking trails. As one parent pointed out, even if the thing breaks, you can go through three LiteRiders before you approach the cost of one Combi or Aprica.

Maclaren .... ★★★
Distributed by KidCo., 901 E. Orchard Ave. #E, Mundelein, IL 60060-3016. For a dealer near you, call (800) 553-5529 or (847) 970-9100. Maclaren is a British-made brand that sells 500,000 strollers each year in 30 countries worldwide. Their specialty? High-quality umbrella strollers made from lightweight aluminum. Maclaren's distribution is limited to the East Coast and the brand has many fans in New York City and Boston. You might wonder whether these parents (who fork over $200 to $300 for a Maclaren) have lost their minds—can't they just go down to a discount store and buy an umbrella stroller for $30? Well, unlike the cheap-o umbrella strollers you find at Toys R Us, Maclaren strollers are packed with good features (five-point safety harnesses, reclining seats) and are built to last, withstanding all the abuse an urban jungle can dish out.

The models. Maclaren's entry-level model (the "Sprinter," $250) weighs 10 pounds and features a fully enclosed protective hood. If you want a model with a reclining seat, check out the "Concorde" ($300, 12 lbs.). It has a three-position, partially reclining seat, full hood and extendable leg rest. The top-of-the-line Cruiser ($360, 16 lbs.) includes a full-reclining seat, full-size mesh basket, bumper bar, larger wheels and dual brakes. A more plush version of this stroller (the Cruiser DX, $420, 17 lbs.) has a full boot and a removable machine-washable seat insert. If you need a side-by-side stroller (preferred by parents of twins), Maclaren offers a partial-recline model (Majestic Double, $520) and a full-recline model (Cruiser Double, $620).

Our view. While those prices are hard to swallow, let us note that we've seen Maclaren discounted in mail-order catalogs like the Baby Catalog of America (800) PLAY-PEN. For example, we've seen the Sprinter for $160 and the Concorde for $200. While those prices are still pretty high, we can understand why parents on Manhattan's Upper West Side think they're well worth the money—few strollers can maneuver around Zabar's *and* outlast those giant potholes on Broadway. We do have one criticism, though: for that money, you'd think Maclaren would throw in a storage basket. Nope, you have to shell out another $10 for that option (they do come standard on Cruisers, though). It's not like $10 would break the bank, but we're still irked by this "nickel and dime them to death" philosophy.

Peg Perego ....★★★★
3625 Independence Dr., Ft. Wayne, IN 46808. For a dealer near you, call (219) 482-8191. Perhaps the biggest frustration with buying a Peg Perego stroller is simply deciding what model to purchase—this hot-selling Italian brand offers a bewildering list of 16 different models, from simple compact-folding strollers to European-style prams to strollers for twins or triplets. Why is Peg Perego so popular? In a word: quality. These are possibly the best made strollers on the planet, loaded with features to please both parent and baby. And, unlike other European brands, Perego doesn't overprice their strollers (full featured styles start at $160). Peg Perego's durability has made it a favorite in New York City, where strollers are your primary vehicle and take quite a beating. In fact, we recently walked into a Barnes & Noble on the Upper West Side and noticed the cafe looked like a Peg Perego showroom—quite a testimonial. Since we don't have the space to review every Peg Perego model here, we'll hit the highlights of the line. Meanwhile, we've posted a chart that compares and contrasts each Perego model on our web page (www.windsor-peak.com). (Note: all the discounted prices quoted here are from the Baby Catalog of America 800-PLAYPEN).

The models. A good starting point with this line is the new "Amalfi " (17.4 lbs) an entry-level model that is still packed with features—reversible handle, full reclining seat, boot, machine-washable upholstery, and storage basket. It retails for about $220. If you want something more plush, the "Roma" ($300-$350, 20 lbs.) is a good bet. This model has the Amalfi's features plus a zippered hood for ventilation, shock absorbers, and boot. The "Milano" ($310, 19 lbs.) and "Elba" ($280, 21 lbs.) are basically variations of the "Roma" with different padding or wheels. Want a traditional European-style pram with wire spoke wheels (similar to Emmaljunga, reviewed earlier)? Perego's got four models in this category. A typical offering is the "Classica" ($370, 20 lbs.), which includes a bassinet, carriage and stroller. If that weren't enough, Perego also offers compact-folding models (the Pliko Matic), tandem strollers (Tender Twin), side by side models (Micro Twin), and even the all-terrain Amico Country with knobby wheels.

Our view. Peg Perego's popularity has been a double edge sword. On the upside, many stores and catalogs discount this brand heavily. On the downside, there are often shortages of popular Perego models. The company also seems perpetually behind in production and slow shipping from Italy doesn't help either. Each year, Perego promises juvenile retailers it's going to step up production and fix the shortage problem . . . and each year, nothing happens. We wonder if they doesn't intentionally short-ship the U.S., artificially creating shortages to give its brand "cache." Despite this gripe, we still think Peg Perego's strollers are tops. We give them our top recommendation.

Peg Perego at a Discount

Sure, Peg Perego makes great strollers, but how can you get them at a discount? Surprisingly, we found several sources. Mail order sources like Kids in Motion of Kokomo, IN (800) 890-8960 and Kid's Factory (317) 864-9405 sell Peg Perego and other brands at deep discounts. One readers said they bought a Peg Perego "Elba" for $239 from Kid's Factory, after seeing it in a store for $299. Yes, says the reader, you pay for shipping ($12, and it arrived in four days) but in most states there is no sales tax—and that can outweigh the shipping charges. Of course, the Baby Catalog of America 800-PLAYPEN also sells Peg Perego at very attractive prices—their most recent catalog features more than a dozen choices (including the "Roma" at $289, compared to $400 in some stores). Another idea: look for last year's fabrics. Each year, Perego comes out with new fabrics and then discontinues the old stuff—and many of the previously mentioned mail-order sources will pick up these strollers at close-out prices. You can also find such deals at baby discount stores like Baby Superstore and LiL' Things (mentioned in Chapter 2).

Other brands to consider

Baby Trend *(800-328-7363, 909-902-5568, internet: www.babytrend.com)* has enjoyed success with a couple of innovative products. It's Snap & Go ($40) is a simple stroller frame that lets parents snap in any major-brand infant car seat—pressto! Instant stroller. Another innovative idea is the Sit N Stand LX ($125), a concept imported from England. This "pushcart" is a regular stroller (with reclining seat, canopy and basket) that has a place for an older child to stand (or sit in a jumpseat) in back. An all-terrain version of the Sit N Stand (the LX II) includes bigger wheels and a padded jumpseat. Of course, Baby Trend also makes several other models, which seem comparable to Graco in price, features and quality.

Fisher Price *(800) 433-5437* has joined the all-terrain stroller craze with two offerings—the ATS 4000 and the tri-wheel

Town & Country. The teal and yellow ATS 4000 is similar to Graco's Navigator, complete with knobby oversized tires, extra-large shock absorbers, and giant storage basket. Yet there is one major difference—it's front wheels swivel for maneuvering. The Town & Country is similar to the ATS-4000, except that it has three wheels (with a front wheel that swivels). We give the edge to the ATS-4000—it has a better storage basket. If you want a more traditional stroller, Fisher Price also offers the "Perfect Fit," which has an adjustable cushion to "provide support where baby needs it most." The stroller features a giant storage basket (and we mean giant), lockable footrest for full enclosure of an infant, three-position reclining seat, canopy and removable washable cushions. The only negative: Fisher Price's choice of fabrics (bright teals, purples) are too loud for some parents.

Well, we have to give it to *Gerry (800) 362-3200, (303) 457-0926* for at least trying something innovative. Their new "Convenience Stroller" features "one-hand steering, a convenient console on handle for drinks and other items, removable front snack tray for safety and convenience and side basket pockets for extra storage." Whew! If you can't pack your entire nursery into this thing, then you're just not trying hard enough. Gerry is also somewhat famous for their affordable jogging strollers, including the Roller Baby ($150). There's even a Double Roller Baby ($220), one of the few side-by-side jogging strollers available on the market.

Parents of multiples should check out *Inglesina (630) 690-6143, Internet: www.x-land.it/inglesina/,* an Italian-made brand of strollers with options for twins, triplets and even quadruplets (and you thought you had challenges with just one). Distributed in the U.S. by Pali (the crib brand), Inglesina offers traditional European-style prams, combo strollers/carriages, and the aforementioned strollers for multiples (overall, prices range from $280 to $550). The new side-by-side "Twin Jet" ($360, no canopy or $480 with canopy) is a compact-folding model with four-position reclining seat and full boot. We like Inglesina and hope their new distributor can expand the success of this often overlooked line.

Kolcraft (773) 247-4494 has joined the "4 in 1" craze with their own infant car seat/stroller combo. Their "Plus 5" combines their Travel About infant car seat with smart handle and a basic toddler stroller in several different trim levels. The stroller isn't that special, though the seat reclines and the storage basket is large. Of course, Kolcraft also makes just strollers too, with entries in both the carriage, lightweight, umbrella and tandem categories. New this year is the Imperial, a carriage stroller with reversible handle that telescopes for taller parents (which is pretty nifty). This stroller has large all-terrain wheels, as does the K-2000 model.

Our Picks: Brand Recommendations

Unlike other chapters, we've broken up our stroller recommendations into several "lifestyle" categories. Since many parents end up with two strollers (one that's full-featured and another that's lighter for quick trips), we'll recommend a primary stroller and a secondary option. For more specifics on the models mentioned below, read each manufacturer's review earlier in this chapter. Let's break it down:

Mall Crawler

You live in the suburbs and drive just about everywhere you go. A stroller needs to be packed with features, yet convenient enough to haul in and out of a trunk. Our top recommendation is a combo unit that includes both an infant car seat and stroller—and our top pick here is the *Evenflo Travel System* ($150). We like the On My Way infant car seat better than the competition and the well-designed carriage/stroller is superior. Good second bets are the Century 4-in-1 Pro Sport ($150) or the Cosco Rock N Stroller car seat/stroller ($140). If you're on a tight budget, the original Century 4-in-1 is a good deal at $100.

Second stroller. This is somewhat more difficult of a recommendation. Generally, we'd recommend a super-light weight stroller that folds compactly. At the budget end, the *Graco LiteRider* ($79) boasts a large number of features at an affordable price. In the middle, *Peg Perego's Pilko Matic* ($190 with hood, 15 lbs.) features a three-position reclining seat, shock absorbers and a compact umbrella fold. We're also excited about *Combi's Gem*, a new model that will weight only 11.5 pounds and retail for around $100.

If you plan to do air travel with baby or just desire something better, consider investing in a top-quality lightweight stroller. In this category, there are only two contenders—*Combi Savvy Z* and the *Aprica Flash EP*. The Combi Savvy Z ($180 at discounters) is a 7.7 lbs. stroller that's high-quality. Aprica goes one step-further with the Flash EP ($230)—not only does it weigh just seven pounds, it also has plusher fabric and an "one touch" one-hand open/close.

Another option with a second stroller for folks in the suburbs is an all-terrain model. If you want to hike on gravel paths or go on other outdoor adventures, consider the *Graco Navigator or Outrider*, the *Fisher Price ATS-4000* or the *Peg Perego Amico Country*. Each has knobby wheels, shock absorbers and more of a "go anywhere" attitude. The Graco and Fisher Price models are around $100, while the Peg Perego is $250 to $300.

Urban Jungle

 When you live in a city like New York City, Boston or Washington D.C., your stroller is more than just baby transportation—it's your primary vehicle. You stroll to the market, on outings to a park or longer trips on weekend getaways. Since you're not lugging this thing in and out of a trunk as much as suburbanites, weight is not as much of a factor. This stroller better take all the abuse a big city can dish out—giant potholes, uneven sidewalks . . . you name it.

We have two words for you: Peg Perego. A full-featured model like *Perego's Roma* (about $300 retail, under that on sale) is plush, yet weatherized to fight the elements. Shock absorbers make for a smooth ride. The only problem—it's too wide to fit down the check-out aisles at some of those grocery stores in New York City (sorry, you can't have everything). Of course, Perego makes a wide range of models in several price ranges. If money is tight, an entry-level Perego can be had from discount catalogs at $150 to $200.

Second stroller. While Peg Peregos' are all nice, they do have one disadvantage. They're heavy (many are 20 to 30 pounds) and most don't fold compactly. Sometimes, all you need is a lightweight stroller that folds like an umbrella (for taxis, etc.), yet can still take stand up to big city abuse. Hence, we recommend Maclaren—their strollers weigh just 10 to 14 pounds, fold compactly, yet offer top-quality construction and durability.

Discounted through mail-order catalogs, you can find Maclarens that start at $160. The Concord and Cruiser models combine great features (reclining seats, etc.) and extra weather-proofing for $200 to $270.

While it's easy to spend less money than a Maclaren or Peg Perego, don't be penny-wise and pound foolish. Less-expensive strollers lack the weather-proofing that living in an East Coast city requires. And since baby spends more time in the stroller than tots in the suburbs, plush fabrics and padding is more of a necessity than a luxury.

Green Acres

 If you live on a dirt or gravel road or a neighborhood with no sidewalks, you need a stroller to do double duty. First, it must handle rough surfaces without bouncing baby all over the place. Second, it must be able to "go to town," folding easily to go into a trunk for a trip to a mall or other store.

There are three stroller solutions we'd recommend: all-terrain, joggers or European-style prams. As we mentioned earlier, good all-terrain models include the *Graco Navigator* or *Outrider*, the *Fisher Price ATS-4000* or the *Peg Perego Amico Country*. For around $100, you get rugged construction, large knobby wheels and shock absorbers . . . yet each easily folds for transport and doesn't weigh a zillion pounds. (The Perego is the exception on the cost side: it's $250 to $300). We'd suggest you get a model that has swivel front wheels for maneuverability, but also can be locked in a forward position for rougher rides.

Another possible solution is a jogging stroller. The two best bets here are *Baby Jogger* ($300, call 509-457-0925 for more info) or *Kool Stop's Kool Stride* ($300, call 503-636-4673). Each has large bicycle tires to handle the roughest roads, yet folds compactly with quick release wheels to fit into a trunk. (More on these models later in this section). The only disadvantage: jogging strollers have fixed front wheels, making them difficult to maneuver. These strollers large size makes them impractical to use in a mall or store.

The final option is a European-style pram. Yes, we realize this sounds like an oxymoron, but many of these well-built carriage strollers boast big, all-terrain wheels—perfect for handing a gravel road. *Emmaljunga's Viking* (retail $380, mail order $250) comes complete with shock absorbers, adjustable seat and many more features. The only disadvantage: most of these strollers are very heavy, tipping the scales at over 30 lbs.

Exercise This

If you like to walk or jog, you don't have to leave baby at home. Many models today let you take junior along for that power walk or merely a jog in the park. (As a side note, most safety experts suggest waiting until your baby is a year old before taking him along on a jog).

Most jogging strollers have three wheels and are built like bicycles—they boast large rubber wheels with rugged tread that can handle any terrain, yet smoothly move along at a fast clip. What's the best jogging stroller? To be honest, we'd stay away from those low-price models made by "juvenile products companies." Instead, consider a company that specializes in just making high quality models (many are also in the bike business). Why? Those cheap-o strollers can't compare to the quality of the better-made brands. If you're serious about jogging, you should invest in a good jogging stroller.

To that end, there are just two contenders: *Baby Jogger* (call 800-241-1848 or 509-457-0925 for a dealer near you) and *Kool Stop* (call 503-636-4673). Each makes a jogging stroller that sells for about $300 to $400 (but are discounted to $225 in superstores and mail-order catalogs). We give the edge to Kool Stop's "Kool Stride" (model KS-S). While Baby Jogger has the better-known name (and larger distribution), the Kool Stride is designed better—it features a five-point safety harness, reclining seat, and retractable hood. Another plus: the Kool Stride's rear wheels are angled by five degrees for improved tracking. Quick release wheels and easy fold up make the stroller easy to transport.

Of course, when you look at those prices, you have to ask yourself—is this overkill? If you like to do occasional walks in the park but aren't training for a marathon, a simpler stroller may do. One parent in San Diego we interviewed liked the *Emmaljunga "Rio"* (about $200 to $250), which glided easily for power walks but also worked for a trip to the mall. On the lower end, all of the all-terrain strollers mentioned in the "Green Acres" lifestyle earlier in this chapter would also work for folks who like to walk at a nice pace.

Strollers for Two

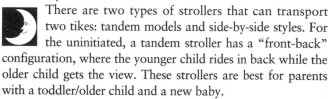 There are two types of strollers that can transport two tikes: tandem models and side-by-side styles. For the uninitiated, a tandem stroller has a "front-back" configuration, where the younger child rides in back while the older child gets the view. These strollers are best for parents with a toddler/older child and a new baby.

Side-by-side strollers, on the other hand, are best for parents of twins. In this case, there's never any competition to see who gets to sit in front. The only downside: many of these strollers are so wide, they can't fit through narrow doorways or store aisles.

Like any stroller choice, you can go cheap or expensive. But, remember when you're considering a stroller for two, it must take twice the weight, twice the abuse and more. Hence, we're only going to recommend the better-quality options and skip the low-price offerings by Graco and others.

As for tandem strollers, your big choice is weight—do you want a lower price stroller that weighs over 30 lbs. or do you want to shell out another $100 to $200 for a lighter-weight option? On the heavy side, we like the *Peg Perego Tender Twin* ($400 retail, $330 mail order, 27 lbs.). For the money, it's a top-quality stroller with plush fabric and a compact fold. If you want to go light, try out the *Combi Twin Spin* ($350 retail, $280 mail order). This amazing stroller weighs a mere 20 pounds, yet features a height adjustable handle, reclining rear seat, removable front guard rail, removable washable cushions and more. As a side note, Combi also makes a more plush version of this stroller called the Twin Star ($400 retail, $310 mail order).

A dark horse contender for the tandem stroller crown is the *Cosco "Two Ways."* This new model features a reversible front seat so the children can face one another. For $120, you get full reclining seats, shock absorbers, quilted hoods and more. While we don't except the quality on this model to be the same as Peg Perego, we do expect Cosco to give Graco (and other low-priced tandem makers) a run for their money.

What about side by side strollers? Once again, we have to give the nod to Peg Perego and Maclaren—each makes lightweight models that are top-quality. The least expensive option is **Peg Perego's Micro Twin** (21 lbs., $400 retail, $290 mail order). This model has reclining seats, shock absorbers and a full-size double hood. Maclaren offers two options: the bare-bones **Majestic Double** (20 lbs., $400 retail, $330 mail order) or the more deluxe **Cruiser Double** (23 lbs., $500 retail, $400 mail order). The latter model has full reclining seats, but both are just 29" wide, which will enable them to fit through more doorways that most side-by-sides.

Of course, don't forget the **Emmaljunga "Monaco Duet"** ($450 retail, $300 mail order). At 38 lbs., it isn't lightweight, but offers parents the advantages of a full stroller/carriage. This model includes a full boot.

Safe & Sound

Next to walkers, the most dangerous juvenile products on the market today are strollers. That's according to the U.S. Consumer Product Safety Commission, which estimates that over 10,000 injuries a year occur from improper use or defects. The problems? Babies can slide out of the stroller, and small parts can be a choking hazard. Seat belts have broken in some models, while other babies are injured when a stroller's brakes fail on a slope. Here are some safety tips:

♣ *Never hang bags from the stroller handle*—it's a tipping hazard.

♣ *Don't leave your baby asleep unattended in a stroller.* Many injuries happen when infants who are lying down in a stroller roll or creep and then manage to get their head stuck in the stroller's leg openings.

♣ *The brakes shouldn't be trusted.* The best stroller models have brakes on two wheels; cheaper ones just have one wheel that brakes. Even with the best brakes, don't leave the stroller unattended on an incline.

♣ *Follow the weight limits.* Most strollers shouldn't be used for babies over 35 pounds.

♣ *Check for the JPMA certification.* The JPMA (the Juvenile Products Manufacturers Association) has a pretty good safety certification program. They require that strollers must have a locking device to prevent accidental folding and meet other safety standards, such as those for brakes. You can contact the JPMA for a list of certified strollers at (609) 231-8500.

Recalls: Where to Find Information

The U.S. Consumer Product Safety Commission has a toll-free hotline at (800) 638-2772 for the latest recall information on strollers and other juvenile products. It's easy to use—the hotline is a series of recorded voice mail messages that you access by following the prompts. You can also report any potential hazard you've discovered or an injury to your child caused by a product. If you prefer, you can write to the U.S. Consumer Products Safety Commission, Washington, D.C. 20207. Another source: check out the CPSC's web site (www.cpsc.gov) for the recalls and safety information.

Money-Saving Tips

1 CHECK OUT THE DISCOUNTERS. Later in this chapter, we'll spotlight the Baby Catalog of America, which offers great discounts on such well-known brands as Peg Perego, Combi and Aprica. Also, we'd be remiss not to mention the baby mega-stores LiL' Things (for the store nearest you, call 817-649-6100), Babies R Us/Baby Superstore and the Burlington Coat Factory's Baby Depot (800) 444-COAT. All carry famous names at rock-bottom prices. Special kudos are due to the Baby Depot—their frequent sales mean even bigger deals on strollers.

2 WHY NOT A BASIC UMBRELLA STROLLER? If you only plan to use a stroller on infrequent trips to the mall, then a plain umbrella stroller for $30 to $40 will suffice. One caveat: make sure you get one that is JPMA certified (see above section for details). Some cheap umbrella strollers have been involved in safety recalls.

3 CONSIDER THE ALTERNATIVES. Some smart inventors have come up with alternatives to strollers. For example, the Snap N Go Lite (also called Kar Seat Karriage) from Baby Trend (800) 328-7363 or (909) 902-5568 turns major brands of infant car seats into a stroller—you just put the car seat in the frame. The cost: about $35.

4 CHECK FOR SALES. We're always amazed by the number of sales on strollers. We've seen frequent sales at the Burlington Coat Factory's Baby Depot, with good markdowns on Aprica and Peg Perego strollers, to name a few.

And just the other week we received a coupon booklet from Toys R Us that featured a $10 off coupon on any Graco stroller over $70. That's nearly a 15% savings off the already low prices. Another reason strollers go on sale: the manufacturers are constantly coming out with new models and have to clear out the old.

4 LOOK FOR DISCONTINUED FABRICS. If you don't feel comfortable buying a discontinued stroller, consider buying one with discontinued *fabric*. Yes, many stroller manufacturers sell the same models year after year . . . they just occasionally add new fabrics. When this happens, they'll discount strollers still in inventory that have the old fabric. You'll find these models heavily discounted (as much as 50% off) in stores and mail-order sources like the ones listed earlier. A reader in Vermont found an Emmaljunga Viking Plus with discontinued fabric for just $229—that's a steep discount off the regular $480 retail. And it's not like stroller fabric fashion varies much from year to year—is there really much difference between "navy pin dot" and "navy with a raspberry diamond"?

5 SCOPE OUT FACTORY SECONDS. Believe it or not, some stroller manufacturers sell "factory seconds" at good discounts—these "cosmetically imperfect" models might have a few blemishes, but are otherwise fine. An example: one reader told us Combi occasionally has "showroom models" that are offered to the public at good discounts. She found a factory second for just $199—that's much less than the $350 retail price. Call Combi at (800) 992-6624 or (708) 350-0101 for more info. Another reader told us Baby Jogger (800) 241-1848, (509) 457-0925 has factory seconds that are sold at $60 off the retail price.

6 DON'T FALL VICTIM TO STROLLER OVERKILL. Seriously evaluate how you'll use the stroller and don't over buy. Flashy strollers can be status symbols for some parents—try to avoid "stroller envy" if at all possible.

7 REJUVENATE A SECOND-HAND STROLLER. You're browsing a neighborhood garage sale when suddenly you see it—the perfect stroller at a bargain price. The only problem? The fabric is dirty, stained . . . or worse. We have an answer: renew that garage sale find or hand-me-down with a new set of pads. Nojo makes an entire line of stroller fabric covers in a variety of patterns. For $30 to $35, you can give an older stroller new life. For a Nojo dealer near you, call (800) 854-8760 or (714) 858-9717.

Wastes of Money

1 GIVE THE "BOOT" THE BOOT. Some expensive strollers offer a "boot" or apron that fits over the baby's feet. This padded cover is supposed to keep the baby's feet dry and warm when it rains or snows. But how many parents walk their baby in the rain or snow anyway? We say save the $20 to $60 extra cost and buy a blanket instead.

2 SILLY ACCESSORIES. Entrepreneurs have worked over time to invent all kinds of silly accessories that you "must have" for your stroller. We've seen stroller "snack trays" ($15) for babies who like to eat on the run. Another company made a clip-on bug repellent which used sound waves to scare away insects. Yet another money-waster: extra seat cushions or head supports for infants made in your stroller's matching fabric. You can find these same items in solid colors at discount stores for 40% less.

One accessory we do recommend is a toy bar (about $20), which attaches to the stroller. Why is this a good buy? If toys are not attached, your baby will probably punt them out the stroller. Another affordable idea: Rinky Links ($9) from the Right Start Catalog (800-548-8531) enable you to snap toys to plastic rings that attach to the stroller.

Do It By Mail

The Baby Catalog of America

To Order Call: (800) PLAYPEN (1-800-752-9736) or
(203) 931-7760; Fax (203) 931-7764
Or write to: Baby Catalog of America 719-721 Campbell Ave.,
West Haven, CT 06516.
Credit Cards Accepted: MC, VISA, AMEX, Discover.

 If you're tired of high prices for strollers and carriages, you've got to get a copy of the Baby Catalog of America. Granted, the catalog itself is nothing fancy (just black and white pictures), but the prices are fantastic. And, best of all, the Baby Catalog sells such premium brand names as Peg Perego, Aprica, Inglesina, and even Emmaljunga.

In fact, it's the sheer variety of different brand names available that really impressed us. From the basic (Century, Graco) to the super-expensive, the selection is expansive (including some of our top picks from Aprica and Combi). Unfortunately, the catalog doesn't list or show all the strollers available you have to call for a quote on most brands.

However, we did see quite a few of the Perego strollers listed, and the prices were discounted 10% to 30% off retail.

Of course, you have to pay shipping and handling. Thanks to the heavy package weight of some strollers (up to 35 pounds), this runs $10 to $20 extra. Yet, you don't pay any sales tax (unless you live in Connecticut) and that may outweigh the shipping. You can also join the Baby Club of America (the Baby Catalog's parent company) for $25 per year. Members get an additional 10% off the catalog price, special deals and other perks.

The Well-Stocked Diaper Bag

We consider ourselves experts at diaper bags—we got *five* of them as gifts. While you don't need five, this important piece of luggage may feel like an extra appendage after your baby's first year. And diaper bags are for more than just holding diapers—many include compartments for baby bottles, clothes, and changing pads. With that in mind, let's take a look at what separates the great diaper bags from the rest of the pack. In addition, we'll give you our list of nine items for a well-stocked diaper bag.

Smart Shopper Tips

Smart Shopper Tip #1

DIAPER BAG SCIENCE

"*I was in a store the other day, and they had about one zillion different diaper bags. Some had cute prints and others were more plain. Should I buy the cheapest one or invest a little more money?*"

The best diaper bags are made of tear-resistant fabric. Contrast that with low-quality brands that are made of cheap, thin vinyl—after a couple of uses, they start to split and crack. Yes, high-quality diaper bags will cost more ($30 to $40 versus $15 to $20), but you'll be much happier in the long run.

Here's our best piece of advice: buy a diaper bag that doesn't look like a diaper bag. Sure those bags with dinosaurs and pastel animal prints look cute now, but what are you going to do with it when your baby gets older? A well-made diaper bag that doesn't look like a diaper bag will make a great piece of carry-on luggage later in life.

The best bets: Lands' End's or Eddie Bauer's high-quality diaper bags (see reviews later). Another option: the Designer Diaper bag from the Right Start Catalog (800-548-8531) is cleverly designed like a purse, complete with designer fabric. Inside you get a changing pad, storage pouch, bottle pockets, and a waterproof bag. Cost: $40. A mini version of the bag is available for $20.

Smart Shopper Tip #2
MAKE YOUR OWN

"Who needs a fancy diaper bag? I just put all the necessary changing items into my favorite backpack."

That's a good point. Most folks have a favorite bag or backpack that can double as a diaper bag. Besides the obvious (wipes and diapers), put in a large zip-lock bag as a holder for dirty/wet items. Add a couple of receiving blankets (as changing pads) and the key items listed below, and you have a complete diaper bag.

Another idea: check out the "Everything But The Bag" ($30) from McKenzie Kids (call 503-238-7675 for a store near you). This gift box includes everything you need for a diaper bag (insulated bottle holder, changing pad, dirty duds bag, toiletry kit, etc.) but the bag itself.

Top Nine Items for a Well-Stocked Diaper Bag

After much scientific experimentation, we believe we have perfected the exact mix of ingredients for the best-equipped diaper bag. Here's our recipe:

1 GO FOR TWO DIAPER BAGS—one that is a full-size, all-option big hummer for longer trips and the other that is a mini-bag for a short hop to dinner or shopping. Here's what each should have:

The full-size bag: This needs a waterproof changing pad that folds up, waterproof pouch or pocket for wet clothes, a couple compartments for diapers, blankets/clothes, etc. Super-deluxe brands have bottle compartments with Thinsulate (a type of insulation) to keep bottles warm or cold. Another plus are outside pockets for books and small toys. A zippered outside pocket is good for change or your wallet.

The small bag: This has enough room for a few diapers, travel wipe package, keys, wallet, and/or a checkbook. Some models have a bottle pocket and room for one change of clothes. If money is tight, just go for the small bag. To be honest, the full-size bag is often just a security blanket for first-time parents—they think if they lug around every possible item they'll need, no catastrophes will happen. But, in the real world, you'll quickly discover schlepping that big full-size bag everywhere isn't practical. While a big bag is nice for overnight or long trips, we'll bet you will be using the small bag much more often.

2 STOCK EXTRA DIAPERS. Put a dozen in the big bag, two or three in the small one. Why so many? Babies can go through quite a few in a very short time. Of course, when baby gets older (say over a year), you can cut back on the number of diapers you need for a trip. Another wise tip: put whole packages of diapers and wipes in your car(s). We did this after we forgot our diaper bag one too many times and needed an emergency diaper.

3 A TRAVEL-SIZE WIPE PACKAGE. We find the best are the plastic cases that you can refill. Some wipe makers sell travel packs that are allegedly "re-sealable"; we found that they aren't.

4 BLANKET AND CHANGE OF CLOTHES. Despite the reams of scientists who work on diapers, they still aren't leak-proof—plan for it. A change of clothes is most useful for babies under a year of age, when leaks are more common. After that point, this becomes less necessary.

5 PAIR OF SUNGLASSES AND A HAT. We like the safari-type hats that have flaps to cover your baby's ears (about $10 to $20). Baby sunglasses serve two purposes: one, they shield your baby's eyes from damaging ultraviolet light; two, they look so darn cute in pictures.

6 BABY TOILETRIES. Babies can't take much direct expo-sure to sunlight—sunscreen is a good bet for babies over six months of age (doctors advise against it for younger infants). Besides sunscreen, other optional acces-sories include bottles of lotion and diaper rash creme. The best bet: buy these in small travel or trial sizes.

7 DON'T FORGET THE TOYS. We like compact rattles, board books, teethers, etc.

8 SNACKS. When your baby starts to eat solid foods, hav-ing a few snacks in the diaper bag (a bottle of juice, crackers, a small box of Cheerios®) is a smart move.

9 YOUR OWN PERSONAL STUFF. We put our wallet, check-book, and keys in the diaper bag. If we ever lose this thing, we're sunk.

Our Picks: Brand Recommendations

We've looked the world over and have come up with two top choices for diapers bags: Land's End and Eddie Bauer. They both meet our criteria for a great diaper bag—

each offers both full-size and smaller bags, they don't look like diaper bags, each uses high-quality materials and, best of all, they are affordably priced. Let's take a look at each:

Land's End (800) 356-4444 sells not one but three diaper bags: The Do-It-All Diaper bag ($29.50), the Deluxe ($45), and the Little Tripper ($20).

The Do-it-All is a best buy. Made of tough heavy-duty nylon fabric (the same as Lands' End's luggage), the diaper bag features a large main compartment for diapers and wipes, a clip for your keys, and a detachable waterproof pouch for wet clothes. Then there's another zippered compartment for a blanket or change of clothes, a waterproof changing pad and an expandable outside pocket for books and small toys. Outside, you'll find a zippered pocket on the other side and a small pouch with a Velcro closure. And, if that weren't enough, the bag also has two large pockets for bottles on each end of the bag.

Whew! That's a lot of stuff. But how does it work in the real world? Wonderful, as a matter of fact. We've hauled this thing on cross-country airline trips, on major treks to the mountains, and more. It still looks new. At $29.50, it isn't cheap, but considering the extra features and durability, we think it's worth the money.

How about those quick trips to the store? We bought the Little Tripper for this purpose and have been quite happy. It has a changing pad, waterproof pouch and bottle pocket. With just enough room for a few diapers, wipes and other personal items, it's perfect for short outings. And, at $19.50, it's a good value.

In case you need more room, the Deluxe ($45) is a bigger version of the Do-It-All (about 20% larger). It has a bigger changing pad, two zippered pouches for wet clothes and other items, a zippered compartment on the outside, built-in toiletry kit and larger bottle pockets lined with Thinsulate to keep food cool or warm.

Not to be outdone, *Eddie Bauer* (800) 426-8020 offers *four* diaper bags. Each is made of high-quality nylon that's easy to clean and contains a removable changing pad, two exterior bottle pockets, and a detachable pocket for damp items. Bauer's full-size option is the Diaper Shoulder Bag ($40), but you can also buy a diaper back-pack for $55. Our favorite is the smaller-size "Diaper Day Bag" ($28). Yes, it's more than the Little Tripper, but it's also larger and well-designed. We bought an Eddie Bauer Diaper Day Bag and swear by it.

Carriers

Strollers are nice, but you'll soon discover that your baby doesn't want to sit in one for a long time. No, they really want to be with you. So, how do you cart around a baby for long distances without throwing out your back?

Several companies have come to the rescue with dozens of different carriers, all designed to make your little one more portable. Carriers come in two flavors: soft carriers (for everyday use) and backpack carriers (for outdoor adventures like hiking and more).

As for the soft carriers, one of the more famous is Nojo's *Baby Sling* (about $40; call 714-858-9496 for a dealer near you). The Sling enables you to hold your baby horizontally or upright. Babies seem to run hot or cold about the Baby Sling—we used one and found that our baby would go to sleep in it if he was really tired. However, he was less thrilled about the Sling when he was awake. And that experience pretty much paralleled the experiences of the parents we interviewed—some had babies who loved the Sling and others panned.

So, what's the best soft carrier on the market? We have two words for you: *Baby Bjorn*. Quite simply, we love this thing! In a Bjorn, baby can face forward or backward and is positioned for easy carrying. Adjusting the straps is also easy, since everything is up front. And best of all, you can snap off the front of the Bjorn to put a sleeping baby down. Imported from Europe by Regal Lager (for a store near you, call 800-593-5522), the Baby Bjorn isn't cheap ($70 retail, $57 in catalogs like Kid's Club, 800-363-0500) but it's vastly superior to other carriers on the market.

Yes, there are other brands of carriers on the market (notably, Kappochi and Snugli), but we've heard mixed reviews about these cheaper options. The only carrier parents unanimously can agree on is the Bjorn.

What about back-pack carriers? If you plan a hiking adventure, serious outdoor enthusiasts go nuts over the *Tough Traveler Back Pack* ($79.95, call 800-GO-TOUGH or 518-377-8526). Adjustable for just the right fit, the Tough Traveler features cushioned pads, tough nylon cloth, and two-shoulder harnesses for baby. A comfortable seat provides head and neck protection for smaller children— you even get a zippered pouch for storage. For infants through four years. Another source of outdoor baby gear is the Campmor catalog (800) 226-7667. So, how do decide which carrier is best for you and your baby? The best advice is to borrow different models from your friends and give them a test drive.

Restaurant Trips—

We live in a town with wonderful restaurants—hence, when we became parents, we were loathe to forego eating out. Granted, some parents don't want to be bothered with restaurants; one couple we interviewed didn't eat out with their baby until he was seven months old! However, it's not as difficult as you might think. Newborns and infants (up to a year old) can be surprisingly good dinner dates. After that point, things get a little trickier. Before you reach the "terrible twos," it is possible to eat out with your baby—if you master the "surgical strike." Here are our nine tips to eating out with baby:

♣ *Surprisingly, the easiest time to eat out with a baby is when he or she is a newborn.* Why? They tend to sleep all the time anyway. If your baby feeds every two hours, you can easily fit a nice meal (and even dessert) into that interval. Later, when the baby gets more active, is when the fun begins.

♣ *Before the baby is born, scout out restaurants that have booths and high chairs.* Let's be honest: some restaurants are more kid-friendly than others. The best have nice high chairs (not metal death traps), private booths (great for nursing), diaper changing stations in the rest rooms (believe it or not, some places actually do have these), and wait people who are understanding. Create a mental "restaurant map" with spots that have all of the above amenities.

♣ *Make reservations.* Babies hate to wait for a table, or anything else. If you can't make reservations, call ahead to gauge the wait. Some restaurants have call-ahead seating, which puts you on a waiting list *before* you arrive. While you might have been willing to wait 30 minutes or more for a table when you were "without baby," the maximum now should be no more than 15 minutes. Think of this as a surgical strike—you want to get in, eat, and leave . . . not waste time waiting for a table.

Mastering the Surgical Strike

♣ *Go for close parking.* We eliminate restaurants that don't have close, abundant parking. It's no fun searching for that elusive parking spot, dragging Junior three blocks, getting out a stroller, etc.

♣ *If you can't eat out, see if there is a restaurant delivery service in your area.* Not long ago, the only food you could get delivered was pizza. In our town, a new delivery service delivers food from 30 different restaurants. Now we can get our fix of Thai, Southwestern, French, or whatever for just a $3 delivery charge per order.

♣ *Go early.* We like to hit many restaurants in the 5 pm to 6 pm time range. It's less busy, the staff isn't harried, and the kitchen can get the meals out quicker.

♣ *You may have to forget dining out on the weekend.* The wait and crowds may make a home-cooked meal seem like a better deal on Saturday night.

♣ *Do the Cracker Dance.* Here's an all-purpose baby toy: the package of crackers. Not for eating, mind you, for playing. They're shiny, make neat noises, and are quite chewable—and restaurants tend to have them in stock. You'll enjoy this trick so much you'll probably start hauling around packages of crackers just in case your favorite cafe is out.

♣ *Walk your child around before the meal arrives.* Then, when the food hits the table, it's into the high chair (or carrier for young infants). That way you minimize the amount of time sitting in that high chair and the boredom your baby is bound to feel.

Late-breaking news on car seats: As we went to press, the federal government was set to announce a new "universal" car seat design that would address some of the concerns we outlined earlier. The new seat will be phased in over the next few years—we'll post the latest developments on this issue on our web site at *www.windsorpeak.com/*.

THE BOTTOM LINE:
A Wrap-Up of Our Best Buy Picks

 We strongly recommend buying an infant car seat/carrier—the sheer convenience makes it worth the $40 to $60 price tag. The best bet is Evenflo's On My Way car seat (which also comes in a "travel system" package with a stroller), although Century's Smart Fit is a good second choice.

As far as the larger, "convertible" car seats go, we thought Midas' free offer for a Century 1000 STE car seat can't be beat. If you want something more plush, however, we think the safest car seat on the market is Britax's Freeway ($169 to $189)—it meets both the European and U.S. safety standards, plus does away with the dreaded locking clip.

Strollers are a world unto themselves, with prices ranging from $30 for a cheap umbrella style to $500 or more for a deluxe foreign model with all the bells and whistles. The key message here is to buy the right stroller for your lifestyle (see specific recommendations earlier in this chapter). No one model works best for all situations.

In general, the best stroller brands are Peg Perego, Combi, Aprica and Maclaren. For jogging strollers, the Kool Stop is hot, while we thought Fisher Price's all-terrain strollers were good choices for off-road adventures.

Who's got the best deals on strollers and car seats? We like the Baby Depot for their fantastic sales, but both LiL' Things, Baby Superstore/Babies R Us shouldn't be overlooked either. If you want to shop by mail, try the Baby Catalog of America for low prices and a wide selection of name brands.

Now that your baby is mobile, don't forget the diapers—or the diaper bag. The best bets are the high-quality options from Lands' End and Eddie Bauer. For $30 to $40, you can get a full-size bag or consider a smaller "day bag" for $20 to $30. Or who says you need a diaper bag at all—convert your favorite back pack or other bag into a diaper bag with a few small additions like a changing pad and water-proof clothing container.

Baby carriers? Baby Bjorn ($70) runs away with the crown, although some parents like the Nojo's Baby Sling ($40) and serious outdoor enthusiasts consider Tough Traveler's baby backpacks the best.

Chapter 8

Affordable Baby Proofing

I nside this chapter, you'll discover how to baby proof your home on a shoe-string budget. We've got room-by-room advice and several money-saving tips that might surprise you. Which devices work best? We'll give you the answers and share four mail-order catalogs that will save you time and money. Finally, learn what items should be in your baby's first aid kit.

Getting Started: When do you need this stuff?

 Whatever you do, start early. It's never too soon to think about baby proofing your house. Everyone we talked to admitted they waited until their baby "almost did something" (like playing with extension cords or dipping into the dog's dish) before they panicked and began childproofing.

Remember Murphy's Law of Baby Proofing: your baby will be instantly attracted to any object that can cause permanent harm. The more harm it will cause, the more attractive it will be to him or her. A word to the wise: start baby proofing as soon as your child begins to roll over.

Smart Baby Proofing Tips

The statistics are alarming—each year, 100 children die and millions more are injured in avoidable household accidents. Obviously, no parent wants their child to be injured by a preventable accident, yet many folks are not aware of common dangers. Others think if they load up their house with safety gadgets, their baby will be safe. Yet, there is one basic truth about child safety: safety devices are no substitute for adult supervision. While this chapter is packed with all kinds of gizmos and gadgets to keep baby out of harm's way, you still have to watch your baby at all times.

Where do you start? Get down on your hands and knees and look at the house from your baby's point of view. Be sure to go room by room throughout the entire house. As you take your tour, here are some points to keep in mind:

General Tips

♣ *Throw away plastic bags and wrappings*—these are a suffocation hazard. And there are more plastic bags and packing in your house than you might realize—dry cleaning bags, grocery bags and bubble pack are all prime suspects.

♣ *Put window guards on any windows you plan to open.* Otherwise, keep all windows locked.

♣ *Mini-blind cords can be a strangulation hazard.* Put them high off the floor or buy cord shorteners (available from many of the safety catalogs we review later in this chapter). Another money-saver: inexpensive cleats from hardware stores let you wrap up the cords, keeping them far from baby's reach.

♣ *Always use gates at the TOP and BOTTOM of stairs.* Placing a gate two or three steps up from the bottom allows your child to practice climbing without the danger.

♣ *Keep your child out of garages and basements.* There are too many items stored in these areas that can be dangerous (like pesticides and gardening equipment).

♣ *Put the cat's litter box up off the floor.* Even better: install a cat-sized pet door in the laundry room, put the litter box in there, and keep the door closed.

♣ *Keep pet food dishes and water dishes out of baby's reach.* Besides eating dog or cat food (and maybe choking on it), some pets jealously guard their food and might snap at an eager toddler. Water dishes are a drowning hazard.

♣ *Fireplaces can be a major problem.* Never leave your child unattended around a fire. Even if there is no fire in the fireplace, the soot left behind is a toxic snack. Fireplace tools aren't good play toys either; put them away in a locked cabinet. Consider buying a bumper pad to go around the hearth to prevent injuries.

♣ *Cover outlets.* You can buy outlet covers from hardware stores or safety catalogs. Consider moving heavy furniture in front of some of your outlets as well. Safety experts caution that those cheap outlet plugs are a choking hazard.

♣ *Fire escape ladder.* If you live in a two-story home, purchase a portable fire escape ladder. These ladders fold up compactly for storage. The Perfectly Safe catalog (800) 837-KIDS sells one in both two-story ($90) and three-story ($130) versions.

Bathrooms

♣ *Toilets make a convenient stepping stool and can be used to reach the bathroom countertop.* Take hair dryers and curling irons off the counter and put them in a locked cabinet.

♣ *Secure tub spouts or nozzles with protective covers.*

♣ *Set your hot water heater to a lower setting.* The best temperature for baby-friendly bathrooms is 120 degrees or less. As an alternative, you can purchase an anti-scalding device that attaches to showers or sink faucets. We saw one from the Perfectly Safe catalog (800-837-5437) called the ScaldSafe. The shower version sells for $16.95 and the sink model for $9.95. It shuts the water off immediately when it reaches 114 degrees.

♣ *Hide medication* (including vitamins), mouthwash, perfume, and anything else containing alcohol in a cabinet with a latch. Don't think that a childproof cap is really childproof. Junior is much smarter than those rocket scientists at the drug companies think he is. Keeping all items that pose a hazard out of reach is your best defense. Each year, one million children accidentally ingest medicines or chemicals. Sadly, 50 of those cases are fatal.

♣ *Get a toilet lock for all the toilets* (about $10 from hardware stores and safety catalogs). Toddlers are fascinated with the water in the bowl. If they fall in head first, they won't be able to get themselves out. Also, don't use those colored deodorant products in the toilet. Not only are they toxic and therefore inherently dangerous, but they also make the toilet water a more enticing blue color.

♣ *Check out those bath rugs and mats.* Get non-skid versions or buy rubber backing to keep baby from slipping when she starts walking.

♣ *Never leave buckets of water around,* in the bathroom or anywhere in the home. If your baby should fall in head first, the weight of his head makes it impossible for him to leverage himself out. The result could be a tragic drowning, even in an inch or two of water.

♣ *Separate your medicine and vitamins from the baby's.* You don't want to make any mistakes in the middle of the night, when you're sleepy and trying to get your baby's medication.

♣ *Don't store non-medicines in the medicine cabinet.* You might pick up a bottle of rubbing alcohol instead of cough syrup by accident.

Kitchen

♣ *Remember the dishwasher is a fun toyland,* filled with all kinds of interesting objects. The best advice: keep it locked at all times. Lock the oven door as well. Another tip: never put dishwasher detergent in the dishwasher until you're ready to use it (and clean up any left over blobs after it's done). Dishwasher detergents are highly toxic.

♣ *Put all cleaning supplies and poisons into an upper, locked cabinet.*

♣ *Use safety latches on drawers with sharp cutlery and utensils.*

♣ *Latch any cabinets containing glassware.*

♣ *Lock up garbage in a place that's out of sight.*

♣ *Unplug those small appliances*—you don't want Junior playing with the Cuisinart.

♣ *Protect your child from the stove.* We recommend purchasing a device that keeps hands away from the burners. One option: the Stove Guard ($25 to $29, in different sizes) from the Perfectly Safe catalog (800-837-5437). These metal guards are four inches high, wrap around all four sides, and suction to the top of the stove. Of course, you can remove the stove knobs when not in use as extra safety precaution.

♣ *Keep stools and chairs away from countertops, stoves, and sinks.*

♣ *Tablecloths can be yanked off your table* by an overzealous toddler, bringing dishes crashing down on her head. Use placemats instead when you're eating at the table; otherwise, the table should be cleared.

Living Rooms

♣ *Forget using that coffee table for just about anything*—

remove any small objects and potential missiles. If it's break-able, it should go up on a high shelf or in a locked cabinet. Pad that coffee table with bumpers—especially if it's made of glass.

♣ *Anchor bookcases to the wall with nails or brackets.* Shelves present a great challenge to budding rock climbers who might pull them over on themselves.

♣ *Inspect your house plants and get rid of poisonous ones.* Which ones are poisonous, you ask? Check out the book *Baby Safe Houseplants and Cut Flowers*, which is referenced in Chapter 10. This handy reference will give you the answers. Or ask your local nursery for a list of poisonous plants. Of course, even a "safe" plant should be placed out of reach. And don't forget to check silk plants and trees to make sure leaves cannot be detached and swallowed.

♣ *Extension cords are a notorious hazard.* Use as few cords as possible and hide them behind (or under) furniture.

♣ *Make sure the TV or stereo cart can't be pulled over.* Babies also love to play disc jockey, so your stereo equipment should be moved far out of reach.

♣ *Consider buying a VCR lock to keep your little one from feeding the tape player her Cheerios®.*

Bedrooms

♣ *Don't leave small objects like coins, jewelry, cosmetics, or medications on dressers or bureaus.*

♣ *Storing items under the bed is a no-no.* These are easy pick-ings for a baby.

♣ *Check how easily drawers in dressers can be pulled out.* Once babies can open the drawers, they may try using them as step ladders.

Money-Saving Secrets

1 WOOF! GO TO THE DOGS FOR THE BEST PRICES ON GATES. Suspicious that many "baby" safety items would be cheaper if they didn't come from shops that sell baby items? We sure are. As evidence, check out the R.C. Steele Catalog (800-872-3773), a compendium of wholesale pet supplies. Inside, you'll find "pet gates" that are suspiciously similar to baby gates and are made by the

same manufacturers. The only difference is the price.

For example, Pet Gate (made by General Cage) is a 29" high gate that adjusts from 26" to 42" wide. This gate can be pressure mounted or can be installed permanently with included hardware. The cost is only $30. The exact same type of "baby" gate in other catalogs and stores sells for $50.

Here are a few other price comparisons of gates available from R.C. Steele:

♣ *A basic wooden pressure gate* (24" high and 26" to 42" wide) sells for $35 in baby stores but just $17 in R.C. Steele.

♣ *A Gerry walk-through gate* (27" high and 27" to 38" wide) is $70 in stores but just $40 in R.C. Steele.

♣ *An extra-wide wooden gate from Super-Gate* (31" high and five feet wide) retails for $100 but is just $50 in R.C. Steele.

The only disadvantage to ordering from R.C. Steele is that you must order a minimum of $50 worth of merchandise. However, if you plan to buy more than one gate (or you have a lovable pet in need of some new toys), you won't have any trouble meeting this minimum.

Of course, R.C. Steele isn't the only wholesale pet supply catalog that sells safety gates. Readers have written to us to also recommend JB Wholesale (800) 526-0388, Cherrybrook (800) 524-0820, Care-a-lot Pet Supply (800) 343-7680 and Doctors Foster & Smith (800) 826-7206. A reader in Ft. Worth, Texas e-mailed us to say she really liked Care-a-lot's catalog, which had no minimums and rock-bottom prices.

2 OUTLET COVERS ARE EXPENSIVE. Only use them where you will be plugging in items. For unused outlets, buy cheap plate covers (these blank plates have no holes and are screwed into the wall over the plugs). Another option: put heavy furniture in front of unused outlets. What type of outlet cover should you buy? We like Fisher Price's "Safe-Plate" ($4, made by Selfix 312-890-8908), which requires you to slide a small plate over to access the receptacle. In contrast, those that require you to turn a dial are more difficult to use. Also be wary of those cheap plastic outlet plugs—they can be a choking hazard.

3 MANY DISCOUNTERS LIKE TARGET, K-MART, AND WAL-MART SELL A LIMITED SELECTION OF BABY SAFETY ITEMS. We found products like gates, outlet plugs, and more at prices about 5% to 20% less than full-priced hardware stores.

4 SOME OF THE MOST EFFECTIVE BABY PROOFING IS *FREE*. For example, moving items to top shelves, putting dangerous chemicals away, and other common sense ideas don't cost any money and are just as effective as high-tech gadgets.

How safe is Safety 1st?

If you ran a company named "Safety 1st," you'd think it would turn out products that were, well, *safe*. Yet we were troubled to notice Safety 1st (which controls a whopping 70% of the baby proofing market) faired poorly in a test by *Consumer Reports*. In the January 1997 issue, the magazine evaluated 24 Safety 1st products, from cabinet locks to stove guards. While six products were rated good, very good or excellent, the majority (10 products) were rated only "fair." Most troubling was one product that rated poor (their Grip 'N Squeeze Door Knob Cover) and three more "not-acceptable" (Safety 1st's Stove Knob Cover, Balcony Guard, and Stove Guard).

How could these safety products be so unsafe? Unfortunately, no government agency tests safety products to make sure they're actually safe Only after a product causes an accident or injuries will the government consider an investigation.

To be fair, these problems aren't unique to Safety 1st—many companies that make "low-cost" (read: cheap) safety products suffered poor ratings from *Consumer Reports*. Many of these items are made of flimsy plastic or other materials that simply don't work in the real world.

So, what's a parent to do? Use high-quality safety products like the ones featured in the mail-order catalogs listed later in this chapter. Another idea: consider calling a professional baby-proofer who is a member of the International Association for Child Safety (to find a member near you, call 214-824-3964). These folks sell high-quality baby proofing items and offer installation, or you can do-it-yourself. The association is run by (and shares a phone number with) Dr. Baby Proofer, a Dallas-based company headed by Tom Golden—we often turn to Tom when readers ask where they can find obscure items like pool alarms and other safety products. There are about 50 members of the association in both the U.S. and Canada.

Do It By Mail

One Step Ahead.

To Order Call: (800) 274-8440 or (800) 950-5120;
    Fax (708) 615-2162.
Shopping Hours: 24 hours a day, seven days a week.
Or write to: One Step Ahead, 950 North Shore Dr.,
Lake Bluff, IL 60044.
Credit Cards Accepted: MC, VISA, AMEX, Discover, Optima.

 One Step Ahead has a convenient index that lets you zero-in on any product. The catalog's four pages of babyproofing products include such items as gates (Soft Gate by Gerry, for example, is $30), "Tot Lok" cabinet latches ($12.95 for two locks a key), and Toddler Shield coffee table bumpers ($30 to $40). They even offer toilet locks, child-proof room heaters and appliance safety latches. While the catalog doesn't carry as many safety products as some competitors, the selection in One Step Ahead is decent, and the prices are worth comparing.

Perfectly Safe.

To Order Call: (800) 837-5437; Fax (330) 494-0265.
Shopping Hours: Monday-Friday 8 am-10 pm;
Saturday 9 am-7 pm; Sunday 10 am-6 pm Eastern Time.
Or write to: 7245 Whipple Ave. NW, North Canton, OH 44720.
Credit Cards Accepted: MC, VISA, AMEX, Discover.

This well-organized catalog was developed by the author of *The Perfectly Safe Home* book (available in the catalog as well, of course).

Perfectly Safe's latest catalog features over 70 products to "keep your children safe and healthy." A handy index spotlights such topics as the nursery, kitchen, bathroom, toys, windows and doors. We like the extensive kitchen safety section, which includes stove guards, appliance latches, and cabinet locks. There's even a device to check to see if your microwave leaks radiation ($9.95). Another interesting product: a "choke tester" for $2.50. This little gizmo enables you to test toys to see if they present a choking hazard.

Perfectly Safe's prices seem high—for example, the Braun Thermoscan thermometer (which takes your baby's temperature instantly via the ear canal) is $89.95 (we've seen it in stores for $60). Despite the prices, Perfectly Safe is the most comprehensive catalog of safety items available. It's not the cheapest, but the selection is hard to beat.

Right Start Catalog.

To Order Call: (800) LITTLE-1 (800-548-8531);
Fax (800) 762-5501.
Shopping Hours: 24 hours a day, seven days a week.
Or write to: 5334 Sterling Center Dr., Westlake Village, CA 91361.
Credit Cards Accepted: MC, VISA, AMEX, Discover.

Although the Right Start Catalog doesn't carry a huge selection of safety items, we found that the prices on what they do carry were very competitive. For example, Safe-Plate outlet covers with sliding socket guards were $12.95 for a set of three.

Right Start also sells toilet locks, fireplace hearth bumpers, and a plastic stove guard. Altogether, there are about five pages of safety items.

Safety Zone.

To Order Call: (800) 999-3030; Fax (800) 338-1635.
Shopping Hours: 24 hours a day, seven days a week.
Or write to: The Safety Zone, Hanover, PA 17333.
Credit Cards Accepted: MC, VISA, AMEX, Discover.

Finally a catalog for the hypochondriac in all of us. The Safety Zone is not just a catalog for kids' safety products. It also covers everything from travel safety (including a hotel door alarm), to personal health items (a monitor to test your fat), to car and home safety. Within its pages, however, there are quite a few items that may be useful for parents.

For example, we saw several carbon monoxide detectors, a portable fire escape ladder, radon detectors, and more. A pressure-mounted safety gate from Gateway was pricey at $70. Compared to years past, there seem to be fewer kid's items in the catalog, but the sheer variety of offerings makes the Safety Zone an interesting catalog to browse.

Wastes of Money

Waste of Money #1

OUTLET PLUGS
"My friend thought she'd save a bundle by just using outlet plugs instead of those fancy plate covers. Unfortunately, her toddler figured out how to remove the plugs and she had to buy the plates anyway."

It doesn't take an astrophysicist to figure out how to remove those cheap plastic outlet plugs. While the sliding outlet covers are more pricey, they may be well worth the investment. Another problem with those cheap plastic plugs: they can be a choking hazard. If baby removes one (or an adult removes one and forgets to put it back), it can end up in the mouth.

Waste of Money #2

PLASTIC CORNER GUARDS
"The other day I was looking through a safety catalog and saw some corner guards. It occurred to me that they don't look a whole lot softer than the actual corner they cover. Are they worth buying?"

You've hit (so to speak) on a problem we've noticed as well. Our advice: the plastic corner guards are a waste of money. They aren't very soft—and they don't have air bags that pop out when you hit them either. So what's the solution? If you're worried about Junior hitting the corner of your coffee table, you can either store it for a while or look into getting a soft bumper pad ($30 to $65 in catalogs). Similar bumpers are available for your fireplace as well. On the other hand, you may decide that blocking off certain rooms is a more affordable option.

Waste of Money #3

APPLIANCE SAFETY LATCHES

"I can't imagine that my daughter is going to be able to open the refrigerator any time soon. So why do they

---

First Aid Friends

Wonder what should be in your baby first aid kit? Honestly, as a childless couple, you were probably lucky to find a couple of plastic bandages and an ancient bottle of Bactine in your medicine cabinet. Now that you're Dr. Mom (or Nurse Dad) it's time to take a crash course on baby medicine etiquette. Here's a run-down of essentials.

♣ ACETAMINOPHEN (one brand name of this drug is Tylenol). If you suspect your child may have an allergy to dyes or flavorings, you can buy a version without all the additives. You may also want to keep acetaminophen infant suppositories in your medicine cabinet in case your infant persists in vomiting up his drops. Or refuses to take them at all. DO NOT keep baby aspirin in your house. Aspirin has been linked to Reyes Syndrome in children and is no longer recommended by the medical community.

♣ ANTIBIOTIC OINTMENT to help avoid bacterial infection from cuts and scrapes.

♣ BAKING SODA is great for rashes.

♣ A BULB SYRINGE to remove mucus from an infant's nose when she's all stuffed up. One of the top 15 fun parenting activities that no one tells you about.

♣ CALAMINE LOTION to relieve itching.

♣ A COUGH AND COLD REMEDY recommended by your pediatrician.

♣ A GOOD LOTION. Unscented and unmedicated brands are best. If your baby has very dry skin or eczema, buy a jar of Eucerin cream.

♣ MEASURING SPOON or cup for liquid medicine. For small infants, you may want a medicine dropper or syringe.

sell those appliance safety latches in safety catalogs, anyway?"

There must be some super-strong kids out there who have enough torque to open a full-sized refrigerator. At this point, ours isn't one of them so a $6 refrigerator latch isn't on our shopping list. One point to remember: many appliances like stoves and dishwashers have locking mechanisms built in. And, keep all chairs and stools away from the laundry room to prevent your baby from opening the washing machine and dryer.

♣ PETROLEUM JELLY, which is used to lubricate rectal thermometers.

♣ PLASTIC BANDAGES like Band-Aids.

♣ SALINE NOSE DROPS for stuffy noses.

♣ SYRUP OF IPECAC TO INDUCE VOMITING. DO NOT administer this stuff until told to do so by your physician or poison control center. Keep your local Poison Control Center's phone number handy. Syrup of ipecac is especially useful in cases of poisonings (although it may be contraindicated for small infants).

♣ THERMOMETER. There are three types of thermometers you can use to take baby's temperature. A rectal thermometer, the old stand by, is probably the most accurate. On the other hand, an ear thermometer is certainly the most convenient yet can give inaccurate readings if not used properly. The third possibility, especially for infants, is an underarm thermometer—again easy to use, but not as accurate. Some thermometers can be used either rectally or underarm.

When it comes to ear thermometers, certainly the most famous brand is Braun's Thermoscan ($50 to $60 in stores like Target). We've owned a Thermoscan for a couple of years and have been pleased (it works not only on children but also adults). Another possible option is Omron's "Gentle Temp" (800) 922-2959 or (847) 680-6200. This ear thermometer has a few more features than the Thermoscan, including the ability to remember the baby's last temperature readings.

Another new product worth a look will be First Years "Comfortemp Underarm Thermometer" ($50, call 800-225-0382 or 508-588-1220). Set to debut in mid 1997, this thermometer will be able to take a underarm temperature in just three seconds. First Years claims the Comfortemp will be much more accurate than the Thermoscan.

♣ TWEEZERS. For all kinds of fun uses.

Top Ten Safety Must Haves

 To sum up, here's our list of top safety items to have for your home (in no particular order).

♣ FIRE EXTINGUISHERS, rated "ABC," which means they are appropriate for any type of fire.

♣ OUTLET COVERS.

♣ BABY MONITOR—unless your house or apartment is very small, and you don't think it will be useful.

♣ SMOKE ALARMS. The best smoke alarms have two systems for detecting fires—a photoelectronic sensor for early detection of smoldering fires and a dual chamber ionization sensor for early detection of flaming fires. An example of this is the First Alert "Double System" ($25 to $35). We'd recommend one smoke alarm for every bedroom, plus main hallways, basement and living rooms. And don't forget to replace the battery twice a year.

♣ CARBON MONOXIDE DETECTORS. These special detectors sniff out dangerous carbon monoxide (CO) gas, which can result from a malfunctioning furnace. Put one CO detector in your baby's room and another near your home's furnace.

♣ CABINET AND DRAWER LOCKS. For cabinets and drawers containing harmful cleaning supplies or utensils like knives, these are an essential investment. For fun, designate at least one unsecured cabinet or drawer as "safe" and stock it with pots and pans for baby.

♣ SPOUT COVER FOR TUB.

♣ BATH THERMOMETER or anti-scald device.

♣ TOILET LOCKS—so your baby doesn't visit the Tidy Bowl Man.

♣ BABY GATES.

"Home Safe, Not Sorry" video teaches baby-proofing basics

Want to learn more about baby-proofing your house? Check out "Home Safe, Not Sorry," a 45 minutes video produced in conjunction with the National Safety Council. The production takes you on a tour of a typical home, backyard and garage, pointing out common dangers and providing safe solutions. The emphasis is on do-it-yourself tips, complete with tips on installing basic safety devices with minimal effort (or damage to walls, cabinets or doors). It retails for $15. For more info, call 1-800-NO-TEARS or check out their web site at *www.opfer.com/homesafenotsorry*.

THE BOTTOM LINE:
A Wrap-Up of Our Best Buy Picks

 Some of the most affordable baby-proofing tips are free—lowering the setting on your water heater to 120 degrees or less, moving heavy furniture in front of outlets, not leaving plastic bags lying around, etc. Instead of buying expensive childproof outlet covers, just buy blank plates (less than $1) for unused outlets.

Baby gates are cheaper when the exact same product is called a *pet gate*. Order them at wholesale from a pet supply catalog (listed earlier in this chapter). Sample savings if you buy three basic wooden pressure gates: $25.

Most of the brands of baby-proofing products were pretty similar. Safety 1st is probably the best known, although we have mixed feelings about their products. Mail-order catalogs are a good places to shop, with Perfectly Safe and the Safety Zone as two of the best.

 Questions or comments? Did you discover a bargain you'd like to share? Call the authors at (303) 442-8792 or e-mail adfields@aol.com! Updates to this book are posted at *www.windsorpeak.com*

Chapter 9

The Best Gifts for Baby

Wwhat was the best baby gift you received? That was the question we posed to new parents across the U.S. In this chapter, we'll report on the results, some of which might surprise you. In addition to top gifts, we'll fill you in on "gift don'ts," advice on how to avoid wasting money. Finally, learn how to save money on baby announcements and discover a company that custom-designs announcements.

Top 12 Best Gifts for Baby

1 "TEDDY TOES" BLANKET WITH FEET. Seattle-based Sisters 3 (call 800-51-TEDDY or 206-284-3404 for a store near you) makes the "Teddy Toes" blanket with feet,. This soft fleece item is breathable, warmer than wool and absorbs little water. At $40 to $45, it may not seem cheap, but the blanket works from newborn to 18 months. We can't say enough about "Teddy Toes"—it's perfect to bundle up baby in an infant car seat for those cold winter days, but you can also use it in strollers, back packs and swings. (If you live in a warmer climate, Sisters 3 does make a lighter-weight, all-cotton version of the Teddy Toes). Available in specialty stores, department stores like Nordstrom's or you can order it directly from the company (800) 51-TEDDY or (206) 284-3404.

2 HOODED BATH TOWEL. Why buy one of those flimsy hooded bath towels, when you can go for a Beary Warm Creations towel. This small Corona, California-based company makes the best hooded towel on the market—plush, thick terry cloth that's similar to the finest adult towels. Compare that to the cheap towels made from fabric so thin, they soak through quickly. Beary Warm Creations towels retail for $35 to $40; you can find them in stores or order directly from the company by calling (909) 674-6630.

3 FIRE ESCAPE LADDER. It weighs only nine pounds, but this portable fire escape ladder can save the lives of you and your children. When unfurled and hung on a window sill, the ladder instantly positions itself on your home's outside wall. The Perfectly Safe Catalog (800) 837-KIDS sells both a two-story ($90) and three-story ($130) versions. Both fold up compactly for storage.

4 ANYTHING HANDMADE. Moms universally praise gifts of quilts, blankets, embroidered pillows, cradles, or bassinets that were handmade by the gift-giver. There's something about handmade items, no matter how small, that's just more special than store-bought items. If you're handy with a needle and thread or hammer and nails, you know your gift will be loved and cherished. My dad made our son the most beautiful cherry cradle we've ever seen. You can bet it will become a cherished heirloom in our family.

5 FLATOBEARIUS FROM AMERICAN BEAR CO. These plush, stuffed-animal rattles will be your baby's first stuffed friend. For about $11, you can buy the golden bear version, the pink and white FlatJack (rabbit), or the black and white Flatopup. We've also seen giant versions of Flatopup and Flatofant (elephant) for $40 and smaller "Squishy Fish" (marlins, starfish, and sea horses) for $9. Call (800) 682-3427 or (312) 329-0020 for the store nearest you.

6 A COMBO INFANT CAR SEAT/STROLLER. They're all the rage with parents—combo "travel systems" that are infant car seats, carriers, carriages and strollers. Our favorite is the Evenflo Travel System (about $150), which combines our top-rated "On My Way" car seat and a decent carriage/stroller. Compared to other all-in-one systems on the market, Evenflo's product is better-designed and higher quality.

7 HEAD SUPPORT INSERT FOR YOUR CAR SEAT. If you opt for a convertible car seat (instead of an infant car seat), consider this item as a must-have. Since your little one doesn't have much neck control for the first few months, a head support insert in your car seat keeps the baby from flopping from side to side and creates a better fit in the seat. Several manufacturers make head supports, including NoJo (714-858-9717) and The Right Fit by Basic Comfort, Inc. (303-778-7535). Most cost $15 to $25.

8 FISHER PRICE BABY MONITOR. While a baby monitor is a popular gift, buying the wrong monitor can drive new parents crazy. We recommend the Fisher Price "Sound 'N Lights" monitor from personal experience—it's one of the most sensitive monitors on the market. For $40, the Fisher

Price features a sound-activated light display and a range-setting option. Another good bet is the First Years "Crisp and Clear" monitor ($50, call 800-225-0382 for a store near you). This model features rechargeable batteries, 900 Mhz frequency for better reception and a sound/light display. Best of all, the receiver has an all-but-non-existent antenna.

9 STACKING CUPS. *Parenting Magazine* lists stacking cups as one of the all-time great baby toys, and we have to agree. Our son started knocking over the brightly colored stacked cups before he even learned to roll over. Later, he practiced drinking from one of the cups, and now he even takes them into the tub to play with. Someday, he'll probably use them to make sand castles at the beach. For $3 to $10, this is one toy your child will really use.

10 DIAPER GENIE. I dream of the Diaper Genie. Okay, so we're a little obsessive about this innovative "diaper disposal system." If you had to change a hundred stinky diapers a week, you'd love it too. Of course, you don't have to buy this little miracle worker, but you will want to have some sort of diaper pail. The bottom line: we think the deodorized plastic that seals each diaper is safer than the usual deodorant cakes used in conventional diaper pails. The Diaper Genie runs $20 to $30 and refill cartridges are $4 to $7—if you're giving the Diaper Genie as a gift, go ahead and get several refills too. Call (800) 843-6430 for a store near you.

11 BABY BJORN. Quite simply, it's the best baby carrier on the market. For $70, you get a carrier that lets baby ride facing forward or backward, is well-designed and easy to use. The Baby Bjorn has wide shoulder straps to distribute the weight comfortably and evenly, a head support for newborns—heck, even the front snaps off so you can put a sleeping baby down without waking it. The Baby Bjorn is 100% cotton and machine washable. To find a store near you, call Regal+Lager (800) 593-5522 or (770) 955-5060.

12 EAR THERMOMETER. In the past, parents took baby's temperature the "old-fashioned way" (that is with a rectal thermometer). Today, you can use Braun's Thermoscan ($50 to $60 in stores like Target). The Thermoscan takes a baby's temperature in her ear. The only downside? If not used correctly, the Thermoscan can give an inaccurate reading.

Nonetheless, we've owned a Thermoscan for a couple of years and have been pleased (it works not only on children but also adults). Another possible option is Omron's "Gentle Temp" (800) 922-2959 or (708) 680-6200. This ear thermometer has a few more features than the Thermoscan, including the ability to remember the baby's last temperature readings.

Another new product worth a look will be First Years "Comfortemp Underarm Thermometer" ($50, call 800-225-0382 or 508-588-1220). Set to debut in mid 1997, this thermometer will be able to take a underarm temperature in just three seconds. First Years claims the Comfortemp will be much more accurate than the Thermoscan.

Here are a few runners up for best baby gifts:

♣ *Gymfinity.* A play gym with a variety of toy attachments, Gymfinity is another toy that your child can use from infant to toddler age. At first, you'll place your baby under the gym to look at all the hanging toys. Later, you can take some of the pieces off, and he'll play with them separately. Once he's standing and walking, you can adjust this activity gym so he can turn the gears and play with the toys from a standing position. We found this toy in the Baby Catalog of America (1-800-PLAY-PEN) for $38 and have even seen it at Toys R Us for as low as $29.99.

♣ *Baby Swing.* Love 'em or hate 'em, they get used. But, if you're buying this as a gift for someone else, check with the new parents to make sure they want one. Swings are available in a wide price range ($40 to $100; battery-powered models range from $70 to $100). You'll find them at most baby stores, Toys R Us, Target, and other discounters.

♣ *Wipe Warmer.* Sure this item sounds frivolous, but try swabbing your private parts with an ice cold wipe at 3 am and see how you like it. For $20 to $25, you can get a "wipe warmer," a device that wraps around a box of diaper wipes and keeps it at a toasty 99 degrees. The Comfy Wipe Warmer features a machine-washable, quilted cover that attaches to wipe boxes with Velcro. Retail is $24.99, but we found it for as little as $19.50 on sale. Another good brand is Dex (for a store near you, call 800-546-1996 or 707-748-4199), which makes a wipe warmer for about the same price as Comfy. We tried out both the Comfy and Dex wipe warmers and give the edge to Dex— their product kept the wipes warmer and fit the box better.

Top Five Gifts for New Moms & Dads

Let's not forget mom and dad, those tireless worker bees who are making all this baby stuff possible. Here are some suggestions:

1 CORDLESS PHONE. What did parents do before this invention? If you don't have a cordless phone already, consider putting this on your gift list. It's hard to imagine life as a parent without one.

2 MOTHER'S LITTLE MIRACLE. Once you've had a baby, you can bet you'll be encountering some stains you've never seen before. We found this product seems to work wonders on anything that a baby can do. The cost: $9 per quart. Once you use it, you'll be a believer. Call (310) 544-7125 or write to Mother's Little Miracle at 930 Indian Peak Rd., Suite 215, Rolling Hills Estates, CA 90274, to find a store near you.

3 *BOOK LINKS* MAGAZINE. There are a zillion children's books out there. How can a new parent tell what's worth the money? Book Links magazine is a bimonthly publication (published by the American Library Association) that reviews children's literature, from picture books on up. The cost is only $16.95 a year. To order, send a check for $16.95 to Book Links, 434 W. Downer St., Aurora, IL 60506.

4 HOW ABOUT A SUBSCRIPTION TO A PARENTING MAGAZINE? There are plenty of magazines out there to help new parents, including *Parenting*, *Child*, and *American Baby*. Check them out at your local newsstand or bookstore and send in one of the subscription cards for a gift the "keeps on giving."

5 CLOTH DIAPERS. These are not for baby, but for parents, who'll need to clean up all matter of drips, spills and other flying liquid matter. Go for a package or two of the good quality, super-absorbent kind.

Gift Don'ts:

These are gifts you shouldn't buy unless parents specifically ask for them:

♣ *Diaper bags.* As far as gifts go, this one has "been there, done that." People have different ideas about what's useful, so ask before you buy. Better yet, buy something else and leave the choice up to the parents.

♣ *Baby bottle feeding system.* This may be offensive to a breast feeding mom who might feel that her choice to breast-feed is being undermined (remember, new moms have very sensitive feelings!).

♣ *Gender specific clothes for girls.* Just because your friend is having a girl, don't rush out and buy lacy, frilly dresses in cotton-candy pink. Some moms prefer more toned down or less gender-cliché gifts.

♣ *Baby flatware.* A friend of ours received an Onieda Love Lasts baby flatware set that includes utensils for first-time eaters up to toddlers. This gift is useless until a baby is 4 to 6 months old, and even then we wonder about the practicality of baby flatware. Plastic spoons and forks are much more practical because they are gentler on the gums and will get tossed on the floor. In addition, expensive sterling silver spoons are really useless.

♣ *Walkers.* This product is an absolute no-no. There are too many injuries every year (over 25,000 in a recent year) involving walkers. A better bet is the Evenflo Exersaucer (available in various versions, from $50 to $70). The Exersaucer is a stationary toy that rocks, bounces, and approximates all the fun of walkers without the danger. Call Evenflo at (800) 837-9201 or (513) 773-3971 to find the store nearest you.

♣ *The right gift for the wrong season.* Your friend gives birth to a bouncing baby boy in August. Wouldn't a cute shorts and shirt outfit be a perfect gift? The answer is no, if you bought a six-month size. When the baby is the right size to fit into this outfit, it will be the dead of winter. Instead, buy the baby a summer outfit for next summer (in a 12 to 18 month size range).

What if you receive one of the "gift don'ts" for your baby? Don't despair. Consign it at a local thrift shop and buy something you really need. Make sure to keep all the packaging, instructions, tags and so on—it helps the consignment shop sell the item that much quicker.

The Seven Most Ridiculous Baby Products

In our official capacity as your ambassadors to the world of baby stuff, we attend juvenile product trade shows where manufacturers ply us with large amounts of liquor and expensive trinkets.

Just kidding! Actually, we usually collect less-glamorous things like press kits and catalogs. And it's in those kits and catalogs that we discover some of the darndest things—products that make you wonder aloud "What were these guys thinking?!!"

As a public service, we have compiled a list of the items

that are truly hilarious. For your entertainment and amusement, won't you join us as we proudly present the ***Official Fields List of The Seven Most Ridiculous Baby Products***:

1 BOTTLED WATER NIPPLES. When plain tap water just won't do, now babies can slurp their Evian and Perrier direct from the bottle. These nipples attach to those tiny colored bottles . . . and actually won a design award at the last juvenile products convention. What's next? Cappuccino-flavored formula?

2 TIFFANY & CO.'S BARBELL RATTLE. Who needs a silver spoon when your baby can suck on this sterling silver baby rattle for a mere $130? An honorable mention for this category also goes to Tiffany's set of *porcelain* baby dishes for $70.

3 BABY KIMONO. Yes, it's a $25 to $40 "after bath" item every parent needs. After his bath, our baby loves to slip into his kimono, curl up by the fire and read the *The New York Times*.

4 AIR JORDANS FOR BABY. Now your baby can shoot hoops with his friends in style. Spend $35 and you get pint-sized versions of his famous tennis shoes for six-month olds. The only problem? Sorry, Michael . . . babies that young don't *walk*. Most aren't even crawling.

5 BABY BACK PACK. Not a back pack to carry your baby, but a back pack for your *baby* to carry. So, for your next hiking trip, your baby can now lug all his own formula, diapers and bottle water nipples.

6 WOMB SOUND MONITORS. Here's a gift for the truly paranoid mom-to-be: a womb monitor that amplifies baby's first sounds. Listen to baby's first hiccups, burps and belches or record them with the handy "out jack" for posterity. A steal at $40.

7 THE "ALL-IN-ONE POTTY SEAT." Yes, it's the first potty seat with a built-in book/newspaper rack, so baby can read the latest Tom Clancy novel while potty training. For $30, you also get the "I'm Done" button, which allows your child to "pretend to flush while alerting you of his accomplishments."

If you've run across a truly ridiculous baby product, feel free to share it with us and our readers. Call us at (303) 442-8792 or e-mail your suggestion to adfields@aol.com. We won't stop until we've uncovered every last silly baby product available on Planet Earth.

Announcements

Getting Started

 Most printers take between five days and two weeks for delivery of standard announcements. You'll want to begin shopping for your design in advance, preferably when you're six or seven months pregnant. If you know the sex of your baby ahead of time, you can pick just one design. If it's going to be a surprise, however, you may want to either select two designs or one that is suitable for both sexes. When the baby is born, you phone in the vital statistics (length, weight, date, and time), and it's off to the printing process.

Money Saving Secrets

1 ORDER 10% TO 20% MORE THAN YOU NEED. Odds are you will forget that long lost friend or relative. Going back for additional announcements will be very expensive—most companies have minimums of at least 25 pieces. Ordering 75 announcements at the outset will be about 50% cheaper than ordering 50, forgetting some relatives, and then going back for another 25.

2 CHECK YOUR LOCAL NEWSPAPER FOR SALES. Many stationers have periodic sales when they discount 10% to 20% off announcements.

Custom made announcements at affordable prices

Tired of all the generic baby announcements? Check out Original Greetings, created by Texas-based artist Mary Sullivan Taylor. Taylor takes your hobbies, careers and personal interests to create a full color, hand-painted cartoon baby announcement. We've done this for both our children and couldn't have been more impressed—you get a true one-of-a-kind announcement. And, best of all, Taylor's prices are affordable. Each card costs $1.95 (which includes envelopes) and there's a minimum order of 50 cards. You can preview Taylor's portfolio and samples of her work on the Internet at http://www.jump.net/~mstaylor/original_greetings or contact her at (512) 251-9621. Original Greetings address is 501 City Park Rd., Pfluegerville, Texas 78660.

3 COMPARE MAIL-ORDER PRICES. In Chapter 11, we list a couple of catalogs that offer affordable options for baby announcements.

4 LASER IT YOURSELF. Consider ordering a box of 100 sheets of specialty laser paper, designing the announcement on your computer, and then printing it out on your laser printer. Paper Direct catalog (800-272-7377) has a wonderful selection of appropriate stationery. We like the "New Arrival" (order #DT3041) design, with its stork and floral border. Price: $22 for a box of 100. Coordinating envelopes are $8.95 for 50. All in all, there are a half dozen designs that would be appropriate. This requires a little more effort than the standard baby announcement but might be a fun project if you're so inclined. Another source: Kinko's copy shops sells laser compatible papers you could use for birth announcements. The cost is 19¢ per sheet and each sheet has two or four post-card size announcements. Matching envelopes are 10¢ each. With a little effort, you could do an announcement for under $10.

5 GET CREATIVE. Want to put your creative juices to work? Check out "Hello Baby," a great article on do-it-yourself baby announcements in March 1996's *Parenting* magazine (see if your library has a back issue). You'll find complete directions to making an "Alpha-Bits" cereal photo announcement or one with a puff-painted onesie with all of baby's vital stats.

Name Game: Reviews of Selected Brands

While dozens of companies print baby announcements, we think the six companies reviewed in this section are the best of the best. We should note that these printers do not sell directly to the public—you must place your order through one of their dealers (usually a retail stationary store). Call the phone numbers below to find the name of a dealer near you.

The Ratings

★★★★ EXCELLENT—*our top pick!*
  ★★★ GOOD—*above average quality, prices, and creativity.*
    ★★ FAIR—*could stand some improvement.*
      ★ POOR—*yuck! could stand some major improvement.*

Carlson Craft ....★★★
For a dealer near you, (800) 328-1782. Carlson Craft can

deliver your baby announcements in as little as seven days (although expect a 10-day wait for most orders). They cost on average $49 to $89 for 50 announcements. Carlson Craft has wonderful designs; we saw die-cut bunnies and border designs with cartoon baby clothes scattered about.

Chase...★★ *1/2*
For a dealer near you, call (508) 366-4441. Chase's baby announcements include cute cartoons, twin announcements, and more—at very reasonable prices. Prices range from $42 to $92 for 50 announcements. The only negative: Chase takes a whopping three weeks for delivery.

NRN Designs ....★★★
For a dealer near you, call (714) 898-6363. California-based NRN Designs offers an unique option for baby announcements. While the printer doesn't have fancy die-cut designs, embossing or ribbons and bows, they do offer wonderful graphic designs. We were especially impressed with their Noah's Ark announcement—a hard to find design. Some of the envelopes even have coordinating graphics, creating a complete look from start to finish. NRN's prices aren't cheap, but you can buy them in any increment so you don't have to waste money buying more than you need. You can purchase as few as 25 announcements with coordinating envelopes for $3 each. The price per announcement decreases as you buy more. For example, if you buy 125 or more, the price per announcement is only $2.

William Arthur..★★★
For a dealer near you, call (800) 985-6581, (207) 985-6581. No discussion of birth announcements would be complete

---

Adoption Announcements

Sure, standard baby announcements are cute, but what if you adopt? Readers of our first edition shared with us some of their best sources for adoption announcements:

♣ *Cherished Memories*, W16806 Old Farm Rd. Germantown, WI 53022. (414) 251-0189 or (414) 251-2167.
♣ *Artitudes*, PO Box 12408 Cincinnati, OH 45212. (800) 741-0711 or (513) 351-5412.
♣ *Adoption World Specialties Ltd.*, 6920 Wilton Dr. NE, Cedar Rapids, IA 52402. (319) 373-0391. In addition to adoption announcements, this company carries hard-to-find items such as single-parent announcements and older child adoption announcements. For more info, send a self-addressed, stamped (two stamps) business-size envelope to the above address.

without the classic look of William Arthur. These higher quality card stocks feature cool type styles, linings, ink colors and bows. One particular standout: a Beatrix Potter design in the palest of colors, suitable for boy or girl. Although 50 of these were $98, prices start at $75. One note of caution: if you choose the pink parfait ink, select a heavier type style. This ink is a bit too pale for delicate type styles.

If I had a million dollars . . .

Looking for a unique announcement? Is money no object? Consider checking out *Elite* (800-354-8321) and *Encore* (800-526-0497). These printers have fabulous designs with real ribbons and beautiful embossing—we even spotted a die-cut baby shoe with real laces.

Encore's prices start at $73 and range up to $435 for 50 announcements. They require a minimum 50-piece purchase. Elite's designs are priced from $74 to $389 for 50, with a minimum order of 25.

Questions or comments? Did you discover a bargain you'd like to share? Call the authors at (303) 442-8792 or e-mail adfields@aol.com! Updates to this book are posted at *www.windsorpeak.com*

Chapter 10

Etcetera: Books, Web Sites,
Child Care & More

W hat are the best parenting books? What about
cyberspace—how can you use the Internet to get expert
parenting advice, browse discount catalogs or simply chat
with other parents? We'll look at all this, plus discuss day care
hints, tips and advice

Our Favorite Parenting Books

Each year some 40,000 new books are published. And if
you stop by your local bookstore, you'll swear most of these
are in the child care/parenting section. Which books are
best? Which are a waste of time? As two parents who not
only live it full-time but also write about the subject, we'll
give you our best picks.

How do you find many of these titles? There's no need to
fret if you don't see these books in your favorite bookstore.
Remember to check the library—most have extensive parenting collections. Another good source: the Internet. "Virtual"
bookstores like Amazon.com (www.amazon.com) carry a zillion titles you can receive by mail. Most of these books are
paperbacks that retail for $10 to $20.

If you've stumbled across a great parenting title you think
every new mom and dad should read, feel free to share it with
us. Call us at 303-442-8792 or drop us an e-mail at
adfields@aol.com.

Here's a round-up of the books we think are the best parenting titles (in alphabetical order):

♣ *Baby-Safe Houseplants & Cut Flowers* ....
By John & Delores Alber. *Published by:* Storey
Communications, Inc., (800) 827-8673.

This is a great book for plant lovers with a baby on the
way. The first chapters detail important information on eliminating poisoning risks and explain which poisons plants may
contain and their effects. The best part of this book is the

chapter titled "Buyer's Guide to Selecting Safe Houseplants," which includes a listing of all safe house plants by categories such as tall plants, plants suitable for hanging baskets, and plants that do well in indirect light, among others. This list should be carried with you when you shop for house plants or cut flowers. *Baby Safe Houseplants & Cut Flowers* also gives you phone numbers and addresses for poison control centers across the country. The index is wonderfully cross-referenced by Latin name and by common name, so you can find the plants you're looking for.

♣ *The Best Toys, Books & Videos for Kids* ....
By Joanne Oppenheim and Stephanie Oppenheim. *Published by:* HarperCollins

Incredibly comprehensive, this book also covers kid's audiotapes, software and products for children with special needs. Arranged by age, this 336-page guide includes a rating system, descriptions of products, line drawings, prices, and phone numbers for manufacturers. The no-nonsense reviews are clear and concise. Another plus: *The Best Toys, Books & Videos for Kids* will grow with your child since products for kids up to age 10 are covered. In addition, the book has a section called "Using Ordinary Toys for Kids with Special Needs." To round out their commendable political correctness, they even give lists of "green" (ecologically minded) and multi-cultural products.

♣ *Breastfeeding Secrets and Solutions* ....
By Janice Graham. *Published by:* Pocket Books.

Up-to-date and clearly written, this book offers new insights on breast feeding overlooked by other similar titles. For example, *Breast feeding Secrets and Solutions* has a chapter on the seven myths of breast feeding, an excellent and frank discussion of common misconceptions. Illustrations of breast pumps and other visuals round out the book. The best part? Graham doesn't preach. The book doesn't insist that you breastfeed your baby for years but offers gentle support for both extended breast feeding and for women who must or want to end nursing earlier. Three cheers and four stars for this balanced approach.

♣ *Bringing Baby Home: An Owner's Manual for First-Time Parents* ....
By Laura Zahn. *Published by:* Down to Earth Publications. Distributed by Voyageur Press (800) 888-9653 or (612) 430-2210.

This is by far the *best* book we bought during our pregnancy. Being first-time parents, we were pretty clueless about what to expect or do when we brought our baby home. *Bringing Baby Home* offers real-life advice on what to expect, what to buy, and what the heck to do with our little bundle of joy. The book covers such deceptively simple topics as "how to pick up and hold a baby," "dipe 'n wipe," and, our favorite, "Pets—welcome to the family baby. . . maybe." We especially liked the chapter about visitors—Zahn suggests that when you do have visitors, "don't offer refreshments and don't apologize for it." Discourage friends and relatives from popping in to offer help, but if they do anyway, hand them a laundry list of things to do. "After all, if they really are there to help, they won't be offended by such a list." Overall, Zahn's sense of humor and clear directions make this a simple, enjoyable book to read. Real advice for the real world.

♣ *The Complete Baby Checklist: A Total Organizing System for Parents* ....
By Elyse Karline, Daisy Spier, and Mona Brody. *Published by:* Avon Books.

A planner for new parents to keep track of all the various and sundry baby things, *The Complete Baby Checklist* is probably one of the best we've looked at. Easy to read and use, the book starts with the preparations for baby's arrival and goes on to include mail-order sources, health records, even feeding tips and baby food recipes. I liked the total emphasis on the baby rather than on pregnancy. The only bummer: *The Complete Baby Checklist* does not have a "lay flat" binding, making it less convenient when you want to fill in the blanks.

♣ *Eating Expectantly: The Essential Eating Guide and Cookbook for Pregnancy* ....
By Bridget Swinney, with Tracey Anderson. *Published by:* St. Martin's Press.

One of the best nutrition books for pregnant women, *Eating Expectantly* offers common sense advice for real people. The author, a registered dietician, realizes that during your pregnancy you'll find it difficult to eat a completely perfect, well-balanced diet that doesn't contain some fat, chocolate, or fast food. *Eating Expectantly* walks the reader through the three trimesters of pregnancy. We especially like Swinney's ten steps to a healthy diet, guidelines that thankfully don't come off as too preachy. Another realistic aspect of *Eating Expectantly* is the author's unabashed realization that at some point you might visit a fast food restaurant (the horror!). Instead of slamming you for giving into your weakness for Big Macs and large fries, the book talks about which fast food options (as well as convenience foods and regular restaurant fare) are the most healthy. Author Swinney even has provided charts showing which fast foods are the highest in essential nutrients, such as calcium, vitamin C, zinc, etc. She provides menu suggestions for many fast food restaurants, as well as a collection of recipes for nutritious and delicious home-cooked meals. Each recipe is accompanied by the dish's fat, calorie, carbohydrate, and protein content. A must read for any mom-to-be.

♣ *Games Babies Play*...
By Vicki Lanski . *Published by:* The Book Peddlers.

Games Babies Play is a wonderful collection of entertaining games to play with babies, from birth to twelve months. This is the perfect book for the first-time parent who doesn't know or can't remember the words and games from their childhood, like "Eentsy-weensty Spider," "To Market, To Market," and more. Vicki Lansky not only gives you the words to all the best rhymes but also offers instructions for games to develop verbal and physical skills. For example, she recommends helping your baby practice rolling over by laying her on one side of a blanket, picking up the blanket's edge, and then rolling your baby over. All the games in the book are arranged by age and skill level and each section begins with information on the developmental milestones to expect at each age.

♣ *The Girlfriend's Guide to Pregnancy: Or Everything you Doctor Won't Tell You* ....
By Vicki Iovine. *Published by:* Pocket Books

Quite simply, the most hysterical pregnancy book on the market today. Iovine tells it like it is, skewering common fears, the medical establishment and "pregnancy yentas" . . . that is, everyone who doesn't hesitate in telling you exactly how you should parent your new baby. A must read for any mom-to-be.

♣ *Mommy Made and Daddy Too: Home Cooking for a Healthy Baby & Toddler* ....
By Martha and David Kimmel with Suzanne Goldenson . *Published by:* Bantam Books.

As founders of the country's first commercial, fresh baby food business, the authors of *Mommy Made* offer their recipes and expertise to help other parents become baby food chefs. The book's premise is that you can make fresh, nutritious food for your child without a major investment of time and energy. The best part: a removable chart in the back, which lists all the foods that you will be introducing to your child and when each food should be added to his or her diet. Of course, you also get recipes for making your own baby food, whether it's nibbles for beginning eaters, older babies, or toddlers. Another great section: the "psychology of feeding the small," with advice on situations like the toddler who insists on eating *only* peanut butter and jelly sandwiches six days a week.

♣ *The New Child Health Encyclopedia* ....
By Boston Children's Hospital. *Published by:* Dell.

A massive guide to child health and disease, this 700 page opus includes contributions from 100 different medical authorizes, including such heavy-hitters as T. Berry Brazelton. The book starts out with some brief information on child development and accident prevention. The rest of the encyclopedia (over 600 pages) focuses on diseases and their symptoms. Each disease gets the star treatment—with detailed information on its cause, diagnosis, complications, treatment, and prevention. There is even information on obscure maladies such as hair loss and growing pains. We learned that the latter is not actually caused by growing, but by vigorous use of underdeveloped muscles and bones. In some cases the advice seems a little unrealistic; the information on avoiding pet injuries includes advising your child to lie still on the ground when confronted with an aggressive animal. Sure. Despite these peculiarities, *New Child Health's Encyclopedia* is a helpful and comprehensive sourcebook. Even with its large size, we found it quite easy to use.

♣ *Take This Book to the Obstetrician With You* ....
By Karla Morales and Charles Inlander. *Published by:* Addison-Wesley

This book's subtitle is "A Consumer Guide to Pregnancy and Childbirth," and that's exactly what it is—an in-your-face, take-control-of-the-situation primer to navigating the medical establishment during your pregnancy and childbirth. Authors Morales and Inlander are members of the People's Medical Society, a medical consumer group that advocates a much more proactive role for consumers in the childbirth process. This book has one of the best chapters we've seen on choosing a birth practitioner (obstetrician, family practitioner, nurse, or lay midwife), as well an excellent discussion of birth settings (hospital, birth centers, or home births). Instead of merely explaining the differences between the options, *Take This Book* gives you questions to ask during the first visit and opinionated advice as to what is the best answer in each situation. So, should you read it? Yes. The aggressive tone may turn off some readers—this is definitely an anti-hospital book dedicated to exposing common abuses and problems with childbirth in the U.S. Unlike books written by nurses and others who are part of the medical establishment, *Take this Book*'s outsider mentality is a refreshing and needed approach.

♣ *What to Expect When You're Expecting* ....
♣ *What to Eat When You're Expecting*................................
♣ *What to Expect the First Year* ....
♣ *What to Expect the Toddler Years*......................................
By Arlene Eisenberg, Heidi Eisenberg Murkoff, and Sandee Eisenberg Hathaway, RN. *Published by:* Workman.

Unless you live in a closet, you can't be pregnant and escape the phenomena called *What to Expect When You're Expecting*. Apparently, every pregnant mom is issued a copy of this book right after their pregnancy test. And, yes, there is a reason why these books have achieved legendary status—the organization is excellent, with a comprehensive month-by-month format which makes the book(s) easy to read. We liked the charts, illustrations, and absence of medical jargon. What's the worst part of *What to Expect*? Hands down, it's got to be their diet "advice"—and we use that word loosely. The authors' "Best Odds Diet" is similar to the regimen used by prisons in third-world countries to torture inmates. Although the advice has merit (avoid high-fat foods, eat lots of vegetables), just take a look at this piece of advice: "The Best Odds diet recommends eating no refined sugars at all during pregnancy." Excuse me? Are they kidding? While many expectant mothers aspire to cut back on sweets, going nine months without an ice-cream cone just doesn't happen in the real world. Their recommended fat intake is another shocker—the authors advise restricting this to two tablespoons of high fat a day. Basically, one bagel with cream cheese would shoot your fat allowance for the whole day. To add insult to injury, the authors took these nuggets of nutritional knowledge and rolled them into a separate book, a flawed and useless tome which really needs to filed under "Fiction" at your local bookstore. While we liked the other *What to Expect* books (especially the "First Year" spin-off), forget about this one.

Advice for Parents of Multiples

Books are nice, but it's also helpful to read the latest research and advice on raising twins. To the rescue comes *Twins Magazine*, a bi-monthly, full-color magazine published by The Business Word (800) 328-3211 or (303) 290-8500 (internet: *www.twinsmagazine.com*). Inside, you'll discover money-saving tips, parent-to-parent advice and info on twins from infancy through adolescence. A must-have for parents of multiples, a subscription runs $23.95 for six issues.

♣ *Your Pregnancy Companion: A Month by Month Guide to All You Need to Know Before, During & After Pregnancy* ......
By Janis Graham. *Published by:* Pocket Books.

This was one of my favorite books during my pregnancy simply because it was so clear and direct. The book's month-by-month format helps you find your way easily. Each chapter tells you a little bit about what your growing baby is doing, as well as about the changes going on in your body. The author also covers your doctor's appointments, diet, exercise, feelings, and lifestyle changes. Most of the information in the book mirrored what my doctor was telling me, as well as what other pregnancy books mentioned. In fact, when I couldn't find an answer to a question in one of the other books, *Your Pregnancy Companion* almost always filled in the gap. And with its forthright language, it gave me all the facts I needed about any situation.

Parents in Cyberspace

In the old days of parenting, moms got together once a week to discuss their babies, swap tips and discuss the latest trials and tribulations of being a parent. These one-on-one chats helped keep everyone sane.

Alas, the days of mom get-togethers are becoming as rare as manual typewriters. With moms (and dads) working outside the home, the time to sit and idly chat with other parents has dwindled. Yet, in its place comes a new high-tech form of the coffee klatch: the Internet.

Once the domain of scientific researchers and pontificating academicians, the Internet (and specifically, it's well-publicized off-spring, the World Wide Web) has evolved into a fantastic resource for parents. With a few clicks, you can surf on-line catalogs, swap advice with other parents, or merely find someone to chat with who doesn't cry or need her diaper changed.

How do you get started? While it's beyond the scope of this book to go into great detail on getting on-line, we do have a couple of suggestions. First, check out your library. Many now have computers hooked to the Internet and you can get a taste of what's out there. Other libraries may even offer instructional classes on using the 'net. Another idea: start with a commercial on-line service like America On-Line (800) 215-0800. Their easy-to-use software gets you up and running quickly, plus you can access the World Wide Web and e-mail through their own proprietary software.

Once you're wired, here are a couple of ideas on how you can use the 'net:

1 **E-mail it.** Forget the post office and zap messages to friends and relatives with e-mail. You can also e-mail the authors of this book—feel free to ask questions or merely say hello. Our e-mail address is adfields@aol.com.

2 **Surf catalogs on-line.** Many of the companies listed in this book have web addresses (which we note in their contact information). These sites often feature on-line catalogs, news and announcements as well as general background on the manufacturers.

3 **Research a wide range of products.** The web also has several sites that are like the reference section of your local library—you can get info on a wide range of products quickly and easily. One such site is *www.thebabynet.com*, which includes product info, manufacturer contact listings, chat rooms and even baby name suggestions.

4 **Save money.** Yes, there are a few internet-only sites that sell baby products. One of the most comprehensive is *www.internetbaby.com*. Internet Baby sells a wide variety of name-brand products (car seats, strollers, toys, etc.) at deep discounts.

5 **Chat with other parents.** Commercial on-line services like American On-Line have parenting areas with chat rooms where you can converse with other parents.

6 **Post to an on-line parenting bulletin board.** Our favorite part of the Internet is called the "usenet." This section includes a series of bulletin boards where folks post questions and others answer. If you can think of a topic, it's out there on the usenet. For parents (or parents-to-be), we like "misc.kids" group, which has seven sub-topics. Among the more popular is

"misc.kids.pregnancy," where moms-to-be swap pregnancy stories, ask advice and hear other folks' opinions.

7 *Order catalogs.* Pop into *www.catalogsite.com* and you can order catalogs directly via the 'net. Many of the catalogs listed in this book are on the site and some even offer a preview.

8 *Get free updates on this book.* It's the one truth about book publishing: the minute you print a book like this, something will change—products get discontinued, companies change phone numbers, new bargains pop up and more. Now you can read the latest news on *Baby Bargains* by surfing our web page at *www.windsorpeak.com*. Another popular features: our reader "mail bag." You can skim our reader mail, including suggestions and experiences from other parents on the products we recommend.

Child Care

"It's expensive, hard to find and your need for it is constantly changing. Welcome to world of child care," said a recent *Wall Street Journal* article—and we agree. There's nothing more difficult than trying to find the best child care for your baby.

With 57% of moms with children under age one back in the workforce today, wrestling with the choices, costs and availability of child care is a stark reality. Here's a brief overview of the different types of child care available, questions to ask when hiring a provider and money-saving tips.

What are you buying?

On average, parents pay 7.5% of their pre-tax income for child care. And if you live in a high-cost city, expect to shell out even more. As you'll read below, some parents spend $20,000 or more for daycare. Whatever your budget, there are three basic types of child care:

♣ *Family daycare.* In this setting, one adult takes care of a small number of children in her home. Sometimes the children are of mixed ages. Parents who like this option prefer the lower ratio of children to providers and the consistent caregiver. Of course, you'll want to make sure the facility is licensed and ask all the questions we outline later. How much does it cost? Family daycare typically runs $3000 to $10,000 per year—with bigger cities running closer to the top figure. For example, in New York City or San Francisco, family daycare can run $200 to $250 per week (that's $10,000 to $13,000).

♣ *Center care.* Most folks are familiar with this daycare option—commercial facilities that offer a wide variety of childcare options. Convenience is one major factor for center care; you can often find a center that is near your (or your spouse's) place of work. Other parents like the fact that their children are grouped with and exposed to more kids their own age. Centers usually give you a written report each day which details your baby's day (naps, diaper changes, mood). On the downside, turnover can be a problem—some centers lose 40% or more of their employees each year. Yet center car offers parents the most flexibility: unlike nannies or family care, the day care center doesn't take sick or vacation days. Many centers offer drop-off service, in case you need care in a pinch. The cost: $3000 to $13,000 per year, yet some pricey centers can cost over $20,000 in the biggest cities. As with family daycare, the cost varies depending on how many days a week your baby needs care. We pay about $6700 per year for 30 hours of daycare per week in Boulder, CO.

♣ *Nanny care.* No, you don't have to be super-rich to afford a nanny. Many "nanny-referral" services have popped up in most major cities, offering to refer you to a pre-screened nanny for $100 to $200 or so. Parents who prefer nannies like the one-to-one attention, plus baby is taken care of in your own home. The cost varies depending on whether you provide the nanny with room and board or not. Generally, most nannies who don't live with you run $6 to $10 per hour. Hence, the yearly cost would be $10,000 to $20,000. And the nannies salary is just the beginning—you also must pay social security and Medicare taxes, federal unemployment insurance, plus any state-mandated taxes like disability insurance or employment-training taxes. All this may increase the cost of your $20,000 nanny by another $3500 or more per year. The other downside to nannies? You're dependent on one person for child care. If she gets sick, needs time off or quits, you're on your own.

Money Saving Tips

1 ASK YOUR EMPLOYER ABOUT DEPENDENT CARE ACCOUNTS. Many corporations offer this great benefit to employees. Basically, you can set aside pre-tax dollars to pay for child-care. The maximum set aside per child is $5000 and both parents can contribute to that amount. If you're in the 31% tax bracket, that means you'll save $1550 in taxes by paying for childcare with a dependent care account.

2 SHARE A NANNY. As we noted in the above example, a nanny can be expensive. But many parents find they can

halve that cost by sharing a nanny with another family. While this might require some juggling of schedules to make everyone happy, it can work out beautifully.

3 GO FOR A CULTURAL EXCHANGE. The U.S. government authorizes a foreign nanny exchange program. "Parents can hire a young European to provide as much as 45 hours of child care a week as part of a yearlong cultural exchange," says a Wall Street Journal article. The wages are fixed at $138 per week for an nanny arriving after Jan. 1, 1996, although that amount may adjust with any change in the federal minimum wage. You also agree to pay for the nanny's room and board, but that fixed fee is good for any number of children. Eight "au pair" agencies are authorized by the federal government to place foreign nannies in homes (call Au Pair in America 800-727-2437 x6188 for more details). These agencies charge placement fees of $3700 to $4200 which cover health insurance, training and other support services. When you factor this and other fees, an au pair runs about $200 a week (plus room and board) or $11,000 a year.

4 TAKE A TAX CREDIT. The current tax code gives parents a tax credit for child care expenses. The amount, which varies based on your income, equals about 20% to 30% of child care costs up to a certain limit. The credit equals about $500 to $1500, depending on your income. Another tax break: some states also give credits or deductions for child care expenses. Consult your tax preparer to make sure you're taking the maximum allowable credit/deduction.

Questions to ask

 When evaluating child care options, consider asking the following questions of the care provider and yourself:

1 *What are the credentials of the provider(s)?* Obviously, a college degree in education and/or child development is preferred. Additional post-college training is also a plus.

2 *What is the turnover?* High turnover is a concern since consistency of care is one of the keys to successful child care. Any turnover approaching 40% is cause for concern.

3 *What is the ratio of children to care providers?* The recommended national standard is one adult to three babies (age birth to 12 months). After that, the ratios vary depending on a child's age and state regulations. With some day care centers, there is one primary teacher and a couple of assistants (depending on the age of the children and size of class). Compare the ratio to that of other centers to gain an understanding of what's high and low.

4 *Do you have a license?* All states (and many municipalities) require child care providers to be licensed. Yet, that's no guarantee of quality—the standards vary so much from locale to locale that a license may be meaningless. Another point to remember: the standards for family daycare may be lower than those for center daycare. Educate yourself on the various rules and regulations by spending a few minutes on the phone with your state's child care regulatory body. Check on the center's file with the state to make sure there are no complaints or violations on record.

5 *May I visit you during business hours?* The only way you can truly evaluate a child care provider is the on-site visit. Try to time your visit during the late morning, typically the time when the most children are being cared for. Trust your instincts—if the facility seems chaotic, disorganized or poorly-run on one day, take the hint.

6 *Discuss your care philosophy.* Sit down for a half-hour interview with the care provider and make sure they clearly defines their attitudes on breast feeding, diapers, naps, feeding schedules and any other issues of importance to you. The center should have established, written procedures to deal with children who have certain allergies or other medical conditions. Let's be honest: child-rearing philosophies will vary from culture to culture. Make sure you see eye to eye on key issues.

7 *Do you have liability insurance?* Don't just take their word on it—have them provide written documentation or the phone number of an insurance provider for you to call to confirm coverage.

8 *Does the center conduct police background checks on employees?* It's naive to assume that just because employees have good references, they've never been in trouble with law.

9 *Is the center clean, home-like and cheerful?* While it's impossible to expect a child care facility to be spotless, it is important to check for basic cleanliness. Diaper changing stations shouldn't be overflowing with dirty diapers, play areas shouldn't be strewn with a zillion toys, etc.

10 *What type of adjustment period does the center offer?* Phasing in daycare isn't easy—your child may have to have time to adjust to the new situation. Experienced providers should have plans to ease the transition.

Sources for the best child care facilities

Which child care centers have the highest standards? The National Association of Family Child Care (800) 359-3817 and the National Association for the Education of Young Children (800) 424-2460 offer lists of such facilities to parents in every state.

Questions or comments? Did you discover a bargain you'd like to share? Call the authors at (303) 442-8792 or e-mail adfields@aol.com! Updates to this book are posted at *www.windsorpeak.com*

Chapter 11

Do it By Mail: Catalogs for Clothes, Baby Products & More

Tired of the mall? Think those sky-high prices at specialty stores are highway robbery? Sit back in your favorite chair and do all your shopping for your baby by phone. With over 8000 mail-order catalogs out there, you can buy everything from bedding to furniture, clothes to safety items. We've rounded up the best catalogs for baby and you—and they're all free for the asking!

Before we get to the reviews, a word on being a smart catalog shopper. Ordering from a mail-order company that's miles away from you can be a nerve-racking experience— we've all heard the stories of scamsters that bilk money from unsuspecting consumers. As a result, there are a few precautions any smart shopper should take:

1 ALWAYS USE YOUR CREDIT CARD. Credit card purchases are covered by federal consumer protection laws. Basically, the law says if you don't get what you were promised, you must get a refund. Technically known as Federal Regulation C, the rule says you have 60 days to dispute the charge with the company that issued your credit card—but first you must try to work out the problem with the merchant directly. Call your credit card company to determine the exact procedures for disputing a charge.

What if you pay with cash or a check? If the company goes out of business, you're out of luck. We've interviewed some consumers who feel squeamish about giving out their credit card number over the phone. While you always have to be careful, ordering from a reputable mail-order company (like the ones below) with a credit card is very safe, in our opinion. And the consumer protection benefits of using a credit card far outweigh any risks.

2 MOST COMPANIES HAVE RETURN POLICIES that enable you to get a refund or credit within a specified period of time. Make sure to confirm this before you order. Also ask who pays for the shipping on a returned item—some companies pay for this, while others don't.

3 ALWAYS KEEP ALL INVOICES, RECEIPTS, AND ORDER CONFIR-
MATIONS. Inspect all packages thoroughly upon arrival
and keep the original packing, just in case you decide to
return the item.

4 KEEP A LOG OF WHOM YOU SPOKE TO AT THE COMPANY.
Get any names and order confirmation numbers and
keep them in a safe place.

5 CONFIRM DELIVERY METHODS. Some companies use
United Parcel Service to deliver merchandise. The problem? UPS can't deliver to post office boxes and often requires
you to be present when the package is delivered. If you're not
at home, they leave a call slip, and you've got to go to the
nearest UPS office (which could be a long drive) to pick up the
item. A possible solution: give your work address and specify
any floor, suite number, or building location for the delivery.
Or you could request delivery by the U.S. Postal Service.

6 THE TIME REQUIRED FOR SHIPPING WILL VARY WIDELY.
Some companies offer two to three-day delivery, while
others may take weeks. Customized items (like mono-
grammed bedding) take the longest. As for the cost, mail-
order catalogs use a variety of methods to determine shipping
charges. Some charge a flat fee, while others use a sliding scale
based on the dollar amount of the order or the weight of the
package. Please note that the prices we quote below do not
include shipping.

7 USE THAT 24-HOUR FAX NUMBER. Not all catalogs have
operators standing by around the clock. However,
many have fax numbers that you can use to place an order
at any time.

8 NEARLY ALL MAIL-ORDER CATALOGS ARE FREE FOR THE ASK-
ING. Even though some have a price printed on the cover,
we've never had to pay for one.

9 BE PREPARED TO WAIT. Some catalogs take *weeks* to
arrive, so plan ahead. Don't wait until baby arrives to
request catalogs that look interesting.

10 GET A COPY OF *WHOLESALE BY MAIL*. If you're serious
about mail order shopping, you need Wholesale By
Mail (by the Print Project, $17, HarperPerrenial). This thick
book (available in bookstores nationwide) gives mail-order
sources for just about anything you need to buy.

National Parenting Center

Looking for more consumer information on the latest baby products? The National Parenting Center is a California-based group that produces a bi-annual "Seal of Approval" product report. The 10-page book reviews the latest toys, infant and music products, computer programs, and educational products. A one-year membership for $19.95 gets you this report, a monthly subscription to the "Parent Talk" newsletter, and various discounts on child-rearing products. For more information, call (818) 225-8990 or write to The National Parenting Center, 22801 Ventura Blvd., Suite 110, Woodland Hills, CA 91367.

General Catalogs

The Baby Catalog of America. ....
To Order Call: (800) PLAYPEN (1-800-752-9736) or
(203) 931-7760; Fax (203) 931-7764
Or write to: Baby Catalog of America, 719-721 Campbell Ave.,
West Haven, CT 06516.
Credit Cards Accepted: MC, VISA, AMEX, Discover.

 We just love this catalog. With super discounts on everything from baby products to toys, strollers to car seats, the Baby Catalog of America is a must.

Want a stroller by such premium names as Emmaljunga or Peg Perego but don't want to pay full retail? We found these and other strollers in the catalog, including such premium brands as Aprica, Combi and Maclaren.

And that's just the beginning—the catalog also has bedding, monitors, toys, books, bottles and more. The prices are excellent, often 15% to 50% off what you'd see in stores. You can also save an additional 10% if you join their "Baby Club" for a $25 annual membership. Members get a newsletter, information on special closeouts, and exclusive sales. Another plus: you can sign up three "associate members" (family or friends) for free, and they get the same discounts.

We highly recommend this catalog—their latest version includes black and white pictures of many products plus such hot-sellers as Pooh bedding, Avent bottles and Peg Perego's Prima Poppa high chair.

Dr. Possum's World ....
To Order Call: (800) 827-4086; Fax (310) 543-5570.
Shopping Hours: 8 am - 4 pm, Monday through Friday.
Or write to: 4455 Torrance Blvd., #270, Torrance, CA 90503.
Credit Cards Accepted: MC, VISA, AMEX, Discover.

"Nurturing the whole child . . . naturally" is the theme of this California-based catalog that specializes in health, skin care, and homeopathic remedies for children. The catalog also carries many of the items we recommend in this book, including Medela breast pumps. We also noticed a nice selection of cloth diapers and supplies, organic cotton clothing and parenting books. Don't expect any fancy pictures—most of this black and white catalog is text with some line drawings of products. The best part: "Dr. Possum's Remedy Chart," which lists homeopathic remedies for such conditions as cradle cap, colic and colds.

Exposures ....
To Order Call: (800) 222-4947; Fax (414) 231-6942.
Shopping Hours: 8 am-Midnight, seven days a week.
Or write to: Exposures, 1 Memory Ln., P.O. Box 3615, Oshkosh, WI 54903.
Credit Cards Accepted: MC, VISA, AMEX, Discover.

If you're like us, you'll probably snap 10,000 pictures of your baby before she turns one. When our baby was born, the stock price of Kodak must have tripled overnight. But where to put all these wonderful snapshots? Call Exposures, a fantastic catalog that sells an amazing variety of picture frames and photo albums. You'll also find photo-related gifts, curio cabinets, and photograph storage systems.

Frame styles range from the basic (a 8" x 10" wood design for $19.95 in teak or rosewood) to the sophisticated (an oval gold leaf frame for $44). Some of the products geared for new parents include "Baby's First" frame ($100), a set of six frames which highlight memorable moments like baby's first tooth.. They also carry an "archival baby memories book" ($25), a baby photo calendar for $16, and magnetic fridge frames. We love Exposure's photo albums, from the basic leather styles to funky leather and wood combinations. Scrapbooks are also scattered throughout, including oversized options capable of storing 11" x 14" photos ($60).

Our only complaint: the service from Exposures can be inconsistent. The company had so many problems shipping orders one Christmas that they told us in early December that orders wouldn't arrive until January. Phone operators also tend to be a little gruff. Because the catalog's offerings are so unique, we hope they can iron out these wrinkles.

JCPenney ....

To Order Call: (800) 222-6161.
Shopping Hours: 24 hours a day, seven days a week.
Credit Cards Accepted: MC, VISA, JCPenney, AMEX, Discover.

JCPenney has been selling baby products for over 90 years. Their popular mail-order catalog has a couple free "mini-catalogs" of maternity wear and baby items that should be of particular interest to parents-to-be.

Check out Chapter 5 for more info on Penney's maternity clothes. Earlier in the book, we also mention their catalog for cribs, bedding and accessories. You'll find good name brands and prices that are about regular retail.

Kids Club ....

To Order Call: (800) 363-0500; Fax (216) 494-0265.
Shopping Hours: 24 hours a day, seven days a week.
Or write to: Jeanie's Kids Club, 7245 Whipple Ave. NW, North Canton, OH 44720.
Credit Cards Accepted: MC, VISA, Discover, AMEX.

Kids Club offers a great low-price guarantee—if you see a baby item in another catalog at a lower price than Kids Club, they'll meet the price. The catalog offers two prices: "catalog price" and "club price," which is about 10% to 30% less. To get the club price, you buy an $18 yearly membership, which also includes a free monthly newsletter. We found the prices in Kids Club to be excellent—for example, the club price for the Evenflo On My Way Travel System (car seat and stroller) is $150 and the Baby Bjorn is $58. Those are comparable to or lower than prices in other discount stores or catalogs. Kids Club carries bedding, rocking chairs, bath items, closet organizers, high chairs, safety items, toys and more. We noticed the entire Lamaze line of developmental toys, as well as Guardian's car seats, Gerry's Play Top high chair and other products we recommended earlier in this books. Overall, this is a wonderful catalog—the full-color photos let you see most products and the prices can't be beat.

Lands' End ....

To Order Call: (800) 356-4444; Fax (800) 332-0103.
Internet: www.landsend.com
Shopping Hours: 24 hours a day, seven days a week.
Or write to: 1 Lands' End Ln., Dodgeville, WI 53595.
Credit Cards Accepted: MC, VISA, AMEX, Discover.
Discount Outlets: They also have a dozen or so outlet stores in Iowa, Illinois and Wisconsin—call the number above for the location nearest to you.

This great catalog is featured in several places in this book. We discuss their bedding items in Chapter 3 and diaper bags in Chapter 7. Land's End even has a special children's catalog with clothing, layette items and more. For example, a long-sleeve side snap t-shirt is $14.

Lilly's Kids (Lillian Vernon) ....
To Order Call: (800) 285-5555; Fax (804) 430-1010
Shopping Hours: 24 hours a day, seven days a week.
Or write to: Lillian Vernon, Virginia Beach, VA 23479.
Credit Cards Accepted: MC, VISA, AMEX, Discover, Diner's.

An offshoot of the popular Lillian Vernon catalog, Lilly's Kids is a collection of gifts and toys just for kids. At 80 pages, Lilly's Kids is chock full of interesting items.

The Natural Baby Company...
To Order Call: (609) 771-9233; Fax (609) 771-9342.
Shopping Hours: Monday through Saturday, 9am to 11pm Eastern. Sunday 9am to 6pm Eastern.
Or write to: 816 Silvia St. 800-BS, Trenton, NJ 08628.
Credit Cards Accepted: MC, VISA, Discover.
Outlet Store: This catalog has an outlet store in Princeton, NJ and also has occasional sales at their headquarters location in Trenton. Call the above number for more details.

A good (if pricey) catalog of bedding, diapers, clothes and bath items, all with an ecological bent. We review this catalog in depth in Chapter 3.

One Step Ahead ....
To Order Call: (800) 274-8440 or (800) 950-5120;
Fax (708) 615-2162.
Shopping Hours: 24 hours a day, seven days a week.
Or write to: 950 North Shore Dr., Lake Bluff, IL, 60044.
Credit Cards Accepted: MC, VISA, AMEX, Discover, Optima.
Outlet store: Deerbrook, IL (847) 714-1940.

Illinois-based One Step Ahead is a jack-of-all-trades catalog that covers everything from clothes to toys, car seats to organizational items. Similar to the Right Start catalog, One Step Ahead has a slightly heavier emphasis on clothing, shoes, and linens. For example, we thought their selection of shoes was excellent: suede moccasins were $14.95, and Cutiecakes brand shoes cost $7.95. For rainy climates, check out Puddleduckers vinyl boots for $14.95.

This catalog is easier to use than most because of its index, which is organized into sections such as mealtime, bath and health, auto safety, and "just for fun." Prices are very competitive compared to other catalogs (they also have a price guarantee—One Step Ahead will match any price you see in another "children's direct mail catalog"). For example, we saw a Stroller Mate toy bar for the same price as the Right Start ($19.95).

All in all, One Step Ahead is a good all-around catalog. If you can't find it elsewhere, it's worth it to take a look in here. The prices are good, the selection changes frequently, and they do carry some unique items.

The Orange Elephant...

To Order Call: (800) 467-5597 or (304) 744-9323;
Fax (800) 329-6687
Shopping Hours: 9am to 9pm Eastern Time, seven days a week.
Or write to: 90 MacCorkle Ave. SW, South Charleston, WV 25303.
Credit Cards Accepted: MC, VISA, AMEX, Discover.

Orange Elephant uses "real people" to test products for their catalog . . . and we have to agree with many of their selections. You'll see everything from Evenflo's On My Way car seat to the Baby Bjorn carrier, as well as a selection of toys, bedding, bath items and even educational software. Prices are about regular retail—the aforementioned Bjorn is $70, Evenflo's Happy Cabana portable play yard is $130 and the Exersaucer Deluxe walker alternative is $90. The catalog's organization and design is excellent—large color photos let you see the products and in-depth descriptions note age groups and other features.

Right Start Catalog ....

To Order Call: (800) LITTLE-1 (800-548-8531);
Fax (800) 762-5501.
Shopping Hours: 24 hours a day, seven days a week.
Or write to: 5334 Sterling Center Dr., Westlake Village, CA 91361.
Credit Cards Accepted: MC, VISA, AMEX, Discover.
Retail stores: The Right Start has 30+ retail stores in major malls; call the above number for a location near you.

Whether you visit their stores or browse their catalog, the Right Start is jammed packed with all the latest products for baby. We like the emphasis on high-quality brands, like Peg Perego's high chairs. While the prices can be quite high, the company's employees are amazingly helpful and friendly. The Right Start gets new items in all the time (you'll often see cutting-edge products before they hit the stores), and they have periodic sales that make the prices even more reasonable.

Announcements Catalogs

H & F Announcements ....

To Order Call: (800) 964-4002; Fax (913) 752-1222.
Shopping Hours: 24 hours a day, seven days a week.
Or write to: 3734 W. 95th St., Leawood, KS 66206.
Credit Cards Accepted: MC, VISA, AMEX, Discover.

H & F Announcements offers a mail-order birth announcement service that promises to ship within one to four business days of receiving your order, depending on the style of invitation.

All announcements are printed on 4" x 6" or 5" x 7" cards, with your choice of pre-printed designs featuring bunnies, balloons, toys, sailboats, and more. Besides contemporary options, classic designs are also available with plain printing and no border. Another option: consider H & F's photo announcements—you send the negative in and they send back a picture announcement with a decorative border. The catalog also features christening, shower, and birthday invitations.

All designs for invitations and announcements are priced the same. A minimum order of 25 is $21.75. Items are also sold in quantities of 25, 35, 50, 75, 100, and 125. An order of 50 announcements is $32.95. Prices include plain envelopes, colored ink, and 15 different type styles. Additional options are thank-you notes (50 for $18.75), your return address printed on the envelope (50 for $7.50), and ribbon tying (for some invitation styles—50 for $8.75).

If you're looking for basic and affordable baby announcements, H & F's catalog should be on your shopping list.

Heart Thoughts ....

To Order Call: (800) 524-2229; Fax (800) 526-2846.
Shopping Hours: 8am to 5pm Monday through Friday, Central .
Or write to: Heart Thoughts, 6200 E. Central #100,
Wichita, KS 67208.
Credit Cards Accepted: MC, VISA, Discover, AMEX.

Heart Thoughts offers affordable baby announcements in over 100 different styles. Their recent catalog included "classic" birth announcements with black and white line drawings, formal cards with ribbon details, and the usual cutesy, cartooned designs. All are available with quick shipment—just two business days, depending on the design (add an extra day if you want ribbons tied onto the cards).

Heart Thoughts' announcements are very affordable. At the bottom of the price range are the "classic" designs ($26 for 50 announcements); at the top are the "Ribbons & Lace" cards ($115 per 50). Included in the price are colored inks and ribbons, as well as a choice of eight typefaces. For an additional $12 to $50 (depending on the quantity), Heart Thoughts will even address them for you, plus print your return address on the back flap. Shipping prices are also reasonable: for example, it costs just $4 for next day air delivery.

In addition to announcements, Heart Thoughts also carries parenting books, pregnancy exercise videos, and other gift items.

Bedding Catalogs

Check out Chapter 3 for in-depth reviews of these and other bedding catalogs.

The Company Store. ....
To Order Call: (800) 285-3696; (800) 289-8508;
Fax (608) 784-2366.
Shopping Hours: 24 hours a day, seven days a week.
Or write to: 500 Company Store Rd., La Crosse, WI 54601.
Credit Cards Accepted: MC, VISA, AMEX, Discover.

Cuddledown of Maine ....
To Order Call: (800) 323-6793; Fax (207) 761-1948
Internet: www.cuddledown.com
Shopping Hours: 24 hours a day, seven days a week.
Or write to: 312 Canco Rd., PO Box 1910, Portland, ME 04104.
Credit Cards Accepted: MC, VISA, AMEX, Discover.

Schweitzer Linen ....
To Order Call: (800) 554-6367, (212) 249-8361;
Fax (212) 737-6328
Shopping Hours: 10:00 am to 6:00 pm Monday-Friday, Eastern.
Or write to: 457 Columbus Ave., New York, NY 10024.
Credit Cards Accepted: MC, VISA, AMEX.
Retail Outlets: Three stores in the New York City area.

Seventh Generation ....
To Order Call: (800) 456-1177; Fax (800) 456-1139.
Shopping Hours: 24 hours a day, seven days a week.
Or write to: One Mill St. Suite A26, Burlington, VT 05401.
Credit Cards Accepted: MC, VISA, Discover.

Clothing Catalogs

These catalogs are reviewed in depth
in Chapter 4.

After the Stork ....
To Order Call: (800) 333-5437 or (505) 867-7168;
Fax (505) 867-7101.
Shopping Hours: 24 hours a day, seven days a week.
Or write to: 1501 12 St. NW, Rio Rancho, NM 87174.
Internet: www.AftertheStork.com
Credit Cards Accepted: MC, VISA, AMEX, Discover.

Biobottoms ....
To Order Call: (800) 766-1254 (U.S. and Canada) or
(707) 778-7945 or fax (707) 778-0619.
Shopping Hours: Monday-Friday 5 am-9 pm;
Saturday 6 am-6 pm; Sunday 8 am-4 pm Pacific Time.
Or write to: Biobottoms, PO Box 6009, Petaluma, CA 94955.
Internet: www.biobottoms.com/
Credit Cards Accepted: MC, VISA, AMEX, Discover.

Children's Wear Digest ....

To Order Call: (800) 242-5437; Fax (800) 863-3395.
Shopping Hours: 24 hours a day, seven days a week.
Or write to: Children's Wear Digest, 3607 Mayland Ct.,
Richmond, VA 23233.
Credit Cards Accepted: MC, VISA, AMEX, Discover.

Chock ....

To Order Call: (800) 222-0020; or (212) 473-1929; Fax (212)
473-6273.
Shopping Hours: Sunday-Thursday 9:30 am to 5:30 pm Eastern.
Or write to: Chock, 74 Orchard St., New York, NY 10002.
Credit Cards Accepted: MC, VISA, Discover.
Retail store: 74 Orchard St., New York, NY 10002.

Hanna Anderson ....

To Order Call: (800) 222-0544; Fax (503) 321-5289.
Shopping Hours: 5 am to 9 pm Pacific Time, seven
days a week. They have an automated order system after hours to
take your order
Or write to: Hanna Anderson, 1010 NW Flanders, Portland, OR,
97209.
Credit Cards Accepted: MC, VISA, AMEX, Discover.
Retail Stores: 125 Westchester Ave., Suite 3370, White Plains,
NY 10601; (914) 684-2410 and 327 NW Tenth Ave., Portland,
OR 97209; (503) 321-5275.
Outlets Stores: Lake Oswego, OR (503) 697-1953 ; Michigan
City, IN (219) 827-3183; and Portsmouth, NH (603) 433-6642.

Olsen's Mill Direct. ....

To Order Call: (800) 537-4979, (414) 426-6360 or
Fax (414) 426-6369
Shopping Hours: 7:00 am to 11:00 pm Central Time, seven days
a week.
Or write to: Olsen's Mill Direct, 1641 S. Main St,
Oshkosh, WI 54901.
Credit Cards Accepted: MC, VISA, Discover.

Patagonia Kids ....

To Order Call: (800) 638-6464; Fax (800) 543-5522.
Shopping Hours: Monday-Friday 6 am- 6 pm Pacific;
Saturday 8 am- 4 pm Mountain Time.
Or write to: Patagonia, Inc., 8550 White Fir St., PO Box 32050,
Reno, NV 89533.
Credit Cards Accepted: MC, VISA, AMEX, Discover.

Playclothes ....

To Order Call: (800) 362-7529; (800) 222-7725;
Fax (913) 752-1095.
Shopping Hours: 24 hours a day, seven days a week.
Or write to: Playclothes, PO Box 29137, Overland Park, KS
66201.
Credit Cards Accepted: MC, VISA, AMEX, Discover.

Talbot's Kids ....

To Order Call: (800) 543-7123 (U.S. and Canada) or (617) 740-8888; Fax (800) 438-9443.
Shopping Hours: 24 hours a day, 7 days a week.
Or write to: Talbot's Kids, 175 Beal St., Hingham, MA 02043.
Credit Cards Accepted: MC, VISA, AMEX.
Retail stores: 57 stores—call the above number for the location nearest you.

That Lucky Child ....

To Order Call: (800) 755-4852 or (410) 876-9071.
Shopping Hours: 24 hours a day, seven days a week.
Or write to: That Lucky Child Clothing Co., PO Box 245, Hunt Valley, MD 21030.
Credit Cards Accepted: MC, VISA.

Wooden Soldier..

To Order Call: (800) 375-6002 or (603) 356-7041;
Fax (603) 356-3530.
Shopping Hours: Monday-Friday 8:30 am to midnight
Saturday and Sunday 8:30 am to 9 pm Eastern Time.
Or write to: The Wooden Soldier, PO Box 800,
North Conway, NH 03860.
Credit Cards Accepted: MC, VISA, AMEX, Discover.

Maternity & Nursing Catalogs

These catalogs are reviewed in depth in Chapter 5, Maternity and Nursing Clothes.

Garnet Hill ....

To Order Call: (800) 622-6216 or (603) 823-5545;
Fax (603) 823-9578.
Shopping Hours: Monday-Friday 7 am-2 am; Saturday and
Sunday 9 am-11 pm Eastern Time.
Or write to: Box 262 Main St., Franconia, NH 03580.
Credit Cards Accepted: MC, VISA, AMEX, Discover.

MothersWork/Motherhood ....

To Order Call: (800) 825-2268 or (215) 625-9259;
Fax (215) 440-9845.
Shopping Hours: 24 hours a day, seven days a week.
Or write to: MothersWork, 456 N. 5th St., Philadelphia, PA
19123.
Credit Cards Accepted: MC, VISA, AMEX.

La Leche League International Catalog ....

To Order Call: (708) 519-7730; Fax (708) 455-0125.
Shopping Hours: 8:00 am-3:00 pm Central Time,
seven days a week.
Or write to: La Leche League International Catalog, Order
Department, LLLI, PO Box 1209, Franklin Park, IL 60131.
Credit Cards Accepted: MC, VISA.

It ain't glossy, it ain't slick, but La Leche League International's catalog is a treasure trove of information and breastfeeding products. Dozens of books are featured, as are videos, gift items and breast pumps.

Safety Catalogs

Check out Chapter 8 "Baby Proofing" for in-depth reviews of these catalogs.

Perfectly Safe ....
To Order Call: (800) 837-5437; Fax (330) 494-0265.
Shopping Hours: Monday-Friday 8 am-10 pm;
Saturday 9 am-7 pm; Sunday 10 am-6 pm Eastern Time.
Or write to: 7245 Whipple Ave. NW, North Canton, OH 44720.
Credit Cards Accepted: MC, VISA, AMEX, Discover.

Safety Zone ....
To Order Call: (800) 999-3030; Fax (800) 338-1635.
Shopping Hours: 24 hours a day, seven days a week.
Or write to: The Safety Zone, Hanover, PA 17333.
Credit Cards Accepted: MC, VISA, AMEX, Discover.

Toys and Entertainment Catalogs

Back to Basics Toys ....
To Order Call: (800) 356-5360 or (818) 865-8301;
Fax (818) 865-9771.
Shopping Hours: 24 hours a day, seven days a week.
Or write to: 31333 Agoura Rd., Westlake Village, CA 91361.
Credit Cards Accepted: MC, VISA, AMEX, Discover.

In business since 1988, Back to Basics Toys catalog looks for toys that are "built to last, have enduring play value, provide pure playing simple fun and stimulate the mind." Best of all, their prices are very competitive. An excellent index lets you zero in on a certain age group of toys. The "early childhood" section featured such classics as "Alphabet Blocks in a Pull Wagon" ($44), cotton-covered foam blocks for $30 and a Radio Flyer wagon for $53. Altogether, there are over 20 pages of toys for children up to five years, complete with color pictures, great descriptions and age specifications.

Constructive Playthings ....
To Order Call: (800) 832-0572 or (816) 761-5900;
Fax (816) 761-9295.
Shopping Hours: 24 hours a day, seven days a week.
Or write to: 1227 E. 119th St., Grandview, MO 64030.
Credit Cards Accepted: MC, VISA.
Retail Outlets: They have seven retail stores; call the phone number above for a location near you.

In the last edition of our book, we criticized this catalog's organization as cluttered and cumbersome. Well, there here some good news—the latest issue of the catalog we viewed has improved design and expanded information.

Now there are eight pages of "First Playthings," toys for babies under three years old. You'll find the typical items like building blocks and activity gyms, plus musical toys and educational items. A typical offering: the "Light and Sound Rhinoceros" crib toy with 12 songs for $15.

Edutainment Catalog ....
   To Order Call: (800) 338-3844 or (303) 444-3700;
   Fax (800) 226-1942.
   Shopping Hours: 24 hours a day, seven days a week.
   Internet: www.edutainco.com
   Or write to: PO Box 21330, Boulder, CO 80308
   Credit Cards Accepted: MC, VISA, AMEX, Discover.
   Canadian orders: A $5 processing fee is added to all
   Canadian orders.

"The best in PC and Mac Software for the whole family" is the motto of this Boulder, CO-based catalog. The recent issue showcased a good selection of CD-ROM educational and entertainment titles, including Dr. Suess, Curious George, Sesame Street and Berenstain Bears. We liked the organization, which included age group info and computer requirements. Edutainment has occasional specials, a frequent buyer's club and even sells computer accessories like QuickCam and printers.

Gifts for Grandkids ....
   To Order Call: (800) 333-1707, Fax (610) 532-9001.
   Shopping Hours: 24 hours a day, seven days a week.
   Or write to: 100 Pine Ave., Holmes, PA 19043
   Credit Cards Accepted: MC, VISA, AMEX.

Excellent design makes this a great catalog to browse—toys are divided into age appropriate groups, and in-depth descriptions include even more developmental information. Four pages of the catalog spotlight toys for "birth to one year," including the Summer portable play center for $94. Another neat idea: the catalog has a "monthly gift program" ($15 per month) that sends a new age-appropriate toy each month for a baby's first year. Gifts for Grandkids also carries personalized gifts, matching clothing items, pictures frames and more. Don't let the name fool you—this is a great catalog for everyone.

Great Kids Company ....
  To Order Call: (800) 533-2166 or (800) 582-1493;
  Fax (919) 766-9782
  Shopping Hours: 24 hours a day, seven days a week.
  Or write to: The Great Kids Co., PO Box 609,
  Lewisville, NC, 27023.
  Credit Cards Accepted: MC, VISA, AMEX, Discover.

Great Kids Company is an educational toys catalog with the theme "quality products for educating today's kids." This 36-page publication focuses mostly on older children but does have a three-page spread called "Great Beginnings," which spotlights toys for younger children.

Toys are well priced. For example, the popular nine-piece My First Playset is $14.50—we saw it in another catalog for $15.95. Another toy we liked was the activity pots and pans set for $14.95. These six stackable pots and pans incorporate mirrors, rattles, and see-through bottoms. Toys range in age from three months to three years old.

The organization of Great Kids is excellent—the age appropriate listings make shopping easy. And the prices are very reasonable.

Hand in Hand Professional ....
  To Order Call: (800) 872-3841; Fax (207) 539-4415.
  Shopping Hours: Monday-Friday 8:00 am-5:00 pm Eastern Time.
  Or write to: Hand in Hand Professional Catalogue Center,
  Route 26, R.R. 1 Box 1425, Oxford, ME 04270.
  Credit Cards Accepted: MC, VISA, AMEX, Discover.

Here's one of the best catalogs of toys for babies, infants, and toddlers. Maine-based Hand in Hand Professional features a wide variety of mainly educational products that you just can't find everywhere. For example, the Puzzle Path ($109.95) is a set of colored cushions that make into a three-foot circular jig-saw puzzle. The Penguin and Toucan Proppers are cute cushions that help prop up infants.

The catalog's organization is excellent—easy-to-find sections highlight such categories as art, music, bath toys, and the obligatory Barney products. The "All Through the Night" section features a selection of items such as a Moon Night Light ($14.95) and bedtime boardbooks. In "Places to Go," we saw strollers, toys, car seat boosters, and more. There are even safety items, organizational products, and a wide variety of books.

Perhaps the best thing about the Hand in Hand Professional catalog is their large selection of educational toys. For example, the "Puzzling Panda" ($19.95) is a rocking rattle toy and three dimensional puzzle for "laughter and learning." Age appropriate information is provided for each item.

The prices are moderate to high—in line with the Right

Start catalog (whose prices are about the same as regular retail). All in all, we recommend Hand in Hand Professional as one of the best mail-order catalogs for moms and dads-to-be.

Music For Little People ....
   To Order Call: (800) 727-2233; Fax (800) 722-9505.
   Or Write to: Music for Little People, 4320 Marine Ave., Box 1720, Lawndale, CA 90260.
   Shopping hours: 24 hours a day, 7 days a week.
   Credit Cards Accepted: MC, VISA, AMEX, Discover.

Music for Little People is at the top of our list of children's catalogs. We love the huge selection of audiotapes, CDs, and videos, as well as the extensive collection of musical instruments—from electric guitars to harmonicas to autoharps.

Sections include "Fun Around the World," Adventurous Spirit," and "Rockabye Baby," which includes books, toys and several tape and CD collections of lullabies. You'll find both classic and contemporary children's artists, including music by Judy Collins, Kenny Loggins, Bobby McFerrin, and Joe Scruggs, our favorite children's artist.

Besides music, this catalog also carries videos, musical instruments, puppets, toys and more. The catalog is extremely well laid out and colorful, drawing you on to the next page with the promise of more unique products. All the products have information on age appropriateness.

Questions or comments? Did you discover a bargain you'd like to share? Call the authors at (303) 442-8792 or e-mail adfields@aol.com! Updates to this book are posted at *www.windsorpeak.com*

Chapter 12

Conclusion:
What Does it All Mean?

How much money can you save if you follow all the tips and suggestions in this book? Let's take a look at the average cost of having a baby from the introduction and compare it with our *Baby Bargains* budget.

Your Baby's First Year

	AVERAGE	BABY BARGAINS BUDGET
Crib, dresser, changing table, rocker	$1500	$1125
Bedding / Decor	$300	$170
Baby Clothes	$500	$340
Disposable Diapers	$600	$450
Maternity/Nursing Clothes	$1200	$480
Nursery items, high chair, toys	$400	$225
Baby Food/Formula	$600	$250
Stroller, Car Seat, Carrier	$300	$200
Miscellaneous	$500	$500
TOTAL	**$5900**	**$3740**
TOTAL SAVINGS:	**$2160**	

WOW! YOU CAN SAVE OVER $2000!

We hope the savings makes it worth the price of this book. We'd love to hear from you on how much you saved with our book—feel free to write or call the authors at (303) 442-8792.

What does it all mean?

At this point, we usually have something pithy to say as we end the book. But, as parents of a toddler and a newborn, we're just too tired. We're going to bed, so feel free to make up your own ending.

And thanks for reading *Baby Bargains*.

Appendix

Canada:
Car Seat Info, Cribs & More

If you walk into a baby store in Canada, you'll see many of the same baby products for sale in the U.S. There is one exception, however: car seats.

Canada requires child safety seats to meet slightly different safety standards than the U.S. Perhaps the biggest difference is the tether strap, which is used to keep the car seat from flying forward in the event of a head-on crash. One end of the tether strap attaches to the car seat while the other end is bolted to the back seat of the car.

Any child safety seat made after 1987 is required to have tether strap hardware. Furthermore, any *car* made after 1989 that's sold in Canada must have tether anchorage points provided. For older cars, check your owner's manual or car dealership for more info.

Using the tether strap is not an option in Canada; all provinces have laws the not only require a child to be in an approved safety seat but also that the seat be anchored with the tether strap.

What if you have two cars but only one child safety seat? You can purchase an additional anchor bolt at most baby stores and juvenile retailers in Canada.

As a result of these special rules, not all car seats sold in the U.S. will be available in Canada. For more information on this and other issues regarding child safety seats, contact Transport Canada's Road Safety Office at (613) 998-1978 or on the internet at *www.tc.gc.ca/*.

The Canadian Automobile Association (CAA) also works closely with Transport Canada to provide child safety seat info. Contact their headquarters at (613) 247-0117 for more details or check your phone book for the number of a local CAA office. We noticed the British Columbia Automobile Association (800) 663-4636 operates a web site that provides basic safety tips plus recall notices.

General Safety Info

If you have a question about a juvenile product or a safety concern, contact the any of these regional branches of the Canada Consumer and Corporate Affairs Product Safety Office:

Location	Phone
Ottawa/Hull (headquarters)	(819) 953-8082
Halifax	(902) 426-6328
St. John's	(709) 772-4050
Moncton	(506) 851-6638
Montreal	(514) 283-2825
Quebec	(418) 648-4327
Toronto	(416) 973-4705
Hamilton	(416) 572-2845
Winnipeg	(204) 983-3293
Saskatoon	(306) 975-4028
Edmonton	(403) 495-7198
Calgary	(403) 292-5613
Vancouver	(604) 666-5006

Recap of Canadian Sources

Many of the sources mentioned earlier in this book sell or ship to Canada. Here's a recap of specific Canadian juvenile product manufacturers (all prices are in U.S. dollars):

Cribs

Morigeau/Lepine ....★★ ¹/₂
2625 Rossmoor Dr., Pittsburgh, PA 15241. Call (800) 326-2121 or (412) 942-3583 for a dealer near you. Based in Quebec, Canada, this family-run juvenile furniture company has been in business for over 50 years. Their pricey cribs are quite stylish, with a Shaker sensibility. Morigeau cribs run $475 to $750, while a five-drawer dresser topped $579. The cribs (which have just two mattress levels) have a weird locking mechanism that we found awkward. On the upside, Morigeau sells a wide assortment of accessories, including coordinating desks, armoires, and even baby entertainment centers. As for the finishes, we thought the white looked the best, although Morigeau boasts a wide variety of finishes for each crib style (including such interesting options as cinnamon and cognac). One style that caught our eye was a "moon" crib, featuring a crescent shaped moon headboard (style 795) available in a variety of painted finishes for $575. Other innovative headboard styles featured carousel and swan designs. Morigeau's sister line is "Lepine," a smaller collection of cribs at slightly lower prices. Lepine cribs feature

similarly whimsical designs in a smaller number of finishes (white, natural, cherry) for $450 to $660. Morigeau/Lepine is mainly available through baby specialty stores.

Ragazzi .... ★ ¹/₂
8965 Pascal Gagnon, St. Leonard, Quebec H1P 1Z4. Call (514) 324-7886 for a dealer near you. This Canadian import features very adult-looking furniture at very-adult prices. Cribs run a whopping $469 to $510, while a five-drawer dresser will set you back an amazing $749. Ragazzi's claim to fame is their two-tone wood finishes in contemporary colors (forest green, deep burgundy, etc.). For example, the base of the dresser is a natural finish wood, with the knobs and top finished in color. This two-color look has become so popular that almost every other crib manufacturer has knocked it off today. As a result, you can get a Ragazzi look at a much lower price.

As for the cribs themselves, parents we've interviewed say they love Ragazzi's crib rail release—it's one of the quietest in the market. We didn't like the mattress height adjustment system, however, which had metal straps that screwed to the side post (unusual for this price level). The quality of Ragazzi's cribs disappointed us; for the money, you can find a much better crib than this. Even if you can find a Regazzi crib on sale for $300 or so (as some of our readers have reported), they still seem overpriced.

While we liked the style of Ragazzi's furniture, we're less thrilled with Ragazzi's customer service. In a word, it stinks. One baby store owner we interviewed said he dropped Ragazzi after the company shipped the wrong color cribs and was very slow to fix defective products. Also, we encountered Ragazzi's president Jerry Schwartz at a trade show recently and found his arrogant and obnoxious behavior reflected poorly on his company. All in all, if you want a stylish Canadian crib, we suggest buying from Morigeau (reviewed earlier).

Stork Craft ....★★ ¹/₂
11511 No. 5 Road, Richmond, British Columbia, Canada, V7A4E8. For a dealer near you, call (604) 274-5121. Internet: www.storkcraft.com/storkcraft. Unlike other Canadian crib makers that concentrate on the upper-end of the market, Stork Craft's cribs are priced for the rest of us. Most are in the $150 to $250 range (although a few reach $400) and are sold in such places as Baby Superstore and other chain stores. Manufactured in Mississauga, Ontario (just outside Toronto), Stork Craft's cribs feature two different releases. Some models use the standard metal hardware/foot-bar release, similar to Child Craft and Simmons. Others use a two-handed plastic trigger drop-side. As mentioned earlier in this section, we're

concerned such plastic hardware might crack, especially in dry climates where low humidity leads to wood shrinkage. Nonetheless, the styling of Stork Craft cribs is pleasing. Most are plain vanilla, although a few echo Italian cribs with curvy headboards, heavy white wood finishes, etc. A few styles even have under-crib drawers.

Rocker-Glider

Market-leader *Dutailier* (298 Chaput, St-Pie, Quebec, Canada JOH 1WO; call 800-363-9817 or 514-772-2403 for a dealer near you) says their glider-rockers have a "unique bearing system (tested to six million cycles) that ensures the best rocking sensation money can buy!" Wow! Sounds like the same system used on the Stealth bomber.

Basically, what all this hoo-hah means is gliders rock more easily than plain rocking chairs. We were somewhat skeptical about this before we bought our glider, but after doing a test drive we're convinced they're worth the extra money.

And how much money are we talking about here? A basic Dutailier (pronounced due-TAL-yea) glider starts at $210 (without cushions, or $250 with basic cushions), with some leather versions topping out at $600 or more. An optional accessory is the ottoman that glides too. This starts at $99 without a cushion, but most cost $125 to $150 with cushions.

We suggest forgetting the ottoman and ordering an inexpensive "nursing" footstool (about $30 to $40 in catalogs like Motherwear 800-950-2500). Why? Some moms claim the ottoman's height puts additional strain on their backs while breastfeeding. While the nursing footstool doesn't rock, it's lower height puts less strain on your back.

Is a glider-rocker a waste of money? Some parents have written to us with that question, assuming you'd just use the item for the baby's first couple of years. Actually, a glider-rocker can have a much longer life. You can swap the cushions after a couple of years (most companies let you order these items separately) and move the glider-rocker to a family room.

So, how can you get a deal on a Dutailier? Well, the JCPenney catalog (800) 222-6161 sells a few basic styles of Dutailier gliders for $270. We also discovered the Baby Catalog of America (800-PLAYPEN) sells Dutailier at a discount.

Of course, there are several other companies that make glider-rockers for nurseries. While we think these brands are good alternatives, Dutailier is still our pick. Why? Consider the styling—while other glider-rockers make a basic number of styles, Dutailier is the fashion leader. For example, they're the only company with a "sleigh back" glider-rocker that matches similar style cribs. Dutailier also has a much wider choice of fabrics than other brands—just this year, they've released 17 new styles (including a teddy bear tapestry).

Finally, Dutailier does a better job at shipping and customer service than its rivals. In 1996, the company introduced its "Express" line—a selection of 17 chair styles in two or three different fabric choices that are in stock for shipment in two weeks. (Glider-rockers from other makers and Dutailier's regular line must be special ordered and that can take six to eight weeks). As for quality, we've never received a complaint about Dutailier glider-rockers.

Bedding

Grey Fort Quilts ....★★ *1/2*
For a brochure, call (800) 505-2660 or (519) 664-2130. A Canadian mother-to-be e-mailed us with her enthusiastic recommendation for this company. Ontario-based Grey Fort Quilts custom makes baby bedding, including bumpers, sheets, dust ruffles and, yes, quilts. We priced a log-cabin style quilt at just $70 Canadian—that works out to about $52 U.S., which is a great deal. The company will send you fabric swatches or you can use your own fabric.

Oshkosh ....★★ *1/2*
Made by Marimac, 10340 Cote de Liesse, Suite 200, La Chime, Quebec Canada H8T1A3. Call (514) 422-1171 for a dealer near you. With the denim fad sweeping the baby bedding biz, was it any surprise that crib bedding by denim king Oshkosh would be far behind? The Wisconsin company famous for those too-cute overalls has licensed its "Baby B'Gosh" to Canada-based Marimac for a line of crib bedding that's surprisingly affordable. A three-piece set is $89 to $99 and a four-piece set is about $119 to $129. The most expensive design topped out at $199 for a five-piece set. This isn't a big line—we only saw eight collections, which mixed denim fabric with stripes, plaids and lace accents. While you might think Oshkosh's bedding would be a boy thing, there were quite a few feminine looks with frilly bows, lacy accents, etc. While the designs are good, the quality is only average—most of the bedding items are 50/50 cotton/poly blends, except for the denim (which is 100% cotton). The sheets have 160 thread counts, which is higher than some makers but below those of the better-made brands. The company did tell us they plan to introduce an all-cotton seersucker design later in 1997.

Outlet Stores

There is one publication that lists nearly every outlet store in the Canada—*Outlet Bound* magazine, which is published by Outlet Marketing Group ($7.95 plus $3.50 shipping, 800-336-8853). The magazine contains detailed maps noting outlet centers for all areas of the U.S. and Canada, as well as store listings for each outlet center. We liked the index that lists all the manufacturers, and they even have a few coupons in the back. The publication also has an excellent web site (www.outletbound.com) with the most up-to-date info on outlets in the U.S. and Canada.

Maternity Bras

God bless Canada—those Maple Leaf-heads make the best maternity bra in the world. Toronto-based *Bravado Designs* (for a brochure, call 800-590-7802 or 416-466-8652) makes a maternity/nursing bra of the same name that's just incredible. "A godsend!" raved one reader. "It's built like a sports bra with no underwire and supports better than any other bra I've tried . . . and this is my third pregnancy!" The Bravado bra comes in three support levels, sizes up to 42-46 with a F-G cup and a couple of wonderful colors/patterns. Available via mail order, the bra costs $29-$31 U.S. (or $32 to $35 Canadian). Another plus: the Bravado salespeople are knowledgeable and quite helpful with sizing questions.

Nursing Fashions

The Toronto-based *Breast is Best* catalog sells a wide variety of nursing tops, blouses and dresses. For a free catalog and fabric swatches, call (416) 461-3890.

Car Seats

Cosco ....★★
2525 State St., Columbus, IN 47201. Call (812) 372-0141 for a dealer near you (or 514-323-5701 for a dealer in Canada). Internet: www.coscoinc.com Cosco, which is owned by Canadian conglomerate Dorel Industries, makes several car seats that are widely available in both the U.S. and Canada. What makes Cosco's seat's unique this their "auto tighten" belt systems. Instead of manually tightening (or loosening) the belts every time you put baby into the car seat, the belts on some Cosco models automatically retract for a secure fit, sort of like a car's regular seat belts. Why the other major car seat makers (that is, Century and Evenflo) haven't thought of this yet is beyond us. Here's an overview:
Infant car seats. Like Century, Cosco makes infant car seats in two flavors: one with a fancy handle and one without. The

"Turnabout" ($60) features a handle grip that rotates 360 degrees into any position and then locks in place. Our only complaint: one version of the Turnabout (the 02-764) has a canopy that wraps around the handle, making it difficult or impossible to carry the handle under your arm. Oddly enough, this mistake isn't in repeated three other versions of the Turnabout. Another oddity: Cosco's "Auto Reel" belt tightening system (described above) is only available on two of the Turnabouts (the 02-760 and the 02-766). If you want this feature, make sure you shop carefully. (As a side note, Cosco also makes a plain car seat without the fancy handle—the "Arriva" also lacks the Auto Reel feature). Parents of twins or premature babies, take note: Cosco is one of very few manufacturers to make a "travel bed." For babies that need to travel laying down, the Cosco "Dream Ride" is about $90.

Convertible car seats. Cosco a dozen or so car seats, but only their "Olympian" car seats feature the "Auto Retract" harness system. Unfortunately, this upper-end model only comes in t-shield and bar-shield versions—no five point. All Olympians have the option of an extra infant cushion insert and harness covers. Of course, Cosco does make less-expensive car seats too—the entry-level Touriva ($60 to $90) comes in both basic and "deluxe" padding and the Regal Ride, which features even more deluxe padding. Both the Touriva and Regal Ride come in five-point, t-shield and bar-shield versions. All in all, we have to give Cosco a mixed rating. While we liked the auto-retract harness systems, their car seats lack features common with the competition. For example, even their most expensive convertible car seats don't recline, a very handy feature for sleeping infants. Also we've heard little feedback from parents about the quality and durability of these car seats; Cosco seems to been more successful in Canada than the U.S. You don't see these seats in wide distribution.

Baby Proofers

Looking for help baby proofing your house? Consider calling a professional baby-proofer who is a member of the *International Association for Child Safety* (to find a member near you, call 214-824-3964). These folks sell high-quality baby proofing items and offer installation, or you can do-it-yourself. The association is run by (and shares a phone number with) Dr. Baby Proofer, a Dallas-based company headed by Tom Golden—we often turn to Tom when readers ask where they can find obscure items like pool alarms and other safety products. There are about 50 members of the association in both the U.S. and Canada.

About The Authors

~~~~~~

by Benjamin Fields

As the three year old son of the authors, I suppose I was the publisher's natural choice to write the "About the Authors" section. Who else spends more time with the writers than me?

Well, I'd like to point out that negotiations dragged on for days. The publisher was worried that no one would believe that a toddler could actually sit still for five minutes, much less compose a thoughtful and respectable biographical portrait of the authors (my parents). "Look, even great writers like Ernest Hemmingway and Dave Barry didn't write before they were five years old?" they said. And I replied, "Yeah, but they probably weren't breastfed."

Finally, we got to the the the heart of the matter: compensation. The publisher offered me three book choices and a toy to be named later, before finally saying, "Do you want a cookie?" And I said, "Do fish swim?"

So here I am writing this thoughtful and respectable "About the Authors" section. Let's start with my mother, Denise Fields. She grew up in Loveland, Colorado, a town I have visited and have to say looks relatively normal on the surface. Denise (a.k.a. Mom) went to the University of Colorado and majored in Elizabethan English History, a fact I intend to remind her of when I announce my college major: Advanced Computer Game Theory.

While studying at dear old CU, my mom met my dad, Alan Fields. Alan is from Dallas, Texas, or so I'm told. I've only visited this place once and it was (to borrow a phrase from Neil Simon) HOT. Africa hot. While we were there, we visited a Mexican restaurant called Zuzu's. That name rang a bell—I remembered that our dog is named Zuzu. This came as somewhat of a disappointment since I always thought our dog was named after the four-wheel drive sport utility vehicle.

Anyway, Mom and Dad got their start writing weddings guides in Austin, Texas, another place which has truly world class Mexican restaurants. Apparently, my parents became quite the experts at weddings and went on to write a national best-selling book called *Bridal Bargains*. I should say it was first just a "book," with the prefix "best-selling" added one day in June 1991. That was the month a producer from the Oprah Winfrey Show called and invited Dad and Mom to be guests on the show. They tell me life improved dramatically after that.

Next, Mom and Dad wrote a book called *Your New House: The Alert Consumer's Guide to Buying and Building a Quality Home*. This was voted one of the "Top 10 Real Estate Books" for 1993 and 1996, which I think were two very good years indeed. I was born in 1993 and, coincidently, my brother Jack was born in 1996.

Both Jack and I would like to point out it was really us who test drove all those strollers, ate those do-it-yourself baby food experiments and wore all those diapers. And what do we get for all this effort? Top-billing on the cover? A cut of the royalties?

The answer, of course, is zippo, nada, nothing. Oh sure, that's our picture on the back cover, but pictures don't pay for Thomas the Tank Engine collectible series, do they?

So, that's why we're filing a formal complaint with our union . . . right after we finish this cookie.

Index

Notes

Is This Book A Loaner?

*Have you checked this book out
from a library?*

*Borrowed it from a friend
who wants it back?*

**Now, there's an easy and quick way
to get your very own copy of**

BABY
Bargains

Just
$13.95
Plus $3 shipping
(Canada price: $19.75 plus $4 shipping)

Call toll-free
1-800-888-0385
to order!

*Mastercard, VISA, American Express and
Discover Accepted!*

More Books by the Fields

Bridal Bargains

The #1-best selling wedding book!

"If you're getting married, you need this book!"
—Oprah Winfrey

WOW! Finally, a book on weddings you can actually use! With the average U.S. wedding now costing over $18,000, you need creative and innovative solutions to planning a wonderful wedding on a realistic budget. *Bridal Bargains* in the answer! Inside you'll discover:

- ♣ HOW TO SAVE **20%** TO **40%** off brand new, nationally-advertised bridal gowns.

- ♣ FIVE GREAT TIPS to save you hundreds of dollars on your wedding pictures.

- ♣ THREE COSTLY MYTHS about wedding catering plus **Seven** delicious trends in affordable wedding cakes.

- ♣ TWELVE CREATIVE WAYS TO SAVE MONEY on wedding flowers.

- ♣ HOW TO NEGOTIATE THE BEST DEAL on a ceremony and reception site.

- ♣ WHO OFFERS THE BEST BUYS on elegant invitations.

- ♣ PLUS MANY MORE MONEY-SAVING TIPS on wedding videos, entertainment, party favors and **More!**

MONEY BACK GUARANTEE: If *Bridal Bargains* doesn't save you at least $500 on your wedding, then we will give you a complete refund. No kidding.

Just
$11.95
(Plus $3 shipping)

Call toll-free to order!
1-800-888-0385
Mastercard, VISA, American Express and Discover Accepted!

MORE BOOKS BY THE FIELDS
"The Bridal Gown Guide"

The Ultimate Dress Guide!

Reviews and ratings of 40 top designers.

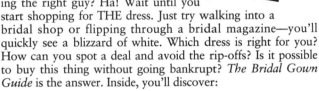

So, you thought the tough part about getting married was finding the right guy? Ha! Wait until you start shopping for THE dress. Just try walking into a bridal shop or flipping through a bridal magazine—you'll quickly see a blizzard of white. Which dress is right for you? How can you spot a deal and avoid the rip-offs? Is it possible to buy this thing without going bankrupt? *The Bridal Gown Guide* is the answer. Inside, you'll discover:

- ♣ **SEVEN STEPS** to finding the perfect bridal gown, from understanding fabrics, laces and silhouettes to what to get in writing when you place an order.

- ♣ **HOW TO SAVE 20% to 70%** off your bridal gown—we've got 21 money-saving strategies to cut the price, not the quality.

- ♣ **DESIGNER-BY-DESIGNER REVIEWS** that tell you all the information bridal magazines don't! Discover actual retail prices, candid reviews, delivery dates and more.

- ♣ **DETAILED SIZING INFO** on over 40 top gown designers. Which ones offer large sizes? Custom changes?

- ♣ **AND DON'T FORGET THE BRIDESMAIDS.** Discover the complete low-down on the best dresses for bridesmaids, with money-saving tips and designer-by-designer reviews.

Just
$11.95
(Plus $3 shipping)

Call toll-free to order!
1-800-888-0385
Mastercard, VISA, American Express and Discover Accepted!

MORE BOOKS BY THE FIELDS

Your New House
The Alert Consumer's Guide To Buying and Building a Quality Home

Picked one of the "Top Real Estate Books" 1993 & 1996

"This is, by far, the best book available on how to buy and build a new home!"
—Robert Bruss,
Chicago Tribune

With the cost of buying a new home these days, you need more than just a little help. And we've got just the book for you: YOUR NEW HOUSE. Just like our other books, we give you page after page of helpful tips, including questions to ask, scams to avoid, and step-by-step strategies. Whether buying a new home is just over the horizon or a long-term goal, get a copy of YOUR NEW HOUSE today.

As featured on ABC's 20/20 and "Good Morning America"

Just
$13.95
(Plus $3 shipping)

Call toll-free to order!
1-800-888-0385
Mastercard, VISA, American Express and Discover Accepted!

How to Reach Us

Have a question about
Baby Bargains?

Want to make a suggestion?
Discovered a great bargain you'd like to share?

Contact the Authors, Denise & Alan Fields
in one of four ways:

1. By phone
(303) 442-8792.

2. By mail
436 Pine Street
Suite 600,
Boulder, CO 80302

3. By fax
(303) 442-3744.

4. By e-mail
Our address is
adfields@aol.com.

Our web page is at
www.windsorpeak.com
(more details on the next page)

Surf for Updates!

POP INTO OUR WEB SITE TO GET THE LATEST UPDATES ON BABY BARGAINS. Things change quickly in the juvenile products business. By surfing our web site (which is updated periodically), you'll stay on top of any changes.

http:// www.windsorpeak.com

You'll read about:

♣ New companies and services that were recommended by moms and dads.

♣ The BABY BARGAINS Mail Bag! Read letters from our readers, giving their opinions about products, new bargains and more!

♣ Corrections and clarifications in our book, especially phone number changes.

♣ The latest in baby news and trends.

♣ Updates on when this book will be revised next, with early bird discounts!

♣ Links to other great parenting sites on the web! With one click, you'll be able to jump to web sites for catalogs mentioned in this book, manufacturers with detailed product info and general sites with even more parenting advice.

Best of all, it's all free!

Join Our Preferred Reader List

We've got lots of new books coming out over the next few years! Just jot down your name and address below, mail in the coupon and we'll keep you up-to-date!

Best of all, we have "early bird" DISCOUNTS especially for BABY BARGAINS preferred readers!

Name _____

Address _____

City _____ State_____ Zip_____

Baby's Name & Birthdate_____

How did you hear about our book?_____

_____

What was your favorite section or tip? _____

_____

How can we improve this book? _____

_____

_____

_____

_____

Mail To:
BABY BARGAINS
436 Pine Street
Boulder, CO 80302
or fax to (303) 442-3744
or e-mail to adfields@aol.com

If this book doesn't save you at least

$250

off your baby expenses, we'll give you a complete refund on the cost of this book!

NO QUESTIONS ASKED!

Just send the book and your mailing address to

Windsor Peak Press • 436 Pine Street, Suite T Boulder, CO, 80302.

If you have any questions, please call (303) 442-8792.

Look at all those other baby books in the bookstore—no other author or publisher is willing to put their money where their mouth is! We are so confident that *Baby Bargains* will save you money that we guarantee it in writing!

Remove this card for **SMART SHOPPER TIPS** to help evaluate baby products.

Is this card missing? Is this book on loan from a friend?

Well, you need your very own copy!

Baby Bargains is available in bookstores nationwide!

Windsor Peak Press

Questions or comments?

Call (800) 888-0385

SMART SHOPPER TIPS
Reprinted from
The *Baby Bargains* book • Fields

CRIBS
❏ Evaluate the mattress support: springs? straps? bars? cardboard?
❏ How easy does the side rail release?
❏ Evaluate the mattress height adjustment: screws or hooked bracket?
❏ How stable is the crib?
❏ Is the crib JPMA safety-certified?
❏ How easy is the crib to assemble?
❏ Does the store offer delivery and set-up?
❏ Are there any danger signs: sharp edges? Fold-down railings? Attached dressers?

BEDDING
❏ What is the thread count of the sheets?
❏ Is the appliqué stiching tight, smooth?
❏ Is there a tag with maker contact info?
❏ Is the bedding sewn with cotton/poly thread (versus nylon)?
❏ Are there ties on the top and bottom of the bumper pads?
❏ Is the design printed on the fabric? Or merely stamped?
❏ Are the ruffles folded over for double thickness?

LAYETTE (CLOTHING)
❏ Choose sizes based on your child's weight and length (not age).
❏ Evaluate the fiber content (all cotton versus blends).
❏ Is the item pre-shrunk?
❏ Are snaps on a reinforced band?
❏ Check for easy diaper access.
❏ Avoid outfits with detachable decoration.
❏ Remove any drawstrings.
❏ Recommended layette:

Quantity	Item
❏ 6	T-shirts/onesies (over the head)
❏ 6	T-shirts (side snap or side tie)
❏ 4-6	Sleepers
❏ 1	Blanket Sleeper
❏ 2-4	Coveralls
❏ 3-4	Booties/socks
❏ 1	Sweater
❏ 2	Hats (safari and caps)
❏ 1	Snowsuit/bunting
❏ 4	Large bibs (for feeding)
❏ 3 sets	Wash clothes and towels
❏ 7-8	Receiving blankets

HIGH CHAIRS
❏ Does the chair have a stable, wide base?
❏ How easily does the tray release?
❏ Is the chair height adjustable?
❏ How easy it is to clean?
❏ Is there any protection to keep the baby from sliding under the tray?

CAR SEATS
❏ Check your vehicle's owner manual to see if you need additional hardware.
❏ How easily do the belts adjust?
❏ Are the installation instructions clear?
❏ Is the pad cover machine washable?
❏ Does it require installation with each use?
❏ New rules to take effect soon! Check our web page at *www.windsorpeak.com* for the latest on changing safety standards.

STROLLERS: KEY FEATURES TO LOOK FOR
For Baby: ❏ Reclining seat. ❏ Front Bar. ❏ Seat Padding. ❏ Weather protection.
For Parents: ❏ Roomy storage basket. ❏ Compact fold. ❏ Removable cushion. ❏ Lockable wheels. ❏ Handle height. ❏ Reversible handle. ❏ Overall weight.

TOP TEN SAFETY MUST HAVES
❏ Outlet covers. ❏ Baby monitor.
❏ Smoke alarms. ❏ Toilet locks.
❏ Cabinet/drawer locks ❏ Tub Spout cover.
❏ Bath thermometer or anti-scald device.
❏ Carbon monoxide detectors.
❏ Fire extinguishers, rated "ABC."
❏ Baby gates.

QUESTION TO ASK A CHILD CARE PROVIDER
❏ What are the credentials/education of the provider(s)?
❏ What is the turnover?
❏ What is the ratio of children to care providers?
❏ Do you have a license? Verify.
❏ May I visit you during business hours?
❏ Discuss your care philosophy.
❏ Do you have liability insurance? Ask for written verification.
❏ Does the center conduct police background checks on employees?
❏ Is the center clean, home-like, cheerful?
❏ What type of adjustment period does the center offer?

Remove this card for **SMART SHOPPER TIPS** to help evaluate baby products.

Is this card missing? Is this book on loan from a friend?

Well, you need your very own copy!

Baby Bargains is available in bookstores nationwide!

Windsor Peak Press

Questions or comments?

Call (800) 888-03